SFSR

| Moldavia | AZ | Azerbaijan | UZ | Uzbekistan |
| Georgia | KA | Kazakhstan | TA | Tadjikistan |
| Armenia | TU | Turkmenistan | KI | Kirghizia |

# THE LOST EMPIRE

*Perceptions of*
*Soviet Policy Shifts in the 1990s*

# THE LOST EMPIRE

*Perceptions of*
*Soviet Policy Shifts in the 1990s*

Edited by

## JOHN HEMSLEY

## BRASSEY'S (UK)

A Member of the Maxwell Macmillan Group

LONDON · OXFORD · WASHINGTON · NEW YORK

UK                      Brassey's (UK) Ltd.,
(Editorial)             50 Fetter Lane, London EC4 1AA, England
(Orders, all except     Brassey's (UK) Ltd.,
North America)          Headington Hill Hall, Oxford OX3 0BW, England
USA                     Brassey's (US) Inc.,
(Editorial)             8000 Westpark Drive, Fourth Floor,
                        McLean, Virginia 22102, USA
(Orders,                Brassey's (US) Inc., Front and Brown Streets,
North America)          Riverside, New Jersey 08075, USA
                        Tel (toll free): 800 257 5755

First edition 1991

**Library of Congress Cataloging in Publication Data**
The Lost Empire : perceptions of Soviet policy shifts in the
1990s / edited by John Hemsley. -- 1st ed.
p. cm.
Includes index.
1. Soviet Union--Politics and government--1985- 2. Soviet Union--
Military policy. 3. Soviet Union--Foreign relations--1985-
I. Hemsley, John, 1935-
DK288.L68    1991        322'.5'0947--dc20        91-593

**British Library Cataloguing in Publication Data**
The Lost Empire : perceptions of Soviet policy shifts in the
1990s.
1. Union of Soviet Socialist Republics. Defence (Military
strategy). Policies
I. Hemsley, John 1935-
355.033547

ISBN 0-08-040981-4

*Printed in Great Britain by B.P.C.C. Wheatons Ltd, Exeter*

# Contents

v

# PART III

# List of Tables and Illustrations

# Glossary of Terms

| | |
|---|---|
| ABM | Anti-ballistic missile |
| ACM | Advanced conventional munitions |
| ATTU | Atlantic to Ural Zone |
| *BMP* | *Boyevaya mashina pekhoty* [infantry battle vehicle] |
| BW | Biological warfare |
| C³ | Command, control, communications |
| CEMA | Council for Economic Mutual Assistance [also known as COMECON] |
| CFE | Conventional forces in Europe |
| COMECON | [see CEMA] |
| CPSU | Communist Party of the Soviet Union |
| CSCE | Conference on Security and Co-operation in Europe |
| CW | Chemical warfare |
| FYP | Five-year plan |
| INF | Intermediate-range nuclear force(s) |
| IRBM | Intermediate-range ballistic missile(s) |
| IRM | Intermediate-range missile(s) |
| MBFR | Mutual and balanced force reductions |
| MD | Military district |
| MRM | Medium range missile(s) [see IRM] |
| MVD | Ministry for Internal Affairs (Soviet) |
| NATO | North Atlantic Treaty Organisation |
| SALT | Strategic Arms Limitation Talks |
| SDI | Strategic Defence Initiative |
| SSBN | Ballistic missile submarine |
| *TVD* | *Teatr voennykh deistvii* [theatre of military operations] |
| UN | United Nations |
| US | United States |
| USSR | Union of Soviet Socialist Republics |
| UTTPA | Ural-to-the-Pacific-Ocean Zone |
| WP | Warsaw Pact |
| WTO | Warsaw Treaty Organisation |

# Notes on the Contributors

**Dr Christopher BELLAMY** is the Defence Correspondent of *The Independent* newspaper in London. His background is an interesting combination of army officer, civil servant at the Ministry of Defence, and academic. He has degrees in history from Oxford, in Russian language studies from the Polytechnic of Central London, and an MA in War Studies from King's College, London. From 1987 – 90 he was the Senior Research Analyst in the Centre for Defence Studies at the University of Edinburgh, where he is now a Fellow, having completed his PhD on the Russian and Soviet view of the character of future war, 1877 – 2017. He is the author of *Red God of War: Soviet Artillery and Rocket Forces* (1986) [Hebrew translation 1990]; *The Evolution of Modern Land Warfare: Theory and Practice* (1990); and was Consultant Editor on the Eastern Front for *The Times Atlas of the Second World War* (1989). He has broadcast extensively on military and Russian/Soviet matters, both contemporary and historical.

**Christopher CVIIC** is a native of Croatia in Yugoslavia and was educated at Zagreb University, gaining his degree in languages. He then attended the University of London obtaining a degree in economics and international relations from the London School of Economics. He carried out post-graduate research in modern Balkan history at St Antony's College, Oxford; and subsequently worked for the BBC External Services from 1954 – 59, and from 1964 – 69. In 1969 he joined *The Economist* as a leader writer and correspondent specialising in Eastern Europe. He retired from this appointment at the age of 60 but still contributes regularly on East European affairs and religious subjects. Since 1984 he has been editor of *The World Today*, published by the Royal Institute of International Affairs. Cviic is the author of numerous studies and articles on Eastern Europe, where he visits regularly. He is currently working on a book on the future of South-Eastern Europe, to be published by the Royal Institute for International Affairs in 1991.

**Professor John ERICKSON** is the Director of Defence Studies at the University of Edinburgh. Following military service at the end of the

Second World War, when he served in The King's Own Regiment and Army Intelligence, he graduated from St John's College, Cambridge, before becoming a Research Fellow at St Antony's College, Oxford. He then lectured in Russian and East European History at St Andrew's University, Scotland prior to being appointed Lecturer, and then Senior Lecturer and Reader, in the Department of Government at Manchester University. He subsequently became Reader in Higher Defence Studies at the University of Edinburgh, in association with the Ministry of Defence. He is Visiting Professor to the Russian Research Centre at the University of Indiana, as well as to Texas A&M University. He is also President of the Association of Civil Defence and Emergency Planning Officers in the United Kingdom. Professor Erickson is the author of many books and published articles, the most notable being: *The Soviet High Command 1918 – 1941: Soviet Ground Forces: an Operational Assessment* (as co-author), and the two volume history of the Soviet-German War, *The Road to Stalingrad* and *The Military-Technical Revolution*, monograph *Soviet Military Power*. His Yale University Lecture Series entitled 'War', and 'Soviet Society 1941 – 1945' is to be published in 1991 as *Blood, Bread and Steel* by Yale University Press. Professor Erickson is an elected Fellow of the Royal Society of Edinburgh and a Fellow of the British Academy.

**Colonel David GLANTZ** is Acting Director and Chief of Research of the Soviet Army Studies Office, Combined Arms Centre at Fort Leavenworth, Kansas, USA. He holds degrees from the Virginia Military Institute and the University of North Carolina at Chapel Hill. He is the author of numerous articles on military affairs and books on Soviet military operations in the Second World War; including *August Storm: The Soviet 1945 Strategic Offensive in Manchuria* (2 volumes); *The Soviet Airborne Experience; Soviet Military Deception in the Second World War; Soviet Military Intelligence in War; Soviet Military Operational Art; In Pursuit of Deep Battle; From the Don to the Dneiper — A Study of Soviet Offensive Operations, December 1942 to August 1943;* and *The Role of Intelligence in Soviet Military Strategy During the Second World War.* He is currently working on a history of Soviet military strategy.

**Ambassador Lynn Marvin HANSEN** currently holds the Chair of John M Olin Distinguished Professor of National Security and Defence Studies at the United States Air Force Academy, Colorado, having previously served in the Bush and Reagan Administrations as Assistant Director of Arms Control and Disarmament Agency. In November 1989 he was appointed Delegate-at-Large on the US Delegation negotiating CFE, advising on Alliance and verification issues. He previously served as Ambassador to the Stockholm CSCE talks, as well as interim representative to the Geneva Conference on Disarmament and on the Delegations to MBFR and Madrid CSCE Review Conference. A former US Air Force officer, he served twice as liaison officer to the Commander, Group of Soviet Forces, Germany, before retiring as a Colonel in 1983. His military decorations include the Defence Superior Service Medal, the Legion of Merit, the Bronze Star, the Meritorious Service Medal, the Air Force Commendation Medal and the Vietnamese Staff Services Medal (First Class). He is a graduate of Utah State University, a Fulbright Scholar at the Free University of Berlin and a Fellow of the University of Edinburgh, where he studied Soviet Military Doctrine. Dr Hansen is a widely published author on issues of European security and arms control. He is fluent in German, Danish, Swedish and Russian. A native of Idaho Falls, he now lives with his family in Monument, Colorado.

**Brigadier John HEMSLEY** is described as traveller, author, international rally driver, and ex-soldier, having taken early retirement from the British Army to form his own consultancy business in International Project Research. He was educated at Wellington College, Edinburgh University and the Royal Military Academy, Sandhurst, as well as being a graduate of the Defence Services Staff College in India, the NATO Defence College in Rome, and an instructor at the British Army Command & Staff College. He commanded the 24th (Independent) Infantry Brigade in North-West Germany, before serving on the staff of Northern Army Group as Assistant Chief of Staff, responsible for Intelligence. Author of three books on Soviet affairs, he has contributed to four other major works and published widely in journals, newspapers and magazines, as well as lecturing in Europe and the USA. His work and travel has taken him to over 80 countries around the world, including Africa, Australia, Canada, Europe, Eastern Mediterranean, South America, the USA and the USSR. He is a Fellow of the Royal Geographical Society and a Research Fellow of Edinburgh University. Listing his main interests as exploration, the countryside, sailing, ornithology, music and line-engraved philately, he represented both County and Army at chess and hockey; and now lives on the Mendip Hills with his Australian wife and two young children.

**Dr Jacob KIPP** is a Senior Analyst for the Soviet Army Studies Office, Combined Arms Center at Fort Leavenworth, Kansas, USA. Born in Harrisburg, Pennsylvania, he graduated from Shippensburg State College and completed his MA and PhD in Russian History at

Pennsylvania State University. He has conducted extensive research in both Poland and the Soviet Union, where he met and married his wife, Dr Maria Kipp. He joined the History Department of Kansas State University in 1971 and taught there until 1985 when he moved to his present job. Dr Kipp was Associate Editor of *Military Affairs* from 1979 to 1983, and now holds the rank of Adjunct Professor of History with the University of Kansas, teaching in the Soviet and East European Studies programme. He has published extensively in Russian and Soviet military and naval history.

**Michael MccGWIRE** was a Senior Fellow with the Foreign Policy Programme at the Brookings Institution, Washington from 1979 – 90, following which he returned to England where he is currently working with the Global Security Programme at Cambridge University. A former British Naval Officer, he entered the Royal Naval College, Dartmouth at the age of 13, from where he was duly commissioned into the Royal Navy. He saw active service in the Mediterranean and in the Channel from 1942 – 45. His peacetime service included two years as Assistant Naval Attaché in Moscow, followed by a period as a War Planner at SACLANT where he headed the Soviet Naval Section of British Defence Intelligence. He retired from the Royal Navy in 1966 and went to the University of Aberystwyth to take a degree in economics and international politics. Having also lectured there for a year, he spent the period from 1970 – 79 in the Centre for Foreign Policy Studies at Dalhousie University, Nova Scotia, as Professor of Maritime and Strategic Studies, before working in Washington, DC. He is married with five grown-up children, and lives at Swanage in Dorset.

**Captain John MOORE, RN** (*retd*) was born in Italy in 1921 and educated at Sherborne School, before joining the Royal Navy as a Special Entry Cadet on 1 September 1939. He served both at home and abroad, specialising in submarines. After six commands followed by command of a squadron, he was appointed Chief of Staff to Commander-in-Chief Naval Home Command, taking charge of Soviet Naval Intelligence at the Ministry of Defence. He retired at his own request in 1972 and subsequently edited *Jane's Fighting Ships* until 1987. He is author or co-author of nine books on naval subjects. At present he is Honorary Professor of International Relations at St Andrews University and has two books in preparation.

**Professor Amnon SELLA** was born in Israel in 1934 and graduated in 1969 from the Hebrew University in Russian Studies and English

Literature. He received his PhD from Edinburgh University in 1973, after which he returned to the Hebrew University in Israel where he is now an Associate Professor and Head of the Leonard Davis Institute for International Relations. He is the author of *Soviet Political and Military Conduct in the Middle East* (1981), and *Israel the Peaceful Belligerent* (1986), as well as being a co-author of *Organising for War: Soviet Military Establishment Viewed Through the Prism of the Military District* (1984). He has also had numerous articles published in various journals in the Middle East, Britain and the United States.

**Dr Henry SPETTER** took a Bachelor's degree in law from Sofia State University in Bulgaria and his doctorate in economics at the Höchschule für Oekonomie in Berlin. He has a solid background in research, having started as a research associate at the Institute of Economics at the Bulgarian Academy of Sciences in Sofia. After a spell with the United Nations, he was invited to be a Guest Researcher at the Vienna Institute for Comparative Economic Studies. He then made his way to Israel and became an economic researcher for the Israel Export Institute in Tel Aviv. He is currently an economic consultant to AEI Trading Ltd, as well as being a freelance correspondent for *Radio Free Europe* in Munich. His sphere of activities covers research into export promotion and marketing; problems of East – West trade and co-operation; trends and problems of the Bulgarian economy; and economic aspects of environmental protection in Eastern Europe. He has published three books and a number of papers, articles and studies in Bulgaria, Germany, Israel and the United States.

**Keith R TITUS** was for many years a military officer and civilian employee of the United States Army, serving in a variety of armour and intelligence assignments in Europe, the Middle East and the USA. He left to join the private sector and is now President of International Business Strategies Ltd, a consultancy specialising in strategic planning on behalf of firms entering into international business ventures. He is a major in the US Army Reserve and his last civilian posting was as the Senior Intelligence Officer, US Army Material Systems Analysis Activity, where he specialised in weapons systems development. Keith Titus received his undergraduate education at Georgetown University, the University of Salzburg, and the American University of Beirut. He is also a graduate of the Defence Intelligence Agency Post-graduate Intelligence Programme.

**Iván VOLGYES** was born in Hungary and emigrated to the USA in 1956. Since receiving his PhD at the American University, Professor

Volgyes taught at various universities including the University of Arizona and Rutgers University. He has been a Professor of Political Science at the University of Nebraska–Lincoln since 1966. His specialisations include political culture, political socialisation, security studies and the Warsaw Treaty Organisation. He is the author/editor of more than thirty books and nearly two hundred articles. Professor Volgyes is also the President of the Erasmus Foundation for Democracy and the Centre for Security and Defence Studies in Budapest.


**Lieutenant Commander James T WESTWOOD USN** (*retd*) is a full-time, self-employed systems scientist and Sovietologist, enjoying a reputation as a widely published author, lecturer and analyst with a broad military, academic and industrial experience. In particular he has been credited with a degree of innovation and discovery in Soviet studies and defence science. He graduated in Modern History, having also studied politics, management science and economic policy and strategy. During the Carter Administration, he was a principal for-mulator of and contributor to US and NATO intelligence estimates on the Soviet Union and Eastern Europe. Since he left the Navy 10 years ago, Westwood has served as a military operations research analyst at Headquarters, US Central Command, as a senior programme analyst at the Office of the US Secretary of Defence, as a scientific and technical intelligence analyst for the US Material Command, and a principal defence analyst of a major US defence electronics contractor. He currently teaches Soviet military science and technology at the George Washington University's School of Engineering and Applied Science, and is technical consultant to various US government agencies and US firms. He is an invited lecturer at the US Naval War College, the US Naval Post-Graduate School, the Marine Corps Command & Staff College, several universities and the US foreign Service Institute. At present he is investigating Soviet defence economic behaviour, trends and directions in Soviet R&D, and is working on the construction of a new model on which to base further research into the Soviet system. His overall interest is to make Sovietology a predictive as well as an interpretative science.


**Dr Stephen WHITE** is a Reader in Politics and a Member of the Institute of Soviet and East European Studies at Glasgow University, Scotland. A graduate of Dublin, Glasgow and Oxford Universities, he is the author of *The Origin of Detente* (1986); *The Bolshevik Poster* (1988); and *Gorbachev in Power* (1990), among other works. He is a member of the Editorial Boards of *Soviet Studies*, the *Journal of Communist Studies* and the *Nordic Journal of Soviet and East European Studies*. In 1990 he served as General Editor of the proceedings of the 4th World Congress for Soviet and East European Studies held at Harrogate, UK.

**Dr Ze'ev WOLFSON** was born in 1944 in Frunze City in the USSR and graduated in Bio-Geography from Moscow State University. From 1976 – 78 he was a senior researcher with the Nature Reserves Authority in Moscow, after which he became Senior Lecturer affiliated to the Biological and Environmental Department of Educational TV Programmes in Moscow. He was awarded his PhD by the Moscow State University in 1978 with a thesis on *The Development of Environmental Conservation in the USSR between 1956 – 1974*. After working in the Centre for Information at the Academy of Sciences in Moscow he emigrated to Israel in 1981, first becoming Adviser to the Israel Environmental Protection Agency, and then taking up a lecturing appointment in the Department of Geography at Bar-Ilan University in Tel Aviv. Since 1986 he has worked at the Centre for Soviet and East European Studies at the Hebrew University. He is best known for his book written in 1978 under the pseudonym 'Boris Komarov' and entitled *The Destruction of the Soviet Union*. Originally smuggled out of the USSR and printed in West Germany, this book was subsequently translated into seven different languages and published around the world. He has also had many articles published in Israel, the Soviet Union, the USA and Europe. Dr Wolfson is the editor of *Environmental Policy Review*. He now lives in Israel where he is married with two children.

# Foreword

MANFRED WÖRNER

AMONG the rich harvest of political and military writings on the significance of the developments which have transformed Europe since
1989, this collection of authoritative essays must stand out as one of the
best. Highly informative and well-researched, as one would expect
from its distinguished authors, the book sets out to examine the true
nature of the process now underway in the Soviet Union and in the
countries of Central and Eastern Europe. In doing so it seeks to
predict, with what might already be seen as a measure of prophetic
insight, how that process may evolve during the next five to ten years.

This is an ambitious undertaking. Given the number of unknowns
and variables which inevitably beset any such analysis in a fast-
changing political environment, it might almost seem an impossible
task. Undeterred, each of the contributors draws upon past history,
present factual evidence and a certain amount of informed speculation
to produce a comprehensive analysis, challenging the popular notion
that because much is uncertain there are no longer any certainties
whatever. Indeed, it has been easy to be distracted, first by the euphoria
which accompanied the advent of change and more recently by the
pessimism to which the realisation of the scale of the obstacles to
change has given rise. Many of those in policy-making roles, for whom
a deep understanding of the developments now taking place is of
critical importance, must be indebted to the contributors for this call
to order.

This novel approach offers unexpected advantages. Often penetrating
Soviet thinking and evoking traditional patterns of policy formulation,
these essays draw the reader away from the immediate impact of the
issues which today occupy the political and military high ground, in
order to focus on their longer-term significance. It is spurious to single
our particular chapters since this is an integrated collection of writings
which complement each other. Purely by way of illustration, however,
let me point the reader to David Glantz's remarkable discussion of the
variants which will provide the foundation for future Soviet military —
and political — strategy and to his summary of the basic realities which
that strategy can be expected to reflect; to Christopher Bellamy's

disciplined historical overview; to Ivan Volgyes' essay on Soviet relations with Eastern Europe; and to the thought-provoking inquiries by Stephen White, Amnon Sella and others into the adaptiveness of the Soviet system, economic and environmental issues, collective security perceptions including 'reasonable sufficiency', and different facets of military doctrine.

In a compilation of this nature the emergence of common themes may seem fortuitous. There are nevertheless many to be found in these pages. There are for example, many expressions of confidence in the ability of Soviet and Russian society to survive — not perhaps with the same characteristics, nor without experiencing a period of severe disruption — but to pull through, to make its proper rich contribution to European and global affairs, and to continue to surprise the world by the choices it makes and the solutions it espouses.

Secondly, from my particular perspective as Secretary General of NATO, a recurring theme is the underlying importance of preserving a modernised but dynamic and effective security structure centered on a proven partnership — that of the North American and European democracies. Readers would of course expect me to say that and had it not been made clear enough in these pages, I would have happily obliged in any case. Fortunately I can content myself with a simple restatement of what is unmistakably the sub-plot of this book.

We wish the Soviet peoples well. We are confident in their ability to succeed. We are willing to help. But our most effective contribution to that process must continue to be the pursuit of our own long-standing objective of a safer, more stable world with guarantees based on realistic negotiated conditions to diminish risks, improve confidence and manage crises. If it is true, as Ivan Volgyes reminds us, that conflict may be endemic to international relations, this is no time to relax our efforts to disprove the theory. Nor is it a time to forget that the Soviet leadership is fully aware that what is at stake is the long-term future. It recognises the importance of reconciling different views about what that future should contain and is enmeshed in a process of unprecedented complexity as it confronts these realities. It is most important that we understand this process and keep abreast of it. The reasons are obvious. Today we are facing the exciting challenge of developing the cooperation at all levels which will ensure that in fulfilling their ambitions East and West are not again setting out along roads which can never meet. This is the value of a book like this. Its reminders are timely and well-directed.

When the world stands at the threshold of a new order, the need for vigorous intellectual leadership is paramount. It is this necessity which is the impetus behind the Alliance's intensive programme of strategic, political and structural rethinking. It is less concerned with 'feeling its way towards a new mission' — and here I do take issue with an interpretation offered within these covers — than it is with developing the right concepts for the future European and international security environment. Of course they must be translated into flexible and creative policies and equipped with the firm political will to implement them and the proper institutional mechanisms to make them effective. If such policies are to carry conviction they must enjoy the enthusiastic support — and participation in their formulation — of all those countries which will be putting them into effect, as well as the respect of those which may be indirectly affected by them.

    This is by any standards an important book. It is also one which will not fall victim to the next change in the course of events, for it is itself predicated upon the exterior manifestations of change, while seeking to pin down the constants which remain. If it contributes, as it should, to our understanding of the future political and military environment in which our policies must be made to succeed, it will have achieved all that its authors may have wished.

# Introduction

JOHN HEMSLEY

IN LATE August 1987, after an absence from the Kremlin of several weeks, Gorbachev emerged from his retreat near Moscow having penned his *locus classicus* for reform. His book entitled *Perestroika*[1] was to be the blueprint for a transformation of the Soviet system; although in the process it could be said to have provided the catalyst which set in motion a chain reaction of events which have shaken the very foundations of the post-war political systems in Central and Eastern Europe.

As we enter the closing stages of the 20th century, portentous and uncertain times loom ahead, casting long shadows across the European political scene. Future historians may well look back to the four decades following the end of the Second World War and depict the Cold War, with its accompanying bi-polar, superpower alliances, as representing a comfortable predictability from which derived a certain stability. Now, whatever structures emerge from the present uncertainty, we can only be sure of two things: first, that there will be no return to the *status quo ante*; and second, and much more significant, there will be no fundamental change to the Russian social psyche.

This is because Russia, in the sense of being an imperial heartland, is more than just a geographical entity — it is a way of life; indeed it can almost be termed a concept in itself. Russia, in a geo-ethnic context and all that this embraces, is far greater than Communism. However what it has historically had in common with Communism is centralism. The very size and nature of both the old Tzarist Russian empire and the present Soviet Union dictate a strong centralised system of control. It is no accident of history that Russia was the one country in which Communism took hold at a time when its philosophical attraction as a political concept was on the decline throughout the remainder of Europe. By its theoretical nature, Communism takes the place of a creed or religion — call it what you will; but its ideality is open to an interpretation which can be subtly adapted to meet changing circumstances. This dialectic philosophy actually makes Communism a more flexible ideology than frequently its detractors give it credit for. Therefore it is important that we in the West should neither misunderstand nor underestimate this capacity for what the Russians term *adaptivnost'*.

In particular we need to appreciate the Soviet understanding of the nature of change. Change is regarded as part of the inevitable process of historical materialism. Nevertheless part of the Soviet paradox is that the Politburo in the Kremlin has always been a highly conservative body. It prefers change to be gradual. Abrupt and rapid change invariably leads to political uncertainty, resulting in events and situations which, more often than not, are characterised by a degree of unpredictability and loss of control. Despite this, the concept of one-party rule has lost credibility in the USSR. The transfer of power by Gorbachev from the Politburo to a presidential system of government was as much an attempt to distance himself from party politics as it was to exercise a more responsive measure of control over rapidly moving events. Although by the end of the 1980s the pace of change might have indicated an ideological retreat of Communism, the Soviet intellectual would argue that socialism has not failed but was merely undergoing a dialectic process of renewal based on humanism.

An appreciation of contemporary Soviet political philosophy is fundamental to our understanding of the Soviet system as a whole, since the latter is bound up with Russian institutions as well as being responsive to political doctrine; and institutions are more important than the weapon systems that support them. By the close of the 1980s, there had been a great deal of discussion and speculation in the West about the imminent break-up of the Soviet empire and the extinction of Communism. A disarmament euphoria had gripped many Western countries and the Soviet bear was suddenly perceived in a benevolent guise. This view was encouraged by a series of exceptional Soviet international propaganda coups in the disarmament field which for a while wrested the initiative from the United States, leaving it in the unaccustomed position of having constantly to react to events. In fact, from 1985 to 1988 the USSR was really facing a crisis of effectiveness, not one of survival. However, by the end of the decade it had become apparent that the USSR was in even deeper economic trouble than perhaps had generally been realised in the West. Consequently there was now an opening gap between Soviet long-term institutional perspectives in the international political and strategic military fields, and the internal concerns created by increasing domestic economic and nationalistic pressures.

Nevertheless, there are reasonable grounds for retaining a certain scepticism over Soviet intentions. So far there are many indications that the paramount concern of the USSR is to retain its collective security policy. In any case, one only has to reflect on the continuity and consistency of Soviet strategic thinking over the past 60 years (and Russian perceptions for 300 years before that). Therefore, it would be foolish not to ask ourselves the question the Russians ask themselves:

what are the determinants of military power? What strategies are required, and what control systems are needed to support them?

One of the Soviet Union's major preoccupations is the search for acceptability through recognition of legitimacy. Whatever the colour of the glass Western analysts use through which to view the Russian colossus, for the foreseeable future the man in control at the Kremlin will have been steeped in the theory of Marxist-Leninism. His policy will be to make the USSR a political and economic superpower as well as a military power. In the light of the probable development of a multi-polar global scenario for the next century, his vision will be of a socialist Europe, dominated by the Soviet Union in the long term, whilst possibly shifting to the West in the medium term, the economic burden of developing the peripheral COMECON countries. As a process of consolidation, this retreat from Eastern Europe, together with the 15 year breathing space required by the USSR to attain some semblance of economic viability and high-tech implementation, is almost certainly the prime motive behind the current apparent softer attitude towards traditional Soviet imperialism. However this cannot disguise the fact that an economically resource-poor civil sector produces little prospect of supporting a strong economic expansion. Therefore Soviet expansionist imperatives can, in the short term, still only be expressed in politico-military or territorial terms. Either way this requires underwriting by credible military power, and the strength and sophistication of Soviet military potential, coupled with the growth of real strategic capability over the past 15 years, has given the USSR the foundation on which to base a significant potential increase in global political influence. The implications of this for the West were aptly summed up by a sometime Supreme Allied Commander of NATO Forces in Europe, General Lemnitzer, who said:

> Military planning must be orientated only to the capabilities of a potential enemy, not his assumed intentions. Intentions can change overnight.

There are three basic components to any strategic threat — capability, likelihood and intent. The first of these is a straightforward matter of the collection, collation and provenance of political, economic and military information, from which an objective assessment can be made. Forecasting any degree of likelihood is a much more complex and difficult matter, since it is based upon a thorough appreciation of the whole intelligence picture, related to current imperatives and national perceptions. The question of intent, however, is notoriously difficult to predict as it is time-sensitive and can normally only be proved by the event itself.

Therefore, when addressing developments in the Soviet Union, it is important to look beneath the surface to determine what it is that we are really seeing, and then to evaluate the significance in relation to Soviet perceptions, uncertainties, capabilities and long-term planning.

The purpose of this book is to look at the way the USSR is likely to develop over the next 10 years or so in terms of its requirements and plans for the first decade of the next century. This implies an examina-ion of some of the instabilities currently facing the Soviet Union, in order to try to deduce Soviet interpretations, debate and response to these uncertainties. To provide such an insight involves many diverse disciplines; consequently this book has been compiled under collective authorship by assembling an international team of specialists on Soviet studies.

An obvious editorial concern lies with the prophetic element, whereby much of the material in this volume will inevitably be concerned with the way that the Soviet Union sees itself in relation to likely develop-ments elsewhere in the world over the coming decade. The science of 'futurology' is notoriously speculative: wherever possible the authors have tried to avoid falling into this trap. Therefore this is not just another dated anthology, speculating on the future of the USSR at a time of rapid change, but rather an attempt at a scholarly investigation into the mechanisms of change as a means of examining their probable impact on the institutional processes of the Soviet Union. These pro-cesses are then carefully defined to establish how much inertia exists and why, and to what extent they may be responsive to the require-ments of *perestroika*. The book seeks to establish the constraints and limitations operating on *perestroika*, as well as looking at the penalties of failure and the effects on the 'system' as a whole. The approach is therefore based on a properly-structured treatment, designed to narrow the parameters for speculation in order to produce a credible forecast regarding Soviet political, economic and security options to the end of this century.

To achieve this, the work has been presented in three main sections by grouping the subject material into broad categories. Part I sets out to investigate Soviet security concerns, economic strategies and political forecasts up to and beyond the end of this century, all of which point to the probable practical effects of *perestroika* and *glasnost'* in terms of internal political and institutional reforms, along with the economic restructuring which will largely influence external policies. Much of this will depend upon many external factors which pose questions, the answers to which are as yet difficult to determine. For instance what are the roles likely to be adopted by the USSR and the USA as self-appointed world leaders and guarantors in global arms control within the context of shifting power blocs and new alliances? In the same context, to what extent will either country be prepared to assume, or allow the other to engage in, the role of an international constabulary to police regional conflict? Or is it possible that a total fragmentation of the Soviet Union will lead to the emergence of latent American isolationism? Will there be an end to the bi-polar, superpower balance which has characterised the last 40 years in favour of a multi-polar world, with some new regional powers emerging? Will the developing nations' dependency on Middle East oil continue to make that part of the world a potential international flashpoint? Is it possible that there will be a realignment of the global strategic centre of gravity to the Pacific? How will Soviet institutions adapt to meet new political, social and economic imperatives? A central question to the whole of this study concerns the future political and economic cohesion of the USSR itself; and, a major matter of concern to the Soviet Union as well as some others in Europe, the future long-term aspirations of a united Germany. It is from some or all of these considerations that future Soviet prescriptions for their national security will be generated, leading to a revision of political doctrine.

This forms a substantial background against which Part II examines a range of issues involving the potential of the Soviet Union for self-defence as well as options for exercising power projection by the end of this century. The result is a cogent appreciation of the Soviet High Command's approach to long-term planning and preparation, within the framework of political and economic constraints, to meet a range of contingencies and involving matters of military doctrine, sea-power, force structures, organisations, techniques, equipment and technology. Although to some extent events may temporarily have overtaken military preferences, the Soviet military remains one of the few institutions which cuts across national, ethnic and cultural lines.

Part III provides support for many of the issues already discussed by looking at some political and economic models, as well as the social dimension on which the system is based. Probably the greatest concern lies in the escalating problem of environmental pollution and an approaching catastrophic ecological destruction. The cost of implementing a damage limitation programme in this area means that it will become increasingly linked to domestic economic considerations. Finally the prospects for arms control are examined in the light of a new European security structure influenced by the changing nature of warfare, new military doctrines, emerging technology and improved procedures for verification.

This collection of 15 essays by individual authors, each of whom is an acknowledged specialist in his field, attempts to answer many of the questions currently being asked in the West regarding what is happening in the Soviet Union today and, more importantly, points the way to understanding what sort of Russia might emerge at the end of this century.

Finally, it must be remembered that the majority of the authors are not British; consequently English may not be their natural written language. Excessive editing is frequently liable to result in an undesirable uniformity of style, not to mention changing the author's original emphasis, and some of the more subtle inflexions of meaning. Therefore, although some passages may justifiably be criticised for some constructional inelegancies, my editorial policy has been to leave each contribution as close to its author's original manuscript as possible.

## Note

[1] *Perestroika* means restructuring, although much of Gorbachev's book is devoted to 'new political thinking', especially in the context of foreign policy.

# PART I

CHAPTER 1

# Historical Perspectives

CHRISTOPHER BELLAMY

A high-spirited people in a land that does not like doing things by
halves, but has spread in a vast smooth plain over half the world,
and you may count the milestones until your eyes are dizzy. . . .
Is it not like that that you, too, Russia, are speeding along like
a spirited *troika* that nothing can overtake? . . . What is the meaning
of this terrifying motion? And what mysterious force is hidden in
these horses, the like of which the world has never seen? . . .
Russia, where are you flying to? Answer! She gives no answer. . .[1]

NEVER was the uncertain track of Nikolai Gogol's three-horsed sleigh,
the speeding *troika*, more apt an image than now. Wherever Russia is
flying to, maybe over a precipice, it is the old Russia. Seventy years
of socialism are but a thin neo-cortex on over a thousand years of state-
hood, shaped by the same climate, the same land, the same people, the
same pattern of life enforced by the seasons. The changes of the last
few years, and most notably since the sudden collapse of the Soviet
East European empire, are the most radical since 1917. The gathering
movement towards parliamentary democracy recalls the previous,
unsuccessful attempt from 1905 – 14. With the socialist topsoil stripped
away, the firmer ground of pre-revolutionary Russian history is exposed.
It has become more relevant than ever, and no-one is more aware of
that than the Russians themselves.

Common sense apart, that is the overwhelming justification for taking
a perspective of Russia's past, present and future which would be
difficult to justify when talking about some other people. It is quite
acceptable to talk about the 'Russian soul', the timeless sweep of
Russian history, or Russia's destiny, because the Russians themselves
do. The British do not. The Russian fondness for eschatology and
contempt for time, as for space, is not only evident in literature. In
1900, General Kuropatkin, the War Minister, drew up the first of a
number of reports on Russia's strategy for the twentieth century.

3

Elements of the reports, transferred via 'a faint carbon copy of a type-script', — no doubt in a suitably James Bond fashion — were translated and published in English in 1909. The editor was suitably impressed:

> The forethought and care with which the possible price of Empire in the twentieth century was worked out by the Russian War Ministry is enlightening, for who has estimated the possible cost in blood and treasure of the expansion or maintenance of the British Empire during the next hundred years?[2]

Who indeed? Kuropatkin used as his database all the wars fought by Russia during the previous 200 years. He advised that the Empire avoided involvement in Afghanistan, and predicted that 'the internal pacification and administration of Poland [then part of the Empire] will doubtless prove one of the problems of this [20th] century'.[3] History is not such a bad database, used sensibly. Still more significant, however, is the astonishing ambition of attempting to predict the conditions and problems of the next hundred years.

Russia has produced more than its fair share of dreamers, and attracted the interest of others. Of the futuristic writers of this century, two, Yevgeniy Zamyatin (1884 – 1937) and Isaac Asimov (born 1920), were Russian by birth, although Asimov left Russia as a baby and Zamyatin was an exile and outcast from Soviet Russia. Zamyatin's novel *We* anticipated Huxley's *Brave New World* and Orwell's *Nineteen Eighty-Four*, and it is almost certain that both the English-language writers were influenced by Zamyatin.[4] H G Wells was fascinated by Russia and corresponded with Lenin and Stalin. In his works before the First World War, Wells anticipated the current round of *glasnost'* (itself a word used, with the same implications of openness and intellectual freedom in the 1850s). Without freedom to think and develop ideas, Russia would be doomed to remain technologically second-rate. The imperative for liberalisation and reform was as much military as philanthropic. Only by 'liberalising on the western model', said Wells, could Russia compete with Germany in terms of technology and military technique.[5]

Yet even before the First World War Russia's technological achievements were impressive. Another widespread myth is that pre-revolutionary Russia was always backward, dependent on foreign expertise for everything. This is not so. Some things had to be obtained from abroad, but Russian inventiveness could use them in ways that their originators never dreamed of. A striking example is the work of the young aircraft designer, Igor Sikorskiy, (1889 – 1972) better known for his work on helicopters after he emigrated to the United States in 1919. But Sikorskiy designed the world's most extraordinary and advanced aircraft, the first four-engined aerial behemoth, later used as a bomber. This was the *Russkiy Vityaz'* — Russian Knight (another example of patriotic Russian folklore) — completed in 1913 which evolved into the *Il'ya Muromets* — another medieval Russian hero. Besides four engines, these aircraft had completely enclosed cabins with lightweight furniture and even a lavatory. The bomber version was armoured, was the first aircraft ever to have a tail gun, and eventually carried up to seven machine guns. Before the First World War, in June, 1914, Sikorskiy made a record-breaking flight from St Petersburg to Kiev. About 80 *Muromets* were operational during the war, of which only three were lost to enemy action. Having four engines (first French, later British), they were uniquely reliable and, for the time, astonishingly heavily armed.[6]

The *Il'ya Muromets* exemplifies several points about Russian creativity, design and technology: use of foreign parts where necessary; ruggedness; and a sense of the grandiose, of showmanship; maybe a certain meretricious swagger. There is something engagingly child-like about the Russian passion for scale. It sometimes irritates Westerners. One crusty observer muttered, after witnessing the sensational film of a huge simulated Soviet parachute assault in 1935, that it confirmed his view that 'the Russians are a nation of incorrigible dreamers'.[7]

Besides such enduring characteristics, Russian history does seem strikingly cyclical. The medieval Russian state, beleaguered by Swedes and the Teutonic knights on one side, the Mongols on the other, occupied an area almost identical to the Russian Republic in the darkest days of the Civil War, in 1918. In the Civil War, as in the Middle Ages, Russia's adversaries, and identity, were determined not just by nationalistic and economic factors, but by ideology also, adding a peculiar bitterness to the struggle. The Orthodox Russians were regarded as heretics by the Catholics to the west. The world's first Communist state, the Bolsheviks as they were referred to during the Civil War, was an ideological pariah, atheistic to boot. And then, by means of little short of miraculous, in a handful of years, the new government's writ had expanded to run through the full extent of the former Russian Empire, with the exception of Poland and Finland.[8]

Understanding the current phase of Russian history is a lot easier if you look at the past. We are faced with the paradox of Mr Gorbachev acquiring more and more dictatorial powers to enforce modernisation, westernisation, even liberalisation, on a reluctant administration and, increasingly, a reluctant populace. But Mr Gorbachev is simply doing what successive Russian leaders, all great, in their own way, have done before, though not necessarily humanely.

Peter the Great dragged Russia, kicking and screaming — and belatedly — into the Enlightenment. Alexander II, who liberated the serfs in 1861, dragged it kicking and screaming into the 19th century: an act virtually simultaneous with the liberalisation of the slaves in the United States, and with similarly mixed short-term results. Lenin, Trotsky and Stalin dragged Russia kicking and screaming into the industrial era, although there were impressive advances at the end of the 19th century. Mr Gorbachev is trying to drag Russia, kicking and screaming, into the post-industrial era: the information era.

But even those who profess to be experts on Russia, or for whom things Russian are of obvious occasional importance — defence analysts, for example — may be baffled by straightforward allusions to Russian history. With rising anti-Russian nationalism in Georgia, Azerbaijan and Latvia, it made sense this year to rename three aircraft carriers which embarrassingly bore the names of their capitals: *Tbilisi*, *Baku* and *Riga*. The first two were renamed after great Admirals, *Kuznetsov* and *Gorshkov*, and the third, *Varyag*.[9] But the significance of the latter was perhaps lost on the reporter. *Varyag*, — Varangian — refers to the Vikings who pushed down to the Black Sea and Constantinople via the Neva, Volkhov and Dnepr rivers. Some finished up in Constantinople, guarding the Byzantine emperors. One, Rurik, was invited by the inhabitants of Novgorod to become their lord in the 9th century and is regarded as one of the founders of the Russian state. Varyag is as Russian as Robin Hood or Alfred the Great is English: another example of the swelling tide of *Russian* nationalism in the country.

Why 'Russians'? The correct term for citizens of the Soviet Union is, one supposes, 'Soviet people' — a translation of *sovetskiye*, meaning small committees, sitting, one assumes round tables. (Soviets (*sovety*) meaning people is an Americanism.) When referring to the Empire before 1917, scholars are allowed to talk about the Russians, and things Russian, even though that Empire was just as heterogeneous and occupied much the same territory, including the Ukraine, as its Soviet successor, as well as, for a time, Poland and Finland. Ukrainians and Belorussians, Tadzhiks and Tatars, Kalmyks and Georgians are just as infuriated about being referred to as 'Russians' as the Scots, Irish and Welsh are at being lumped together with the English — as they invariably are by the Russians, who call them all *angliyskiy*, unless they are being particularly punctilious.

But Russia was always at the heart of the Empire. Russians dominated its government and administration, as they still do (until break-up, at any rate). Russian was the language of the government. Now, Russia is falling back into itself. The Russian Soviet Federative Socialist Republic — the heartland of Russia in Europe and Russia in Asia — looks set to go it alone, if it has to. And even if it loses the territory, agricultural and mineral wealth of the Ukraine — with 50 million people, a major European state in its own right — Russia will still be Europe's most extensive, populous and militarily powerful state.

When Gogol wrote the mystical, wildly chauvinistic passage at the head of this Chapter in the late 1830s, the Russian Empire was indeed 'a vast smooth plain over half the world', as to a lesser extent it still is. No major mountain ranges running north-south intersect it; the Urals are not a significant barrier. The Empire stretched more than half way round the world, and embraced three continents, from Kalisz, near the frontier of Russian Poland, 18 degrees east of Greenwich, to 140 degrees west, with scattered islands beyond. Three continents because it included the vast unexploited and indefensible land of Alaska, sold to the United States for a song in 1867. The spread of latitude was less staggering, but at one point it still occupied nearly half the hemisphere, from the polar ice-cap down to 45 degrees. Within a few years, it would swallow independent Tartary, take Tashkent and Khiva, and touch the Himalayas and the Persian border, just one short pull, so it seemed from India and the Gulf. The Russian Tzar appeared to worried foreign observers 'the mighty behemoth of Muscovy, the potentate who counts 300 languages round the footsteps of his throne'.[10]

The Russian Empire came to fill the centre of the Eurasian land mass because there was nothing much in the way. The same is true, indeed, of Canada and the United States in North America. As in North America, the most militarily potent and organised state in the region was of European origin. But Eurasia is bigger than North and South America put together. And Russia occupies the central position.

Geopolitics is an unfashionable notion in western intellectual circles these days. But when a senior consultant to the Soviet Communist Party publishes an article called 'Russia: the Earth's Heartland' in an influential journal, even the hardened western liberal has to take note. The idea of Eurasia as the world's heartland is associated with Sir Halford Mackinder (1861 – 1947). As Igor Malashenko reminded readers in July 1990, Mackinder believed that 'those who control Eastern Europe dominate the Heartland; those who rule the Heartland dominate the World Island (that is, Eurasia); those who rule the World Island dominate the world'.[11]

Throughout Russian history, in spite of periodic violent clashes, Russia and Germany have been drawn together. The *Dreikaiserbund* — the three Emperors' League — in the 19th century, the German-Soviet co-operation in the 1920s, and the remarkable rapprochement that has now taken place in spite of the unimaginably bitter memory of 1941 – 45, bear witness to the centripetal tendencies of the 'heartland'. Now, Malashenko points out,

The weakening of the USSR in Central Europe is accompanied

by a reduction of its military presence in that region. In the meantime, the unification of Germany is going on by leaps and bounds [it occurred politically on 3 October, 1990 but true economic unification will take years]. Sooner or later, that country will succeed in translating its enormous economic strength into political influence, acquiring the status of a European superpower.[12]

The idea of greater Germany and Russia uniting to wield economic and perhaps political control over the heartland cannot be ruled out. There may be other states — Poland, Belorussia and the Ukraine (which could conceivably separate from Russia) — between them. But political, economic and geographical realities suggest that the Ukraine and Belorussia will remain in some sort of union with Russia. Once again, Poland finds itself in the unenviable position of being squeezed between Russia and Germany.

It is not impossible that Poland and the Ukraine (whose joint population would be greater than that of United Germany) might form a united power base. This would return eastern Europe to the situation before Peter the Great, where it was touch and go whether Poland-Lithuania, and not Russia, would become the principal Slav power. One might expect Russia to resist such a trend, unlikely though it may be.

The idea that Russian dominion in the Eurasian heartland must be preserved is clearly a powerful influence on Soviet — and Russian — policy. One can see why the Soviet government (and particularly the General Staff) were concerned about the arrival of huge American forces in the Middle East as part of operation *Desert Shield* in the latter part of 1990. From Moscow, this must have looked like giving the United States a threatening and fairly secure toe-hold on the rim of Eurasia.

It is clear that Russia's domination of the centre of Eurasia will be assured, in the last resort, by military power, particularly by Russia's still colossal nuclear arsenal. It is perhaps surprising that the Soviet Union gave up Eastern Europe so easily, as the same time as completing its withdrawal from Afghanistan. Malashenko explains why.

There need be no fear that the withdrawal of Soviet troops from Afghanistan and Czechoslovakia, Mongolia and Hungary, and the reduction of the armed forces and munitions production will diminish this country's security: the Soviet Union's colossal nuclear potential is a reliable shield capable of resisting attempts at obtaining domination in the heart of Eurasia by force of arms. Conversely a further over-extension of all forces and resources for the sake of maintaining military-political control over vast territories can deplete the nation's richest potential and undermine the source of its strength and security from within.[13]

Malashenko adds that the USSR 'is losing its status of a superpower and is becoming merely one of the power centres of Eurasia. In its turn, the United States, which retains its power in absolute parameters, will be increasingly operating as an external balance-wheel averting the rise of a pan-Eurasian centre of power'.[14]

In other words, just as Britain sought to prevent any one power or group of powers becoming too strong in 18th and 19th century Europe, so the same aim will apply to the whole of Eurasia in the next century. Russia will remain one of those great powers. In a sense, its position will be more like that which it enjoyed in 18th century Europe, before the asiatic imperial expansion of the 19th century. By the time of the Seven Years' War (1756 – 63) Russia was a European power to be reckoned with on the same scale as France, Austria and Prussia. By 1914, it was already showing signs of becoming a superpower. Norman Stone, now Professor of Modern History at Oxford, formed the view that this was, possibly, one reason why the Germans were anxious to break Russia before it grew any stronger.[15]

But will Russia itself hold together? The areas which are attempting to break away from the Union are those acquired by conquest, fairly recently. The Baltic states were independent until 1940, when they were incorporated in the Union under the wing of the Nazi-Soviet pact of August, 1939. Central Asia and the Caucasus were acquired by force of arms in the 19th century, and these are areas of particular trouble. But the elements of Russia itself, like those of a giant planet, have a certain mutual attraction. Lev Gumilëv called it a 'superethnos', 'a Eurasian country in the true sense of the word, but also a powerful centre of attraction for numerous ethnoses'.[16]

Against this, however, one must balance the enormously strong pull of the neighbouring European 'superethnos'. Clearly, this counteracts, and may eventually triumph over, Russia's own coherence. And, furthermore, as Malashenko warns:

> One cannot rule out the possibility that decades of coercion by the state, deportation of ethnic communities and destruction of culture could have reduced to nought the forces of ethnocultural attraction which had made Russia what it was, rather than just a 'Russian Empire'. If confidence between our ethnic communities turns out to have been irreparably damaged and the repulsive forces prevail in relations between them, we will have only one prospect in store, that of a nationalistic upheaval in the heartland of Eurasia, beside which even the most macabre versions of the German question will have paled into insignificance.[17]

There is a good parallel with the future position of Russia and the Soviet Union in the Ottoman Empire. Like the Russian Empire, that of the Ottoman Turks grew partly by osmosis, partly by military force. It was a vast super-ethnos, bridging Europe and Asia as Russia does. Inhabitants of all its provinces might participate in its government: indeed some, like Christian boys called up under the *devsirme* system, formed the élite corps of Janissaries. The Cossacks provide a partial parallel. Even when European technology was beginning to surpass that of the Ottoman Empire, the latter's armed forces, maintained and supplied through a superb system of taxation and administration, remained formidable.[18] The Ottoman Empire eventually sickened. But it stumbled on into the 20th century and as late as 1917 was still a formidable military power.

After the First World War, Ataturk strove to make Turkey into a modern, European, secular state. The question is whether the Soviet Union, or Russia, if the Union breaks up, will have to sicken and stumble on for centuries before such a revitalisation, or whether Gorbachev can effect it now, before a catastrophic decline sets in.

A final, necessary perspective, is to remember that the Russians are very like us — though more like the British than the Americans. As with the British, there is a strong Nordic element in the Russian make-up. The slavic element, on the other hand, is very Mediterranean. Like the British, furthermore, they have had a long period of contact with Asia and Islam, which makes them different from the solid inhabitants of *Mitteleuropa*. They drink tea. They like getting drunk. They have rotten weather. Partly for this reason, they love bright, garish colours, particularly red (London buses on a gloomy December day). They are intrinsically anarchistic, so they need to be kept in order. They are not like the Germans, who like being organised and will get on with a job if told to. They will take a tea-break, skive off, go down to the pub. They have to be kept at it. At home, they 'slag themselves off' (to use the current vernacular) constantly, but, deep down, they are utterly proud to be Russian, and hold foreigners in that strange mixture of awe and contempt. So far, few Russians have reached Torremolinos, but when they do they will be indistinguishable from the British.

The parallels are endless. The Emperor Charles V once said he spoke Spanish to God, French to his friends, German to his enemies, and Italian to the ladies. Numerous English and Russian speakers have contemptuously pointed out that, of course, he could have spoken English — or Russian — to all of them.

Like the British, too, the Russians bumble along when things are not too bad, grumbling and putting up with inefficiency. When things get really bad, they have tended to come into their own. So far, that

particular characteristic has not reasserted itself. But if the crisis gets
worse, maybe. . . 'Russia, where are you flying to? Answer! She gives
no answer. . .'

## Notes

[1] Nikolai Gogol, *Mertvye dushi*, trans. as Dead Souls by David Magarshack, (Penguin,
Harmondsworth, 1961), pp. 258 – 59. Dead Souls was written between 1834 and
1842, but mostly in 1818 – 39. Gogol is, of course, the surname of the KGB
General in the James Bond films.

[2] General A N Kuropatkin, *The Russian Army and the Japanese War*, trans. Captain A
B Lindsay, ed. Maj. E D Swinton, (2 Vols., John Murray), London, 1909),
Editor's Introduction, Vol. 1, p. xi. At this stage, Kuropatkin had been unable to
publish his work. However, much of the same material appears in Kuropatkin's
*Zadachi russkoy armii* (The Role of the Russian Army), (3 Vols., V A Berezovskiy,
Commissioner of Military-Educational Establishments, St Petersburg, 1910). A
condensed version of the analysis also appeared in the first four Chapters of A
Morskoy (ed.), *Voyennaya mosch' Rossii. Predskazaniya Gen.-Ad. A N Kuropatkina i ikh
kritika Gr. S. Yu. Vitte* (The Military Power of Russia. Adjutant General A N
Kuropatkin's Predictions and Criticism by Count S Yu Witte), (M Popov, Petrograd,
1915) (signed Petrograd 24 August, 1914).

[3] Quote, Kuropatkin, *The Russian Army*, Vol. 1, p. 11. See also Kuropatkin, *Zadachi. . .*,
Vol. 2, pp. 269 – 70.

[4] Yevgeniy Zamyatin, *We* [My], trans. Bernard Guilbert Guerney, Introduction and
Bibliography by Michael Glenny, (Jonathan Cape, London, 1970), esp. pp. 21, 285;
E J Brown, Brave New World, 1984 and *We. An Essay on Anti-Utopia* [Zamyatin
and English Literature], (Ardis, Ann Arbor, 1976), esp. p. 19; D J Richards,
Zamyatin. A Soviet Heretic, (Bowes and Bowes, London, 1962), esp. p. 13.
Asimov is a prolific writer of science fiction and other work in the field of futures
studies: see especially Isaac Asimov, *A Choice of Catastrophes*, (Hutchinson, London,
1980).

[5] See H G Wells, *The Discovery of the Future. A Discourse Delivered to the Royal Institution
on January 24, 1902*, (T Fisher Unwin, London, 1902); *War and Common Sense*,
(articles from the *Daily Mail*, 7, 8, & 9 April, 1913, reprinted, London, 1913); *The
War that will end war*, (Frank Cecil and Palmer, London, 1914); *What is Coming, a
Forecast of Things after the War*, (Cassell, London, 1916).

[6] See K H Finne, *Igor Sikorsky: the Russian Years*, ed. Carl J Bobrow, Von Hardesty,
Trans. and adapted Von Hardesty, (originally published as *Vozdushniye bogatyry I
Sikorskogo — I Sikorskiy's Winged Knights*, Belgrade, 1930), (Smithsonian Institution
Press, Washington, 1987).

[7] The film shown in 1935 recorded the 1934 Minsk manoeuvres. Comment by
General Knox, a former military attaché in Petrograd (formerly until 1914, St
Petersburg: from 1924, Leningrad). Ivan Maisky, (Soviet Ambassador to the UK),
*V Londone*, ('In London'), in N I Koritskiy, ed., *Marshal Tukhachevskiy: vospominaniya
druzyey i soratnikov*, (Marshal Tukhachevskiy: Memoirs of Friends and Comrades in
Arms), (Voyenizdat, Moscow, 1965), p. 229.

[8] See the author's 'British Views of Russia: Russian views of Britain' in Philip
Towle, ed., *Estimating Foreign Military Power*, (Croom Helm, Beckenham, 1982).

[9] See 'Ships renamed as nationalism rises', *Jane's Defence Weekly*, 8 December, 1990,
p. 1150. The one form of 'nationalism' the analysis does not mention is Russian
nationalism. See also recent editions of *Voyennoistoricheskiy zhurnal* (Military-
Historical Journal), formerly a serious military-scientific publication which has

increasingly degenerated into a catalogue of re-enactments of Tzarist battles by societies in fancy dress and is increasingly filled with illustrations of Russian (not Soviet) decorations. The Interior Ministry (*MVD*) Journal, *Sovetskaya militsiya* covers police matters, also features numerous references to Russian patriotism. See, for example, K Mikhaylov, '*Moy lyubov*', *moya Rossiya*' ('My Love, My Russia'), *SM*, 9/1990, between pp. 32, 33, and G Chagin, '*Verivshiy v Rossiyu*', ('Believing in Russia'), *ibid.*, p. 33. Also, for example, Mark Galeotti, 'Eternal Mother Russia', *Jane's Soviet Intelligence Review*, October 1990, pp. 461 – 64.

[10] Quoted in Francis McCullagh, *With the Cossacks, Being the Story of an Irishman who rode with the Cossacks throughout the Russo-Japanese War*, (Eveleigh Nash, London, 1906), p. 164.

[11] Igor Malashenko, 'Russia: the Earth's Heartland', *International Affairs*, (Moscow, in English, ISSN 0130-9641), July 1990, pp. 46.

[12] *Ibid.*, p. 48.

[13] *Ibid.*, p. 50.

[14] *Ibid.*, p. 51.

[15] See Norman Stone, *The Eastern Front, 1914 – 17*, (Hodder and Stoughton, London, 1975).

[16] Malashenko, p. 52.

[17] *Ibid.*, pp. 53 – 54.

[18] See J M Rogers and R M Ward, *Suleiman the Magnificent*, (British Museum Publications, London, 1988), pp. 36 – 37).

# CHAPTER 2

# Evolving Soviet Political Doctrine[1]

## MICHAEL MCCGWIRE

HAVING endured largely unchanged for 70 years, the Soviet theory of international relations was radically reshaped and the focus of military doctrine was redefined in the 18 months up to mid-1988. Given the fundamental nature of these changes and bearing in mind the uncertain future of the Soviet state, before discussing the possible evolution of its political doctrine, the subject must be placed in some kind of historical context.

This chapter starts by reviewing possible political outcomes to the far-reaching changes that have been underway in the Soviet Union since 1987, and considering which of those outcomes could be termed a coherent doctrine, either Soviet or Russian. It then surveys relevant aspects of Tzarist and Soviet history to provide a plausible basis for prognostication. Next, it reviews the *perestroika* process that led to the fundamental change in Soviet policies and doctrine. Lastly, it considers the constraints on future Soviet policy and suggests two main directions in which doctrine might evolve.

## Relevant Outcomes

There are many possible outcomes to the attempt to restructure the Soviet political economy. Gorbachev may be fully successful and it is conceivable that the Soviet Union will emerge intact as a powerful nation with a fully developed economy which would be a strong competitor in the world economy. It is also possible that the attempt will fail utterly, resulting in political, social and economic disintegration, which could lead to anarchy, brigandage, and perhaps even full-scale civil war.

Many scenarios lie between these extremes, including a state of repressive stagnation, with similarities to the final century of the Ottoman empire or to Spain once it started its imperial decline. There is, therefore, a strong possibility that some or all of the ethnically distinct republics that lie on the Soviet periphery and were later accretions to the Russian empire, will break away, either completely or through some constitutional rearrangement. Many within Soviet government and academic circles see such a breakup as inevitable and some see it as ultimately beneficial. Some believe that only Belorussia can be counted on to remain linked with the Russian republic (RSFSR), while others include the eastern (non-Catholic) part of Ukraine and the northern (non-Muslim) part of Khazakhstan, and there are other variants.

Popular feelings are more difficult to gauge. Among the Russians, who make up about half the Soviet population, there are certainly those who strongly favour preserving the imperial borders of the USSR. These would include many, if not most, of those serving in all-Union military and internal security organisations, the party bureaucracies, state institutions and industries, and professional and trade unions. But there are others who see 'Russia' as a nation rather than an empire, and while the various protagonists may differ on its essential character and postulated boundaries, they agree that such a nation could even profit from relinquishing the non-Russian areas.

From this array of possible outcomes, only two are really relevant to the focus of this book. One is that something approximating the present-day USSR will persist as a more or less effective political entity. The other outcome is the disintegration of the Union, leaving a predominantly slavic nation with a population 50 – 70% of the present size of the USSR, depending on whether either or both the Ukraine and Belorussia break away. I label these alternative outcomes a Soviet and a Russian state.

The nature of these two potential states (and hence their underlying political doctrine) will to some extent depend on how the break-up of the Soviet Union comes about or is prevented, and that in turn will depend on the type of regime in power at the critical period. Drawing on the situation that existed in the second half of 1990, possible types of regime can be specified in terms of their relative position on a continuum between populist democracy and private enterprise at one end, and authoritarian control and state collectivism at the other. Boris Yeltsin and Egor Ligachev can be taken as the opposite ends of this domestic axis, with a Gorbachev-type regime located somewhere between them. The latter would be firmly opposed to Ligachev-type ideas, but also be opposed to populism and to the Yeltsinite rejection of socialist values and embrace of the market as an economic and social panacea.

These three alternative regimes can be further defined in terms of their location on axes measuring nationalistic fervour (high/low) and international stance (outward/inward and active/passive). These are, however, theoretical dimensions whose practical implications are less significant in terms of potential foreign policy than might at first appear.

In respect of nationalism, one must distinguish between the patriotic and cultural forms. There is evidence of a patriotic backlash against Gorbachev's over-conciliatory foreign policy and against the intellectual establishment's readiness to blame the Soviet Union for all unfavourable developments since the Second World War and for much that went wrong in the inter-war years. A restoration of Soviet military might is not a practical option for a future Russian or Soviet state, but it would encourage a more intransigent if not actively confrontational foreign policy that was jealous of the nation's rights and prestige and unwilling to make unilateral concessions or to compromise.

The cultural form of nationalism, which was prominent in the 19th century and was mostly evident in the disagreement between the slavophiles and the westernisers over Russia's future orientation, has implications for the nature of domestic politics and the type of the regime in Moscow. If Solzhenitsyn's ideas are any guide, a slavophile regime would be more authoritarian, hierarchical and less democratic. Cultural nationalism would be a disruptive force in relation to the national aspirations of the other republics and would make a Russian Union comprising Belorussia and the Ukraine unlikely, unless a strong slavophile movement emerged in those republics.

Russian nationalism would tend to be constrained and contained by the countervailing nationalism of other groups. While this could lead to inter-ethnic or inter-republic conflict, there is no reason why that should prompt 'foreign adventures' beyond the borders of the Soviet Union as they exist today, if only because the necessary surplus military capability would be lacking. Besides, the Russians' 'historic urge to aggression' is largely a Western-inspired myth.

## Relevant Background

Russia, whether ruled by Tzars or Communists, has not been unusual in its aggressive or expansionist tendencies. It is true that Tzarist Russia joined the other European nations in the global expansion that got underway at the end of the 15th century. And in the 17th or 18th centuries it jostled for power in Europe, pushing back the Swedish and Polish-Lithuanian empires to the west and the Ottoman empire to the south. But Russia's territorial aspirations in Europe had been effectively satisfied by the middle of the 19th century.

It was England that attached the expansionist label to its imperial rival, along with the continuing 'drive for warm water ports', a Russian requirement that had, however, been largely met by the end of the 18th century. These assertions were resurrected after 1945 and recruited to the cause of inflating a Soviet threat that was said to derive from a Communist urge for military world domination. But that, too, was mainly myth. Certainly, the Communists believed that the socialist system would prevail, but that would be the result of what was believed to be an inevitable historical process. Once the Soviet Union went beyond the arguments of the early 1920s, it was accepted that world revolution could not be exported on Red Army bayonets. Armed forces would, however, be needed to defend the Soviet Union, the revolution's home base, and to rebuff capitalist attempts to reverse future gains of socialism.

It was not Russia, but the three 'unsatisfied' powers, Germany, Italy and Japan, whose expansionist drive led to the Second World War. The Soviet forces entered Eastern Europe in the process of defeating Germany and its willing allies, Romania and Hungary. Having finally achieved victory on German soil, the Soviet Union withdrew its forces from Norway, Finland, Czechoslavakia and Yugoslavia; they agreed to four-power control of Berlin, a city captured at great cost by Russian forces and lying well behind their lines; at British request, they made Bulgaria withdraw its army from Thrace and the Aegean coast; and they withheld support from the grassroots Communist uprising in Greece. Not unreasonably, they sought to establish a buffer zone to their west. But military expansion of the kind sought and partly achieved by Germany and Japan was never on the Soviet agenda.

What, then, of the Soviet forces in Eastern Europe that, until 1989, were postured for a westwards offensive? These are explained by Soviet planning for the contingency of world war and the legitimate objective (shared with the West) of not losing such a war, should it be unavoidable. The important difference was that for the Soviet Union not to lose they had to deny the United States a bridgehead by defeating NATO and evicting US forces from Europe. For NATO not to lose, it needed only retain a bridgehead, which allowed a 'virtuous' defensive posture. The USSR required an offensive posture and a measure of ground-air superiority.

Contingency planning for a world war provides the only satisfactory explanation of the totality of Soviet military behaviour for the 40 years to 1988. That behaviour does not support the claim of a Soviet Union set on military world domination, a claim that relies on highly selective use of evidence, and ignores the several occasions when the Soviets failed to exploit opportunities for military expansion.

As the Second World War drew to a close, the Russians were not alone in seeing the future threat as a resurgent Germany within 15 – 20 years. This sanguine assessment was, however, replaced in 1947 – 48 by what the USSR had good reason to perceive as the more immediate threat of a capitalist coalition that would be ready for war by 1953, built around a radical new partnership between France and Germany (the recognised proponents of large ground force) and led by the Anglo-Saxon powers, who enjoyed a virtual monopoly of naval and strategic air power. The objective of such a war would be to deny the Soviet Union an atomic capability, to contain Communism within Russia's borders, and (if possible) to effect a change in the nature of the Soviet state.

War, initiated by the capitalists in the relatively near future, was seen in 1948 as being inevitable. But as the Soviet Union rebuilt its war shattered economy and modernised its forces, this gloomy prognosis was modified and in 1956 it was ruled that world war was no longer inevitable. By the end of the decade the likelihood of a premeditated US attack had been largely discounted, but the possibility of war remained inherent in the antagonisms of the two social systems. The military was therefore required to continue preparing for the worst case of world war — a war the Soviet Union absolutely wanted to avoid but could not afford to lose.

Initially, Soviet military requirements had not been excessively burdensome, and in the 1950s were mainly an extension of those that had been met so successfully in the war. The nuclear factor was added in the 1960s but, while this complicated immeasurably the actual waging of war, it did not greatly increase the costs of preparing for it. This changed with the 1970s strategy, which required the USSR to replicate its theatre nuclear capability with conventional firepower. This stemmed from the doctrinal decision in December 1966 that a world war would not necessarily be nuclear or involve massive strikes on the Soviet Union. This doctrinal adjustment allowed (and required) the Soviet Union to adopt the objective avoiding the nuclear devastation of Russia, which meant forgoing nuclear attacks on the United States. The US military-industrial base would therefore be left undamaged, and it would only be a matter of time before America built up the capability for a successful land offensive in Europe.

The military problem was how to evict US troops from Europe without precipitating intercontinental nuclear escalation. Part of the answer was to restructure Soviet ground and air forces so that, with conventional means only, they could disrupt NATO's means of nuclear delivery and at the same time blitz their way to the Channel. Although the Soviet Union lacked most of the means to implement such plans at that date, NATO's adoption of 'flexible response', France's withdrawal from its military structure, and American involvement in Vietnam had significantly improved the chances of a conventional blitzkreig being successful. Thus in 1967 – 68 the USSR embarked on the costly process of restructuring its forces in order to be in a position by 1976 to implement the new strategy, should world war be inescapable.

The other part of the answer was to deter the United States from striking at the Soviet Union as US forces went down to defeat in Europe. The necessary ICBM capability would be in place by the end of the 1960s, but it was quite likely that such wartime deterrence would be unsuccessful. If deterrence failed, the smaller the US nuclear arsenal, the less the devastation of Russia.

Whereas the 1960s strategy had required strategic superiority, the logic of the 1970s strategy decreed that Soviet interests would now be served best by nuclear parity at as low a level as possible. This provided a military rationale for negotiating limits on strategic arms (SALT), reinforcing the case of those in Moscow who saw this as fostering detente and relieving the burden of defence. And if less was better, then zero was best, an argument that 15 years later would be reinforced by Gorbachev's conviction that in the existence of nuclear weapons lay the danger of nuclear war.

The argument that less was better did not, however, apply to Soviet conventional forces. The 1970s strategy envisaged a two-phase war: during the first, which would be relatively short and extremely violent, the USSR would defeat NATO in Europe and evict US forces from the Continent; in a subsequent and more unpredictable phase, an extended defence perimeter, reaching from the Atlantic to the Pacific would be established. In 1967 – 68 the Soviet Union therefore began to restructure and strengthen its ground and supporting air forces to enable a successful offensive against NATO in the west and to defend against China in the east, all without resort to nuclear weapons. This meant that they could not engage in serious negotiations to reduce force levels in Europe in the 1970s, or agree to forgo their conventional superiority over NATO. Hence the 15 year stalemate at the MBFR negotiations. This also justified the United States dragging its feet in negotiating reductions in strategic nuclear weapons on the grounds that they were needed to deter the aggressive urge implicit in Soviet ground force superiority.

The Soviet Union faced a dilemma. By the first half of the 1980s it was clear that existing military policies were counter-productive, as well as prohibitively expensive. On the other hand, perceptions of the danger of world war had been heightened by the Reagan administration's confrontational policies. In any case, Marxist-Leninist theory held that until socialism became the predominant system, the possibility of world war remained, and since the capitalist objective would be to destroy the socialist system, the Soviet Union could not afford to lose. It was Gorbachev's genius to find a way out of this logical impasse.

## The Perestroika Process

When Gorbachev took office in March 1985, he was determined to introduce a new approach to international relations that would reduce the danger of nuclear war and facilitate the restructuring of the Soviet economy by alleviating the burden of defence. It was, however, another 18 months before he fully understood the fundamental nature of the changes that would be needed.

The catalyst was his realisation that economic *perestroika* would fail if he did not 'enlist the energies of the Soviet people directly', a conclusion that changed the very nature of the process. By January 1987 he had sufficient support in the Politburo to announce a new policy of democratisation at the thrice-deferred Central Committee plenum. After that (to quote Gorbachev) 'events went in a completely different direction'.

Supporters and opponents alike knew that democratisation meant political destabilisation, in Eastern Europe as well as inside the Soviet Union. Gorbachev was proposing to re-rig the ship of state on the high seas, and success required a calm environment, a compliant crew, and external assistance. This meant harnessing the body of US opinion which favoured 'new political thinking about international relations', recognised 'the new realities of the nuclear age', realised that there was no longer 'national security, only international security', and acknowledged reliance 'above all on political and not military means'.

The breakthrough came with acceptance that in 1947 the Soviet Union had been unwise to respond in kind to the Truman doctrine of military containment and the build-up of US strategic nuclear forces, thus creating the threat that was the life blood of the US military-industrial complex and allowing itself to be dragged into a ruinous arms race. The prescription was clear. Get out of the arms race at whatever cost in pride or fairness, although not by sacrificing security; take active measures to de-demonise the Soviet Union, thereby denying Western militarists their 'threat'; and instruct the General staff to plan on the assumption that world war could and would be prevented by political means.

There remained the problem of Marxist-Leninist ideology and a theory of international relations that saw the world in terms of opposing social systems, where capitalism's gain is socialism's loss. This zero sum view of the world was reflected in Soviet calculations of the correlation of forces and a definition of peaceful coexistence that required the ideological struggle to continue. The conflictual effects of that view were magnified by the analytical precedence given to class interests over national interests. The failure of *détente* in the 1970s argued that this whole body of theory would have to be rethought if good relations with the United States were to endure.

By November-December 1986 Gorbachev and his supporters had concluded that political democratisation, withdrawing from Afghanistan, recasting Soviet military doctrine, redefining Marxist-Leninist theory, reshaping policy in Eastern Europe and reversing policy towards the United States were all essential if economic *perestroika* was not to fail. It was an ambitious agenda and its timing was geared to the 13th Five-Year Plan (1991 – 96), which meant that the more important reforms would need to be in place by the end of 1988.

By mid-1988, debate on reformulating Marxist-Leninist theory on international relations would have run its course and the new body of theory could be legitimated by the special Party Conference in June, which would also authorise the fundamental restructuring of governance to allow genuine democratic processes. Similarly, the size of the force cuts enabled by the new military doctrine (decreed in January 1987) would have been worked out; these unilateral cuts were essential for priming the pump of large-scale mutual force reductions.

East European party chiefs had already been warned in late 1986 not to expect Soviet military intervention if their regimes ran into trouble. In May 1987 a Warsaw Pact commission was set up to consider the implications of Soviet withdrawal; by then the Soviet leadership was already debating the future of the two Germanies.

In other words, in January 1987 a process was set in motion that would lead to the collapse of the Communist rule throughout Eastern Europe by the end of 1989. This was deliberate. The desanctification of Marxist-Leninist dogma, rethinking the meaning and substance of socialism, the emphasis on democratising both the state and the party, and the plans for unilateral force reductions and the withdrawal of Soviet forces, were all radical developments. In combination, their implications were revolutionary.

In 1989, Moscow actively abetted the popular process that removed existing Communist Party regimes from power in East Germany, Czechoslovakia and Bulgaria — a reversal of Soviet policy made possible by the shift in military doctrine.

For 40 years, Eastern Europe had been seen as a defensive glacis and a springboard for offensive operations against Western Europe in the event of war. The salience of this second role increased with the 1970s strategy, and almost all members of the Warsaw Pact had their parts to play, parts that became more important following the 1984 decision to remain on the defensive for 20 – 30 days. The assumption of 'no world war' changed the plot and wrote out those parts.

Now, the Warsaw Pact was not even needed as a physical buffer against invasion, because that implied world war. And since the idea of an ideological or economic empire was clearly dead, then why remain in Eastern Europe? Afghanistan had shown that the area's potential as a political buffer would be hindered rather than helped by the continuing presence of Soviet troops. Meanwhile, Western 'aggressive circles' would be hard put to sustain the image of a Soviet military threat when faced by the voluntary withdrawal of Soviet forces and the democratisation of the Warsaw Pact.

In 1989, the Soviet military embarked on a protracted rearguard action, both metaphorically and in concrete terms. It was required to withdraw from well-known and long-established positions, intellectual as well as territorial, to some new location in totally unfamiliar territory at some unknown distance to the rear. This withdrawal would be carried out in an increasingly unfriendly environment, where the formerly deferential and supportive populace would become increasingly disrespectful and obstructionist. It was a withdrawal from a situation where military objectives and strategy were clearly defined, to one where nothing was clear and most things could not be decided until some unspecified time in the future.

Henceforth, the military would prepare only for lesser contingencies of limited conflict on the Soviet periphery. This was no mean task, given the length and variety of the Soviet Union's land and sea frontiers and the diversity of the countries ranged against them, but in the past had been subsumed under the larger problem of world war. They would have to plan on the basis of an unknowable future, whose parameters were the subject of continuing negotiation and where the nature and level of the threat remained uncertain.

It was relatively easy for the Soviet Union to set about dismantling the vast military machine restructured so laboriously in the 1970s and early 1980s. But when should they halt the process? The final size and shape of the Soviet armed forces had been specified in principle in numerous declarations and statements. The stated objective was to eliminate nuclear weapons along with chemical and any other weapons of mass destruction. For general purpose forces, the objective was a level sufficient to ensure a secure defence with greatly reduced forces, while forgoing the option of a surprise attack or offensive operations in general.

In practice there were major problems with both objectives. It was clear that the US political-military establishment set great store by large nuclear arsenals, particularly at the strategic level. As for general purpose forces, even if a counter-offensive capability were ruled out and the emphasis placed on non-offensive means of defence, sufficiency would still depend on the military capability of possible opponents and their potential political alignment. The final size and shape of the general purpose forces would therefore depend on political decisions about international trends, about the balance between political and military means of ensuring security, about the nature of the threat, and about the level of defence expenditure the economy would be able to sustain.

These decisions could not be made for at least two to three years, and probably longer, when political trends in Europe and the progress in arms control negotiations would be clearer. By then it might also be possible to judge whether the United States was likely to subscribe to the new political thinking about international relations, or would continue to strive to preserve its military superiority and seek to act as the gendarme of the world.

While Gorbachev had been reasonably specific about the outcome he sought, it was heavily dependent on co-operation by the West, particularly the United States. He was prepared to make concessions to start the process and keep it moving, but domestic political considerations as well as national security requirements would necessarily impose limits on asymmetrical concessions. At some stage the Soviet leadership would have to decide whether its stated objectives were fully realistic and, if not, what lesser objectives were acceptable. At that stage, it should be possible to give the military precise directions.

### Future Policy: Predictables

By combining what is known of traditional Russian and Soviet behaviour with developments in the Soviet Union during the last 10 years, one can identify with reasonable confidence various aspects of Russian/ Soviet defence and foreign policy in the 1990s that will not depend on the nature of the regime in power.

A central assumption is that the economy will be the major preoccupation of any government which finally emerges. A second assumption is that the government will not resort to foreign adventures in response to domestic unrest.

### *Restoring Soviet Military Capability*

Irrespective of what group or individual comes to power in Moscow, there is no combination of domestic or personal circumstances that would cause a reversion to the military policies of the previous 35 years. There are, however, external developments that could prompt a reversal of the present trend.

This categorical assertion is possible because the size, structure and posture of Soviet forces during the last 35 years were determined by the objective of not losing a world war. The consequential requirements had increased incrementally over the years, driven by new technology, changes in threat, and adjustments to strategy. During the 1970s and early 1980s, the burden became increasingly intolerable, while the contingency became steadily less plausible. It is conceivable that, for domestic political reasons, a future leader would reshoulder the burden of preparing for world war, whatever his ideological persuasion.

It is necessary to be clear about what is being said. By the second half of the 1970s, preparing for the contingency of world war required the Soviet Union to be able to defeat NATO in Europe using conventional means only, evict US forces from the Continent, and prevent their return. This last required an extended defence perimeter and the capability to establish political control over the western half of the Eurasian land mass, the northern parts of Africa, and the Arabian peninsula. In the eastern half of Eurasia the USSR needed the conventional capability to deter Chinese involvement and subsequently to seize Manchuria. The Soviet navy had to be prepared for global war against a coalition of maritime powers. And since it was unlikely that it would be able to avert NATO's resort to nuclear weapons in Europe, it had to be prepared for theatre nuclear war and that wartime deterrence would fail, leading to intercontinental escalation.

It was the Soviet capability to fight this kind of war that so worried the West. It is this burden that the Soviets will not reshoulder for domestic political reasons. It took political courage to assume the possibility of world war, but Gorbachev will have been proven right if events show that political means can, indeed, dissolve the military threat to Russia.

If, however, negotiations on the mutual reduction of forces bog down or the United States persists in seeking to preserve strategic superiority and on deploying strike weapons in space, Gorbachev would be proved wrong. It would support the case of those in Moscow who had argued that the possibility of world war should not be excluded from contingency planning and from formulating Soviet military requirements.

Not surprisingly, Soviet perceptions of the danger of world war are directly related to US behaviour. If at some future date, for whatever reasons, the US were to deny the legitimacy of the Soviet state and seek to undermine it; if it were to embark on arms racing as a way of impoverishing the Soviet Union while reinforcing its own military superiority; if it were to seek to emplace strike weapons in space that would, in practice, provide the key to a first strike capability while posing a continuous threat of instantaneous political decapitation; in circumstances such as these the threat of world war would resurface in Moscow.

Such circumstances are not fanciful, since it is what the first Reagan administration sought to achieve in 1981 – 84. The re-emergence of such policy would prove that those who resisted Gorbachev's policies in the 1980s had been right all along. It would confirm that the United States mistook conciliation for weakness and that the security of the

Soviet Union could not be entrusted primarily to political means. World war remained a live possibility and must be prepared for, whatever the cost.

## Re-establishing Control over Eastern Europe

Assuming no world war, Eastern Europe is no longer needed as a defensive glacis or a springboard for a western offensive in the event of war. Meanwhile the Warsaw Pact has disintegrated, a process that is irreversible in the short to medium term.

In 1944, Soviet forces entered Eastern Europe in the course of defeating Germany, and in many countries they were welcomed as liberators. It was their military presence that allowed the USSR to establish political hegemony in particularly favourable circumstances, not least because their system could be seen to have prevailed in the crucial test of war. To reimpose that hegemony in the 1990s would require the Soviet Union to go to war with the states of Eastern Europe, invading and occupying countries whose people would now be active enemies rather than nominal allies.

In the longer term, given the experience of the last 200 years, it is most unlikely that a regime would emerge in Moscow that had autonomous territorial ambitions. One can, however, visualise three kinds of situation in which Soviet forces could be drawn back into Eastern Europe. In the event of internal or inter-state conflict in the region, Soviet forces might become involved in conflict resolution, peace-keeping or re-establishing political order. Secondly, in a replay of the 1930s, an East European state would call for Soviet support against a resurgent Germany. And third, the threat of a world war might re-emerge.

## Marxist-Leninist Theory

There is no likelihood that Marxist-Leninist theory will regain its former hold on the Soviet world view or shape the approach to foreign affairs. There was always a disjunction between Soviet theory and practice and, as a general rule, national interests took precedence over ideological considerations. Nevertheless, theory did play an important part in shaping assumptions about the likelihood of world war and separating out the ideological struggle as something that must not be sacrificed to the exigencies of arms control or detente. By 1981, however, Marxist-Leninist theory had been shown to be largely invalid in respect to the Third World, and the existence of a single world economy had been acknowledged, undermining the case for competing social systems. In 1987 – 88 the Gorbachev leadership subsumed the interests of the working class under the universal interests of mankind, allowing the emergence of national interests as the central factor in international relations.

These redefinitions served to bring theory into line with reality, but, while the Soviet Union no longer holds an over-simplified, dichotomous view of a world where a decaying and inherently wicked capitalist system is locked in a struggle for its survival with an emerging and inherently virtuous socialist system, they do not see the West as necessarily benevolent. Furthermore, while a desperate need for external assistance and for a relaxed international environment has, since 1987, caused the Russians to adopt a policy towards the United States that has at times verged on the ingratiating, they continue to have strong reservations about the US approach to world affairs. This could be seen in the Soviet response to US policy on the Gulf crisis in summer 1990, and the different priorities of the then foreign minister Edouard Shevardnadze, who focused on maintaining good relations with the United States, and the Middle East expert Evgeniy Primakov, who focused on the regional concerns of the Soviet Union.

## Future Policy: Regime Dependent

Within these predictable constraints, the political complexion of the regime in Moscow will obviously be important in defining the world view that will shape the style and direction of the policies pursued by some future Russian/Soviet state. That view will influence who are seen as allies, non-aligned, and enemies; it will also determine where those policies are located on the continuum between co-operation and confrontation.

The type of regime will also be important in shaping Soviet reactions to problems or opportunities on its borders where the use of military force might be appropriate. A reactionary regime would be more likely to resort to force than a Gorbachev-type leadership, with its remarkably consistent emphasis on non-intervention and its primary reliance on political instruments of policy. Such a regime would also be more likely to resist the secession of the Union Republics.

It would, however, be wrong to conclude that because a conservative regime, particularly one that had strong military support, would be likely to place greater value on military power, it would therefore respond to domestic unrest by embarking on foreign adventures. While Soviet behaviour in many circumstances will be regime-dependent, the issues involved are generally situation-specific and none of the underlying considerations justify the label of doctrine. The exception concerns the continuing acceptability in Moscow of the 'new political thinking about international relations' that Gorbachev was advocating even before he took office.

## A Different Approach to International Relations

There was nothing particularly original in the new political thinking, and its novelty lay in its being adopted by a great power and applied with beneficial effects to itself and to the world community. As Gorbachev noted, it reflected the principles underlying the UN Charter and drew on a wide body of ideas, both Western and non-aligned. The approach to national security was specifically linked to that put forward by Olaf Palme when Prime Minister of Sweden and fleshed out in the report of the UN-sponsored Palme Commission, published in 1982.

The shift in Soviet thinking can be traced back to their experience in the Third World in the second half of the 1970s. Acceptance of the idea of a single world economy, and recognition that backwardness was a global problem and that underdevelopment threatened world civilisation, brought the globalists to prominence. They emphasised the existence of global problems that required global solutions, the interconnection of these problems, and the interdependence of the different actors in the international arena.

According to Gorbachev, the new political thinking reflected the new reality that mankind faced the very real possibility of extinction. The central reality was that nuclear weapons had the inherent capacity to annihilate the human race. The more distant threat came from the onrush of technology and growth in world population which, separately and together, laid the grounds for a global ecological disaster. Meanwhile, the growing contradictions between world poverty and wealth threatened to spark a global explosion.

From these realities the new Soviet leadership drew the general conclusion that the present way of thinking about international relations was not only obsolete but extremely dangerous. It acknowledged that what it was advocating was not only profoundly revolutionary but also smacked of utopianism. There was, however, no alternative and the time for corrective action was running out.

Since the need for security was the essence of international relations, it was essential to forgo the search for national security and think in terms of international security. A state that unilaterally sought to improve its own security must automatically reduce the security of others, diminishing overall security by increasing the danger of war. In any case, modern weapons capability meant that physical security could no longer be ensured by military-technical means. National security could now only be achieved by co-operating with other states to provide mutual or universal security.

Furthermore, security had to extend beyond political-military security to encompass the economic and cultural aspects. There could be no gain in security unless it was equal for all. This implied a shift in emphasis from inter-state competition to international co-operation. Peaceful coexistence had to become a universal principle of relations between states. The concepts of mutual interdependence and universal security required a recognition that other countries had legitimate interests which must be respected. Thus, intervention by great powers in the internal affairs of other states was impermissible.

The immediate threat of nuclear annihilation could be neutralised by averting war and eliminating nuclear weapons. The first imperative was to prevent an arms race in space and to terminate it on earth. Halting and then reversing the arms race was not only a primary goal of Soviet foreign policy; it was also the main level in the field of security and a prerequisite for a new world order. The ultimate objective was a demilitarised world, a world without war. External involvement in regional conflicts carried the risk of great power confrontation.. Competition between social systems had therefore to rely primarily on example and avoid military means.

In 1987 the Gorbachev leadership set Soviet defence and foreign policy firmly on the course prescribed by the new political thinking, and was supported by the military high command. By 1990, however, there was growing criticism of the new policy, which seemed to involve endless Soviet concessions which the West were happy to pocket while offering nothing in return. Proponents of the new political thinking could argue that the danger of war had receded sharply and that international security (and hence Soviet security) had therefore been increased. But it was irrefutable that the process had been very one-sided, and not all agreed that Soviet security had in fact been enhanced. Army General Albert Makashov caught the mood of the opposition in his address to the founding congress of the Russian Communist Party in June 1990. He noted that 'Germany is reuniting and will probably become a member of NATO; Japan is becoming the decisive force in the Pacific. Only our wise peacocks are crowing that no one is going to attack us'.

## Two Very Different Doctrines

There exists within the Soviet Union a fundamental cleavage of opinion on the appropriate approach to foreign policy: the traditional approach, whose theoretical roots go back to Machiavelli and Thucydides, and the new political thinking advocated and to a large extent practised by the Gorbachev leadership.

The traditional approach is essentially zero-sum, where one side's gain is the other's loss. So, too, was Marxist-Leninist theory, which defined international relations in terms of a competition between two social systems. In other words, the opposing sides in the Cold War shared the same approach to international relations and, in essence, the competition did not differ from the imperial rivalries of the 19th century.

The tendency in the West has been to dismiss Gorbachev's new political thinking as utopian and to denigrate it as a propaganda ploy. It is, however, firmly anchored in a well-established body of Western theory that began to diverge from the traditional approach to foreign policy in the second half of the 19th century. This new trend, which was later labelled the 'idealist' school of thought, had gathered momentum by the end of the century and its argument that war between industrialised states was dysfunctional was borne out in the First World War.

The League of Nations was a formal attempt to develop co-operative procedures for dealing with conflicts of national interest and collective measures for responding to aggression, but circumstances were not then ripe for that Utopian approach. But as the Soviet commentator Aleksandr Bovin put it, Utopia is merely history waiting to be written, and the failure of these concepts in the 1930s could be blamed on prematurity rather than impracticability.

The so-called idealist school re-emerged in the 1960s in the guise of peace research, conflict resolution, and the study of international organisations. It gradually gained intellectual substance and then political credibility in the West as an alternative to the traditional approach to international relations, which seemed to justify an endless arms race while staggering from crisis to the next. It was on this body of Western thought that Gorbachev drew when developing his ideas about the need for new political thinking in the nuclear age.

Concepts dismissed as Utopian in the 1930s had meanwhile begun to take concrete form. One such expression was the European Community, which brought long-standing enemies like Britain, France and Germany together in a supranational organisation. Another was the continually growing family of organisations institutions, and initiatives under the general umbrella of the United Nations. But the most unexpected was the Soviet withdrawal from Eastern Europe, a political decision that was based on the 'utopian' assessment that world war could and would be prevented by political means.

Through 1990, Moscow continued to advocate and implement the 'idealist' approach to foreign policy. In the future, however, the choice of doctrine will be heavily dependent on the nature of the regime in power. A regime that tends towards the more authoritarian end of the continuum will be more likely to favour the traditional approach to foreign policy. But this may also apply at the populist end, where an appeal to nationalist sentiments may yield domestic dividends.

A second determinant will be the nature of the future international environment and the readiness of the West to subscribe to the new political thinking. Part of the difference between the new and the traditional approach to foreign policy is that which distinguishes the zero-sum from the expanding sum view of international relations.

It may be possible to resolve that particular difference, since both sides are divided on the issue. Traditional elements in the Soviet polity share the zero-sum views of the political-military establishments of the major Western powers. On the other side is an unexpected alliance between the new thinkers in Moscow and like-minded people around the world, including important Western élites and some political parties, who challenge the emphasis that has been placed on military power in post-war Western policy and stress international over national security.

But the difference in the two approaches goes beyond this, and beyond the attitudes implied by the labels 'realist' and 'idealist'. It includes a basic disagreement on the realities of the nuclear age and extends to questions concerning the risk of war, the role of force, and the danger inherent in nuclear weapons. The Gorbachev leadership claims that the danger of nuclear war lies in the existence of such weapons; the Western political-military establishment claims that nuclear weapons actually prevent war. This disagreement is fundamental.

## Note

1   This essay draws on the analysis in Michael MccGwire *Military Objectives in Soviet Foreign Policy* (Brookings Institution, 1987) and *Perestroika and Soviet National Security* (Brookings, 1991).

CHAPTER 3

# The Adaptiveness of the Soviet System

STEPHEN WHITE

THERE were two key issues involved in *perestroika*, Gorbachev told his audience on the 70th anniversary of the October Revolution in November 1987: the 'democratisation of all public life and a radical economic reform'. Economic reform, so far, has made little headway beyond plans and proclamations. But reform of the Soviet political system has been advancing at an accelerating pace since the plenary meeting of the CPSU Central Committee in January 1987, and has already brought about what Gorbachev and others have described as the greatest advance in socialist democracy since the October Revolution itself. Addressing the January plenum, Gorbachev made clear that economic reform was conceivable only in association with far-reaching changes in the political system. Control 'from above' would remain, and even be strengthened; but it was likely to prove effective only when combined with control 'from below', based upon the widest possible popular participation. There were still 'forbidden' subjects, officials who did their best to suppress criticism, and stagnation and corruption at leading levels of party and state. All of this, in Gorbachev's view, argued the need for a 'profound democratisation' of Soviet society, designed to ensure that ordinary people once again felt themselves to be masters of their own destinies.

Gorbachev elaborated upon the reasons for these changes in subsequent speeches. Democratisation, he told the Soviet trade union congress in February 1987, was a 'guarantee against the repetition of past errors, and consequently a guarantee that the restructuring process is irreversible'. There was no choice — it was 'either democracy or social inertia and conservatism'.

The June 1987 Central Committee plenum agreed to his proposal that a party conference — the first for nearly 50 years — should be called in the summer of 1988 to consider further democratising measures.

31

Addressing the conference, Gorbachev called for 'radical reform' of the Soviet political system, not just 'democratisation', and argued that it was 'crucial' to the solution of all the other problems that faced Soviet society. The political system established by the October Revolution, he maintained, had undergone 'serious distortions'. A massive bureaucratic apparatus had developed, which had begun to 'dictate its will' in political as well as economic matters. Many millions of working people, elected to state and non-state bodies, had been 'removed from real participation in handling state and public affairs'. Public life had become unduly governmentalised, and ordinary working people had been 'alienated'. It was this 'ossified system of government' that was now the main obstacle to *perestroika*.

The process of political reform has involved both a critique of the Stalinist past and an attempt to delineate a democratic socialist future. In 1986, responding to a question from the French Communist newspaper, *L'Humanité*, Gorbachev refused to accept that there could be such a phenomenon as Stalinism. But in 1987, in his speech on the 70th anniversary, there were references to the 'wanton repression' of the 1930s, and shortly afterwards a Politburo commission was set up which, by the spring of 1989, had already rehabilitated 47,000 victims of the purges.

The vision of the future has been much less clear; but, broadly speaking, Gorbachev and the reformers have called for a new model of socialism, one that discloses the creative potential of the Soviet people and the socialist system, one that is centred on society rather than the state, and one that involves co-operation with societies elsewhere in the resolution of common problems. Central to the achievement of such a society is a political system that is responsive to its citizens not simply to its rulers, and this in turn explains the priority that has been attached to political reform since at least the January 1987 plenum. What mechanisms of popular control have been developed over this period? To what extent have they established a balance between party control from above and popular control from below? And to what extent is the system that has now developed likely to be able to adapt to the different circumstances of the 1990s?

## Reforming the Soviet System

The political reforms that have now been agreed include an entirely new electoral law, approved on 1 December 1988. The faults of the existing system were apparent not just to outside observers but also, and increasingly, to Soviet citizens themselves. Most obviously, there was no choice of candidate, still less of party or programme. The single slate of candidates was often all but entirely unknown to the electorate,

not surprisingly as many of them had little connection with the constituency for which they had been nominated; (in a survey of October
1988, for instance, only 5% of those who were taking part in a by-
election could even name the candidate). Nor could this situation easily
be remedied, as the right of nomination was reserved under the
Constitution for the CPSU and other party-controlled organisations.

Voters could, in theory, delete the name of the single candidate, and
at the local level there were occasional defeats of this kind in response
to particularly unpopular nominations. Such a practice, however, was
strongly discouraged by the need to make use of the screened-off booth
for this purpose, and at the national level no candidate had ever been
unsuccessful since the first elections under this system were held in
1937. The candidates, moreover, were chosen so that they conformed
to certain centrally-specified guidelines. This 'modelling' could be
alarmingly precise. One local official, for instance, told *Izvestiya* what
his 'programme' was in this respect: he was to ensure that 4.6% of
the successful candidates were enterprise directors, 1.1% were to be
employed in culture and the arts, and 45.9% were to be returned for
the first time. In another instance, a notorious prostitute had to be
returned as she was the only person in the constituency who satisfied
the relevant criteria: female, aged 35 – 40, unmarried, and a factory
worker. If all this failed the results were simply falsified: Stalin, in an
early exercise, once secured a vote of over 100% (voters in other constituencies, it was explained, had insisted on casting their votes in his
favour), and there was abundant evidence in more recent times of
family members voting on each others' behalf and officials voting for
anyone who seemed likely to 'spoil the percentages'.

There had been expressions of dissatisfaction with these arrangements
for some time and Gorbachev, in his speech to the 27th CPSU Congress
in February 1986, promised that the 'necessary correctives' would be
made. A limited experiment took place in the local elections in June
1987, by which more candidates were nominated than seats available
in about 1% of all constituencies, and a new electoral law, published
in draft in *Pravda* on 23 October 1988 and adopted in its final form the
following December, has since made these practices universal. The
right to nominate has been extended to electors' meetings of 500 or
more, and an unlimited number of candidates may be nominated.
Deputies must 'as a rule' live or work in the area they represent, and
they cannot hold governmental posts at the same time. Candidates are
now required to present a 'programme of their future activity' to the
electorate, and have the right to appoint up to 10 campaign staff to
assist them. Electors, for their part, have to pass through a booth and
must cast an 'active' rather than a 'passive' vote by marking the ballot
paper in line with their preferences, unless (exceptionally) just a single

candidate is standing. The new law was to apply to all future elections, beginning with the national elections in March 1989; these, the Central Committee promised at its meeting in November 1988, would be 'unlike all those that had preceded them'.

The Central Committee, in fact, can hardly have guessed how different the new electoral arrangements would prove to be. A whole series of party and state leaders were successfully returned, and there were some striking victories for individual first secretaries: the Tambov party secretary, for instance, won more than 90% of the vote, and the first secretary in earthquake-stricken Spitak took more than 93%. The proportion of party members among the new deputies was substantially higher than in the outgoing Supreme Soviet, and slightly higher even than the level of party membership among the candidates that had been nominated. Much more striking, however, were the defeats suffered by official candidates, even when there was no direct competitor. The Prime Ministers of Latvia and Lithuania were both defeated, as were the mayors of Moscow and Kiev, and about 38 district and regional party officials. The most spectacular defeats were in Leningrad, where the list of casualties included the regional first secretary (a candidate Politburo member), the regional second secretary, the chairman of the city soviet and his deputy, the chairman of the regional soviet and the city party secretary. Many party leaders, understandably, found themselves too busy to be able to contest the local and republican elections which took place throughout the USSR in late 1989 and 1990.

The process of reform could scarcely limit itself to the electoral system: at least as important, the deputies that were elected would have to have a meaningful role to perform. The old Supreme Soviet had met for three or four days a year, making it among the world's least frequently convened assemblies. Its members, all of them working on a part-time basis, had approved every proposal of the Soviet government without a dissenting voice at least since 1955, when there was a single abstention. The same was true at local levels. Nominally, under this system, all power belonged to the people themselves through the soviets of deputies to which they elected their representatives. In fact these arrangements meant the virtually unconstrained power of the apparatus, since deputies served for lengthy periods of office with scarcely any need to defend their decisions or their personal integrity. The result, inevitably, was incompetence and inertia, and sometimes straightforward crime. Hardly less significant, the policies that emerged from such a system were often misconceived and wasteful. One of these misconceived decisions was the Baikal-Amur railway, started in the 1970s, which has never had a level of traffic sufficient to justify the enormous resources that were poured into it. Another was the long-standing plan to divert the Siberian rivers, with incalculable consequences for the Soviet and global environment. The new objective was 'all power to the soviets', but this time in real rather than formal terms, so that state bodies would exercise the full range of powers with which they had nominally been invested.

The soviets, in Gorbachev's view, had served as the basis of a system of genuinely socialist democracy during the revolutionary years, but had then fallen victim to bureaucratisation and over-detailed regulation by party committees. One of the problems was the often honorific character of the membership. In the 1984 Supreme Soviet, it was calculated, about 40% of the deputies owed their place to the official function they performed. These *ex officio* deputies, mostly party and state bureaucrats, were balanced by large numbers of manual workers, leaving very few deputies to represent the white collar professions. Would it be so bad, it was asked, if there were fewer milkmaids and party secretaries in the new Supreme Soviet, but rather more popular and articulate economists, historians, actors and writers? Three jurists, Barabashev, Sheremet and Vasil'ev, pointed out that surveys had found low levels of satisfaction with the work of the soviets, and even deputies themselves appeared to be unsure of their own usefulness. They had access to legislation only in its final stages, sessions were far too brief, and even the plan and budget could scarcely be seriously considered. According to the Soviet jurist Boris Kuirashvili, writing in *Kommunist* in May 1988, nothing less than 'Soviet parliamentarianism' was needed, backed up by a separation of powers, a constitutional court and a system of smaller, full-time soviets staffed by salaried politicians.

A number of these proposals found favour in Gorbachev's speech to the 19th Party Conference a month later and were duly passed into law in the package of constitutional amendments approved by the Supreme Soviet in December 1988 after some weeks of public discussion. The reforms that were agreed included a Committee of Constitutional Supervision (not quite a court) to monitor the legality of government actions. Judges, it was established, were to be elected by higher-level soviets and would hold office for 10 rather than five years at a time in order to strengthen their independence. Soviets at all levels would be elected for five-year terms rather than for two-and-a-half years so that the deputies could accumulate more experience; and government officials were to hold office for two five-year terms at the most, subject to recall at any time if those who elected them so decided. Deputies themselves could serve on no more than two soviets at the same time. Much more controversially, the soviets were to be given chairmen, elected deputies who would also be the party leaders of the area in question; this would, for the first time, expose them to the indirect control of ordinary citizens.

The centrepiece of the new changes, however, was undoubtedly the formation of an entirely new representative body, the Congress of People's Deputies, based upon the Congress of Soviets that had exercised legislative authority in the 1920s and 1930s. The Congress of People's Deputies was to be elected in three different ways. Ordinary constituencies were to return 750 members, as before, and national-territorial areas such as the union republics would continue to return a further 750 members. They would however be joined by a wholly new group of 750 deputies who were to be elected by a wide range of nationally-based organisations, including the Communist Party, the trade unions, and women's councils. The Congress of People's Deputies, which was to meet at least annually, would in turn elect from among its members a working Supreme Soviet of 542, a fifth of whom would meet for six to eight months every year and its members would 'as a rule' carry out their duties on a full-time basis. The Congress was also to elect to an entirely new post, the Chairmanship of the USSR Supreme Soviet, which would normally be combined with the party leadership. In March 1990, after a rather perfunctory public debate, the new state structure was completed with the institution of an executive Presidency with wide-ranging powers, including the nomination of leading public officials, a suspensory veto on legislation and the right to rule by decree.

The representative institutions that emerged from this process of reform were certainly very different from the 'supreme state organs' they replaced. The proportion of women and workers was down by about half, but there were many more figures from the academic and cultural world, and the first-ever religious leaders, rural leaseholders and commercial co-operators. Gorbachev, as expected, was elected to the chairmanship of the Supreme Soviet and then to the newly-established Presidency, but by a less than unanimous vote. There were attacks upon the leadership, the party-state apparatus and the KGB — this last for 'crimes unprecedented in the history of humanity'. An elaborate committee system was set up to cover *glasnost*, rights, defence and state security as well as other matters. An organisational base, with a library and electronic services, came into existence in central Moscow. Together with the expenses of deputies, the new parliament was expected to cost about 40 million rubles a year to run, as compared with seven million a year for its predecessor. Organised caucuses of deputies began to emerge, particularly the Inter-Regional Group, whose first meeting attracted an audience of nearly 400. No less important, the new institutions of government attracted a massive public audience through radio and television: from 61% (in Alta-Ata) to 92% (in Tbilisi) claimed to be following the first Congress of People's Deputies 'constantly' or 'more or less constantly', and very large majorities thought it was operating 'completely' or 'more or less democratically'. The Communist Party has undergone a corresponding process of political reform, the substance of which was agreed at the 19th Party Conference in mid-1988. The central thrust of these changes was, as *Kommunist* put it in January 1988, that there should be a kind of 'division of labour' in which the party would stand aside from direct management of the economy and exercise a more general co-ordinating role. The discussion that preceded the Conference saw very widespread support for changes of this kind. There were calls, for instance, for party officials to spend more time working with ordinary people and less time in their offices, and for more frequent conferences of this kind. The most widely supported proposals, however, concerned democratic change in the party's own organisation. There should, for instance, be a choice of candidate at all elections to party office; officers should serve for a limited period and should perhaps be subject to an age limit; more should be known about the party's finances; and the party's bureaucracy should be smaller, and less obviously duplicate the ministerial hierarchy.

Most of these themes found a place in Gorbachev's speech to the Party Conference on 28 June, 1988. Democratic centralism within the party, he complained, had become bureaucratic centralism. The rank-and-file had lost control over the leaderships that spoke in their name; and an atmosphere of comradeship had been replaced by one of commands and instructions. The Conference agreed with his suggestion that the party's whole existing membership should be reaccredited, so that the unworthy and inactive should be removed from its ranks. A less bureaucratic approach to membership was to be adopted, with more emphasis being placed upon the personal qualities of new recruits than upon their social background. Central Committee members, it was agreed, must also be involved in a more regular way in the work of the leadership, and the rank-and-file in the work of the leaderships at all levels. Party officials, moreover, like their state counterparts, were to be elected by secret ballot from a choice of candidates, and were to hold office for no more than two five-year terms in a row.

These changes, again, have become at least a partial reality. Six new commissions, for instance, were established under the auspices of the Central Committee in the autumn of 1988. Each headed by a senior member of the leadership, they were intended, at least in principle, to involve a wider party élite in the process of central decision-making. The party apparatus was slimmed down from 20 to just nine departments, losing about a third of its staff and much more information was made available about the party's operations and finances, not least for the benefit of its own members. A new Central Committee journal, *Izvestiya Tsk*, appeared in 1989, covering all kinds of matters from unpublished

Leniniana to the number of Eskimos that were party members. The
new party rules, as adopted by the 28th Congress in 1990, extend these
changes further: party branches, for instance, receive a greater degree
of independence, and a Control Commission, elected by the Congress,
restores the practice of the 1920s by which a body of this kind provided
a continuing check on behalf of the membership over the actions of the
central leadership. Members, equally, are allowed to develop 'platforms'
if not organised factions, and minority rights have been significantly
strengthened.

Finally and perhaps most fundamentally, the process of political
reform has involved a reassertion of the role of law in Soviet society,
and a greater place for political activity initiated by citizens themselves
rather than by the state on their behalf. Gorbachev, a lawyer himself,
told interviewers from *Der Spiegel* that *perestroika* was as much a 'legal
revolution' as a reform of the political system. The changes centred
around the concept of the 'socialist law-based state', first mentioned by
Gorbachev at a meeting with media workers in May 1988 and later the
centrepiece of a resolution on legal reform adopted at the 19th Party
Conference. This called for 'large-scale legal reform' including a review
of existing codes of law, greater safeguards for the independence of
judges, and an extensive programme of legal education for the public.
Criminal and court reform took place during 1989, and Soviet penal and
psychiatric institutions were opened to outside observers. Gorbachev's
principle was that everything that was not prohibited by law should be
allowed; recommending the changes in the Constitution that took place
at the end of 1988, he argued that they represented a distinctive
'socialist system of checks and balances', protecting society from the
abuse of power by those who held the highest offices of state. Whatever
its limitations, this is certainly the most sustained attempt that has yet
been made to institute a Soviet-style government of laws rather than
men.

## Political Change and Political Adaptation

It must obviously be premature to judge a political system that is still
evolving. Formal legislation may in any case be beside the point; for
many reformers there can be no alternative to the slow process of
'learning democracy', developing a civic culture that can sustain processes of bargaining and accommodation rather than commands
backed up by coercion. The evidence that is available — attitude
surveys, and the conduct of demonstrations and public discussions
generally — certainly suggests there is still a fairly limited attachment
to the democratic norms of toleration and accountability. Kurashvili,
among Soviet reformers, has suggested that the transition from a harshly

authoritarian to a democratic-authoritarian regime may take at least 10 – 15 years; a group of specialists at the Institute of State and Law has pointed out that the establishment of a rule of law in capitalist countries took 'hundreds of years' and doubted if that period could be significantly reduced under Soviet conditions. The evidence nonetheless suggests that a political order developed in the Gorbachev years which was an uneasy amalgam of two conflicting principles: Leninism, or party rule from above, and democracy, or popular rule from below, (which had always been a fiction but which the Gorbachev reforms have now attempted to strengthen).

The tension between these two principles takes many forms. Voters, for instance, can reject party officials, but not (as yet) elect a different administration. Deputies, reflecting the wishes of their electors, can resist unpopular policies such as a reduction in the subsidies on food but, elected as individuals, they can hardly put forward an alternative programme of government. The new representative system, with its inclusion of a range of organised interests, lends itself to the articulation of grievances rather than the formulation of solutions. Tensions of this kind go back to the revolution itself, in which power had been taken in the name of the Soviets but in fact by a small and organised Bolshevik minority. Article 2, in the 1977 Constitution, embodied the first of these principles with its references to popular sovereignty; but Article 6, until its reformulation in March 1990, embodied the rival principle of party monopoly. The tension between these two principles became particularly acute after the 1989 elections had led to the defeat of so many of the party's official representatives. Why, it was argued, should the Communist Party have any guaranteed seats in the Congress of People's Deputies? Why should it have 100, when its numbers were so much smaller than the trade unions, which also had 100? And what was the relationship between the newly-elected Congress and the CPSU: was the party subordinate to the Congress, or the Congress to the party?

The tension between these two principles, indeed, began to generate more than questions in the late 1980s and early 1990s. Deputies, for instance, began to reject the nominations to ministerial positions that were offered to them by the Soviet government. At least 10 of Ryzhkov's original list were voted down, and some positions (such as that of minister of culture) remained unfilled for months. Where did this leave the party's vital power of *nomenklatura*, or the right to fill such key positions? And how could it control the actions of officials when increasing numbers were outside the party's ranks and thus outside its disciplinary reach? There were conflicts on policy, with deputies, mandated to increase social spending and resist higher prices, voting extra fund for their constituents but refusing to accept the increase in prices required to pay for these measures. The bill on social security, for instance, approved in 1990, was amended by deputies to include a further 46 billion rubles of public expenditure. This increased the planned budgetary deficit by 76% but why should deputies worry when reconciling income and expenditure was the responsibility of government? There were conflicts about the nature of the state itself, as nationalists in the Baltic and elsewhere secured a popular mandate to press for greater independence and even separation. The party leadership, armed with the much less impressive mandate of history, had no alternative but to concede at least the principle of their demands, proposing a law on secession in 1990 while hoping to keep the USSR together through some kind of new 'union treaty'.

This was, arguably, the tension upon which the Communist Party itself began to founder in the late 1980s and early 1990s. Having monopolised power throughout the Soviet period, it monopolised the blame for the mistakes and even crimes it belatedly acknowledged. More generally, as economic and other difficulties mounted, the party began to doubt its ability to continue to guide the whole life of the society. Some party members went on strike and rose to prominence in the popular fronts; others opposed them and called for discipline and central control. Members began to resign in significant numbers, the circulation of party newspapers began to fall, and posts in the apparatus became increasingly difficult to fill. Factions began to develop, with as many as eight different groupings — including the 'silent majority' — identified in party writings. The party's standing in the wider society began to decline, and fewer and fewer professed to see Marxism-Leninism as an answer to society's problems. The biggest shortage of all, the Central Committee was told in 1990, was the 'deficit of trust' in the party itself.

The changes of early 1990, and the abandonment of the leading role in particular, represented the logical completion of these changes. There was virtually no opposition within the Central Committee to the abandonment of the party's monopoly; as Gorbachev pointed out that monopoly had already disappeared. A wide range of political forces had come into existence and could not be wished away; the party had to recognise that reality and hope to retain at least a position of political dominance, co-operating with those 'healthy forces' that recognised the Constitution and the social order it embodied. The aim, once again, was to reconcile Leninism and popular sovereignty, retaining party leadership but this time with the consent of the governed. The outcome, in fact, was likely to be rather different: a demoralised and fragmented party losing its majority at the polls as most of its counterparts had already done in Eastern Europe. Gorbachev, originally, had sought to develop a model of 'socialist pluralism', and at the 1990 Congress he persuaded the party to adopt a programme of 'humane, democratic socialism', based upon popular consent but led by a CPSU that was committed to a 'Communist perspective'. The experience of the Gorbachev years had shown the difficulty in practice of combining these various elements, and little support at present remains for the Leninist alternative to democracy to which successive Soviet governments have committed themselves for more than 70 years.

## Economic Performance and System Adaptation

The decisive factor in the evolution of the Soviet system has been the performance of the Soviet economy. The collapse in the authority of the Communist Party was largely a result of the apparent failure to improve Soviet living standards. Slower rates of economic growth mean slower rates of social mobility, and slower rates of improvement or even stagnation in housing, medical services and education. Slower rates of economic growth were one of the most important reasons for the increasing pressure by more prosperous or better endowed republics to leave the rest of the USSR, or at least to increase their independent decision-making powers within it. Slower rates of economic growth undermined the claims of the official ideology, and weakened the attractiveness of the Soviet Union to outside powers. Above all, slower economic growth placed a heavy strain upon the 'social contract' between the Soviet authorities and the population, under which the Soviet public had notionally exchanged some of their civil rights for a modest but assured standard of living — and particularly for stable prices, full employment and cheap housing. Steadily falling rates of economic growth, which Gorbachev inherited from his predecessors, placed all of this in doubt; and Gorbachev's attempt to deal with this problem would in turn determine the future shape of the Soviet system.

Historically, the Soviet economic record has in fact been impressive. Russia in 1913 was a backward country, the 'poorest of the civilised countries' as it was described in a contemporary account. There was a small but active manufacturing sector, and levels of production in some areas, such as oil and textiles, were high by world standards. The overwhelming majority of the population, however, were engaged in agriculture, only a quarter of them could read and write, levels of infant mortality were high, and living standards were very low. National income in pre-revolutionary Russia is estimated to have been about 15% of that in the USA and 22% of that in the United Kingdom; labour productivity in industry, according to Soviet sources, was probably about 10% of the level attained in the United States. And living standards were improving less rapidly than elsewhere in Europe. Seventy years later, the contrast could hardly have been greater.

The USSR was one of the world's economic superpowers with a level of industrial output that was exceeded only by that of the USA (and probably Japan). In many areas — oil, gas, cast iron, steel and tractors, for instance — Soviet levels of production were the highest in the world. The USSR had pioneered the exploration of outer space, and led the world in the number of its scientific personnel. Soviet national income, 58% of that of the USA in 1960, had increased to 67% by 1980. Soviet industrial production, about 3% of the world total in 1917, had increased to 20% by 1987; by this date, indeed, the USSR produced more than the whole world had done in 1950. These achievements, moreover, had taken place in historical circumstances that could hardly have been more difficult. As Gorbachev told *Time* magazine in 1985, the old regime had left Soviet Russia a 'grim legacy: a backward economy, strong vestiges of feudalism, millions of illiterate people'. To this had to be added two devastating world wars, in the second of which (according to 1990 estimates) more than 26 million had been killed and many more maimed and wounded. The arms race, after the Second World War, had placed a further burden on the domestic economy, pre-empting resources that could otherwise have been devoted to the improvement of living standards.

Yet if the economic achievements of the USSR over the longer term were clear, particularly when war and other factors were taken into account, it was equally apparent by the late 1970s that there were deep-seated difficulties still to be resolved. The most striking indicator of these difficulties was the rate of economic growth, which fell consistently from the 1950s to the early 1980s with only a slight reversal in the late 1960s (see *Table 3.1*). Levels of economic growth in the late 1970s and early 1980s, in fact, were the lowest ever recorded in Soviet

TABLE 3.1 *Soviet Economic Growth, 1951 – 1985 (average annual rate of growth, official data, %)*

| Years | Produced national income | Gross industrial output | Gross agricultural output | Real incomes per head |
|---|---|---|---|---|
| 1951 – 55 | 11.4 | 13.2 | 4.2 | 7.3 |
| 1956 – 60 | 9.2 | 10.4 | 6.0 | 5.7 |
| 1961 – 65 | 6.5 | 8.6 | 7.2 | 3.6 |
| 1966 – 70 | 7.8 | 8.5 | 3.9 | 5.9 |
| 1871 – 75 | 5.7 | 7.4 | 2.5 | 4.4 |
| 1976 – 80 | 4.3 | 4.4 | 1.7 | 3.4 |
| 1981 – 85 | 3.6 | 3.7 | 1.0 | 2.1 |

Sources: Based upon *Narodnoe khozyaistvo SSSR 1922 – 1972 gg.* (Moscow: Statistika, 1972), p. 56, and *Narodnoe khozyaistvo SSSR za 70 let* (Moscow: Finansy i statistika, 1987), pp. 58 – 9.

peacetime history. In 1979, for instance, national income (in the Soviet definition) rose just 2.2% and living standards per head of population a bare 1.9%. Some Soviet as well as Western scholars were prepared to argue that, in real terms, growth had altogether ceased during these years. The 11th Five-Year Plan, covering the first half of the 1980s, was in turn substantially underfulfilled; the 26th Party Congress, in 1981, had approved directives providing that national income should increase 18 – 20% by 1985, but the actual increase was 16.5%, and each extra unit of output had been bought at the cost of an increasing consumption of energy, raw material and investment funds, unlike the experience of other industrialised nations. If this was the legacy of Brezhnev it was not a happy one.

Even these figures, moreover, overstated the real level of Soviet economic achievement. They normally left out the rate of growth of population — about 0.9% annually in the 1970s and 1980s. They also concealed a steady increase in over-reporting, amounting to 3% or more of total production in the 1980s and up to a third or more in certain sectors (the Central Asian cotton crop, in particular, became increasingly fictitious). Nor did the figures allow adequately for price increases and changes in specification. According to a highly controversial reassessment of official figures published in 1987, taking such factors into account Soviet national income from 1928 to 1985 had increased six or seven times — a highly creditable performance in comparative terms, but well short of the 90-fold increase recorded in official sources. Much of Soviet economic output was in any case hardly a contribution to real wealth. More tractors and combine harvesters were produced, for instance, than there were people available to operate them. And more than twice as many shoes were produced as in the USA, but the quality was so poor that millions more had to be imported. Even on the official figures some alarming developments were occurring. Soviet national income, for instance 67% of that of the USA in 1980, had slipped to 64% by 1988, and labour productivity in agriculture, about 20% of that of the United States in the 1970s, had fallen to 16% by the late 1980s.

The broad framework of Gorbachev's approach to economic reform was set out in his speech to the 27th Party Congress in 1986. The top priority, in his view, was to overcome the factors that had been holding back the country's socio-economic development and to resume the growth of earlier decades. Not only was it necessary to accelerate the rate of growth: it must be a new quality of growth, based upon scientific and technical progress, structural change and new forms of management and labour incentives. A change of this kind — from extensive growth, based upon the use of additional resources, to intensive growth, based upon the better use of existing resources — was not simply desirable: for Gorbachev, there was 'no other way'. The revised Party Programme and the Guidelines for the new 12th Five-Year Plan, both of which were adopted at the Congress, therefore set their central objective as the doubling of national income by the year 2000, based upon scientific progress, decentralised management, more 'flexible' prices and greater participation in the running of enterprises.

More detailed guidelines for economic reform were approved by a Central Committee meeting in June 1987, at which Gorbachev delivered the key address. There had, he suggested, been outstanding successes in the years after the revolution, but the established centralised and detailed forms of management had now outlived their usefulness. Attempts at reform, from the 1950s onwards, had been unsuccessful. Now, in the 1980s, the Soviet economy was in a 'pre-crisis' situation. The rate of economic growth had dropped to a level that 'virtually signified the onset of economic stagnation'. Resources were being wasted, and technological levels were lagging increasingly behind those of the rest of the developed world. Budget deficits were being covered by the sale of oil and other raw materials on world markets and by tax returns on the sale of alcohol, which had more than doubled over the previous 15 years. Spending on wages had systematically exceeded plan targets, while increases of output and productivity had been less than predicted. This meant that money incomes were increasingly outstripping the supply of goods and services. There was a shortage of everything, from metal and cement to consumer goods and manpower. Nothing less than a 'radical reform' in the whole system of economic management was needed to reverse these alarming trends.

In agriculture, Gorbachev suggested, greater use should be made of the 'collective' or 'family contract', by which a small group of workers obtained the use of an area of land for a fixed price and received in return the right to sell their surplus produce on the open market. Storage and processing facilities should be modernised (up to 30% of agricultural output was being lost in this way); and, more generally, the management of agriculture should be shifted away from officials at the central and local levels and into the hands of the workers. Comparable changes were needed in the housing and construction industries, which were operating well below capacity. Still more important, consumer goods should be given a higher priority, and so should services. Gorbachev quoted an official estimate that the size of the black economy was at least 1.5 billion rubles a year. Local officials could not escape their responsibility for such matters; nor could national-level ministers, a number of whom were directly named.

Above all, an attempt must be made to establish an 'integrated, efficient and flexible system of economic management', relying less on administrative or 'command' forms of direction and more on market-based or 'economic' methods. Enterprises should be more autonomous, with more responsibility for their own production and finances, leaving Gosplan and other bodies to set the broad strategy of economic development. Plans would continue to be produced, but they would be concerned with long-term objectives and major state programmes, not with the day-to-day functioning of industries and enterprises. Economic management at this level would in future be based more upon commercial 'state orders' (*goszakazy*), which would be allocated on a competitive basis by the central planners, and upon the orders of other enterprises. In extreme cases, if an enterprise became unprofitable it might be liquidated. There should also be a much closer relationship between the Soviet and the world economy, including joint ventures and other forms of co-operation. These principles were embodied in a set of 'Guidelines for the radical restructuring of economic management', adopted by the plenum, and were carried further by a Law on the State Enterprise, adopted by the Supreme Soviet later in the year.

Other elements to the programme of economic reform were added over the months that followed. Under legislation approved in November 1986, for instance, a wide variety of forms of 'individual labour activity' was specifically legalised. The main aims as set out by the chairman of the State Committee on Labour and Social Questions, were that the activities concerned should not detract from production in the state sector, and that the income obtained should correspond to the work performed. Those who were eligible to engage in such activities included housewives, students, invalids and ordinary employees in their free time; work they could undertake included car repairs, translation, photography, typing and handicrafts (but not pornography or the manufacture of armaments). A further, potentially more significant, change was the adoption in May 1988 of a new Law on Co-operatives widely seen as the most radical of all Gorbachev's changes. The new co-operatives were, in principle, exempted from obligatory state plans and state orders, although they were required to inform the relevant authorities of their intentions. Co-operatives could fix their own prices, except when they were producing for state orders or using state-supplied materials (in practice, a considerable limitation). They were entitled to conduct foreign trade operations, and to keep a significant part of the hard currency they earned; and they could form joint ventures with foreign companies. By January 1990 the new co-operatives employed 4.5 million workers on a full-time or part-time basis and were increasing rapidly in number, although they still accounted for no more than 1.5% of retail trade and services.

If the central objective of the Gorbachev reform strategy was to recover the economy's growth dynamic, it was clear it fell far short of success in its early years. The 12th Five-Year Plan called for a 4.2%

annual rate of growth in produced national income, as compared with the rate of 3.6% achieved in the first half of the decade. The Guidelines adopted by the 27th CPSU Congress stipulated a still higher rate of growth in the 1990s, 5% p.a., in order to double national income by the year 2000. The rate of growth achieved in 1986 – 88 in fact averaged a modest 3.6%, exactly as had been achieved in the late Brezhnev, Andropov and Chernenko years. The 1988 plan results,

TABLE 3.2 *Soviet Economic Growth, 1981 – 89 (official data, %)*

|  | 1981 – 5 average | 1986 – 90 average (plan) | 1986 | 1987 | 1988 | 1989 |
|---|---|---|---|---|---|---|
| National income produced | 3.6 | 4.2 | 4.1 | 2.3 | 4.4 | 2.4 |
| Industrial output | 3.7 | 4.6 | 4.9 | 3.9 | 3.9 | 1.7 |
| Agricultural output | 1.0 | 2.7 | 5.1 | 0.6 | 0.7 | 1.0 |

Sources: As for Table 3.1; and *Kommunist*, 1989, no. 2, p. 23; *Pravda*, 28 January, 1990, p. 1.

compared with the others, were relatively more satisfactory: national income rose by 4.4% and gross national product (which was much closer to the definitions of economic activity used in the West) rose by 5%. The figure for national income, however impressive, still left economic growth for the first three full Gorbachev years below the Five-Year Plan target; grain production was particularly poor (substantial foreign purchases had to be made), and wages were still increasing much more rapidly than output. The 1989 results showed a lower rate of growth of GNP, just 3%, and there were falls in housing, transportation, oil and coal. In the view of reform-minded economists the overall economic performance of the late 1980s represented a stagnation or even a decline, not the resumption of growth as the leadership had intended; and in the first half of 1990, even on the official figures, national income actually declined.

Admittedly, many of the difficulties the economy had experienced were the result of exogenous factors of various kinds. One of these was a change in the terms of trade, particularly a fall in the value of Soviet oil exports. Further heavy losses were incurred by a series of natural disasters including the Chernobyl nuclear explosion of April 1986 and the Armenian earthquake of December 1988. The reforms, in any case, often made relatively little difference to the realities of economic management, perhaps the most conspicuous example being the state orders which were supposed to replace ministerial directives under the Law on the State Enterprise. It soon became apparent that the Law was largely a dead letter; ministries continued to issue directives but simply renamed them state orders, and these directives in turn continued to account for the overwhelming share of output. Enterprises, for their part, often sought to obtain a high level of state orders so that their sources of supply could be secured. As a result, *val* or gross output rather than market-related success criteria, continued to determine the pattern of production, much as it had done ever since the command economy had been established. In the absence of a comprehensive price reform and in conditions of shortage and monopoly, the profitability of enterprises was in any case a poor guide to their efficiency.

More fundamentally, the reform programme led to tensions between the traditional mechanism of central planning, which still defined the framework of economic activity, and market criteria of various kinds. Their greater autonomy, for instance, allowed enterprises more freedom to choose their output mix in a way that met their obligations in the easiest way. One general response was to reduce or discontinue the production of less profitable items and concentrate on other products. This led to shortages of children's goods and many other necessities. The lack of soap and washing powder, in the late 1980s, was a source of particular indignation. Quality was a related concern. An increasing proportion of sausage, for instance, included fat or additives. The weekly paper *Literaturnaya gazeta* experimented on 30 cats who knew 'nothing of chemistry, bureaucracy or economies of scale'; 24 of them refused all the varieties of sausage they were offered, and five more refused most of them.

One result of shortages was queues, sometimes of wartime proportions, and the widespread use of coupons for rationing purposes. Another was a rapid increase in prices as producers took advantage of their new ability to exploit market conditions. Inflation, according to the State Statistics Committee, reached a level of 7.5% in 1989; unofficial estimates suggested a level of up to 20%. The greater the shortages, the more shoppers had to make use of collective farm markets and co-operatives where prices were still higher. The prices that were charged by co-operatives, often for goods that had originally been bought in the state sector, and the huge incomes they were able to pay their workers, aroused particular resentment. Some co-operatives were paying their members twice as much in a day as an ordinary workers was able to make in a month. There was strong public support for the restrictions upon the activity of co-operatives that were imposed at the end of 1988, and taken further in 1989.

Greater enterprise autonomy led to increasing difficulties of a different but related kind: it made it easier for management to put up wages more rapidly than would otherwise have been possible, covering their costs by higher prices. The result was a rapid increase in inflationary pressures, as rising incomes chased a much less rapidly increasing supply of commodities. In 1988 the average monthly income of workers and white-collar staff in the state sector rose by 7%, but productivity in the economy as a whole by just 5.1%. In 1989 the same tendencies were even more apparent: money wages rose by 9.5% but labour productivity by a much more modest 2.3%. As a regional party first secretary told the Central Committee, wages were increasing ahead of production at such a rate that soon the whole economy would be devoted to printing paper. If individuals and enterprises had financial difficulties, so too did the state. With increasing levels of consumption and unchanged prices, the subsidies that were paid particularly for foodstuffs shot up. Heavy costs fell directly upon the state budget from the Chernobyl explosion and the Armenian earthquake. Meanwhile, income was reduced with the fall in the world price of oil, and the vigorous campaign against alcohol abuse, launched in 1985, led to a massive loss of revenue without significantly affecting the consumption of alcohol itself (black marketeers pocketed the difference).

## The Economics and Politics of Adaptation

If political reform, by the early 1990s, had led to an uneasy combination of Leninism and democracy, economic reform had similarly resulted in an unhappy compromise between the traditional system of central planning and the market-oriented principles promoted by the new leadership. Commentators in the early 1990s saw at least two clear ways forward. For one group, including most economists, the continuing problems of the Soviet economy stemmed from too little reform, not too much. Like the 'radical right' in other countries, they called for cuts in public spending, the elimination of indiscriminate subsidies, privatisation of state assets, wider inequalities of income and, if necessary, limited forms of unemployment. For Nikolai Shmelev, for instance, an economist and a member of the Congress of People's Deputies, better living standards would come about only through satisfying the market. The way forward in agriculture was through the private and co-operative sector. In industry, enterprises should be compelled to operate in free market conditions. Fears that this would result in massive unemployment were 'greatly exaggerated'; people were continually changing jobs as it was, nor could they close their eyes to the 'great harm being done by our parasitic reliance on guaranteed employment'. If disorderliness, drunkenness and poor workmanship were really to be eliminated, there was probably no alternative to the establishment of a 'comparatively small reserve army of labour'. Foreign firms should be given greater access to the Soviet market so as to force Soviet enterprise to become competitive; the role of Gosplan and the ministries should be reduced drastically; and prices should be brought into line with those that prevailed internationally.

There was, however, another view, more directly linked with the industrial working class and articulated with considerable force by politicians such as the former Moscow party leader and later President of the Russian Republic, Boris Yeltsin. Seen from this perspective, the source of the country's economic difficulties lay much more in the distribution of benefits and the relations between social groups on which that distribution was based. The Soviet working class, they pointed out, was poorly remunerated, even in relative terms. Spending on the health service, once at a high level, had dropped to 3 – 4% of national income as compared with 8 – 12% in most other developed nations. Public spending on education, housing and other programmes had also fallen steadily to levels that were often far below those of comparable nations. Subsidies, it was argued, were not necessarily regressive. In some cases, such as housing and meat, those with higher incomes also had a higher level of consumption, and thus of public support; but in other cases, such as bread and potatoes, the better-off did not on the whole, consume more than the poor and the subsidy which kept the price down was in effect a form of income redistribution in their favour.

For many radicals, in fact, the monetarist diagnosis was not simply on shaky ground empirically: it was actually an attempt to solve the nation's economic difficulties at the expense of ordinary workers. Yeltsin, for instance, speaking to the Congress of People's Deputies in 1989, argued that there had been no real advance in social justice in the 70 years of Soviet rule, and that there was every reason to speak of an 'élite stratum' of society, 'wallowing in luxury' while tens of millions lived in abject poverty. The radical sociological Tatiana Zaslavskaya, also a people's deputy, referred in a newspaper interview to 'indirect exploitation' of the working class by the full-time party and state bureaucracy. Indeed for some Soviet writers, in the late 1980s, social relations in the USSR were best understood in straightforwardly Marxist terms, with a bureaucratic 'class' exploiting the labour of ordinary workers.

Gorbachev and the party leadership distanced themselves from the more extreme monetarist prescriptions, but also from a class analysis of this kind. For Gorbachev personally, speaking in 1989, there could be no talk of private property — did they really want to work for the capitalists, he asked a group of Leningrad workers? — and he promised the Party Congress in 1990 that price increases, where they occurred, would be discussed widely and introduced in a form that would protect the living standards of the least affluent. There was much that could be done, in any case, within the existing framework, such as reductions in military expenditure and eliminating waste. In the long run, however, it was likely to be difficult to avoid a choice: either a revolution 'from above', made in the name of working people but without their participation and possibly against their interests, or a popular movement 'from below', in a form that was likely to challenge the power, and not simply the fairly modest privileges, of Soviet officials. Entering the 1990s, it was this delicate and unpredictable balance of social forces that was most likely to determine the adaptiveness of Soviet socialism and the future of *perestroika*.

# References

Aslund, Anders *Gorbachev's Struggle for Economic Reform*. (1989, London: Pinter).

Gorbachev, Mikhail *Perestroika: New Thinking for Our Country and the World*. (1987, London: Collins).

Hewett, Edward A *Reforming the Soviet Economy*. (1988, Washington DC: Brookings).

Hill, Ronald J *The Soviet Union: Politics, Economics and Society*. (1989, 2nd ed., London: Pinter).

Hill, Ronald J and Frank, Peter *The Soviet Communist Party*. (1987, 3rd ed. London: Allen and Unwin).

Hosking, Geoffrey A *A History of the Soviet Union*. (1990, 2nd ed. London: Fontana).

Lane, David *Soviet Society under Perestroika*. (1990, Boston: Unwin Hyman).

Lewin, Moshe *The Gorbachev Phenomenon*. (1988, London: Radius).

Medvedev, Zhores *Gorbachev*, (1988, rev. ed. Oxford: Blackwell).

Nahajlo, Bohdan and Swoboda, Victor *Soviet Disunion: A History of the Nationalities Problem in the USSR*. (1990, London: Hamish Hamilton).

Nove, Alec *An Economic History of the USSR*, (1989, 2nd ed. Harmondsworth, Mx.: Penguin).

Sakwa, Richard *Gorbachev and his Reforms*. (1990, London: Simon and Schuster).

White, Stephen *Soviet Communism: Programme and Rules*. (1989, London: Routledge).

White, Stephen *Gorbachev in Power*. (1990, Cambridge and New York: Cambridge University Press).

White, Stephen, Pravda, Alex and Gitelman, Zvi, eds. *Developments in Soviet Politics*. (1990, London: Macmillan).

Wilson, Andrew and Bachkatov, Nina *Living with Glasnost*. (1988, Harmondsworth, Mx.: Penguin).

CHAPTER 4

# Soviet Collective Security Perception

AMNON SELLA

THE SOVIET armed forces, rich in experience, abundant in arms, both conventional and nuclear, will virtually have to start again from scratch. It is bad enough when a country has no allies; it is worse when the enemy is within. The basic concept of the USSR's defence has long been based on the unity of the Soviet people, the Soviet State and the Soviet armed forces. After the events of Azerbaijan, Lithuania, Moldavia and Kirghizia this concept is a shambles. Since 1955 the basic concept of Soviet collective security was formally founded on the unity of the socialist countries, locked in fraternity and in the Warsaw Pact Treaty. This idea, erroneous as it may have been from its inception, and half-baked as it may have been in its implementation, has been, never-theless, the centrepiece of Soviet official defence policy, sucking in many resources. It is now in ruins. Both NATO and the Warsaw Pact were based on a certain ambivalence in overall strategy as well as in the division of labour between their member states. Whether NATO is a tool of the 'free world' to contain expansionist designs of Communism the world over, or an umbrella to protect Western Europe from Soviet threats and to prevent a deterrence failure in Europe which might deteriorate into a global crisis has never been resolved. According to the first assumption non-American NATO forces were supposed to assist US forces to protect 'indivisible peace' everywhere: in Korea, in Vietnam, or in the Gulf; according to the second, US forces in Europe were supposed to form a 'trip-wire' in case of a rapid Soviet advance to the Channel. Tactical nuclear missiles, as well as cruise missiles based on European soil, were supposed to have deterred Soviet nuclear adventures.

The Warsaw Pact's ambivalence derived from the fact that the Soviet government has never resolved whether it wanted a political organisation with a military back-up to defend socialism in Eastern Europe, or a

51

military organisation with some political attributes to assist the Soviet armed forces in case of a major crisis in Europe. In effect the Soviet armed forces were never dependent on Warsaw Pact forces. At best they trained and exercised with specialised units that in case of war were supposed to be incorporated into the main body of the Soviet armed forces. Consequently, Soviet forces in Eastern Europe formed a shield for local governments that by and large were imposed on their people and as such served more as police than as military forces. The political aspect was very one-sided since the Soviet forces in Eastern Europe wielded great political influence by their sheer presence and under the cloak of the Brezhnev doctrine, whereas the political organisation of the Warsaw Pact was of little significance. As soon as the Brezhnev doctrine was abrogated, in 1989, signifying Moscow's acquiescence in the 'democratisation' of East Europe, the walls came tumbling down, literally and figuratively, forcing Moscow and the Eastern bloc to face for the first time the external implications of Soviet domestic *perestroika*.

It has been suggested above that the whole idea of the Warsaw Pact was strategically erroneous and, in the nuclear age, obsolete. In due course it proved also to be politically unsound. The only military actions ever taken by the Pact have been against its own members: in 1956 in Budapest and in 1968 in Prague. All it managed to do was to alienate the Soviet Union in Eastern Europe and cause concern in the USA and NATO. From a strategic point of view the years of the Cold War were a frightening exercise in nuclear arms race and in nuclear and conventional deployment, masquerading as an American effort to contain Communism in order to defend democracy and a Soviet effort to achieve parity and to defend socialism. The conventional build-up of NATO and WTO were taken extremely seriously by the parties concerned until the INF agreement was signed, revealing that the Soviet conventional advantage and alleged threat in Europe had been a chimera. Apparently the Soviet Union volunteered willingly to get rid of its 'advantage', indeed as willingly as the USA volunteered to remove the intermediate-range nuclear missiles that since 1985, were supposed to have served as the immediate deterrence against a Soviet rapid advance into Western Europe. Now, more than ever, the USSR must look for a new strategy in Europe, indeed, a new strategy for its armed forces.

## A New Strategy for the 1990s and Beyond

The Soviet Union seems to be looking not only for a new strategy but also for a new type of army. In many respects the current dispute within the military élite, and between the military and political élites, recalls a similar dispute in the first years after the Revolution. Then the leadership was groping for new ideas in the military field, torn between ideological aversion to 'militarism' on the one hand and the need to defend the new regime on the other. All we have to do is to substitute the old idea of 'militia' or paramilitary force for the 'new' idea of a volunteer army and the old aversion to militarism for the 'new thinking' about 'the common European home'. The differences however, outweigh the similarities. The traditional balance of forces was based on a bipolar system with a superpower at each pole. The definition of a superpower incorporated a dynamic economic structure, a stable political system and a large military power. The Soviet system, which had been in force from 1917 – 85, crumbled because the economic structure proved unable to sustain either the political system or the military machine. In order to form a new strategy the Soviet leadership must redress two sets of equations: the domestic and the external. On the domestic front a 'realistic' assessment of the challenges to Soviet national security lay not in the outside world but inside the country, in its stagnating economy, falling living standards, growing technological backwardness and in the deterioration of the environment.[1] A realistic reassessment is a necessary diagnostic and psychological process at the end of which the problem may only be aggravated and lead to further weakening of the political system. This compound strain of a deteriorating economic system leading to political instability is exacerbated by the growing dependence on external goodwill. In short, the weaker the Soviet system and the less menacing it becomes to its environment, the less capable it is of coming up with a new strategy. The dilemma of the new strategy is how to reduce the armour without affecting the armature. There is no argument between the political leadership and the military that the armed forces must be reduced in size; the main argument is the severity of threat and the likelihood of a war 'unleashed by the imperialists'. Given the economic constraints of the Soviet Union, the collapse of the Eastern bloc and the Soviet-American agreements, a shift from the current military system to a much smaller professional army seems not an illogical conclusion.

Such a shift recalls another dispute from the 1930s of which Soviet military strategists are well aware — the smaller professional army versus the mass army. The difference is that during the USSR's formative years it was easier to reach a decision, whereas now there are many vested interests, many jobs that may become redundant, many privileges that would disappear. In the past

'the decision-making procedure was in the hands of a small group of politicians who consulted neither the people nor the Supreme Soviet. They did not even bother to study the view of the military. In the era of *perestroika* it is impossible to make a decision without the supreme state organs. Generals and Marshals never had a free hand, they do not have it at present and they shall not have it in the future'.[2]

The military in the USSR has never had a free rein; but for several decades it was consulted as its share of the national resources grew larger each year. The same applies when reductions of the armed forces are in the offing. Indeed, in the best traditions of recent Soviet practice, the ideas about planned reductions were discussed in military academies; and the military leadership shares the burden of responsibility for today's planned reductions. However, the recent and current upsurge of national sentiments present the military and political leadership of the Soviet Union with problems greater than merely the size of the army. One such problem is whether, by the end of the 1990s the government will still deal with a Soviet Union, a Soviet people and a Soviet armed forces, or with a confederation of autonomous and semi-autonomous entities and a Russian army. The recent Ukrainian declaration about the supremacy of their law over that of the Soviet Union and their wish to have their own army is an ominous sign.

On 22 September, 1989 *Krasnaya Zvezda* suggested as much. Not only that some 15% of all new draftees could not or would not speak Russian, but also that many officers complained that they were treated as occupiers in some provinces and that the local Party organs refused to deal with them. It went on to say that, whereas in the Military Districts some 90% of the units were composed of several nationalities, in the combat divisions it was only 40%, and in the navy 30%. Discreetly, the air force is not even mentioned. In sum, the main strategic problems have strong political overtones. A new perception of national and collective security will have to take into consideration the following questions about the armed forces:

- size;
- type; professional, regular, volunteer, or some mix of all three; and
- ethnic composition.

If these problems are resolved, there will be other sociological problems such as new vocations for redundant career officers and absorption by the labour market of youngsters who will no longer be conscripted. Noteworthy in this respect are Soviet announcements that by January 1991 the Soviet armed forces would number 3,760,000 instead of the then current approximate 4,200,000, and that by 1995 security expenditure will be 2 – 2.5% less than at present.

Of a rather more strategic-operational nature is the problem of nuclear arsenals and missile sites that may be outside the direct control of the Soviet government as we know it now, in Kazakhstan for instance. Future strategy will have to come to grips with the possibility of a huge nuclear arsenal under the control of a less stable political centre, a phenomenon which should cause both the Soviet government and the West to be cautious in the agreements and verification procedures they sign. The USSR has already proposed to establish a centre to deal with reducing the danger of war and surprise attack which could in turn pave the way for an 'all-European committee of foreign ministers, for an Institute of Annual Summits of the 35'.[3] Soviet and Hungarian diplomatic representation in NATO may be harbingers of a salutary change.

Furthermore, if the tendency of at least part of the Soviet leadership is to withdraw back into 'fortress Russia', with the Russian Republic as the hard core of a new and looser confederation of the other 14 Republics, the strategy of the armed forces must undergo a radical change. If the army that emerges retains the name Soviet Armed Forces, a complete reshuffle must take place in the proportion of Slavic to non-Slavic members of the officer corps. However, if current tendencies persist it is probable that the confederated Republics will be reluctant to send draftees to the Soviet Armed Forces, and may prefer to have their own national forces even if only to parade their national flags and to defend their separatist national interests. In either case the Soviet or the Russian army may be much smaller than it is now and, in an emergency, will have to count on reservists. In other words, the military will have to work out a system of mobilisation for both men and equipment and a system of arsenals and depots of large capacity. It may also have to come to terms with several other national armies of the loose confederation on equal terms. Collective security in the future will depend on the success of the confidence-building measures that are being worked out now, on stabilisation of the Soviet political system, on the results of German and European unification and on the lingering uncertainty of nuclear weapons. The new balance of forces in Europe suggests a brighter future, with less proclivity for global crisis in the relationships between the superpowers.

So far we have dealt with the domestic aspect of possible changes of Soviet strategy. However, to be able to produce a new strategy for the next decade the Soviet government will also have to take into account both European and 'out of area' global events in terms of space and time. The official Soviet aim is worldwide elimination of nuclear military power, coupled with a semi-official line regarding 'open skies, open seas and open land'. The government does, however, make allowances for the Western approach of 'minimal deterrence' and is unlikely to give up its nuclear capability unilaterally. The US and

NATO remain the main concern of USSR strategists, in particular of the military establishment, but there is also concern about nuclear and missile technology proliferation and the possible rise of new potential alliances armed with nuclear capability around the southern borders of the USSR.

For methodological reasons it is better to examine the strategic problems that carry a crisis potential in three separate sections: the USSR, WTO and NATO; the USSR and the Middle East; and South-east Asia and China.

## The USSR, WTO and NATO

The WTO is now obsolete for two reasons: first, it lost its political purpose when the Brezhnev doctrine was abrogated; secondly, its military uselessness came into a sharp relief when the USSR was asked to pull out its forces from Eastern Europe. The withdrawal of Soviet forces from Eastern Europe is now in progress and, if all goes to plan, by 1992 there will be only a few Soviet divisions outside Soviet territory, and by the year 2000 only a few outside Russian territory and those may have to have special permission to stay.

However, it must be borne in mind that, under Soviet tutelage, the Eastern bloc was stable and quiet as far as inter-bloc relations were concerned. National and ethnic animosities were kept tight under the Soviet lid. As long as *perestroika* remains the official policy, the withdrawal of Soviet forces from Eastern Europe will go on; and on 25 February, 1991 the military structure of the Warsaw Pact was disbanded.

Far more complex and uncertain are the futures of NATO and USSR-NATO relations. Soviet strategists pointed with great accuracy at the bones of contention, 'forward defence' and 'flexible response'. The London Declaration on 6 July, 1990, at the end of a two-day NATO summit meeting, struggled with these and other issues. The Soviet Union and NATO have now declared that neither would be the first to use force. The London Declaration states that: '. . . the Alliance's integrated force structure and its strategy will change fundamentally. . . '. NATO seems to be satisfied with the changes in Soviet strategy and the implementation of the new doctrine: 'reasonable sufficiency'. However, the ambiguity concerning the use of nuclear weapons still hovers over Europe:

> Finally, with the total withdrawal of Soviet stationed forces and the implementation of a CFE agreement, the allies concerned can reduce their reliance on nuclear weapons. These will continue to fulfil an essential role in the overall strategy of the Alliance to prevent war by ensuring that there are no circumstances in

which nuclear retaliation in response to military action might be discounted.

Europe as a 'common European home' or as 'an integrated free Europe' will face a different future as far as the 'delicate balance of terror' is concerned. The nuclear arsenal will be smaller and under more supervision, namely 'verification'. It is most likely that conventional forces will also be smaller in size with fewer and smaller military exercises. However, imponderable circumstances will remain in which nuclear retaliation cannot be discounted. With the demise of the Warsaw Pact suspended for a while and NATO feeling its way for a new mission, the Conference on Security and Co-operation in Europe (CSCE) is beginning to claim its own military identity. The Soviet strategic agenda will have to deal with the organisation and purpose of its armed forces in the face of a volatile home front, defence of new and perhaps not yet final borders and a lingering uncertainty concerning a possible use of nuclear retaliation.

The uncertainty over nuclear retaliation is further complicated by the reunification of Germany. Both Germany and the Soviet Union are well aware of the complications, the drawbacks and the benefits thereof and a new dimension has been added to Gorbachev's definition of the new Europe. In a Soviet-German declaration on 21 June, 1989, both governments resolved to build a common home 'in which the United States and Canada have a place as well'. At the introduction to this Chapter it was stated that economic power, a stable political system and military might make a superpower. The question now is whether these three are necessary and sufficient conditions. After some US-Soviet bargaining and a great deal of German persuasion, Moscow agreed to Germany's membership of NATO. This concession raises an interesting problem which pertains not only to security in Europe but also to the wider question of the nature of sovereignty and the face of future superpowers. Will Germany as a member of NATO have access to nuclear weapons, or will it give up a portion of its sovereignty by disclaiming such access? Germany is going out of its way to reassure its neighbours of its goodwill. It boldly recognised the Oder-Neisse as the permanent border between Germany and Poland, as though proof were needed that the spectre of the marching Wehrmacht was laid to eternal rest. However the price Germany paid to the Soviet Union by financing a residual Soviet force in East Germany, even if this is only for a short period of time, adds further complications to the problem of sovereignty. The Soviet-German agreement which incorporates a lucrative financial boost to Soviet economy, does not settle the question about the nature of superpowers. How long can a country enjoy a robust economic infrastructure and a stable political system without aspiring also to become a strong military power? Is there a guarantee in the new framework of Europe and in the new international atmosphere against irrational forces?

## Conventional Forces in Europe

The military powers, both European and non-European, would have us believe that security and confidence in Europe are predicated on the CFE. On the face of it agreements on conventional forces seem to be easier than on nuclear ones, but the world lost its innocence with the invention of the atom bomb. With a fair amount of confidence nuclear weapons may be put under control, but even if the Soviet idealistic demand were accepted and there was complete nuclear disarmament it would not end the problem. The knowledge cannot be eradicated, proliferation cannot be stopped and both superpowers retain a strong element of military conservatism which genuinely fears the traditional enemy, as well as having a vested interest in maintaining a credible opposition.

However, purely conventional forces also present the strategists with many problems. In the transitional period, that is when the need to think in 'Pan-European' terms is pressing and popular, and while old suspicions and some new ones still pervade the traditional blocs, there is a sense of vacillation between collective security and individual susceptibilities. The WTO disintegrated for practical as well as ideological reasons. The practical reasons are the abrogation of the Brezhnev doctrine and the incapability of the USSR to sustain the burden of such a huge military organisation. The ideological reasons are inherent in the Treaty, and have been from its inception. The preamble to the WTO called for the establishment of a system of European collective and Article 11 stipulates that the treaty will stop functioning when a treaty of collective security is signed in Europe.[4] Such a treaty seems now within grasp. However, the Soviet Union is not unambiguous in its statements about the need to dissolve the blocs. On the one hand it has taken many steps towards this end and Gorbachev has made it clear that he wished to put an end to the division of Europe. On the other hand, there are several Soviet statements to the effect that the blocs actually help to stabilise the international political arena during a period of transition. The dissonance between collective security and concerns of individual countries led to an arrangement of two sets of talks: one among the 23 states (17 NATO and 6 WTO countries) dealing with CFE, and another among the 35 states dealing with Confidence and Security Building Measures (CSBM). Thus, two forums deal with the security problems of Europe: the forum of the 23, respecting the wishes of most NATO countries, still acknowledges the old alliances, while the forum of the 35 was assembled in respect of the French, Swedish and the WTO wish to do away with old alliances. As soon as negotiations started, old unsettled feuds surfaced between Greece and Turkey and between Bulgaria and Turkey. Italy complained that the problems of the Mediterranean were not being addressed with due circumspection, and Spain demanded closer ties with France.

Notwithstanding all these difficulties, the talks are moving apace. The USSR is prepared to reduce its conventional forces which, in turn, will ensure a radical change in organisation and deployment of forces in the ATTU (Atlantic-to-Urals Zone). In many respects the organisation and deployment of Soviet armed forces in the next decade will indeed be defensive. If all goes according to plan motorised infantry divisions would lose 40% of their tanks and the armoured divisions would lose 20%. Coupled with the reductions in the number of warplanes, this may remove the fear of a conventional surprise attack in Europe which has been at the core of so much suspicion during the years of the Cold War. The question now is what are the effects of new technologies on the balance of conventional forces that is emerging out of the CFE and the CSBM?

Many risks are involved in the use and implementation of new technologies. In the first place they do not carry the stigma attached to nuclear weapons and therefore the temptation to use them against enemy forces reduced in size may be irresistible at a time of acute crisis. On the one hand reducing manpower is becoming operationally meaningless in view of modern technological capabilities; on the other, if 'conventional deterrence' fails the temptation to use Advanced Conventional Munitions (ACMs) to annihilate swiftly and efficiently small professional enemy forces will be enormous. The whole idea of 'conventional deterrence' has not yet been worked out and the parties perhaps reluctantly must retain nuclear power as a weapon of last resort. The 28th CPSU Congress still pointed to the danger emanating from the 'imperialists' presumably noting carefully the clause in the London Declaration stating: 'NATO will rely more on the ability to build up larger forces if and when they might be needed'.

The future of security in Europe does not depend entirely on the physical withdrawal, redeployment, reduction of forces or even the scrapping of weapon systems, but on the combination of CFE with CSBM. Insecurity, instability, suspicion and lack of confidence are not, and probably have never been, a result of ill intentions *per se*, but of the interpretation of the intentions and assessment of the capabilities of one side by the other, leading to worst case analyses. Alliances and their relationships have left their imprint on post-war history. The delicate balance of terror was fraught with many dangers apart from being costly, but at least in the eyes of its proponents it had one obvious advantage: it was an effective deterrent against nuclear adventures. However, the options for peace or war in Europe in the coming decade will depend on diverse forces, like national feelings, ethnic animosities and old disputes that respectable and reasonable governments do not control. NATO and the USSR will retain enough military capability not only as a sop to their respective military establishments but also as residual caution at a time of transition. The 'revolution' in East Europe and the instability in some of the Soviet republics is so far-reaching that the Soviet government will have, sooner or later, to address the legal problems involved. For instance Article 37 of the law of the 'State borders of the USSR', states:

> The state borders of the USSR adjacent to the borders of other socialist countries are guarded by border guards together with the border guards of these countries. Mutual means to guard the USSR state border adjacent to countries of the socialist community are based on agreement and co-ordination.

If this somewhat sanctimonious statement failed to stand the test of the Sino-Soviet split when China was considered to be socialist, can it stand the test of future possible tensions with countries around the USSR that might repudiate socialism?

## The USSR and the Middle East

War in the Middle East is an ever-present danger. It has already been proved that the superpowers could not prevent the outbreak of war; the most they could do was to influence its intensity and duration by regulating arms delivery to the region. In the light of the emerging global balance of forces, the USSR is even less likely to carry much weight in the area. The USA and the USSR have never managed to work out a plan for regional co-operation, either in Central America or in the Middle East. However, they did manage to tackle some of the most important problems such as chemical weapons and proliferation of missile technology. In the coming decade the Middle East may become a military theatre of chemical devices, intermediate-range missiles and nuclear weapons. The two superpowers agreed that:

> When the CW convention enters into force, the sides will further reduce their CW stocks to equal levels at a very small fraction of their present holdings over the first eight years of operation of the convention. All remaining CW stocks should be eliminated over the subsequent two years. Of course, all CW-capable states must adhere to the convention.

Superpowers, European powers and regional powers are well aware of the fact that without limitation on the delivery and production of arms there can be no peace in the Middle East. So far there have been few ideas for negotiations on this subject. The superpowers cannot agree on a machinery to enforce their own agreements on the region and the regional countries cannot resolve either their differences on the Israeli-Palestinian issue or the issue of arms limitation. When CFE is eventually implemented in Europe, the arms market may be flooded with redundant advanced weapon systems even after the scrapping of so many tanks and missiles. If political stability in the Soviet Union deteriorates, the temptation to sell arms in the open market may grow. Although the USSR no longer supports Syrian aspirations for strategic parity with Israel, a further impoverished USSR might be tempted to sell arms for hard currency. Even now the combination of SU-24 and MIG-29 in the arsenals of Syria, Libya and Iraq (probably also Iran at the time of writing) put Israeli conventional deterrence at risk. However, partly as a result of economic difficulties, Syria, Egypt, Iran and Israel, at least, reduced their arms purchases in 1989. Only Libya (not strictly speaking a Middle Eastern country) increased its arms purchases in 1989.

Although the USSR has signed several treaties with Middle East countries incorporating military clauses, despite its past involvement in skirmishes between the Arab countries and Israel, there has never been a large scale intervention of Soviet armed forces in the region. For several reasons, such intervention is even less likely in the future. Past experience did not convince the Soviet government of the prudence of deep military involvement. Domestic instability, particularly in the Muslim republics, will make it extremely difficult to use force in countries adjacent to Soviet southern borders. In the past, the Soviet command post for possible Middle Eastern operations was in the Za-Kavkaz *oblast* of the Trans-Caucasus Military District, but by the end of the decade the Soviet government may have to negotiate with one or more local governments the right of stationing and passage of forces through the Caucasus. The strategic significance of the Middle East seemed to diminish until the crisis created by Iraq in the Gulf. We shall have to wait to see if the parties concerned will have learned how to deal with the problem of rising oil prices as indeed they learned soon after the end of the energy crisis of 1973. In all likelihood the competition for power in the Middle East from the Mediterranean to the Gulf and from the Soviet border to the Indian Ocean, will be more of an economic than strategic-military nature. Even when the Soviet Union eventually becomes a net importer of energy, it is not very likely to try to obtain it by force.

With the Soviet force reductions, there will be fewer forces available for operations outside the borders of the Soviet Union. Even in a catastrophic case of a world war it will not be easy for the Soviet Union (or Russia) to send forces for operations in the Middle Eastern theatre. Nevertheless the area harbours enormous pent-up tension and it is arming with missiles and possible nuclear deployment in the near future. Both the USA and the USSR have some influence to arrest the dangerous tendency to solve problems by force. Some of the regional parties are prepared to seek security in collective agreements, but so far this has been done only within sub-systems in the area and not between systems. Each of these sub-systems used to ally itself with one or other superpower as an insurance. The European model suggests itself as a way out, but it is doubtful whether the regional parties on their own are capable of emulating this model, while it seems certain that neither of the superpowers on its own is capable of reducing the danger of another war in the area within the coming decade.

## South-East Asia and China

It seems that the European powers have found a way of dealing with the ATTU zone while the Asian powers have not found a way of dealing with the Ural to the Pacific Ocean zone (UTTPA). China will probably remain a major concern of Soviet strategists. Since 1959 the number of Soviet divisions on the Chinese border has increased gradually and now reaches over 50. Even though many of these are not of the best quality and are maintained at a low state of readiness, they are backed up by a system of airfields, missile sites and radar installations. The Soviet military deployment (conventional, nuclear and electronic) indicates the degree of Soviet concern and presents a permanent warning to the Chinese.

*Perestroika* has not left the Soviet Far East unaffected. On 3 March, 1990 the Soviet Union and Mongolia agreed that all Soviet forces would be withdrawn from Mongolia in two stages: most combat forces by the end of 1991 and other forces by the end of 1992. Other units in the Soviet Far East will also go along with many military installations, but the Soviet government will no doubt remain cautious about the military balance in the Far East, chiefly because of the preponderance of population on the two sides of the Soviet border but also due to logistical difficulties that will probably bother Soviet strategists well into the 21st century.

However, the Soviet government has made diplomatic attempts to improve its relationship with China. After the agreement signed in Moscow by Li Peng concerning mutual reduction of military forces, the two sides tackled the sensitive problem of the disputed border between the two states. In June 1990 Soviet and Chinese experts met in Beijing to discuss this centuries-old Chinese grievance, and a settlement seems possible. With Soviet forces out of Afghanistan, Vietnamese forces out of Cambodia and an improvement in trade between the two countries, a lowering of tension along the longest border in the world may be expected.

The Malta summit meeting between Bush and Gorbachev was instrumental in bridging some of the difficulties in Soviet-Korean relationships. South Korea, which used to be viewed as a pariah state in Moscow, now enjoys diplomatic relations, a development which has already induced North Korea to improve its relationships with South Korea.

The Soviet Union will no doubt persist in its attempt for an agreement to make the Indian Ocean a nuclear free zone. Costly naval operations consume resources in which the USSR is less and less capable of investing. At the end of 1989 the first of the new Tbilisi Class of aircraft-carriers carried out its initial sea trials, a second has been fitted out and work on a third has just begun. But naval operations in general are on the decline: naval exercises have been shortened, ships spend longer periods in ports, submarine patrols off the UK and western Africa have ceased and patrols in the Indian Ocean have been cut back. There is an urgent need to conclude further agreements that would limit the dangers of war at sea but, if the USSR is accepted as an equal member in the 'European common home', it is not likely that it will enhance dramatically its naval activities in the coming decade. It seems that the Soviet government will make great efforts to sign many diplomatic agreements with countries in South-east Asia in order to reduce tension and precipitate better trade.

Some sensitive problems, such as Soviet-Japanese relations, have not yet been fully addressed. Japan is a model of a new economic superpower. It enjoys an enormous economic capability, a relatively stable political system and spend little on military power. Although it is not a member of any military bloc, it could count on American support in case of emergency. If American naval activities in the Sea of Japan are cut back it is likely that the four Kurile islands, held by the USSR since the end of the Second World War, may lose their operational significance in the eyes of the Soviet military establishment, thus paving the way for a peace treaty between the two countries.

## Conclusion

The strategic agenda for the coming decade is to restructure Soviet security, building on a reduction of forces, both Soviet and non-Soviet. Such a strategy for stability and confidence may be achieved only through collective security by agreement and consent. Soviet policy in Europe, the Middle East and in South-east Asia seems to be directed at just that. Furthermore it seems to aim at achieving such agreements in co-operation with the USA and other forces.

If *perestroika* breaks through the lethargy of the current Soviet economic system while the international climate continues to improve, the USSR (or even Russia) may come closer to developing a better choice of strategies. Economic autarky was long ago thrown overboard. The USSR is in dire need of international goodwill and economic aid. Gorbachev seems temporarily to have traded off his country's reluctance to see Germany as member of NATO in return for German promises of economic aid of gigantic order. If Japan can be induced to help the USSR, or even only the Russian republic, we may see a new alliance — Berlin, Moscow and Tokyo — that may change the face of the world. This prospect must be of concern to many countries because it cuts across several existing programmes, including the European Common Market.

Even if only part of this strategy is implemented the Soviet Union will be, by the end of the coming decade, in a better position to choose between the option of becoming a superpower of the old model, an economic-political and military giant, or the new model, namely enjoying economic prosperity and political stability without a correspondingly huge military expenditure.

## Notes

[1] Sergei A Karaganov, 'The year of Europe: a Soviet view', *Survival*, No. 2, March-April, 1990, p. 122.

[2] *Ogonek*, '*Kakaya armiya nam nuzhna?*', p. 31.

[3] Sergei A Karaganov, 'The year of Europe: a Soviet view', *Survival*, No. 2, March-April, 1990, p. 127.

[4] K I Savinov, *Varshavskii dogovor*, (M. 1986), p. 225.

## References

*SSSR v bor'be za bezopasnost' i sotrudnichestvo v Evrope 1964 – 1987*, Sbornik dokumentov, (M. 1988).

*Zakon soyuza sovetskikh sotsialisticheskikh respublik o gosudarstvennoi granitse SSSR*, (M. 1986).

F I Kozhevnikov (Otvets. redaktor), *Kurs mezhdunarodnogo prava* (M. 1972).

*Vneshnyaya politika sovetskogo soyuza 1985*, Sbornik dokumentov, (M. 1986).

V V Ermoshin, *Problema voinyi i mira*, (M. 1989).

K e Savinov, *Varshavskii dogovor*, (M. 1986).

Mikhail Gorbachev, *Perestroika*.

Sean M Lynn-Jones, Steven E Miller and Stephen Van Evera, (eds), *Soviet Military Policy*, (Princeton University Press, 1989).

George Hudson (ed.), *Soviet National Security Policy under Perestroika*, (Boston, 1989).

Seweryn Bialer, (ed.) *Inside Gorbachev's Russia*, (Westview Press, 1989).

Nicholas N Kittrie and Ivan Volgyes, (Eds.), *The Uncertain Future, Gorbachev's Eastern Bloc*, (Paragon House, 1988).

Henry S Rowen and Charles Wolf, Jr. (Eds.), *The Impoverished Superpower*, (Institute for Contemporary Studies, 1990).

SIPRI Yearbook 1990.

'Armia na poroge reformyi', *Literaturnaya gazeta*, No. 10, 7 March, 1990.

A A Kokoshin, A A Konovalov, V V Larionov, V A Mazing, *Voprosyi obespecheniya pri radikal'nykh sokrashcheniyakh vooruzhennykh sil i obuchnikh vooruzhenii v Evrope*, (M. 1989).

(a) Georgi Arbatov, 'Armiya dlya stranyi ili srana dlya armii?'

(b) 'Kakaya armiya nam nuzhna'.

(c) Marshal Akhromyeev, 'Kakie vooruzhennyi silyi nuzhnyi sovetskomu soyuzu'.

(d) 'Pis'ma marshalu'.

(e) Aleksei Kireev 'Skol'ko tratit' na oboronu'.

*Ogonek*, December 1989 – March 1990.

*Voenno-istoricheskii zhurnal*, No. 2, 1990.

'Armiya druzhbyi i bratsva narodov' *Krasnaya zvezda*, September 22, 1989.

Sergei A Karaganov, 'The year of Europe: a Soviet view', *Survival* No. 2, March/April 1990.

Andrei Kudryavtsev and Romil Shchenin, 'A Common European Home: the Soviet View', *International Relations*, No. 6, November 1989.

*National Security Strategy of the United States*, March 1990.

Neil Malcolm, The 'Common European Home' and Soviet European Policy'; General of the Army Dmitry Yazov, 'Warsaw Treaty Military Doctrine for Defence of Peace and Socialism'.

*International Affairs*, Nos. 4, 1989 and No. 10, 1987.

Wojciech Lamentowicz, 'The Warsaw Pact, An uncertain Alliance', *International Defense Review*, No. 2, 1990.

Mark Kramer, 'Beyond the Brezhnev Doctrine', *International Security*, Vol. 14, No. 3, 1989 – 1990.

CHAPTER 5

# Alternative Politico-Military Futures

JACOB KIPP

THERE IS a certain element of audacity involved in any effort to foresee the future of the Soviet military in a period of such profound and far-reaching internal, domestic and international change. This systemic crisis, which involves the economy, political legitimacy of the existing order, the cohesion of a multi-national empire, and the integration of the state into the international system, is the result of the arrested development which the Stalinist order imposed upon the Soviet Union.[1] The fact that the mature Soviet state was a totalitarian order best adapted for preparing and fighting total war but ill-adapted to fostering economic development, social integration, and technological change calls into question the very military system which it created. Military power advanced at the expense of societal interests. In the end the society could not meet the very needs of military modernisation. The command system created a false image of economic reality which bred a social inertia among the population and promoted faith in bureaucratic solutions, if only 'good' officials might be found. The state appeared to house the worker and feed him, when, in fact, it was the worker who grudgingly served the state.[2]

Given the complexity of the current problems and the intensity of the dislocations, it is quite conceivable that the Soviet experiment of the last seven decades may be coming to an end. However, the end of Soviet history does not mean the end of Russian history. The qualities of the people, the level of their culture and their past achievements make any forecast of an end of their history quite shortsighted. Moreover, this pattern of a state and social order adapted to military requirements but unequal to the demands of political and socio-economic reform and development has a parallel in other periods of Russian history. In each case military reform was part of a much more comprehensive process of social transformation.[3] It shaped, and was shaped by, far-reaching changes in the state and society. For much of Russian history the outcome of such periods of reform has strengthened the

67

power of the central state at the expense of society. The power of the centralised state has been expressed in its arbitrariness and its definition of security as *raison d'état*. The issue now before us is whether the current crisis will be but a continuation of that trend or whether the alternative of a military subordinated to a lawful state and protecting a vital civic society might prevail.

## The Economic Crisis

The future nature of the Soviet military is, then, caught up and will be determined in large measure by the resolution of the multiple crises now confronting Soviet society. Moreover, the resolution of each aspect of this crisis will impinge upon the solution to other aspects of the problem. Of the four systemic problems confronting the Soviet Union, this Chapter will examine three alternatives and relate these solutions in each area to a final end state at an arbitrary future point, 2010. While the range of alternative futures is quite wide, it will focus on three of the more probable outcomes, define each one's salient features and discuss the resulting military order.

In the area of the national economy there are three clear options. The first is a continuation of the current 'muddling through' with a mix of weakened command elements and immature market instruments. The outcome of this would be a continuation of the economic chaos and disorder of the last five years with a sustained decline in gross national product (GNP), a further breakdown in the distribution system, and the likelihood of a serious social-political crisis in the not-too-distant future. Should this mixed system weather such a crisis, it might achieve the levels of slow growth of the East European economies of the 1970s and early 1980s, falling further behind in relative economic development and entering another period of stagnation in the first years of the next century. Foreign investment would be low because of the low rates of growth. Muddling through economically would carry political costs as well, undermining the legitimacy of the new political institutions and reducing incentive for voluntary association among republics and regions. Indeed, it would strengthen those elements who are seeking to make each republic both politically and economically sovereign, which, in turn, would undermine the development of national markets. Given the uneven economic development within the various regions of the USSR, muddling through would have the additional impact of politicising all issues of economic equity. Does Russia bear a fair share of the economic burden and do the central authorities which planned and executed the environmental disasters in Central Asia, bear a responsibility for undoing the ecological damage?

The second economic option is a successful conversion to a full market economy and the transformation of the existing command infrastructure into one adapted to its needs. This task will be formidable, involving wrenching socio-economic adjustments, imposing significant social costs, and demanding a radical change in attitudes to work, unemployment, property and saving. If successful such a market economy would still involve a decline in GNP during the transition period and would bring only slow growth in the subsequent period of adjustment. The closing of many state-subsidised enterprises, appearance of mass unemployment, and massive dislocations in agriculture would impose economic and political costs. The adaptation of the infrastructure of a command economy, with its emphasis upon hierarchic channels of communication and control, to the needs of a market economy would be a severe challenge. It would require a massive expansion of lateral channels of communication and the expansion of feedback mechanisms in all sectors of economic life. However, once the new economy was functioning effectively, the size of the economy, the skills of its labour force, and the availability of a wide range of natural resources would lead to very high rates of economic growth, attracting foreign capital. The successful construction of national markets would act as a powerful engine for political integration and would probably strengthen the power of the central government in its role as protector of commerce among the republics through control of the money supply, banking, and regulation of inter-republic commerce. The political integration of a market-oriented state into the international system would be relatively simple and would provide another source of stability in the international order. Western interest in Soviet integration would go hand-in-hand with Soviet interests.

The political costs of creating a market economy are quite high, and the short-term risks of economic breakdown and collapse, if the existing command infrastructure either sabotages or simply fails to adapt to markets, have to be taken into account. The recent debates over the Shatalin, Ryzhkov and Gorbachev plans for marketisation only underscore the dilemma. The transition to a market economy must be rapid and evident — within something like 500 days — but the risks are high and the results open to question. Soviet economic reformers are well aware that external shocks could prove fatal to the effort. They need look no further than the Polish 'cold turkey' approach under the current Solidarity government, which has run into a deep crisis over escalating oil prices, which could not be foreseen and for which the economy was ill-prepared.

Thus, while marketisation offers the best prospect for the future of the Soviet economy and could serve as a powerful engine of national integration, the Soviet Union may be too sick for the medicine to work. Even supporters of marketisation wonder whether the distortions of six decades of a command economy have not undermined the psychological prerequisites for entrepreneurship. The most glaring example of this problem is to be found in the agricultural sector where collectivisation destroyed a peasantry with organic ties to the land and replaced it with rural proletarians, who not only lack the skills and initiative to be independent farmers but who also are hostile towards any fellow workers ambitious enough to accept the risks. The whisper of *kulak*, with all that this implies in rural Russia, can again be heard. In the cities the same sounds can be heard about the 'co-operatives' and their 'speculation'. Without the rapid development of markets, there is a real danger of the collapse of the old command system in agriculture. In that case the *kolkhozy* and *sovkhozy* will cease to function because they are so dependent on the command system's ability to engage in extra-economic mobilisation, i.e. the deployment of 'voluntary' labour and material from the urban economy and the employment of military personnel and equipment to bring in the harvest. The crisis of late 1990, when an abundant harvest rotted in the fields because the command system would not or could not bring these extra-economic forces into play in a timely fashion, makes it quite clear that the Stalinist linkages between town and country are breaking down at a time when market mechanisms and infrastructure are not yet in place. The sight of military helicopters being used to bring in sugar beets demonstrates just how desperate the situation has become.[4]

Unsuccessful marketisation could set off further political disintegration and might put into motion forces seeking to re-establish a command system under the guise of a bureaucratic-technocratic rationality. A model for this third option was that adopted by General Jaruzelski in Poland following the imposition of martial law in 1981, when the military replaced the PZPR as the co-ordinating institution for the polity and economy.

This third course of restoring 'order' and reverting to a command economy promises to arrest the decline in GNP but at best offers prospects for very slow, long-term economic growth. The USSR would fall further and further behind in the transition to an information society, because the reimposition of totalitarian controls would undercut the free flow of information. A repeat of the Stalinist 'revolution from above' does not seem to be in the cards. The Party-state élite and the ideology simply have no credibility. Even the military-industrial complex, which was touted early in *perestroika* as an island of efficiency in a sea of sloth, has been shown to lack the skills to manage conversion to the production of civilian goods. Moreover, it is inconceivable that the retreat to a central, command economy could be carried out without the use of force to silence opposition and to retain the unity of the union. Repression would undercut the climate for Western investment, heighten tensions on the international scene, and set in motion yet another round of civil war. This reactionary order would in all probability retrench its international position still further, in order to concentrate on internal cohesion and order. It would, however, be heavily engaged in policing its own borderlands, and this could bring about its own share of confrontations, especially in Eastern Europe, the Caucasus and Central Asia.

## The Crisis of Soviet Federalism

The second crisis affecting the Soviet polity concerns its federal nature. Four conceivable variants need to be addressed. The first is maintenance of the current Union system. Political pressures among the republics, ethnic groups, and regions call this outcome into question. Moreover, the Leninist concept of federalism — national in form but socialist in content — has been so betrayed by seven decades of Moscow's hegemony that it has no ideological appeal or credit. One result of the 28th Party Congress was to reassert the Party's role as an agent of multinational integration through the appointment of the leaders of the republican parties to the Presidium. But this comes at a time when the Party has abandoned its constitutionally-stipulated 'leading role' in Soviet society. Without the cement of Party-enforced centralism, the concept of Union has lost its legitimacy and appeal. Many of the institutions of all-Union control are seen as agencies of oppression, including *Gosplan* [State Planning Agency], *Gossnab* [State Supply Agency], the central ministries, the KGB, and the armed forces. Such an order might be reimposed but only by the overt use of force and would have to involve the overt or covert co-operation of the *nomenklatura* in protecting their positions. Stripped of even the fig-leaf of 'internationalism' and 'fraternal relations among peoples', the local careerists serving Moscow's interests would simply be the agents of a russified and russifying centralism. As the experience of the Brezhnev period makes clear, such careerists, if they are granted enough privileges and allowed enough opportunity for graft and corruption, can be recruited. Their following, however, is confined to their clients, and their authority and power can be sustained only by Moscow's control of the instruments of intimidation and violence.

A much-debated alternative is the creation of a new federal system based upon the sovereignty of the republics. In some cases initial declarations of sovereignty were, in fact, only convenient half-way points on the preferred road to complete independence. This certainly was the case with the three Baltic Republics, Estonia, Latvia and Lithuania. The case in other areas is more problematic. In the Caucasus, Armenia, Georgia and Azerbaijan seem to be moving towards independence but are constrained by their own internal and external conflicts. Moldavia has moved towards embracing its Romanian ties, but not without internal disputes and inter-ethnic conflict. Central Asia, in the face of all the talk about a Pan-Muslim revival, has seen ethnic politics take on primary importance and feed communal violence. The Slavic core of Russia, the Ukraine and Belorussia, have also proclaimed their sovereignty but have yet to redefine their relationships with the central authorities, among themselves, or with the other republics. The conspicuous claims of President Boris Yeltsin in defence of the sovereign rights of the RSFSR have been challenged not only by Gorbachev and the all-Union institutions, but also by ethnic communities within the RSFSR who see no more claim to legitimacy in the RSFSR's institutions than those of the Union.

The path to a new federalism will not be easy. At the very least, this process will require granting independence to the Baltic Republics; at the most it could also involve the Caucasus, Moldavia, and Central Asia. It might even call into question the unity of the two largest Slavic republics, the Ukraine and RSFSR, where regionalism, cultural-religious differences and ethnic conflicts are potentially explosive. The new federalism, thus, may, if successful, lead to a very different political landscape from the existing 15 republics with their current boundaries. The chances for the success of a new federal system are highest if the process of marketisation succeeds. In that case the centripetal forces of national markets and economic integration would serve to counter the centrifugal forces of nationalism and the antagonisms created by 70 years of Soviet centralism, disguised in the slogans of federalism. The great economic dilemma confronting any new federal experiment at present is the fact that the old command economy, which consciously fostered a dependence of the new periphery upon the centre, did so by means of strengthening vertical channels of communication at the expense of horizontal channels, those most needed for the creation of an effective and vital national market.

This situation puts into sharp relief a third option for the resolution of the present crisis of federalism: the disintegration of the Union as a polity and economy. Such a disintegration, a remote prospect only a few years ago, now looms as a real possibility. Indeed, the discussions of such an outcome have focused upon two alternatives. One is a gradual collapse of the centre in the process of economic and political muddling through in which Moscow becomes increasingly irrelevant. In this case the command economy would keep issuing orders but they would not be obeyed; instead, the republican and local governments would embark upon their own reform programme, meeting local needs and making their own deals with other governments. In such a gradual process there is at least the hope that local and regional markets over time might fuse into a single market.

The other alternative, which seems more remote but cannot be excluded in the event of political crisis and civil war, would be the catastrophic collapse of all economic activities, a curtailment of deliveries between town and country and the reduction of the national economy to a combination of barter and forced expropriation. While this case is extreme, it does have a historic parallel with the situation under War Communism. In the more gradual case of collapse, some regions, notably the Baltic Republics with their high level of economic and social development and their ties to Western market economies, seem well adapted to such a process.

In the Caucasus, both Georgia and Armenia have a tradition of economic autonomy and cultural-political identity which would make such a course appealing. However, inter-ethnic tensions and the possibility of external intervention by hostile foreign states — both republics have Moslem minorities and Armenian hopes of reviving claims to a Greater Armenia would bring about increased tensions with both Turkey and Iran — make such a course of action problematic. In Central Asia economic backwardness, ecological disaster, and inter-ethnic tensions undercut regional co-operation and foster grudging ties with Moscow. At least some of the reformers in Moscow see Central Asia as so serious a social, national, economic and ecological disaster that they may be willing to consign those parts of the region without large ethnic Russian minorities to a benign neglect, granting considerable political autonomy and even independence to free themselves of the considerable costs associated with rehabilitating the region, bringing about economic development and fostering socio-political integration. Even in the case of a successful marketisation of the Soviet economy, much of this region would still be a poor step-child, left with an economy based on a cotton mono-culture and facing the ecological disaster of 60 years of exploitation of a colonial region to fulfil the needs of the metropolis.

Even within the so-called Slavic core, the possibility of collapse cannot be ignored. The RSFSR, with its vast territories, population, and resources, seems the one political unit which might profit from such a collapse. Indeed, some Russian nationalists, who see the Soviet period as a disaster for the Russian nation, during which it lost its national identity and institutions and saw its wealth used to maintain a foreign empire, seem to find solace in such an outcome, a 'Russia for the Russians'. However, the RSFSR is itself a multinational state and will have to find a means of dealing with the minorities within its own borders. Moreover, there are the 25 million Russians who do not live within the RSFSR and whose fate must concern any Russian national government. It is one thing to proclaim a regime of national self-absorption and another to abandon fellow nationals to their fate on the periphery.

Furthermore, there is a serious element of regional conflict in the RSFSR. The western part, with its huge cities, ageing industrial plant, and massive, resource-consuming, command apparatus, needs the support of its two regional partners, Siberia and the Far East, but will have to negotiate new political and economic terms for their integration. Siberians of whatever nationality see themselves as victims of Moscow's centralism and they are not likely to be any more sympathetic to Russian centralism than they were to Soviet centralism. Lake Baikal, 'the Pearl of Siberia', as the author Valentin Rasputin called it, has become a symbol of the old and new rejected relationship, of the abuse of nature and of custom, which makes up the indictment of the old centralism.[5] The maritime region with its potential ties to the Far East and its vast resource base, likewise, has a distinct orientation, drawing it towards Asia and the Pacific, even as it remains dependent on centre for capital and to finance its development and food to feed its population. But its resources make it an attractive field for market-directed investment by the new economic giants in the region, and there is a logic to a division of labour among the Soviet Far East, Japan and Korea, and Manchuria, if regional peace and stability will let market forces develop.

In the case of the Ukraine and Belorussia, cultural, economic and political tensions pull towards the centre and away at the same time. The Ukraine remains three historic regions. The east is tied economically and ethnically to Russia, the centre, with a unique cultural and historical identity and significant agricultural wealth, has its own self-identity and roots in a Ukrainian nation with an unrealised claim to the status of a nation-state and full partnership in any new political order. Galicia in the west, with its Uniate church and ties to a Habsburgian Central Europe, must face the problem of turning east to Kiev without being drawn into the legacy of border changes and ethnic minorities, which have been such fertile ground for conflict in the region since the First World War. The collapse of a Stalinist Union offers both prospects for co-operation and sources of conflict, especially between Poles and Ruthenians in Galicia. This split makes the situation in the Ukraine particularly volatile and has recently placed pressure on the Ukrainian nationalist movement *Rukh* to be more confrontational in its dealings with the central government in Moscow. For Belorussia the last few years have sharpened the issue of national identity.

The likely independence of Lithuania, and the emergence of a national Poland has raised the question of the fate of the Republic and the Belorussian minorities outside its borders. Chernobyl and the associated widespread radioactive contamination has made ecological issues a vital concern. Both the Ukraine and Belorussia would best be served by a new definition of federalism, which granted them sovereign powers as members of a confederation. However, a legacy of national oppression and the discovery of more and more mass graves to remind each nation of its losses at the hands of Soviet power makes such compromise more and more politically difficult to achieve. Confrontation seems to be replacing dialogue. It remains to be seen whether Yeltsin's government in the RSFSR can sustain the confidence to erect and maintain even republic-to-republic ties and contacts.

The recent publication of Alexander Solzhenitsyn's programme to reconstitute Russia, *Kak nam obustroit' Rossiyu*, posed the dilemma of state-building within the Slavic core most pointedly. The author's conservative nationalist message acknowledged the sin of 'the great power approach, of the imperialist narcotic' in poisoning past relations among Russians, Belorussians, and Ukrainians and speaks of a series of regional *oblast'* plebiscites to define new relations with a unitary Russian *Rossiiskoye* state.[6] While his views echo those of the late Russian Slavophiles of the 19th century, who sought first a moral regeneration of the nation in the name of a conservative utopia, the practical politics of such plebiscites would be votes for or against partition with all the prospects for communal violence and pogroms.

## The Political Crisis

In the final analysis the successful or unsuccessful resolution of the two crises mentioned above depends upon the outcome of the political crisis. If the command economy was the heart of Soviet totalitarianism and its bastard federalism the skeleton, the single-party, monocratic order provided its brain. Since Lenin, the Party had been the guiding and directing entity of the polity. As a vanguard party representing the interests of the working class, it claimed for itself the right to direct society along the path to Communism under 'mature socialism' it had become an aggregator of the interests of the privileged layers of Soviet society, who formed the *nomenklatura* and ran the nation. In the years of stagnation and decay its leadership, long used to deceiving the outside world and its own citizens about the real situation in the USSR, began even to deceive itself. It was this process of self-deception which made *glasnost'* necessary — and such a sharp break with the past. Gorbachev's initial efforts to revive the Party, restore discipline, and speed up production failed because no acceleration *uskoreniye* was possible. Confronted by this reality, Gorbachev set out on a pragmatic set of reforms to seek new levers to move society. *Perestroika* was an admission of past failure and a desperate attempt to deal with an unravelling order. In the end it came to mean a more open society, based upon representative institutions, and the rule of law. Yet, the success of this political experiment was in the hands of those very elements of the old élite who had the most to lose from such reform. The Party-state regime still controlled the instruments of violence, the KGB, the internal troops and the armed forces, and could use them in Tbilisi and Baku to repress nationalist challenges. But with each passing day the Party's claim to a monopoly of power declined.

Within the Party, factionalism, which had been outlawed since the 10th Party Congress, has reappeared. Party membership declined by more than 2.3 million in 1990.[7] At the plenum in February 1990 the Central Committee renounced its vanguard role. In the local elections which followed, non-Party candidates scored key successes. New parties covering the entire political spectrum not only made their appearance but emerged as powerful alternatives to the Communist Party. This was especially the case where national fronts became the spokesman for republican sovereignty and independence, as in the Baltic Republics, in the Caucasus, and in the Ukraine.

In the spring of 1990 Gorbachev faced and survived a revolt of Russian Communists, leading to the founding of a Russian Communist Party and its first Congress in June. At its 28th All-Union Congress in July the CPSU managed to avoid an open split into separate organisations and began the task of adapting its institutions to the new role of 'generator of ideas' as opposed to ruling party. There were sweeping changes of leadership in the Politburo and Central Committee as Gorbachev tried to adapt the Party to the task of maintaining the Union. But the most conspicuous event of the Congress was Boris Yeltsin's political instincts, which had repeatedly shown him adept at reading new trends, had a solid basis in Party demographics. More and more members were leaving the Party — over 1.2 million in the first 10 months of the year.

For the last three years Gorbachev has been guiding political *perestroika* towards a new system, in which political legitimacy would be in all-Union state institutions, based upon limited popular representation as embodied in the Supreme Soviet and the Congress of People's Deputies. From those institutions he has sought to create a new and powerful executive authority, the Presidency, to guide and direct the process of reform. In this fashion he has kept nominal control of the state's instruments of violence and control, i.e. the KGB, the internal troops, and the armed forces. However, the very processes of reform, *glasnost'* and pluralism, which were set in motion by this process, have fostered the development of alternative political centres of power in the republics, which, freed of Party discipline and control, have sought their own definitions of reform and proclaimed their own basis of legitimacy. The clashes over sovereignty between the central and republican institutions have taken on the character of a power struggle, complete with periodic crises, confrontations, and rumours of armed intervention in the form of a coup or counter-coup.

These waves of rumours began in February 1990 in association with the appearance of the first mass demonstration by democratic forces and were a feature of the repeated politico-economic crises throughout the year. In September, when the Congress of People's Deputies was considering alternative plans for the marketisation of the economy, a new wave of rumours about military manoeuvres around Moscow in conjunction with a coup attempt by the military leadership were met by counter-rumours of plans, the so-called 'Programme 90' of an unknown 'Russian Democratic Front', to seize power. Another wave of rumour about coups and counter-coups appeared in October in conjunction with the 73rd anniversary of the Bolshevik Revolution and the military parades which traditionally celebrate the event. While no political party or group has openly proclaimed a willingness to use violence to seize state power in the manner of the Bolsheviks in 1917, the rumours and counter-rumours reflect the growing anxiety and distrust within the polity and a perception that, unless the decline into anarchy is arrested, such a forceful transfer of power may gain in appeal as the only viable way to restore 'order'.

On 13 November, 1990, President Gorbachev met over 1,000 military personnel serving as people's deputies in various Soviets. In a stormy session, he again stated that military reform was necessary to meet the requirements of the new international environment. But he also heard from the assembled officers about their grave concerns for the fate of the military and the deepening crisis within the country. On 14 November, *TASS* reported that Gorbachev had sided with the 'party of order' and was prepared to act against recalcitrant republican governments seeking independence.[8] In a matter of days the government's shift towards a much harder line against domestic opponents was evident. In January 1991 it authorised a crackdown against the democratically-elected governments of the Lithuanian and Latvian Republics.

Three possible outcomes of this political crisis can be foreseen. One is the triumph of a pluralist, multi-party system with competing, but integrated, centres of power. This would mean the end of the Leninist Party and the triumph of an open polity. The relative success of such an experiment at the all-Union level depends in good measure upon the maturity of the civic societies which make up the USSR. Given the fact that the most mature polities (those in the Baltic Republics) are bent upon independence and the less mature polities (those of Central Asia) are dominated by a tribal protectionism, a single, successful resolution along these lines seems difficult to imagine. The core issue will be the attitude of the Russian population which composes about half of the population of the USSR towards such a civic culture. However, over the last year pluralism as 'multiple-power' and anarchy has discredited itself and made the case for a restitution of 'order' stronger, especially within the military. Commenting on the future of military reform before the 4th Session of the Congress of People's Deputies, Colonel V. N. Ochirov, Deputy Chairman of the USSR Supreme Soviet's Committee on Defence and State Security, summed up the situation in this manner.

> The aims of the reforms here are splendid. But now we are coming up against a situation where they could be destroyed. Instead of reforms, it is possible that we — or more likely, someone else — will have to gather stones together and rebuild the edifice from scratch. Therefore the tasks of preserving the armed forces and state security organs come first, and the tasks of reforming them come second. These tasks must be tackled simultaneously, but the former takes priority.[9]

Colonel Ochirov, a Kalmyk by birth, commander of a helicopter squadron in Afghanistan, Hero of the Soviet Union and one of those officers elected to the Supreme Soviet in spite of the existing military-political order, played a leading role in drafting and editing recent proposals for military reform. His assessment of the current crisis, especially concerning the fate of the armed forces, sheds light on the perceived depth of the crisis and the appeal of violent means to end an intolerable situation.

An alternative scenario is the reimposition of authoritarian controls in the name of such 'order'. While it is difficult to imagine a bankrupt CPSU playing such a role, it is possible to imagine a 'national bolshevik' alternative, based upon a militarised 'order' and supported by the military as the only alternative to chaos and disintegration. Such an order would be Russian in form and authoritarian in content. It would strive to maintain the empire even as it undermined any basis of long-range co-operation by attacking political pluralism, ethnic tolerance, and economic decentralisation. At best it would offer a return to tech-nocratic control and bureaucratic rationality. This would be a short-term solution without long-term prospects.

There is at present some debate among those in favour of using force to restore order regarding means and ends. The more moderate position, taken by people like Marshal Sergei Akhromeyev, Gorbachev's National Security Adviser, is that force should be used to maintain constitutional order. This implies limitations on both means and ends and an unwillingness to return to pure arbitrary exercise of power.[10]

The more extreme position, taken by members of *Soyuz* and the pro-moters of an All-Union Committee of National Salvation, involves the suspension of all elected institutions and the subordination of all civic institutions to that committee. This invitation to government by decree for the duration of the crisis places the military under no effective legal checks in the use of violence.[11] The real danger is that once the Soviet state has embarked upon this course the momentum towards dictatorship may prove impossible to stop. This certainly was a part of Foreign Minister Shevardnadze's warning when he resigned from the govern-ment in December 1990. While it is clear that liberals abhorred the recent bloodshed in Vilnius and reactionaries applauded it, the support of conservatives for such an arbitrary course of action is less clear.

The third proposition would involve the triumph of pluralism in a decentralised polity and a gradual process of political adjustment within the individual republics and between them. This pattern seems to be what is offered by Yeltsin's proposal for bilateral negotiations among the republics and a very loose, confederative order of limited co-operation. It would take time to mature, would be based on regional patterns of co-operation, and would require decades to bring about the political, economic, and social reintegration of the polity. It would mean legitimising 'multiple-power' among the republics at the expense of all-Union institutions. It would leave a host of security issues un-resolved and would subsume a long-term benign international environ-ment. Indeed, because a political disintegration would be associated with a protracted economic crisis, it is to be expected that major parts of the western borderlands would drift off into other politico-economic spheres. Regarding military power, in the face of the current crack-down, such a course is only viable if violence can be avoided. This, however, is becoming increasingly difficult. Yeltsin's proposal to create a Russian army to protect democratic institutions in the RSFSR has met with sharp protests from within the armed forces. His support for the Baltic Republics has been met with the counter-charge that he has abandoned his fellow nationals into the hands of revengeful separatists. 'Russia always had and has one great right and obligation — to defend its co-nationals and blood brothers anywhere that they might live.'[12]

Which of these various political features triumphs in the end will depend in good measure upon internal Soviet developments relating to the other two crises and to the nature of the external environment. It is a certainty that the chances for a pluralist, democratic outcome, whether based upon a new federalism or disintegration, will depend upon the sense of external threat confronting the Soviet Union. One of the conspicuous lessons of the Stalin era is that the perception of encirclement by hostile powers eager to unleash a 'counter-revolution' and the definition of whole social groups and ethnic communities as the sources of an 'internal counter-revolution' provided the rationale for the authoritarian-bureaucratic revolution from above that created the modern Soviet system. Like Tzarist Russia during its break with serfdom, Soviet Russia needs peace defined as the absence of an external meta-threat. As in the 1920s, however, there are important groups within the polity who have a conspicuous interest in promoting such a vision of threat as a justification for current privilege and as a rationale for restoring internal order. This question of threat perception, thus, stands at the very heart of the various military systems which might emerge over the next two decades.

## Alternative Military Futures

To understand the alternative futures before the Soviet military it is necessary to begin with the long-existing military order, its place in Soviet society, and its role in the international system. It is the collapse of that military order which has set the stage for the wide range of alternative futures before us.

The internal features of the Soviet military were defined by the geo-strategic context of the state, the national-demographic realities of Soviet society, the Party-state system of rule, and the ideological premises and assumptions of Marxism – Leninism. To some extent the mature Soviet military institution built upon legacies of the old imperial Russian Army, especially its system of universal conscription, its military districts for peacetime administration and wartime mobilisation, and its General Staff to serve as the 'brain of the armed forces'. Geostrategic realities were reflected in both the emphasis upon mobilisation capability and the concern for a military 'buffer' along the Soviet Union's western border. Like Tzarist Russia, the Soviet Union had to adapt a military system to fit its trans-continental extent and multiple-theatre warfare in Eurasia.

Although nominally a federal system of government, the Soviet Union's military system under Stalin became and remained russified. It was based upon the hegemony of the Russian/Slavic core populations and sought to russify non-Slavic conscripts and use the armed forces as a school-room of Soviet patriotism.

The Soviet military, arising out of the traditions of the Red Army and other revolutionary armies, was politicised early in its existence and remains so. In many ways it was much closer to Cromwell's New Model Army, than to the armies of the French Republic, from which it borrowed the institution of the commissar. This was a politicised army, armed with a militant ideology, and guided by vanguard party. The Party, through its military policy, not only set the political side of military doctrine but also penetrated the military through its nearly universal recruitment of members for the Party and Komsomol organisations within the officer corps and the existence of the Main Political Administration to direct the activities of political officers in the process of educating, propagandising, and agitating among military personnel. Senior officers frequently held leading posts in the Party's Politburo and Central Committee, served in the nominal representative institutions at the All-Union and republic levels of government, and even held the post of Minister of Defence. These relations made for a highly politicised military, operating under the guidance and direction of the Party, not only socialising the military leadership to the Party but also building ties between Party and state officials and the military.

Since the Party was the 'vanguard of the working class' in a state which was supposed to serve the interests of workers and peasants, the Party's leading role in military affairs complemented its leading role in every other area of national life. In this regard the Party tied the military into the centrally-planned economy and saw to it that it was organised so as to enhance a socialist war economy (*voyennaia ekonomika*). Through Marxist-Leninist ideology the Party-state élite provided a context and explanation for Soviet military power, stressing the elements of class struggle, the threat of war from capitalism and imperialism, and providing a theory upon which to base a concept of just war in defence of socialism. In a backward society, under extreme pressure to modernise in a surrounding world viewed as implicitly hostile and implacable, the ideology carried with it the necessity for militarisation (*voyennizatsiva*) as a means of survival. For those generations which lived through the Great Patriotic War, the terrible costs of that war and the final victory served to legitimise not only the military system but the entire Stalinist state edifice with its totalitarian controls. This system, which offered security and order at the expense of innovation, survived for five decades. As one senior Soviet scientist pointed out, it was well adapted to the requirements of winning a total war, but had become a brake on social development and a source of stagnation by its last decades. Its continued existence threatened the Soviet Union with a condition of perpetual and increasing backwardness as a dynamic capitalist world moved rapidly from an industrial order to an information society.[13] While the critics of the Soviet system often found themes very similar to those found in Paul Kennedy's recent work on the rise and decline of the great powers, their emphasis is more upon the social costs of political stability bought at the price of stagnation in scientific and technical innovation than the explicit costs of the military burden. They have defined the chief threat to the USSR in economic, not military, terms. Economic reform and marketisation or a declining GNP, increasing technological backwardness, and a failure to make the leap to an information society are the stark alternatives presented by reformers.[14]

At the present time one can foresee a set of distinct military futures based upon the resolutions of the three, above-mentioned crises. If one assumes the victory of a market system, federalism, and political democracy — clearly the most promising but also the most remote outcome of the current crisis — then one can envision a very different threat environment. Market relations will lead to great economic integration and interdependence. A new federal order, based upon voluntary union and broad autonomy for the constituent republics, will provide much more internal stability. Combined with a democratic polity rooted in the consent of the governed, such a system would have a radically reduced need for the internal function of the military. This system is not only the most optimistic; it also requires the greatest degree of social peace and harmony for its realisation. Both commodities are very scarce.

Such a system would require both the de-politisation and de-partyisation of the Soviet armed forces. It would require not only the abolition or transformation of the Main Political Administration into a Morale and Education Directorate, as has happened in Eastern Europe, but also that the officer corps accept an apolitical role as guardians of a constitutional order based upon popular sovereignty. One sure sign of the development of such a system would be the appointment of a civilian Minister of Defence, the subordination of the General Staff to his control, and the expansion of the powers of the Supreme Soviet and its Committees in dealing with defence issues, including budget process, the promotion of senior officers, and the power to subpoena and take testimony under oath. Serving officers on active duty would have to be precluded from standing for election. The armed forces would abandon their internal security role and would be replaced by professional Internal Troops, especially trained to deal with crowd control and terrorism. If the economic reforms were successful the internal function of even these troops would decline as sources of social and ethnic tensions were reduced and as the need to mobilise soldiers each year to bring in the harvest became irrelevant.[15]

The new state would have radically less need for standing military power, could well reform the system of mass mobilisation, based on universal conscription, and shift to a professional force in the more technical arms and services, backed up by territorial units serving in their own home regions. General-Major V. Ivanov of the Academy of the General Staff has proposed such a shift to a three-part force structure, which would include the Strategic Forces Command, the General Purpose Forces, and the Forces Undergoing Training and Alternative Service. The total force would number about 2.3 – 2.4

million men, with the centre of gravity of the standing force concentrated in the Strategic Forces Command, which would include the existing Strategic Rocket Forces, plus air force and naval units capable of engaging in nuclear strikes. Air Defence, ABM defence, and anti-space defence forces would also be part of this command as would 'Space Troops' which would be armed with weapons systems capable of destroying enemy installations from space.[16] These forces collectively would form the 'nuclear and space' component of the Strategic Forces Command. Finally, this command would also include some portion of the navy and highly-mobile ground forces. The General Purpose Forces would be the 'most massive' portion of the force and would include the men, equipment and weapons composing the Soviet strategic reserve. The third part of 'training and alternative service' would be to provide the instrument for 'conducting rapid military service for all the country's citizens on the basis of Law on Universal Military Service'.[17] The mobilisation base of this force would be relatively slow and require a protracted period of post mobilisation training prior to introduction into combat. The fundamental nature of these reforms and the time required for their execution imply an explicit acceptance of an international security environment in which a general war is not imminent.

The force posture could shift away from a large conventional force and emphasise the high-tech means which would complement the modernisation of the Soviet economy. The Soviet war economy of the Stalinist model would give way to a Western-style military-industrial complex. A state-industrial alliance in areas of high technology would go hand-in-hand with economic needs and new threat requirements. The Soviet Union would substitute a military potential in being, that is its standing forces and scientific-technical potential backed by a solid national economy for conversion to military needs, providing the basis for force expansion in case the threat of war became more imminent, for its existing mass forces and war economy.

These forces would focus on the threat along the southern periphery, especially the expansion of the number of states which are likely to possess effective delivery systems and weapons of mass destruction in the next two decades. This would put a high premium on $C^3I$ assets with real-time capabilities and ballistic-missile defence systems to deal with low-end threats. Space-based $C^3I$ systems and their modernisation would be a high priority to deal with 'nuclear jumpers', as one Soviet author described this problem.[18] This would include meeting any danger posed by US strategic modernisation and reconstituting the force to deal with a wider range of threats from other powers. The current Soviet policy in the Gulf War would in this case be a harbinger of a very different role in the Third World and would reflect a very different evaluation of the threat posed by aggressive, militarised regimes along the USSR's southern border which have developed or are developing weapons of mass destruction.[19]

A second alternative military future would come into view if the process of disintegration continued unchecked and degenerated into civil war with the army emerging as the key defender of 'order'. Until late Autumn 1990 no group or faction had proclaimed this outcome as a desired end-state. However, the growing crisis over sovereignty and the rising tide of bitterness and frustration are the breeding ground for such a 'time of troubles' *smutnoye vremya*. Now the unthinkable has become the topic of conversation and analysis. Colonel Viktor Alksnis, one of the most vocal leaders of *Soyuz*, declared in November 1990 that civil war had already begun and that only the armed forces could prevent a slide into chaos and anarchy.[20] Under such conditions the first priority of the Soviet military establishment would be to retain control of all nuclear and strategic assets, to bring back Soviet forces abroad with a minimal amount of chaos and conflict, to focus on the internal function of maintaining order in those portions of the country which remained under Moscow's control and to engage in a struggle for the periphery, which would encompass both the internal and external functions of the armed forces. The loyalty of the officer corps would be divided, and much would depend on the ability of various groups and movements to forge ties with the General Staff as the brain of the armed forces and the key institutional repository of military profes- sionalism. The most likely ideological foundation would be some form of 'national bolshevism' which would seek to protect the unity of the state and its claim to great power status, and accept the armed forces as the embodiment of the forces of national salvation. The international environment would be assumed to be hostile, the force posture would have to be constituted in such a fashion as to sustain a civil war and deter foreign intervention. The force itself would be subject to division into hostile forces, loyal to competing power centres. The economic disorder and general destruction would disrupt the economy and undermine the scientific-technical base for the modernisation of the force. The Soviet military would be self-absorbed, but the threat environment would be quite volatile and would probably lead to confrontations with bordering states which have claims to irredentas against the USSR or its successor states, or which would seek to provide protection for co-nationals now living within the territories of the USSR. Such a collapse of a superpower would be a new and very destabilising factor in an already unstable, multi-polar system.

A third alternative future would be one of a successful use of force to reassert order to prevent just such a decline into chaos and civil war. In this case the military would be the instrument for restoring order and maintaining the existing system. The Party lacks the strength and unity to provide effective leadership. For all effective purposes the long-established relationship of Party and army as subject and object, controller and controllee, has given way to a politicised army in which the control of the organs of politicisation are in the hands of the Minister of Defence himself. The Main Political Administration and its subordinate organs, which long functioned as a department of the CPSU Central Committee, have been directly subordinated to the Minister of Defence.[21]

National bolsheviks like Nina Andreyevna who see the Party as a corrupted force since Khrushchev's efforts at de-Stalinisation, have put their faith in the army as the force in which they have placed their trust. This military alternative would be marked by self-absorption as well. But the focus would be upon the military's role as a force for maintaining enforced order, while the bureaucracy tried to rejuvenate the economy by technocratic means. The armed forces would remain large and conscript. Specialised units for internal control and counter-terrorist operations would be further expanded in the armed forces, KGB, and the internal Troops of the Ministry of Internal Affairs. The politicisation of the armed forces would be complete; they would cease to be under either party or state guidance as the military assumed the function of guiding society itself.

The armed forces might provide order but only on the basis of the threat of force. This might suppress the disintegration of the Soviet Union but it could not solve those basic problems exposed by *perestroika*. A military regime following such a restoration of order would be in a double bind. On the one hand, the use of force would alienate Western opinion and bring about the renewed isolation of the state; on the other hand to justify the internal crack-down the regime would be tempted to fall back upon the Stalinist device of linking the internal and external threats to order. This would increase tension in the international system and could stimulate a real external threat. Whether such a regime could practise totalitarian controls or would be satisfied with a Brezhnevesque authoritarianism is unclear. Neither approach would deal with the key problem of overcoming the Soviet Union's economic backwardness. Thus, while the armed forces might remain quite large and even retain their current nuclear capabilities, the forces themselves would decline as the military leadership found itself drawn into administering the nation, rather than preparing to defend it. The military would find itself drawn increasingly into those 'other duties' which make the Soviet system work. Digging potatoes would go hand-in-hand with running the nation, and that degrading and depressing function for combat troops would grow.

Finally, in this alternative, the military would have to try to replace a law-based civic society with one founded upon military discipline. As the poet Zhukovsky pointed out 150 years ago, such a confusion of discipline with the role of law is dangerous to the very state itself. What is lost is the rule of law. After seven decades in which Soviet power used arbitrary power ruthlessly in the name of building socialism and Communism, it would be a great national tragedy to again sink back into the mentality of 'civil war' and a barrack order. The long-term prospects for such a militarised order are fortunately not bright. But under the influence of a steady drift to anarchy and chaos it may appear to be the lesser evil.

There are, of course, a wide range of alternative outcomes for the three basic crises and the resulting military futures. However, an assessment of the inter-relationship of those crises and their probable impact on the military's role in Soviet Union seems the best point of departure for further analysis. There can be no question that the West is best served by an outcome which will strengthen democratic institutions, market relations, and a federal system upon the consent of the constituent parts of the Union. In the final analysis, however, the peoples of the Soviet Union, especially the Russians, who have endured so much tragedy from the totalitarian excesses of this century, should decide the outcome of these crises and the role of their polity in the international system.

## Notes

1. These issues were at the very centre of the dilemmas of modernisation confronting the Russian autocracy during its last century of existence. For a brief discussion of the reform process, its legacy, and the significance of the Stalinist solution see: W. Bruce Lincoln and Jacob W. Kipp, 'Autocracy and Reform: Bureaucratic Absolutism and Political Modernisation in Nineteenth-Century Russia', *Russian History*, VI, P. 1, (1979), 1 – 21.

2. Vasilii Selyunin, 'Istoki', *Novyy Mir*, No. 5 (May 1988), P. 189.

3. This point was explicitly acknowledged by the editors of *Voyennaya mysl'* when they offered a short historical guide to periods of military reform in Russia in which they identified five periods: the reforms of Ivan Groznyi, the reforms of Peter the Great, the reforms of the 1860s and 1870s, the reforms of 1905 – 1912, and the reforms of 1924 – 1925. See: *Voyennaya mysl' Special'nyy vypusk* [December 1990], pp. 3 – 4.

4. *Vremya* [television news report] (21 October, 1990).

5. Valentin Rasputin, 'Baikal', in: Valentin Rasputin, *Siberia on Fire*, Translated by Gerald Mikkelson and Margaret Winchell, (DeKalb: Northern Illinois University Press, 1989), pp. 186 – 193.

6. Alexander Solzhenitsyn, 'Kak nam obustroit' Rossiyu', *Komsomolskaya Pravda*, (8 September, 1990).

7. SOVSET RFE/RL No. 23 (1 February, 1991).

8. *TASS*, (14 November, 1990).

9. *Fourth Congress of USSR People's Deputies* [FBIS-SOV-91-005-S, 8 January, 1991], p. 26.

10. *Sovetskaya Rossiya*, (24 November, 1990).

11. *Sovetskaya Rossiya*, (30 January, 1990).

87

12 *Krasnaya Zvezda*, (19 January, 1991), p. 1.

13 N. N. Moiseyev, *Sotsializm i informatika* (Moscow: Izdatel'stvo politicheskoy literatury, 1988), p. 136.

14 V. Rubanov, 'Oboronyy dostatok i ekonomicheskiy ostatok', *Mezhdunarodnaya zhizn*, No. 12 (December 1990), pp. 5 – 17.

15 V. Lopatin, 'O podgotovke i provedenii voyennoy reformy', *pravitel'stvennyy vestnik, Dos'be*, No. 48 (November 1990), p. 5. See also: G. Sturua, 'Perepetii voyennoy reformy', No. 7 (July 1990), pp. 87 – 92.

16 V. Ivanov, 'Korennoye obnovleniye a ne 'kosmeticheskiy remont', *kommunist vooruzhennykh Sil* No. 15 (August 1990), pp. 15 – 20.

17 *Ibid.*, p. 16.

18 A. Dukuchayev, 'Uzdechka dlya yadernykh 'skakunov', *Krasnaya zvezda*, (27 September, 1990, 5 October, 1990, 10 October, 1990).

19 'Kontseptsii voyennoy reformy (Proekt)', *Voyennaya mysl' Spetsial'nyy vypusk*, [December 1990], pp. 4 – 5. See also: V. Makareskiy, 'Chto delat' s 'ugrozoy s Iuga?' *Novoye vremya*, No. 34, (September 1990), p. 12.

20 SOVSET, *Radio Liberty Daily Report*, (23 November, 1990).

21 *Krasnaya Zvezda*, (16 January, 1991).

# PART II

CHAPTER 6

# The Future Shape of Warfare

KEITH TITUS

SOVIET PREDICTIONS regarding military art, science and doctrine essentially depend upon Soviet contemporary views concerning the causes, prosecution, effect and result of war. Until the end of the last decade, Soviet military literature grouped warfare into three main categories. First, the strategic dimension involving General War which was envisioned as being conducted on a theatre basis; almost certainly encompassing several theatres simultaneously, or quite likely, being waged globally. By the early 1980s it was envisioned that General War could be fought under either nuclear or conventional conditions, both of which might well also include a bio-chemical component. More recently the space element has been added to the equation. This has been accorded great importance in Soviet military thinking for the last 20 years, although it only achieved public prominence in the early 1980s when President Reagan unveiled his Strategic Defence Initiative or 'Star Wars' concept. Although a war of this nature might not necessarily be initiated by one of the two superpower blocs, it has been tacitly assumed that superpower interests and imperatives could drive them into opposite camps and force an escalation to the level of General War.

The second category concerns Limited War such as those which have occurred over the past 40 years in the Middle East, Vietnam and Afghanistan, amongst many others. These are more commonly termed 'regional conflicts' by the West, and known as 'local wars' in Soviet terminology. The superpowers have always been careful to respect each other's spheres of influence in order to prevent a polarisation which might lead to escalation to General War through provocation. Many thousands of books and articles can be found in the Soviet Union on this subject.

A less extensively covered area is the third category involving violent armed struggle which falls short of limited war status, but would include counter-terrorism, internal insurrection and the battle against the international drug trade. The disparity of treatment accorded by Soviet military writers to these phenomena is perhaps indicative of the relative recent importance accorded to them in the USSR.

It is not the purpose of this chapter to detail the historical Soviet view of warfare or the military doctrine developed to meet such views. Those perspectives can be found in many sources outside the intent of this chapter which is not a re-look at the postwar world but an attempt to preview the first decade of the post-Cold War Era.

We intend to look at the future of war as that perception is shaped by radical changes to policy-making in the Soviet Union which alter the rules in dramatically different, and revolutionary, ways. The very systems used to study and analyse war and the institutions which do the work are being replaced at the same time as the basic assumptions about war have been changed. What systems and assumptions are we talking about? Quite simply, we need to focus on the Soviet army and its General Staff to see how the changes made by Mikhail Gorbachev had dismantled the mechanisms used since the Second World War to answer questions of war — its nature and conduct, and the preparations needed to wage it effectively.

We stated earlier that it was, until recently, relatively easy to ascertain the Soviet view of war. The threats to peace were delineated by the Communist Party of the Soviet Union (CPSU) and the Ministry of Defence under CPSU guidance went through a complex, but systematised, process to develop strategies of organisation, planning and technical responses to fight that war. Since 1945 some basic assumptions have been made that provided a fixed base from which such doctrine developed and which allowed perceptions of war to evolve over long periods of time.

## Soviet Assumptions—Cold War Era

**Internal Factors**
- Primacy of CPSU to exercise power and make policy
- Internal Stability
- Prestige of the Military
- Increasing and High Priority Military Budgets
- Technology Base Equal or Better than the West
- Conscript Army amenable to discipline

**External Factors**
- Bi-polar strategic confrontation with US
- Superpower status
- Warsaw Pact nations as a buffer zone and allies in war with NATO.

- NATO as a military alliance
- Germany divided between East and West
- Ideology as a factor in Local Wars
- Protracted and Limited Arms Control Progress

Some reflection on the table of assumptions above leads to some uneasy feelings. It takes little scholarly research to see that all these assumptions have changed in the last year. Enough press evidence exists which indicates that the military in the Soviet Union today must feel that its worst nightmares are coming true. Imagine what it must be like for a generation of military officers who were raised on a steady diet of lessons from the 'Great Patriotic War'. The very idea of a united Germany as a member of NATO and a dismantled Warsaw Pact embracing market economies with multi-party governments in power has been a major strain on the Soviet military mind. These phenomena, along with the increasing social and economic disorder within the Soviet Union, has created a totally new set of internal and external assumptions affecting the view of future war.

## Soviet Assumptions—Post-Cold War Era

### Internal Factors
- Creation of central government power with multi-party membership
- Republic movements for independence and the rise of ethnic unrest and nationalism.
- Military viewed as a drain on the economy and a general loss of prestige
- Reductions in military spending for economic and arms control reasons
- Technology base non-competitive in the global economy
- Military personnel reflecting general mood of the population due to economic problems and the new era of *glasnost'*

### External Factors
- Rapprochement with US and the West
- Economic requirements to seek help from the West
- Loss of Warsaw Pact as geographical buffer and military alliance
- NATO overshadowed by European economic integration
- Unified, democratic Germany as a member of NATO alliance
- Economic issues replace communism versus imperialism conflict in the Third World.
- Rapid movement of unilateral, bilateral, and multilateral arms control agreements.

All these new assumptions have arisen in varying degrees of reality in an incredibly short period of time. The whole issue of German re-unification played itself out in only a few months in our newspapers and evening newscasts. In 1989 the Soviet Union was steadfast in pronouncing that NATO membership for a united Germany was out of the question. Within two weeks of the 28th Party Congress, however, President (and General Secretary of the CPSU) Gorbachev gave his blessing to the proposal.

These immense changes and the pace under which they are occurring are placing enormous strains on the military's ability to cope and to plan for the future. A particularly disturbing piece of evidence of these problems arose in an interview with the Chief of the General Staff, Marshal Moiseyev, in March 1990. Moiseyev was responding to questions concerning the national defence powers of the office of President of the USSR. While approving the general provisions of the law as approved by the USSR Congress of People's Deputies, Moiseyev listed several areas requiring clarification including the legal status of the President to authorise the release and use of nuclear weapons. He went on to say that 'defence policy is now being made simultaneously by the heads of the Communist Party, the USSR Supreme Soviet and the Council of Ministers, and several different government agencies'.[1]

That interview with the Chief of the General Staff is an incredible commentary on the condition of the Soviet defence establishment. In essence, the Chief Military officer of the USSR has said that he does not know who is legally in charge to plan either for or initiate hostilities. That kind of legal and organisational confusion, coupled with the changed assumptions given earlier, argues that fundamental and revolutionary changes are being forced in institutions which are ill-equipped for such rapid shifts of policy.

Our hypothesis, therefore, is that the bureaucracy of Soviet military planning and thought will itself undergo the same painful introspection as is going on across the state and party organs of the USSR. That introspection will result in some fragmentation of effort and, certainly, divisive debate as to how to approach the future.

Historically, the professional corps of officers comprising the General Staff of the armed Forces of the USSR provided the institutional expertise used to organise, equip, train, and control Soviet military forces. These officers occupy senior positions in all staff and military organisations. The training these officers undergo

> is built on the basis of Marxist–Leninist methodology and the military-theoretical legacy of V.I. Lenin, and is aimed at creative implementation of the decisions of CPSU congresses and decrees of the CPSU Central Committee and Soviet government on

military issues, and on the directives and orders of the USSR Minister of Defence, the General Staff and the Main Political Directorate of the Soviet army and Navy.[2]

The actual analytical work which supports developments in military art, equipment requirements, plans and organisational development is accomplished by the USSR Armed Forces General Staff. The General Staff

> is the principal military command and control organ. It comprehensively analyses and estimates the military-political situation; determines trends in the development of weapons of warfare, organises training of the Armed Forces, ensures their constant combat readiness, directs military scientific work and so on.[3]

The weight, therefore, of the increasing chaos within the Soviet Union and the changes internationally which affect the view of war in the future falls on the officers of the General Staff. Add to this confusion the fact that 90% of Soviet officers are members of the CPSU and you have an atmosphere unlike any the Soviet military has faced since the German invasion of 1941.

At this point it is valid to pose the question: What is the future of war in an era where, geopolitically, peace is breaking out all over? President Bush and the other NATO leaders have declared an end to the Cold War so the Soviet military establishment is not alone in wrestling with the new realities. The Soviet Union does have a more difficult institutional crisis developing which not only will change its views of future war but will also change the very institutions that decide those issues. Professional military officers in both East and West have to evaluate a new order where the possibility of war does not have the same priority for national leaders as it did during the 40 or so years of Cold War.

The content and pace of change as it affects Soviet military thinking has created and will continue to create a period of indecision which may last several years. Although the great majority of Soviet officers are Party members they are also citizens of the USSR. One of the results of *glasnost'* is that both military conscripts and professionals have a much better feel for the increasing economic and social chaos in the country. All members of the military come from some village or city in one of the 15 Soviet Republics. Ethnic violence, food shortages, poor housing, and non-existent consumer goods are real issues for all citizens, in or out of uniform. Military involvement in Georgia, Azerbaijian, Kirghizia, and the Baltic Republics created new missions and responsibilities not taken account of in Soviet military plans and studies of the past. The prospect of internal threats are a new dimension for thought and action. It must be very difficult to concentrate attention on such issues as the loss of the Warsaw Pact to analyse how a future war in Europe might be fought, when finding jobs and housing for several hundred thousand returning troops is a problem without solution. Real world problems now will be much more important than future 'what ifs'.

The internal problems in the Soviet Union will increasingly fragment the military in other areas, affecting their ability to plan for the future. How do they look at a Western world threat when those same countries are being asked to lend billions in capital and technology to save the Soviet economy and bring it into the global family of market economies? What weapons do they want to build when the technological capability of Soviet science and industry is collapsing, as ever scarcer resources move from military budgets to civilian needs? Finally, what system of thought will replace Marxism–Leninism and the loss of Communist Party control over ideology? The 'precision' of Soviet military thought has been based on a system which has been rendered irrelevant by the CPSU 28th Party Congress held in July 1990.

The 28th Congress of the Communist Party will be seen as a pivotal event in Soviet military affairs in the decade to come, even though military questions were not a primary agenda item. Soviet and Western commentators alike viewed this Congress as the ultimate test for Mikhail Gorbachev's challenge to party conservatives and they were proved correct. Would the predominantly hard-line 'old guard' communists embrace his view of Soviet crisis management or attempt to turn back the clock to preserve Party privileges? Without an alternative programme or leader, the conservatives were forced to accede to pressure from the President who was re-elected General Secretary. The change in Politburo membership to include the Republic party chiefs and the more infrequent Politburo meetings mandated *de jure* CPSU support or government control of the USSR. Add the Party's approval of the moves toward a market economy with aid from the West and it would appear that the 28th Congress delegates realise that the primacy of the CPSU as the holder of exclusive truth and power has ended.

If there is any debate about the status of the Party coming only from what was decided in session, the events of the following two weeks should have put those debates to rest. It must be remembered that the Congress was in session when the NATO summit concluded in London that the Cold War was dead. The following week in Houston at the Economic Summit there was an 'agreement to disagree' on the crucial question of aid to the Soviet Union. What emerged was a green light to the Germans and French to make their own policies about aid to the Soviet Union without US interference. The Houston deal made it possible for Chancellor Helmut Kohl to make his visit to President Gorbachev after the 28th Congress, which resulted in Gorbachev's endorsement of NATO membership for the new unified Germany. Gorbachev's victory in the Congress could be no more symbolic than his statement on Germany. That single act signalled Soviet acceptance of the end of the Cold War.

Marxist – Leninist thought could not have provided such an outcome. Communists, military and civilian, had been put on notice that a new era was underway. Serious problems of war and peace could not be answered with old words, plans, or institutions. *Perestroika* would have to turn old ways into new just to survive the crises engulfing the USSR.

The reaction of the military old guard to the 28th Congress and the events immediately after was of shock and dismay. Certainly the senior officer delegation to the Congress shared the conservative view that events under Gorbachev were getting out of hand. Shrinking military budgets, rapid-fire arms control initiatives, internal unrest, the loss of the Warsaw Pact, and the rise of a unified Germany were all cogent reasons for an unhappy military leadership. They must have hoped that the Congress would force Gorbachev to back down somewhat on his reform efforts. Now that the results are in, it would seem obvious that many of the older military generation will follow Ligachev into retirement.

Any exodus of military officers from the armed forces would appear to have two main components based on actions during, and immediately after, the 28th Congress. Two brands of Party members resigned or retired in response to the Congress. While older conservative members like Ligachev admitted defeat by retiring, a more radical faction, unhappy with the slow pace of reforms and led by Boris Yeltsin, left the Party in protest against their inability to contribute positively to efforts at reform. If similar events occur in the military, it could create severe shortages of trained leaders at precisely the time when radical transitions require the best talent to solve the problems of both near and far term import. We may not see this exodus as a public phenomenon, nevertheless the reported decreases in Soviet military active duty strength will affect officer strength. It is the quality and outlook of those who stay which will determine the future of military thought.

The purpose of this Chapter is to examine the view of war in the future from the Soviet perspective. Certain assumptions have been discussed which form the basis upon which threats are postulated. For war to occur, there must be a threat. Threats are represented by capabilities which must be prepared for in case potential aggressors implement them initiating or causing hostilities to occur. Revolutionary changes such as have occurred internally and externally to the Soviet Union within the last two years result in both short and longer term responses by the Soviet military. It will be necessary, therefore, to consider both short and longer term views of warfare in the Soviet view.

Probable changes in the Soviet officer corps and other military personnel are very relevant as the people who fight the wars and the officers who plan and lead must be considered a factor in the short and longer term view of warfare. It is not just Soviet policy in transition but Soviet society as well. The Soviet military will undergo transition under revolutionary circumstances which have already begun to affect the economy, the government (at both national and republic levels), the Party, and individual citizens. It would be a mistake to think that we can reduce the study of future war to the belief that the Soviet General Staff process of developing theory would be immune to the general disruption in the Soviet Union today. Indeed, a real danger in the short term is a pandemic crisis caused by a synergism of internal stresses in this transition period where Gorbachev seems to be tearing down the old order with no clearly identifiable alternative in sight.

Gorbachev in his May 1990 Victory Day speech, set the challenge for military thinkers:

> For the first time, the eternal dream of peace seems possible today in the growing integrity of modern civilisation, and in the economic, ecological and informational interdependence of different countries and peoples, of the political and social systems and of all interests and aspirations. Modern problems can no longer be untangled with weapons. It is high time everyone realised this. They must be patiently unwound, with due respect for the interests of everyone and, most importantly, for the primary value which is human life.

The most interesting aspect of this passage is that it could have just as easily been spoken by President George Bush. Both men have been struggling with the economic and political costs of increasingly dangerous military machines, put at odds by ideologies which are increasingly irrelevant. If the Soviet goal is to create an economy and society with full international legitimacy, it makes little sense to continue the politics of confrontation in the military sphere.

The leaders of both the US and USSR recognise what their military leaders are afraid to see — that war between nation states or coalitions of states (like the Warsaw Pact or NATO) are not viable options in an increasingly interdependent global economy. The irony of economics (remember Marxism?) putting warfare out of business may be lost in these debates, but to the military thinker confusion will be real.

At the strategic level the US and the Soviet Union, as the traditional superpowers, will continue to be concerned with this dimension of war as long as two facts remain — the existence of nuclear weapons and the maintenance of large standing armies. Both nations, and the coalitions they lead, are making progress in gradually reducing those forces which have strategic capabilities. Both nations have adopted arms control programme goals to reduce greatly reduce the political and economic burdens caused by strategic competition.

The Soviet Union will undoubtedly push harder for reductions to such capabilities in the next few years because of its internal economic crisis. The Soviet economy can sustain neither the research and development nor the production costs of a continual arms race when their domestic economy is collapsing. It will be an increasing strain on the military to keep pace with reductions brought on by the leadership. Consequently, the short term view of strategic war for the Soviet Union will not create conditions for any truly long-range planning for war.

It can be argued that the issues of warfare in space should be considered within the context of strategic war. Control of space, either through the deployment of offensive weapons or defensive systems, would be a new dimension of strategic 'high ground'. It is therefore, inconceivable that either the US or USSR would agree to deep cuts in strategic forces on earth and then deploy them in space. The short-term outlook for space ventures would most likely move toward co-operative and peaceful projects. The economics of space technologies alone would seem to dictate co-operation between nations instead of competition. Such co-operation will necessitate technology-sharing which will also serve to negate concerns about one or other achieving some potentially dangerous technological surprise.

There has been no attempt here to separate the matter of nuclear forces from conventional forces simply because it would appear to be irrelevant to the issue of war itself. As economic interdependence replaces ideology as the basis for competition, it would seem that either nuclear or conventional general war would be an unthinkable option for any nation. Modern machines of warfare have the potential to cause destruction of mammoth proportions. While the contamination caused by nuclear war is a phenomenon unique to such weapons, what would be the real difference if Europe was destroyed by a NATO/ Warsaw Pact conventional or nuclear war? Either type of warfare would result in economic devastation of both winner and loser (if it could be decided which was which).

Traditional military views of strategic general war will probably lose importance in the next few years as the means to wage it are removed through arms control processes. As co-operation grows towards arms reduction, so will it increase in areas such as space exploration and other global threats such as poverty, environmental pollution, the Greenhouse effect, over-population, and so forth. These non-traditional 'threats' to international order will create priorities of their own which will further reduce the importance of strategic war as a national option.

It is the category of local wars which will create the greatest challenges to Soviet and and US military thinkers. While both sides face similar issues at the strategic level, there are important differences between nations when it comes to considering local wars. Before these are examined, it is important to see how some common perceptions are shared.

Historically local wars such as Vietnam, Afghanistan, Nicaragua, and the Middle East conflicts have been caused, prolonged, or exacerbated by the Cold War ideological conflict between the US and USSR. Both powers took sides, provided weapons, concluded agreements, and took other measures which added a long-term dimension to many of these Third World conflicts. Local wars became surrogates for the superpower rivalry.

It is already apparent how quickly such local wars can be ended, or forestalled entirely, in the absence of such ideological rivalry. Nicaragua is an example of US and Soviet co-operation where peaceful change is replacing armed conflict under conditions where superpower support to the combatants has been replaced by pressure for peaceful transition. Afghanistan lingers on in conflict but there is no doubt that the Soviet withdrawal has diminished the levels of violence there. Withdrawal of international support and military aid may yet solve similar problems in countries like Cambodia and Burma.

Bad actors in the international community may be more controllable in circumstances where their traditional nation state support is withdrawn. Since 1989, there have been dramatic changes which have gone almost unnoticed as the world has focused on Eastern Europe and the Soviet Union. Nicaragua, Afghanistan, South Africa, Burma, Vietnam, the two Yemens, Namibia and others made changes in foreign policy or resolved internal conflicts of long-standing. Libya and its leader lost the spotlight of world attention. Fidel Castro became increasingly isolated as the Soviet Union backs away from Cuban policies in Latin America. China, although still recalcitrant, was surprised by the level of international condemnation even from its traditional 'socialist' supporters after the 1989 massacre in Tiananmen Square.

The invasion of Kuwait by Iraq may prove a precursor to the resolution of Third World conflicts in the post-Cold War era. Soviet co-operation allowed immediate United Nations condemnation in the Security Council. This crisis provided an example of how quickly support can be organised internationally against regional conflict when ideological competition does not support armed aggression. Indeed, this crisis may yet see military co-operation between the US and the Soviet Union for the first time since the Second World War.

Potential conflicts of this type may even be managed before they become actual conflicts. India and Pakistan represent an excellent example. Since India depends on the Soviet Union for weapons and Pakistan needs US support, it is conceivable that all concerned will reach agreements before conditions for conflict reach crisis stage. The Soviet Union and the US could apply arms control by agreement to limit types and quantities of weapons provided. India and Pakistan would also realise that their respective patrons will not provide political support for conflict. Such variables will increasingly limit warfare as a viable option for Third World antagonists. Since such wars usually require outside support, the limitation of assistance from patron national states can increasingly function as a means of peaceful conflict resolution. In an era of growing appreciation for international order, all sides would benefit from such co-operation, not possible during the Cold War era.

It is in the short term that the Soviet and US military thinkers will experience differences in their approach towards local conflicts in the Third World. The Soviet internal economic and political crises will absorb a great deal of energy during the next few years, and the Soviet military will have to address issues which are Third World problems themselves and which have no counterpart for US planners. Ethnic violence in several Soviet republics is a problem which may increasingly plague the military. Not only has the military found itself using force to control violence in Georgia and Armenia-Azerbaijian, but ethnic conflicts are also reflected within the military itself as its members are also citizens of the groups involved.

It is ironic that the Soviet military may now have to face many of the identical situations it supported in the Third World such as local wars of 'national liberation' in Vietnam and Angola. Now it faces armed insurrections against state power and between rival ethnic factions in the USSR. Third World poverty issues of food shortages, lack of housing, inadequate medical care, and shortages of consumer goods can hardly be blamed on 'imperialism' when they now appear inside the Soviet Union itself. Terms like 'democracy' and 'armed struggle' used so glibly to describe Third World insurrections, will take on new meanings as they occur within Soviet borders. Undoubtedly the Soviet military, with its conscript army, will try to distance itself from such events as much as possible.

The real problem with these internal troubles is that they are likely to occur at a time when the military in the Soviet Union will be searching for new sources of legitimacy. Guidance from the Party is being replaced by control through government and law. Socialism and central planning is be replaced by moves towards a market economy. The 'imperialists' of the West have become the potential sources of the capital and technology needed to rescue the economy. Peace and co-operation are replacing conflict. These monumental changes pose problems for the Soviet military which are not shared by their counterparts in the West. US and NATO officers have not been confronted with a collapse of both their credo and the tangible resources which support their very institutions.

It is this internal conflict inside the Soviet Union which will occupy the Soviet military most in the next few years. They will have to recognise that the very survival of their country is at stake. They will also have to come to terms with the fact that the collapse has not been caused by any external threat but is the result of flaws within their own system.

The military which emerges in the years to come will reflect the values of a new system: whatever the Soviet Union becomes, it is not likely again to claim true legitimacy as a world leader — its failures have been too obvious. The most beneficial by-product of this process will be Soviet understanding that armed conflict has no place in the evolving interdependence of nations and that it will, therefore, co-operate with the West to reduce and manage conflict in the Third World.

So far the subject of the technology of war has not been addressed. The Cold War era was preoccupied with the continual race to acquire new technologies to conduct war. The non-military issues in the years to come, however, will not be technology-driven. Increasing global economic and environmental problems will absorb the resources previously used to support superpower status for both the US and Soviet Union. The new assumptions for geopolitical realities make it possible to redirect such resources. For the USSR it has been forced upon them by economic collapse. For the US it will be forced on them because of continuing debt and budget deficits. Both the major players in this process have military and political machines developed over 40 years of Cold War competition. Habits of expenditure on technological improvements and the production of new weapons will be hard to break. It will take some time for the military cultures of both sides to recognise that this historical moment actually exists and that peace is finally possible. It is possible that the Soviets may recognise this earlier than the West simply because they will not have any choice.

The long-term outlook for war, therefore, depends on many short-term issues. It is to be hoped that the continuing economic problems on both sides will increase the pace of arms control and co-operation on Third World issues. World leaders are being pushed to resolve problems long neglected during the Cold War era when ideological and technological imperatives were paramount. New forces in economics and the environment will increasingly dominate this emerging era and their impact will constrain both the Soviet and the West. Increasing interdependence among the nations of the World will certainly require unprecedented levels of co-operation to solve global problems which were ignored during the Cold War.

## Notes

1  'Chief of Staff Favours Further Expansion of President's Defence Powers', *Krasnaya Zvezda*, No. 61 (15 March 1990), p. 1.
2  Professor Army General M. M. Koslov, *The General Staff Academy. A History of the USSR Armed Forces Order of Lenin and Suvorov 1st Class General Staff Academy imeni K. Ye. Vorshilov*, (Moscow: Voyenizdat, 1987) p. 1.
3  Vyacheslav Filippovich Khalipov, *The Military Policy of the CPSU*. (Moscow: Voyenizdat, 1988), p. 16.
4  Mikhail Gorbachev, Text of Speech: '*The Lesson of War and Victory*'. (Moscow: Novosti Press Agency, 9 May 1990), p. 21.

## References

Dmitriyev, A.P. *New Military–Political Thinking*, Moscow: Izdatelstvo 'Znamya', 1989.

Gayvoronskiy, F.F. (editor), *The Evolution of Military Art: Stages, Tendencies, Principles*, Moscow: Voyenizdat, 1987.

Gorbachev, Mikhail *The Lessons of the War and Victory*, Moscow: Novosti Press Agency, 9 May 1990.

Khalipov, V.F. *The Military Policy of the CPSU*, Moscow: Voyenizdat, 1988.

Kokoshin, A.A. '*The New Soviet Military Doctrine and Unilateral Cuts of the USSR Armed Forces*', Washington, DC: *Statement before Armed Services Committee*, US House of Representatives, 10 March 1989.

Koslov, M.M. *The General Staff Academy. A History of the USSR Armed Forces Order of Lenin and Suvorov 1st Class General Staff Academy imeni K. Ye. Voroshilov*, Moscow: Voyenizdat, 1987.

Laqueur, Walter *Soviet Union 2000*. New York: St. Martin's Press, 1990.

Moiseyev, Mikhail Interview, 'Chief of Staff Favours Further Expansion of President's Defense Powers', Moscow: *Krasnaya Zvezda* (No. 61) 15 March 1990.

Moiseyev, M.A. Speech on Principles of Defence Sufficiency, 28th CPSU Congress. Moscow: *Krasnaya Zvezda*, 6 July 1990.

Philips R. Hyland and Jeffrey Sands. 'Reasonable Sufficiency and Soviet Conventional Defence' *International Security, Vol. XIII, No. 2*, Boston: MIT, Fall 1988.

World Bank. *World Development Report 1990*, New York: Oxford University Press, 1990.

Yazov, D.T. *On Guard Over Socialism and Peace*, Moscow: Voyenizdat, 1987.

Yazov, D.T. '*Technical Training and Organisational Aspects of Military Reform*', Moscow: *Krasnaya Zveda*, 3 June 1990.

Zaykov, L.N. Arms Control Speech, 28th CPSU Party Congress. Moscow: *Pravda*, 4 July 1990.

CHAPTER 7

# The Future of Soviet Military Doctrine

JOHN ERICKSON

THIS CHAPTER is designed to explore the future, both institutional and operational, of Soviet military doctrine, rather than having recourse to the somewhat time-worn Talmudism of narrow textual analysis or even simple extrapolation. Indeed, it might be said that Soviet military doctrine, understood in the widest sense of that term , is 'up for grabs', a situation generated by that 'abundance of uncertainty' espied by General John R. Galvin and a factor potent enough to call into question the very future of 'military doctrine' as it has been previously perceived and interpreted, not to mention the fate of the Soviet Union itself. Past experience is proving to be much less of a reliable guide, least of all since, as Peter Vigor put it, much of what passed for Western 'analysis' was defaced and degraded by presumption, prejudice or dogmatism all pursued with the fervour of 'medieval religious propagandists'.[1]

Now, in many respects, the tables have been turned, for it is Soviet analysts who have donned the mantle of religiosity, engaging in debate and diatribe over 'doctrine' obscured by wordiness, larded with tautology and marred by personal abuse. The opening shots in a war of words soon to be transformed into a bitter institutional struggle were fired by the CPSU General Secretary Mikhail Gorbachev himself during his visit to France in 1985 when he startled the Soviet and non-Soviet world alike with his enunciation of the principle of 'reasonable sufficiency' *razumnaya dostatochnost* in military affairs, all couched in deliberately Delphic terms. This 'new' concept (not without its Western antecedents) suggested restricting military potential to the limits of 'reasonable sufficiency', coupled with the notion of implementing 'non-provocative' or 'defensive' defence, the latter a confusing tautology which seemingly excluded all offensive capability and all offensive operation. In the first instance, such a proposition served the cause of revising an unfavourable image of the Soviet Union abroad and fitted neatly into the peace

offensive. It was also a device or instrument which enabled Gorbachev
and his acolytes to prise open the Soviet 'security agenda' and co-
incidentally break into the arcane mysteries of the Soviet military
budget.[2]

Having taken his propaganda bow abroad, Gorbachev formally
introduced the concept to the 27th Party Congress in February 1986,
followed in turn by his speech to the International Peace Forum in
February 1987, a verbal bandwagon which rolled on and on, drawing
in the Political Consultative Committee of the Warsaw Pact and its
'doctrinal statement' issued in May 1987, affirming the primacy of
'war prevention' (*predotvrashchenie voiny*)[3] and referring in rather vague
terms to 'reasonable sufficiency' as the principle and practice on
which to organise military capabilities. As the terminology proliferated
— reasonable sufficiency, defensive sufficiency, non-provocative defence,
necessary sufficiency or simply and baldly sufficiency — so the lobbies
and interest groups formed up, each choosing its preferred formulation.
But even before Gorbachev's pronouncements the civilian analysts had
unusually begun to breach some of the military's defences and dent its
monopoly of information. The announcement in 1983 of the Strategic
Defence Initiative (SDI) had already precipitated a major crisis in
Soviet defence circles which demanded recourse to civilian and scientific
expertise both to understand and to respond not only to SDI but also
to its underlying challenge, the 'SCI' or 'Strategic Computer Initiative',
leading evidently to the establishment of a highly select *nomenklatura* as
a complementary and subsequently a competitive focus for strategic
estimates and assessments. Emboldened by support and encouragement
from Dobrynin (who had first haltingly hinted at something like
'reasonable sufficiency') and Yakovlev, the civilians — the *institutchikii*
— warmed to their new task, embarking on an increasingly complex
debate with the professional military establishment, disputing 'sufficiency' and probing 'military art', culminating in nothing less than
a full-scale propagandistic assault on the General Staff, initiated in the
summer of 1988 by Shevardnadze and his Foreign Ministry conference
on national security.

The debate has moved steadily from abstract notions, a dash of
utopianism and sheer unrestrained rhetoric to specific issues and particular questions, drawing in an ever-widening circle of contributors
and participants. Though it is possible to distinguish two main groups,
embodying the overall 'civilian-military' relationship, the institutional
alignments are not a little blurred. The 'social science' institutes —
ISKAN (USA and Canada Institute), IMEMO (World Economics
and International Affairs), the recent Europe Institute (*Institut Evropy*)
and the Institute of the Economics of World Socialism each play their
part, coupled with what has come to be called the 'Arbatov school',

part father part son conglomerate. The General Staff can obviously call on the research facilities of the General Staff Academy in addition to those of a whole array of other military academies, and the Research Institute of Systems Sciences. As with the business of advanced military modelling, which has a specific 'civilian-military mix', so elements of that same 'mix' are present in the entire debate over strategy and doctrine dependent on professional military expertise when it comes to technical calculations — in particular, assessments of what comprises 'balance' or evaluation of the correlation of forces — and their civilian institutes discreetly 'seeded' with senior officers nominally retired but installed as 'scientific consultants' .

The entanglement of three fundamental questions has further confused the situation and intensified divergence. The first concerns the question of just what kind of armed forces the Soviet Union needs (and can afford), a debate no longer confined to narrow technical adjustments to existing force structures (upon which the Soviet command had already embarked) but concerned with what type of armed force or 'army' can be justified. The anti-military civilian lobby has no time for the present system, nor indeed has one segment of military opinion, decrying an army 'filled out with sullen, badly trained conscripts' and a 'spineless' officer corps of questionable competence, that 'combat proficiency' is a myth and not even tanks are proof against oafish incompetence.[4]

But if the old does not work, what of the new? Here the 'strategy' of 'war prevention' or 'war avoidance', would seem to oblige the Soviet military to 'deter' with fewer, possibly diminishing resources but at the same time to ensure a favourable outcome — 'a sufficient and *reliable* defence?' — should the unavoidable materialise. Thus, paradoxically, far from displacing the consideration of future war as the core and crux of military doctrine, the espousal of 'war prevention' has actually intensified the relevance and crucial nature of this fundamental doctrinal aspect. Here is also a potent and explosive political argument, with the civilian 'new thinkers' (though they are not quite so novel in their thinking as they would advertise) presupposing that a 'post-reduction environment' implies a *permanent* shift in the 'balance' and, more significantly, in the relationship between political and military means to guarantee Soviet security interest, while the military is generally sceptical of any such transformation. In sum, 'threat assessment' lies at the heart of this matter and it is precisely that 'balance', or rather imbalance, which disturbs the military planners, who perceive a definite technological challenge designed to implement Western military supremacy.

Not surprisingly, the third bone of contention is generated by the vacuity of the concept of 'sufficiency' (openly admitted as inadequately developed within the Soviet strategic community by one civilian analyst, G. Kunadze of IMEMO) and the ambiguities of 'defensivism' and a 'defensive posture'. Here the military is on reasonably strong ground, being able to point out that well before the advent of Gorbachev defensive operations had been under active consideration. That, as we shall see, is a valid point even if it is being somewhat 'economical with the truth': true, advancing technologies obliged the Soviet military to select defensive operational forms but not at the entire cost of relinquishing 'substantial' capabilities for offensive action. If the aim of 'new thinking' and the rhetoric of 'reasonable sufficiency' was to conjure from both civilian and military a workable concept of an operational minimum, then it has failed, not least because of the inconsistencies existing between the rhetoric of 'reasonable sufficiency' and the realities of operational concepts — with a military interest in *maximising* the effectiveness of a 'post-reduction' or a fully restructured force, related to a 'transformation' in military art, itself bound up with projections of the likely course and conduct of war waged with new and advanced weapons. Given such an appreciation, it would seem largely impossible to fit the General Staff's concept of and requirement for 'restructuring' with that which might be understood by Gorbachevian 'defensive defence'.

One further aspect worth mentioning is the question of Soviet forces 'defending' within Soviet territorial limits or even in 'defence' striking beyond them. Here what might best be called the geopolitical school has begun to make itself heard, arguing that military 'restructuring' must furnish forces 'militarily and technologically upgraded . . . geared to resisting not even so much the present war danger as the FUTURE ONE' in a Soviet Union which holds 'the key geopolitical positions' in Eurasia, where the 'colossal nuclear potential of the Soviet Union provides a reliable shield to frustrate attempts to obtain military domination 'in the heart of Eurasia'. Given present and predictable change, 'a balance in Eurasia as a whole' must be maintained, with the USSR duly losing its status as a superpower and becoming merely (!) one of several Eurasian power centres'. That view also takes account of potential dangers arising from prevalent separatist passions, a theme heavily emphasised by Eduard Volodin, a Russian nationalist and conservative, who argued at the beginning of 1990 that the break-up of a 'global superpower', namely the USSR, could not be ruled out, that Russia may have to stand alone, a 'new Russia' itself a Eurasian continent, one possessed of a nuclear armoury and a 'well-equipped, technically advanced army' an 'All-Russian army' deployed and ready on Russian territory.[5]

Not that the military has been content to leave the monopoly of 'new thinking' entirely to the civilian strategists. Nor, for that matter, does the military present itself as an opponent of *perestroika*, the origins of which lay in a recognition of the vital significance of military-factors, above all, the Soviet military-technological lag. Army General Gareyev insists that there has to be a form of 'new thinking' which aims to carry through a redefinition of the 'fundamental military-political and operational-strategic problems of defending the socialist homeland', emphasising not only the importance of advanced technology but also the need for accurate forecasting of military-scientific developments, thus reaffirming the relevance of the 'Ogarkov model' — the reliable mapping of the technological and strategic implications of emerging technologies. Forecasting foresight, *predvidenie* — undertaken with an appropriate methodology is a key element in the battle for the future and it is precisely methodology which creates that deep divide between the professional military and the civilian 'strategists'.[6]

But if Marshal Ogarkov argued that 'established notions' were at risk, a far more radical view has been advanced by the 'artificial intelligence/information technology' lobby, which postulates a whole new world where the much-vaunted 'new means' should not be utilised, simply to pursue and attain objectives which have themselves not changed. Given such circumstances, the polarisation of the 'strategic community' is inevitable, where artificial intelligence (AI) promises nothing less than 'qualitative change' in '*core* military-strategic and political doctrines' which must take account of wholly 'new determinants of military power'[7]

Marshal Ogarkov had also made a similar point rather earlier, namely that 'the military power of the state' could be neither conceived nor construed in traditional terms. Clearly, for all the political and propaganda hullabaloo, 'reasonable sufficiency' is no basis for military doctrine either in the accepted or the predictive sense. Major General Kirilenko, responding to Arbatov senior's sarcasms and excoriations aimed at the military, put the matter succinctly: 'I altogether dislike the phrase 'reasonable defence sufficiency' . . . I cannot conceive of unreasonable sufficiency'. For all practical purposes 'defence sufficiency' is, according to the General, 'the capacity to inflict on any aggressor damage which is unacceptable to him'.[8] Many would simply call that deterrence. So where does Soviet military doctrine go from here?

\*     \*     \*

Though the General Staff has gone far enough to incorporate 'war avoidance' or 'war prevention' in revising what might be called the traditional scope of military doctrine, thus duly making its political obeisance, it has definitely not done so at the cost of the total displacement of considerations of 'future war' or of its professional prerogatives for undertaking threat assessment, strategic analysis and specifying force structure. Little wonder, therefore, that unrestrained military fury met the publication by the younger Aleksei Arbatov of an article on 'sufficiency for defence' which proposed the reduction of Soviet strategic nuclear forces to a minimum deterrent level (10 – 15% of the existing force), the abandonment of the deeply echeloned strategic air defence system and the Moscow ABM system, the restructuring of Soviet general purpose forces to limit their capability purely to *tactical* counter-attack within an unambiguous defensive posture and similarly constricting the Soviet navy to a coastal defence role, eliminating any long-range interdiction or oceanic capability.[9]

Neither this picture of an 'operational minimum' nor the utopian 'vision' of a totally nuclear free world consonant with some grand Gorbachevian design seems to have persuaded the General Staff, bent as it is on elaborating its own operational interpretation of what constitutes not only a 'sufficient' but also a 'reliable' (*nadezhnaya*) defence and by a neat textual trick, the adhesion to 'war prevention' as a primary goal is interpreted as an imperative to be implemented by actual 'improvements' in particular elements of military capability.

Soviet military interest in 'defensivism' certainly predates Gorbachev, indeed it reaches back at least three decades when the development of nuclear weapons and the ICBM fused huge destructive power with long-range, deep strike, leading to an early start on a Soviet SDI programme which continues to this day. A decade or so ago the Soviet military perceived that same threat in a new guise, that of precision-guided weapons and advanced conventional munitions combining lethality with great range of delivery. Over this period Soviet military theorists began to argue for the 'convergence' of the offence with the defence, whereby neither existed in 'pure' form, since the *defender* using the new weapons could deliver his own strikes throughout the depth of the attacker's deployments. Defence continues to assume a new 'quality': while the attacker aims to achieve simultaneous destruction throughout the depth of the defender's deployments, the defender can also launch strikes against the attacker even as, or possibly before, the attack is prepared. Defence, or a 'defensive orientation', can now itself assume the initiative and attain objectives quite as decisive as those hitherto the exclusive province of the offence.[10]

Nevertheless, the 'new quality' of this defence depends essentially upon two factors, attaining fire superiority and command of the air from the outset. An article by Major General A.S. Kulikov and Major General A.D. Nefedov (both students at the General Staff Academy), published in *Voennaya Mysl* in March 1990, discussed the relationship between positional and manoeuvre operations in the defence, arguing for increasing the priority accorded to delivering conventional fire, where the degree of 'activeness' (*aktivnost*) in the defence is commensurate with those 'capabilities in manoeuvring the delivery of conventional fire' and for the pre-emptive destruction of the attacker's 'air echelon' in its concentration areas.[11] Increasing emphasis is placed on the development of 'reconnaissance-strike complexes' (RUKs), designed to co-ordinate sensor, communications and fire systems in order to eliminate targets up to a depth of 500km or even deeper, striking in effect far into the enemy's strategic rear. But perhaps even more significantly, Soviet analysis of the potentialities of these advanced weapons coupled with extended range, improved surveillance and target acquisition, together with speedier information processing encouraged the conclusion that this capability could be described as global and consequently admitted the possibility of non-nuclear warfare on a global scale, all without precise demarcation between defensive and offensive operations.

The military concept of 'restructuring' must therefore make provision for operational effectiveness against the background of this 'offensive-defensive convergence' on a global scale, emphasise manoeuvre operations with the predominance of meeting engagements, cope with the virtual ubiquity of the 'air-land' (or 'land-air') battle and exploit electronic warfare to the utmost. 'Defensivism' as a principle is transmuted into the operational procedures of 'defence activeness' (*aktivnost oborony*) which presupposes attaining fire superiority from the start, which in turn requires command of the air. Thus, defensive stability could be ensured by *surprise* fire (*kontrpodgotovka*), part pre-emption, part spoiling attack, a tried and tested Second World War technique but now vastly enhanced. Already Soviet planners had considered structural changes which envisaged, in a combined arms framework, the creation of independently deployed ACMs, missile and artillery units organised to fight both offensively and defensively, the creation and deployment of dedicated air echelons and the widespread use of 'special forces' (*Spetznaz*) to fight in the enemy rear, as well as the establishment of reserves to counter hostile air-assault forces. In effect, the 'defensivism' embraced by Soviet military planners and military theorists, concentrating as they do upon the critical importance of the 'initial period' of war and the crucial role played by the surprise factor, bears less and less resemblance to the 'defensive defence' notions purveyed and portrayed by civilian analysts. It comes as no surprise that the divide over 'sufficiency' runs both wide and deep.

Indeed, the military prescription of and for 'sufficiency' cannot be dissociated from the General Staff's evaluation of modern warfare and the form of possible (if not actually pending) war *vozmozhnaya voina*. It follows, therefore, that the 'initial period' of a possible war enjoys priority on the list of the considerations of the Main Operations

Directorate of the General Staff, followed by projections of both the intensity and scope of possible operation coupled with studies of particular weapons systems, the possible effects of war upon the Soviet Union itself and developments in Western doctrines relative to the implications of 'reasonable sufficiency'. As for the 'defensive', such operations would not be sustained throughout any such projected war, for there would have to be a turn to 'decisiveness': General Moiseyev in his brochure on military doctrine in the original Russian version (in a passage excised from the English translation) stipulated 20 days only for 'defensivism', before a recourse to the counter-offensive.[12]

The 'character of modern war', to use General Salmanov's term, is essentially one of high intensity operations, globally expansive and *dimensionally extensive to include space*, hugely demanding in efforts to seize the initiative, bereft of front lines with fragmented battlefields where smaller units acting independently will exploit mobility (with sustainability being at a premium), leaving the deep rear open to attack. While the principle of 'combined-arms' continues to pervade such projections, it is significant that attention is increasingly focused on information processing (*informatizatsiya*) and the potentialities of automation (*avtomatika*) for command and control. In fact, if we look closely at both military and civilian work on *upravlenie*, control appears to be the key concept and duly connected with real-time tasks. Mastery of control (one's own and that of the enemy) thus becomes the vital component in 'winning', a term and concept which has undergone radical revision.

New military technologies and new weapons' effects provide the capability to strike deep utilising surprise, where surprise is no longer a passive 'deception' mode but an *active* process exploiting the automation of reconnaissance systems and terminally-guided munitions to strike at enemy concentrations, hit key targets, influence the 'correlation of forces' and disable enemy control systems, in effect to deprive an opponent of control in the very widest sense, rather than simply seizing territory for its own sake. It is clear that at the tactical and operational level and when considering the Soviet 'land/air battle' with its two basic echelons (ground-air), 'defensiveness' in no way precludes the retention and the application of an offensive capability nor, apart from tactical exploitation of positional warfare, do these concepts have anything that might be identified with the 'technological Maginotism' of some civilian strategists.[13]

If we are dealing in the first instance with 'modern war' and its characteristics, exemplified in the 'offensive defensive convergence', this does not fully comprehend the problem of 'future war', though a connection was made by General Salmanov himself in his article on military doctrine. His observation, not merely propagandistic in tone, was that 'space weaponry' designed to fight in space and also to strike terrestrial targets could and eventually would shatter what at present passes for strategic parity. If we pursue certain connections, it is possible to see one 'element' of emerging doctrine as that which is concerned with the 'battle for control' in modern war and the other, a projection, the implications of 'command of space', *gospodstvo v kosmose* for the future war, even outright 'space supremacy'.[14] And what gives added piquancy to this 'defensive-offensive convergence' is the recent confirmation by General Moiseyev himself that henceforth its implementation would be based exclusively in Soviet territory or constrained within Soviet borders (one immediate effect of which is a certain restructuring in border Military Districts, enhancing readiness and improving $C^3$ above all upgrading air/aerospace defence). Not for the military the solace or the supposed sanctuary of the much-touted 'common European home', dismissed by one senior officer at the 28th Party Congress as sheer 'myth'. And, in any event, a united Germany would stalk the corridors.

It is my main contention that what we are seeing in the making with respect to Soviet military 'doctrine' is a *new intellectual amalgam*, in which it would be a mistake to see 'doctrine' as wholly subsumed by technological preoccupation, important though technological considerations are. If the civilian strategists have found their 'guru' in Robert McNamara, the Soviet General Staff has a new-found hero in Friedrich Engels who, as the prophet of military modernisation, has come to displace Clausewitz; now that both the civilian and military sides of the house have recourse to Soviet theoretical writings of the 1920s, most notably those of Svechin.[15] In terms of projections, Soviet military thinking seems to consider the separation of 'modern war' and 'future war' in terms of the phases of advance in technology and weapons systems, with the steady encroachment of new or fundamentally 'new in principle' weapons. The time scale stretches well into the next two decades, with the present decade witnessing the deployment of long-range surveillance systems, those connected with target acquisition and weapon delivery, together with advances in 'stealth' technology, followed by the advent of directed-energy weapons, roboticisation, RF weapons, laser weapons and, not least, biological and genetic weapons. If anything, much of the present Soviet programme is $C^3$ driven, with a widely ramified set of R&D priorities embracing research into multi-spectral senors, high-throughput signal-processing devices, holographic and shape-recognition software and data-processing computer networks, with pronounced emphasis on optical data-processing (since the requirement for near real-time *informatizatsiya* cannot be met by digital microelectronic systems, unable to meet the requirements of data fusion within the time constraints).[16]

I am inclined to conjecture that the Soviet objective, leaving aside utopian visions of a non-nuclear, threat-free world, is the development and deployment of a deeply echeloned global 'defensive system' (where 'global' is not expressly a territorial delineation but rather multi-dimensional, even multi-spatial in the connection between space-based and terrestrial assets, with space-based capabilities utilised for *both* offensive and defensive purposes). This particular form of 'defensive dominance', founded within Soviet territorial confines and only those, would seek to exercise control, offensively and defensively, over the complex of space, the oceans and the electromagnetic spectrum.

Though there is much interest in the revolutionary impact of electronics and microcircuitry, which can themselves accelerate the development and deployment of advanced strategic systems, this is not taken by Soviet specialists to signal the obsolescence of all existing weapons: improved strategic systems already in service will operate side by side with those introduced over the coming decades and embodying 'new physical principles', though the *political* effort to restrict and restrain deployments of advanced space-based offensive systems will continue unabated.

ICBMs with improved accuracy could well be employed with conventional warheads, with much the same being said for long-range cruise missiles, conventionally armed and capable of being directed against hard targets. Follow-on generations of ICBMs will certainly retain utility for specific future strategic *offensive* missions, particularly those aimed at $C^3$ assets (and missile silos). 'Space-strike' weapons, space-based nuclear missiles or re-entry vehicles would not of themselves enjoy the accuracy of the improved ICBM but offsetting that relative disadvantage would be the exemplary time-to-target of such vehicles. Space-based kinetic energy weapons and particle beam weapons could scarcely be employed effectively against terrestrial targets, though these might be directed against hostile space-based $C^3$ or early warning assets.[17] Space and 'future war' seem to be co-terminous, where space steadily becomes the 'principal theatre of operations' involving nothing less than 'constant military control'. But for present purposes 'space and 'modern war' implies its inclusion in a comprehensive, integrated strategic defensive system embracing anti-air, anti-missile and anti-space strike capabilities. Aleksei Arbatov's proposal to dismantle echeloned air defences and abandon the existing ABM system, all in the name of 'reasonable sufficiency', inevitably incensed the professional military who saw nothing either reasonable or sufficient in his arguments.[18]

But while there is much sound and even more fury generated by discussions of doctrines, or pseudo-doctrines of 'defensivism' or 'defensive-offensive convergence', or the emplacement or displacement of this or that weapons system and its propensities, the underlying, nagging question is the future of the military system itself and the implications of what I can only call an eventual 'systems shift', a task now presumably fallen under the aegis of the *Commission on the Development of the Concept of the Organisational Development of the Armed Forces during the period 1991 – 95 and up to the year 2000*. 'Organisational development' can cover a multitude of sins, whether of commission or omission, and here we come back to the cardinal point that the military concept of 'restructuring', the rationalisation of the effectiveness of a post-reduction force, continues to diverge from the imperatives of 'defensive defence' and its associated radicalism or utopianism. 'New thinking' notwithstanding, this will continue to be a nuclear-armed world for the foreseeable future. Changes in the Soviet force structure are known to be inevitable and admitted on both sides of the house, civilian and military, but the radicalism of the former (and that of not a few of the 'Young Turks' within the military itself) encountered the opposition and generated the discontents of senior officers, particularly resistant to calls for a transition to a 'professional' army. Moiseyev and Yazov have resisted calls for the implementation of an all-volunteer system, citing among other things cost, only to be called to account for 'cooking the books'. One Soviet colonel observed sardonically that the high command seemed to prefer an expensive but inefficient army organised round conscription to an expensive but highly professional, well trained volunteer army.

The 28th Party Congress appears to have made little progress in these matters, save for mandating an eventual transition to a 'mixed' manning system, combining voluntary contractual service arrangements with conscription. Otherwise the radicals and the reformers failed to capture any of the commanding heights. But if the Soviet command is to follow its own doctrinal precepts and imperatives, then 'organisational development' must gather speed in order to respond to the new operational environments and the requirements imposed by high-technology conventional warfare and to concentrate on on quality as opposed to quantity. In spite of the acrimony, there is a degree of common ground between the civilian analysts and the military over the diminishing utility of nuclear weapons and the inevitability of force reductions, though the military shows growing concern over the damage to the status of the military institution as a whole, hence the continued stress upon the persistence of external threat, and the struggle to slow further cuts. On the other hand, given the gross economic constraints under which the Soviet Union labours and with the prospect of an eventual price reform which will raise the cost of weapons and equipment, the Soviet military with a limited (and 'real') budget will have to take the greatest care of its pennies. But, of the priorities expressed by doctrine, it would seem that weaponry and organisation to meet the needs of *strategic defence* and modernisation to effect 'defensive stability' (which almost certainly embraces inherent offensive capabilities) stand high on the list, with the requirement to look, as General Moiseyev insisted, towards the long-term future.

A possible 'organisational frame' for that future was furnished by Major General V. Ivanov, Senior Lecturer at the General Staff Academy as recently as July 1990, when he argued that the time for basic re-organisation had arrived. His proposal combines military reform with restructuring, using 'combat readiness' and 'assigned missions' as criteria. He suggests three categories or 'contingents', the first a full readiness/rapid reaction force in terms of manpower, weapons and equipment, combining space and nuclear forces, the bulk of the air/aerospace defence forces (PVO), air force units, 'earmarked' naval forces and the mobile elements of the ground forces. This 'contingent' should be sufficient to carry through a 'defensive resolution' of conflict in any disparate region and be adequate to cover the deployment of the 'second contingent' in time of war.

That second contingent would be numerically the largest, consisting of reserve manpower and stockpiled weapons and equipment, all forming the basis for manning a wartime order of battle. A regular cadre would be maintained side by side with the reservists, its strength *one third* of the first combat-ready contingent. The third contingent, makes provision both for 'military service' and 'alternative service' its main task being to manage universal military service with a cohort of some 600,000 – 700,000 conscripts undergoing a six month training period, after which they would serve the rest of their term in the first or second contingents or an extended term with the military units of the various Soviet republics. This 'third contingent', properly managed, could well become a vital source or pool from which to man the first groups of forces on a voluntary contractual basis and indeed might become *the* main source of professional military volunteers.[19]

But if manning is a problem, the military administration and the military bureaucracy is a nightmare. No country in the world, according to General Ivanov, has such a cumbersome, redundant administration for arms and services as the Soviet Union. Worse, the functions of these administrations have never been formally clarified or established, nor their legal status confirmed. Take, for example, operations in Afghanistan: 40th Army came directly under the army commander, under the 'operational group' of the Turkestan Military District and under the Ministry of Defence's 'operational group', with personnel attached from almost every arm and service. The net result was simple muddle and a flood of curses from commanders of all ranks. By way of rationalisation General Ivanov suggests a complement to his three 'contingents', three forms or echelons of 'command and control' (*upravlenie*), administrative, strategic and operational.

Ivanov's administrative echelon would abolish the present system of C-in-Cs for combat arms, replacing it with committees, collective bodies whose council ('soviet') would be ultimately responsible for most matters, with membership drawn from 100 – 150 representatives from the Defence Ministry, defence industry and scientists working in the defence field. Such committees, overseeing each combat arm, would draft military-technical plans and organisational tables covering a five-year period in the first instance, procure military equipment, monitor its quality and actual delivery, take charge of the manning of formations and units as well as the care and maintenance of troop equipment — all under the direct control of the Ministry of Defence and in close contact with the General Staff and the command of the 'strategic control echelon'.

That 'strategic control echelon', the second in Ivanov's hierarchy, would be responsible for both planning, war plans, and for operational control through functional commands (*komandovanii*) closely tied into the General Staff commands for Strategic Forces (Nuclear and space), Readiness Forces, General Purpose Forces, Training Establishments, Republic and Civil Defence Units and Local Military Administrations. The 'strategic command' would unify and integrate all nuclear-capable elements into Nuclear and Space forces (*Yadernye voiska* and *Kosmicheskie voiska*),[20] with a strength of some 400,000 men. The General Staff would develop plans for their use, confirm them with the President [*sic*], but wartime operational control would be exercised by the Supreme Command (*Verkhovnoe Glavnoe Komandovanie*).

The 'Readiness' command would have forces available either to 'repel aggression' or to intervene in local conflicts, when they would come under the operational control of the *Glavkoms* of the relevant TVDs (theatres of military operations). Their main mission would be to cover the mobilisation and deployment of the General Purpose Command in the time of war or in periods of severe tension. The President would decide on their deployment and the strength would be some 1,250,000 strong. General Purpose Forces, numerically the largest, would draw their manpower from reservists, with the manning rolls kept by the military commissariats (*voenkomats*) and weapons and equipment stockpiled. In peacetime they would have a strength of some 630,000 men part volunteer contract, part fixed-term conscription. Strength would reach 400,000 for the ground forces contingent, 80,000 for air and naval forces, 70,000 for air/aerospace defence.

The 'Training command', with some 300,000 – 350,000 men would implement a 5 – 6 month training programme, after which there would be a choice of 'contract service' on a volunteer principle with other commands, or service with Republic military units. This system is designed to supply 25,000 men to the strategic forces, 200,000 to the ground forces, 30,000 to the air force, 15,000 to air defence and 40,000 to the navy. There might also be manpower for labour and construction battalions. The most controversial of these proposals as General Ivanov himself admits, is the suggestion concerning Republic military organisations and the role of Civil Defence. Many argue that encouraging national Republic military units simply means 'decentralising' the Soviet armed forces, while others insist on the separation of civil defence from the military structure. Republics should be allowed to organise their own national units at company and battalion level, the actual numbers limited to a fixed percentage of the total indigenous population. In peacetime they would render 'aid to the civil power' (harvesting, rescue and emergency services) and in wartime be moved under Military District (or Front) command to hold frontier lines. The local military administration would in effect continue to implement the law on universal military service, though it ought now to come under the competence of the local Soviets of People's Deputies.

Of the three 'control' echelons, there remains the critical question of *operational control*. This independent echelon must come under the direction of the Supreme Commander, closely linked with the Ministry of Defence and the General Staff. In peacetime its main function would be operational planning and preparation in the various TVDs, duties involving the TVD *Glavkoms*, the military districts and the several armies. In war there would be no great change, save for halting the contraction in the numbers of military districts and the creation of a *Glavkom* for the North-Western TVD. In peacetime all military districts would be subordinated to TVD commands, save for the Northern Fleet, the Moscow, North Caucasus, Volga-Urals and Siberian Military Districts which would be subordinated directly to the General Staff.[21] But while there is much talk of cutting troop strength in the interests of economy, a great deal could be saved by eliminating the present top-heavy military bureaucracies.

*      *      *

Let me now return to my main theme, the future of 'doctrine' — even as I would predicate by way of defence of a seeming digression that a consideration of a 'systems shift' is not wholly irrelevant.

Though there is much talk of the relationship between technology and doctrine, indeed they are often treated as if they were synonymous, this does not seem to be the heart of the matter. It is a statement of the obvious that both sides, civilian and military, recognise the significance of technological advance and innovation. The key question is not so much technology as *methodology*, embracing the problem of identifying the 'value' of these new weapons systems and the operational forms which they will generate. To put it another way, for the General Staff to win the battle over doctrine as it undoubtedly thinks it should it must resolve the paradox of how to 'quantify' this new and much-vaunted 'quality'. Much the same applies to those who propound a theory of 'new determinants': they too must furnish 'quantification' for that futuristic quality they ardently profess to espy. In some respects the General Staff has learned its lesson, having recently paid the price for intellectual lassitude, complacency, professional weakness, even downright blimpishness. What was hitherto worked through the Military-Scientific directorate in association with the Main Operations Directorate is now more effectively concentrated in the Centre for Operational and Strategic Studies of the General Staff, much involved with the methodology of modernisation.

What is clear is that the attempt, no doubt politically convenient and propagandistically beneficial, to establish pure 'defensivism' is not only a pretence but pretentious nonsense, which reflects little credit on the acumen of those Western commentators who have taken it all absolutely at its face value. The Soviet military has also obscured the issue with its own 'defensive-offensive convergence' rigmarole, when in fact it wishes to have an unambiguous answer to and formulation of one central issue what combination of military technology or technologies linked to specific operational forms and associated with the requisite 'organisational development' in Soviet force structure will defeat any attempt to intrude on the territorial integrity or the vital interests of the Soviet Union as it exists or might evolve. So far the civilian analysts have failed to come up with persuasive, plausible answers to two questions: what forces, what operational forms? One exception must be made, however, in respect of Andrei Kokoshin, whose acuity and intellectual probity set him apart from the others who are by and large mere civilian scribblers, bemused by their own wordiness in an advocacy of a specious 'defence dominance' and a runic 'reasonable sufficiency'. Their assessment methodology, if indeed methodology fits where much is plagiarism of the American strategic lexicon, is highly questionable, their Achilles heel the inability to define and refine 'stability' save by intellectual mimicry of Western style and terminology.

If it comes down to arms control, perhaps we could do ourselves no small service, by not taking seriously all the verbiage of the civilian 'strategists' and submitting it to endless exegesis, but rather by rendering greater intellectual and professional aid to the General Staff 'modellers', so that they may be more sure in an of their 'assessment methodologies' and we, in our own interest, may better know in whose hands the future of Soviet military doctrine truly lies and will continue to lie, whatever the visions (or nightmares) that unfold over the next two decades. But when it comes to operational military doctrine and force re-structuring, it might be politic for some of the more vociferous would-be Soviet 'strategic analysts' to recall that useful French phrase about matters of moment: *'pas devant les enfants'*. Or, as the British tend to say, don't frighten the horses.

## Notes

1  See Peter Vigor, 'Western Perceptions of Soviet Strategic Thought and Doctrine'. Ch. 2 in Gregory Flynn (Ed.), *Soviet Military Doctrine and Western Policy*, (London, Routledge, 1989.

2  For textual analysis and the significance of terminology, see R. Hyland Phillips and Jeffrey J. Sands, 'Reasonable Sufficiency and Soviet Conventional Defense'. *International Security*, 1988, Vol. 13, No. 2, pp 164 – 178: also Raymond L. Gerthoff, 'New Thinking in Soviet Military Doctrine'. *The Washington Quarterly*, Vol. 11, No. 3 Summer 1988, pp 131 – 158: also David V. Dietrich and Ralph M. Hitchens, 'The Soviet Strategic Debate: Striving for Reasonable Sufficiency', *The Journal of Soviet Military Studies*, Vol. 2 No. 1, March 1989, pp 1 – 16: also V. Zhurkin, S. Karaganov, A. Kortunov, *Razumnaya dostatochnost i novoe politicheskoe myshlenie*, Moscow, Nauka, 1989, 71 pp: also Harry Gelman, *The Soviet Turn Toward Conventional Force Reduction*, RAND Publication R – 3876 – AF, December 1989.

3  See the most recent publication, A.A. Kokoshin and V.V. Larionov, *Predotvrashchenie voiny Doktriny, Kontseptsii, perspektivy*, Moscow, 'Progress', 1990, 184 pp.

4  See Igor Kononov and Yurii Borisov in *Smena*, No. 18 September 1989, pp 6 – 7 and p 18.

5  See Igor Malashenko, Senior Consultant, International Department, Central committee, CPSU, 'Russia: the Earth's Heartland'. *International Affairs*, (Moscow), July, 1990, pp 46 – 54: also Eduard Volodin, 'Novaya Rossiya v menyaushchemsya mire: realisticheskii prognoz', *Literaturnava Rossiya*, 26 January 1990 pp 3 – 4.

6  See especially Dr. Jacob W. Kipp, *From Forecasting to Foresight: the Russian and Soviet Military Experience*, Stratech Studies, Texas A&M University System, College Station, April 1988, 273 pp.

7  See Gennady B. Kochetov *et al*, 'Artificial intelligence and disarmament' in *Arms and Artificial Intelligence*, (Ed. Allan M. Din), SIPRI/OUP, 1987 pp 152 – 162: also Colonel General M.A. Gareyev, *Frunze — voennyi teoretik*, Moscow, Voenizdat, 1985.

8  Major General Kirilenko in *Kommunist vooruzhennykh sil (KVS)*, No. 11, 1990: Admiral of the Fleet Chernavin, equally disenchanted with 'reasonable sufficiency', suggested rather 'sufficient reasonableness'.

9  The English version of Aleksei Arbatov's article, 'How Much Defence is Sufficient?' appeared in *International Affairs* (Moscow) in April, 1989, No. 4, pp 31 – 44 (in the Russian version 'Skol'ko oborony dostatochno?'), Arbatov senior, Georgii, sparked off a blistering row with his own article in *Ogonek*, 1990, No. 5 'Armiya dlya strany ili strana dlya armii?'.

10  See Mary C. FitzGerald's cogently argued study, 'Advanced Conventional Munitions and Moscow's Defensive Force Posture' in *Defense Analysis*, Vol. 6, No. 2, June 1990, pp 167 – 192: also LTC Andrew M. Hulse, 'Soviet Force Development and Nuclear Arms Reductions', *Parameters*, (US Army War College Quarterly), Vol. XVII, No. 4, December 1987, pp 81 – 90.

11  See – Voennaya Mysl, No. 3, March 1990.

12  Army General M. Moiseyev, *The Soviet Military Doctrine: Orientation Towards Defence*, NPA, Moscow, 1898 (abridged from *Pravda*, 13 March 1989.

13  For text and diagrams, see Andrei Kokoshin *et al.*, *Problems of ensuring stability with radical cuts in armed forces and conventional armaments in Europe*, Moscow, (English text), from *Pravda*, 7 and 12 March 1989.

14  Army General G.I. Salmanov, 'Sovetskaya voennaya doktrina i nekotorye vzglyady na kharakter voiny i zashchity sotsializma', *Voennaya Mysl*, 1988, No. 12, pp 3 – 13 for full text.

15  A. Kokoshin, 'Alexander Svechin on War and Politics', *International Affairs*, No. 11, November 1988, p 106, pp 118 – 126: also Colonel General V.N. Lobov, 'Aktual'nye voprosy razvitiya teorii sovetskoi voennoi strategii 20 – kh — serediny 30 – kh godov', – Voenno – istoricheskii Zhurnal, No. 2, 1989.

16  See the important study by Michael A. Pollock, Kevin D. Stubbs, Richard E. Thomas and Steve R. Waddell, – Soviet Optical Data Processing and its Suitability for Troop Control, Stratech Studies, SS90 – 1, 1990: also a Soviet monograph, Yu.R.Nosov, *Optoelektronika*, 2nd Edn., Moscow *Radio i Svyaz*, 1989, 360 pp.

17  For full details see Lawrence R. Fink, 'The Soviet View of War and Military-Technical Progress: Implications for ICBMs', *Comparative Strategy*, Vol. 8, 1989, pp 317 – 333.

18  See the discussion under 'Ob odnom podkhode k otsenke dostatochnosti PVO' in *Voennaya Mysl*, No. 7, 1990. pp 28 – 43.

19  For the whole text, *KVS*, No. 15, August 1990, under 'Korennoe obnovlenie, a nie 'kosmeticheskii remont', pp 15 – 20.

20  Major-General Ivanov mentions '*kosmicheskie voiska*': *Krasnaya zvezda* for 8 September, 1990 publishes the career details of Colonel-General V. L. Ivanov, who is cited as '*nachal'nik kosmicheskikh chastei Ministerstva oborony SSSR*'.

21  Details in *KVS*, No. 15, August, 1990, *loc.cit.*

CHAPTER 8

# Future Directions in Soviet Military Strategy

DAVID M. GLANTZ

SINCE the end of the Second World War, Soviet military strategy has been conditioned by 'experiences of the war and the new distribution of military-political forces in the world'.[1] The Soviet Union claims their policy has been based on the 'fact that the governments of the former allies in the anti-Hitlerite coalition (primarily the United States and England) have departed from the principles agreed upon for the post-war organisation of the world'. During the ensuing Cold War, which the Soviets now infer began in 1949, Soviet military strategy recognised the dual realities of nuclear and conventional war. While their views regarding the domination of nuclear weapons have on several occasions shifted, until recently they have steadfastly insisted that 'the offensive was the main type of strategic operation, in either a nuclear or non-nuclear context'.

During the 1950s Soviet military strategy sought to defend the gains made by Communism in the Second World War and immediate post-war years against what they perceived as a concerted Western effort, led by the US to 'contain' the expansion of Communism. Containment, in their view, was typified by Western political efforts to restore the global *status quo* by the restoration of Germany (western) and Japan, the creation of anti-Communist political-military alliances, such as NATO, CENTO and SEATO, and direct military and political assistance in the form of the Truman Doctrine to nations threatened by Communism such as Turkey and Greece. The economic corollary of these political programmes was the Marshall Plan.

Militarily, the Soviet Union saw the threat as, first the US atomic monopoly (broken in 1949) and, second, the emergence of US-dominated military alliances, the most threatening of which was NATO. The Soviet strategic response was to maintain a large, expandable peacetime military establishment, maintain large military forces in conquered

123

regions of eastern Europe, and cloak these forces in the political guise of an alliance, (the Warsaw Pact), which would contend with NATO on a multilateral basis. The major thrust of Soviet military strategy was to maintain a conventional military force whose offensive capabilities would negate Western atomic and conventional military power.

The growing Western thermonuclear threat caused the USSR in the 1960s to modify its strategy. In the early 1960s Khrushchev adopted a strategy, soon delineated in Marshal V.D. Sokolovsky's work, *Military Strategy (Voennoie strategiia)*, which was based on the Soviet acquisition of a thermonuclear capability equal to that of the West and a presumed reduced Soviet conventional capability, designed, in part, to respond to internal Soviet imperatives and facilitate expansion of the Soviet economy. The central feature of this strategy was the assumption that future war would be inescapably global and nuclear in nature.

Although Khrushchev fell from power in 1964, the 'single option' concept of global nuclear war continued to dominate Soviet military strategy for several years thereafter. Lessons of the 1960s, including the Cuban missile crisis, and the reluctance of key personnel in military-theoretical circles to accept fully the implications of the 'single option', led to a gradual shift in Soviet strategy, which was apparent by the end of the decade. In short, the shift involved a lessened emphasis on the nuclear component of strategy and an acceptance that the role of conventional forces still maintained significance.

From the early 1970s to the mid-1980s, in response to the perceived US and NATO threat, the concept of the theatre-strategic operation dominated Soviet military thought, having replaced the nuclear-dominant strategy of the 1960s. Theatre-strategic operations relied on high-speed combined-arms offensives designed to seize the initiative and achieve strategic objectives quickly and without employment of nuclear weapons. The concept of the theatre-strategic operation provided a broad framework for understanding the full scope and complexity of strategic military endeavours, although the Soviet Union never implied that such a complex and risky concept would be fully implemented in a future war. The theoretical structure of the full theatre-strategic operation provided insights as to what objectives smaller-scale operations over shorter durations could achieve. More importantly, the larger model of the full theatre-strategic operation vividly underscored the possible consequences should the smaller-scale operations fail.

With broadening prospects for larger-scale combined-arms operations occurring in future war, with or without the use of nuclear weapons, the Soviet Union sought to develop concepts which could produce strategic victory within continental theatres of military operations. As a vehicle for understanding the potential for theatre-strategic operations, the Russians thoroughly analysed their Second World War operations, believing that basic principles and combat techniques of that period retained their relevance.

The result was a series of models, which seemed to provide a sounder basis upon which to formulate contemporary concepts for the conduct of theatre-strategic operations. Among the many criteria for selecting models were those features of modern war which the Soviet Union considered most significant. These included great scale and scope of operations, the participation of highly mobile forces as the motive force for development of the operations, rapid development of operations to operational and strategic depths, large-scale conduct of complex missions, and sustainment of the operations in terms of manpower, equipment and logistics to great depths over ever-lengthening periods. The four models focused upon were the Belorussian operation (June – August 1944), the Yassy-Kishinev operation (August 1944), the Vistula-Oder operation (January 1945), and the Manchurian operation (August 1945). The last two, in fact, became virtual models of the theatre-strategic offensive for Soviet strategists in the early 1980s.

During the mid-1980s a range of new influences coalesced to influence Soviet military strategy significantly. First, there was a fundamental reassessment by the Soviet military of the nature and requirements of future war, especially regarding a perceived technological revolution in new weaponry (in particular, high-precision weaponry), whose effects could not readily be predicted. Second, a wave of internal uncertainty swept through the ruling and intellectual circles within the Soviet Union regarding the political, economic and, finally, ideological basis of the Soviet state. Third, there was growing disenchantment with the nature and effects of existing Soviet military, policy and strategy, characterised by Soviet active intervention abroad and an intense and seemingly unlimited arms race, which placed immense burdens on the Soviet economy and seemed to offer little real gain in the Soviet international stature.

All these influences led to the adoption by a new Party Secretary and Premier, Mikhail Gorbachev, of a series of programmes to reform the Soviet state, principally the internal sphere. These internal reform programmes inexorably involved the realm of military policy, doctrine, and, ultimately, strategy as well. In 1987, within the context of these changes, a new defensive military doctrine was adopted which is now producing revolutionary changes in Soviet military strategy.

## Historical Models for Defensiveness

Beginning in 1985, a new period in Soviet military development was designated, soon defined within the context of a recast military doctrine emphasising 'defensiveness' in its political component, but clearly shaped in many of its military-technical aspects by reassessments which had begun during the previous decade. Subsequently, the Soviet Union has articulated several variations of future military strategy couched analogously in historical terms. The Soviet analysts, A. Kokoshin and V. Larionov, have publicly advanced four strategic variants (or models), distinguished by the relative offensiveness or defensiveness of each, and have begun to postulate several additional paradigms as new political realities emerge. It is probable that the debate over strategy and changing political conditions will ensure the strategic realm will remain a topic of uncertainty and redefinition. Quite naturally each model is subject to interpretation.

On a scale of decreasing offensiveness, the four original Soviet models proposed by Kokoshin and Larionov are:

● Opposing coalitions possessing strong, offensively-oriented force groupings, intended to conduct operations on enemy territory. Mutual offensive intent and suspicion of their opponent's motives characterise contending parties in this model, which replicates pre-First World War Europe and, in the Soviet view, the Cold War as well. More important, this model inevitably increases the likelihood of nuclear warfare.

● The Kursk model for premeditated defence, which postulates one side absorbing a major enemy blow and then delivering a decisive counter-offensive that carries into enemy territory. Although labelled by the Soviets as 'defensive', circumstances surrounding the Kursk operation underscore its inherently offensive nature. For this reason, Soviet theorists have recently turned away from the Kursk model as an example of future defensiveness to another which seems more appropriate.

● The Khalkhin-Gol model of 1939 operations against the Japanese and United Nations operations in Korea (1951 – 53) now seem more appropriate to today's doctrinal pronouncements. This model postulates that each side possesses the capability of routing an enemy force on its own territory but is not capable of penetrating enemy territory. Close examination of the circumstance at Khalkhin-Gol, however, indicates other facets of the operation which make it less relevant. These include the secret Soviet force build-up prior to the operation, which accorded the Russians considerable surprise; Soviet numerical advantage; and political circumstances associated with the German threat to the Soviet Union, which restrained the Soviets at Khalkhin-Gol. The Soviets also cite the period 10 June 1951 to 21 July 1953 of the Korean War as representative of this model. During that period warring parties tacitly agreed not to cross a certain demarcation line and not to expand the scale of military operations. Here, difficulties in determining the territorial limits of combat, compensation for losses and degree of restraint on both sides cloud the model's utility.

● Opposing coalitions, possessing only limited tactical capabilities, both of which are unable to undertake any operations of strategic consequence. This model addresses relative capabilities and falters on the amorphous definition of defensive adequacy or, in current parlance, 'sufficiency'. It implies war is considered imminent by neither side, and there is a degree of mutual agreement among opposing parties regarding how 'limited tactical capabilities' are defined.

President Gorbachev's current programme of 'defensiveness' postulates Soviet maintenance of a defensive capability sufficient to absorb and repulse an enemy blow. It leaves several fundamental questions unanswered. First, 'is defensiveness genuine?' Second, if it is genuine, 'is it based upon the Kursk or Khalkhin-Gol models or on yet another model?' And, finally, will events in the USSR permit a rational model based on military considerations to be implemented, and will the General Staff and Ministry of Defence view of military models prevail in the face of other realities?

## Emerging Models

There are additional models which will better suit future Soviet strategic intentions should Soviet defensive doctrine persist. The Soviet Union has already surfaced the first new model concerning future forward defence with their publication in 1989 of a document which they claim was their defensive plan for the Group of Occupation Forces Germany (GOFG) in 1946. Internal discussions have begun on new paradigms related to the Soviet strategic posture from 1921 to the commencement of war on the Eastern Front in 1941. Recent and prospective changes in the Soviet Union and in the European political and economic structure to some extent recall conditions that existed during that period. Close analysis of that period reveals a second and third potential model: the second, regarding Soviet Strategic policy during the 1920s and up to 1935 postulates a Soviet Union beset by severe internal problems, attempting to develop a military strategy to cope with post-Treaty of Versailles realities — specifically, a Europe whose central feature was a militarily weak but dissatisfied Germany bordered on the east by a group of newly-emerged, independent but politically unstable successor states and on the west by war-wearied capitalistic powers bent on maintenance of the post-1919 *status quo*. The reduced threat to the Soviet Union posed by European nations after the First World War and the need to deal with serious internal problems dictated the Soviet adoption of a defensive military strategy characterised by maintenance of a smaller peacetime armed force and a mechanism for a transition to stronger forces in the event of war.

The third paradigm reflects Soviet strategy from roughly 1935 to 1941, when the Russians were compelled to meet the challenge of sharply-changing conditions within the Soviet Union and Europe as a whole. The increased industrial strength of the Soviet state and the emerging threat of German Nazism and Japanese militarism considerably increased the potential external threat and Soviet capabilities for responding to it. The 1930s paradigm was characterised by a more aggressive (although still ostensibly defensive) Soviet military strategy involving the maintenance of a large peacetime military force and a more efficient system for making the transition from peace to war — a system ultimately characterised by the term 'creeping up to war' [*polzanie v voinu*].

These three tentative models address a wide range of emerging military and political realities and provide a framework for analysis of likely political and military implications of future Soviet military strategies. The USSR believed the first model was applicable at a time when it planned to retain the groups of forces in the forward area. That is no longer the case. The two pre-Second World War models provide a framework for analysing Soviet strategy when Soviet forces complete their withdrawal to a national bastion. It is against the backdrop of these models that the following future judgements are made.

## Future Strategy

A wide variety of internal and external political, economic and social factors have coalesced to produce striking change in the Soviet Union and its former satellites. Although no one can predict with any degree of certainty what these changes will ultimately produce, they must be considered as the context for future Soviet military policy, doctrine and strategy.

Within the Soviet Union economic stagnation has reached crisis point. The decay of the Soviet economy and ineffective attempts to deal with it have reduced productivity and, more important in a military sense, excluded the prospect of mastering the rapid technological changes sweeping the developed world. Economic crisis has, in turn, fostered political and social turmoil which threatens the fabric of Soviet political life and society. Democratisation, unleashed in a conscious attempt to legitimise official programme for economic reform, has concurrently released new political forces, which can alter the rigid political structure of the Soviet state, and nationalism, which simultaneously generates both centripetal forces within the Russian nation and centrifugal forces on the part of the Soviet Union's national republics. Democratisation has also severely undermined the power and authority of its natural targets, the Communist party and the *nomenklatura*.[2]

These economic and political crises have, in turn, underscored vividly the class and ethnic nature of the Soviet state, have exacerbated class, ethnic and religious distinctions, and have fostered virtual low-level social warfare among classes and nationalities. This is a particularly vexing problem in light of the impending minority of Great Russians within their Soviet state.

All these forces, singly or in combination, will affect both the nature of the Soviet state and the shape and form of its military establishment in the future, as it strives to achieve a consensus regarding its position in relation to Europe and the rest of the world.

While internal factors will condition the Soviet Union's reaction to the world, in a political and military sense, the main future variable relates to the structure of the international arena itself. There, major changes are occurring that the USSR must take into account in formulating policies and strategies. The Soviet perspective now recognises the following factors:

- The arms race of the 1980s which, while creating enormous economic pressures on both sides, failed to accord military advantage to the Soviet Union (and, in fact, may have accorded advantage to the West);
- The changing international political balance, characterised, in part, by the increased political and economic power of Europe (EEC) and Japan; the opening of China to limited Western influence; the unleashing of politically potent religious forces in the Middle East, and potentially in southern Asia; and the continued poverty and political weakness of friendly Third World governments;
- The new technological revolution, principally in cybernetics, which, because of an inability to compete, places the Soviet Union at increasing disadvantage;
- The worldwide revival of nationalism and its negative effects on the *status quo*;
- The collapse of Communism in Eastern Europe and, with it, diminished Soviet influence in Europe (in a Cold War sense);
- The unification of Germany;
- The limited success of Soviet-sponsored or supported wars of national liberation, the curtailment or asserted abandonment of many military assistance programmes, and the ensuing political and economic enfeebling of Soviet client states.

These complex and inter-related internal and external factors have impelled striking change within the Soviet Union. Gorbachev's initial economic programme of acceleration [*uskorenie*], which was designed to speed up economic activity, failed and instead underscored the need for openness and debate of vital issues. The policy of *perestroika* followed, a revitalisation programme of both the economy and the military, which, like a germ developing in a Petri dish, had to be accompanied by a programme of *glasnost'* to lend it credibility and vitality. When it became clear that institutional constraints threatened to throttle *perestroika*, the ensuing programme of democratisation [*demokratisatsiia*] sought to break the institutional log-jam and legitimise reform.

Each of these stages has reinforced the dialectical truth that all trends are inter-related, and one cannot have genuine progress in one realm without commensurate progress in other important realms. This truth propelled Gorbachev, in the spring of 1990, to embrace reform on all fronts, with inherent risks, while attempting to control the entire process through the new institution of President of the Soviet Union. The military corollary of these fundamental internal and external political, economic and social changes has been a revision of Soviet military policy and declared Soviet intent to implement a defensive military doctrine. That, in turn, requires articulation of a new military strategy.

Soviet future military strategy will reflect four basic realities: first, Soviet national interest and objectives; second, the nature of perceived threats; third, Soviet perception of the nature of future war; and fourth, the potential of the material base (economy, manpower etc.) As the Russians study these realities, they are driven by habit and inclination to consider what the past has to offer in the way of solutions. They understand that study of the past offers no panaceas. But it does offer hints as to proper action at a time when conditions existed similar to those of today.

Once the Soviet leadership fully understands these realities and resolves their most acute problems, their military strategy must address the critical issues of peacetime strategic force posture, force generation, strategic deployment, and the nature and conduct of strategic operations in future wars.

## National Interests and Threat Defining

Whereas in the past many in the West have assumed the USSR's national interests and policy objectives envisioned the ultimate destruction of capitalism, current realities argue that Soviet interests today focus more on ensuring the security and survival of the Soviet state. Whether or not Soviet national interests during the Cold War (1949 – 89) were aggressive, there is now considerable similarity between current and future Soviet interests and similar Soviet interests in the 1920s and 1930s. Specifically, there is a strong case to be made for the defensive nature of Soviet national policy in general and for Soviet military policy in particular. In the last analysis, the future strategic posture of the Soviet Union will settle the issue.

One reality concerning Soviet military strategy which is as true today as it was yesterday is the fact that it reflects the perceived threat. Threat analysis in a time of change is difficult at best, and it inherently involves defining a range of threats and then fashioning a strategy which deals with a combination of the most likely and most dangerous of them. One can postulate a range of future international political relationships distinguished from one another by the degree to which each poses a threat to the Soviet Union. Four principal threat variants based on these relationship may evolve, listed here in descending order of favourability. The listing of nations within each variant are partial, and obviously tentative.

## Threat Variants

### Variant 1 (Best Case)

**Characteristics:** Economically and, to a lesser degree, politically unified Europe with German, Soviet and East European participation. abolition of all military alliances and general disarmament of all European nations. Stability based on *status quo* in Asia. This variant has never before existed.

**National Attitudes**
Group 1: Potentially hostile to the Soviet Union: (Japan, China, Iran, Afghanistan [if Mujahadin rules], Pakistan)
Group 2: Neutral or ambivalent: (Britain, France, Germany, USA, some Eastern European states)
Group 3: Friendly to the Soviet Union (some Eastern European states)

### Variant 2 (Satisfactory Case)

**Characteristics:** NATO as a reduced-scale political alliance without German participation. Unified, neutralised, and partially demilitarised Germany. Soviet Union with limited bilateral political, economic, or military agreements with selected East European nations. Continued US security role in Asia and Pacific with growing Japanese participation. This somewhat resembles political conditions existing in the 1920s.

**National Attitudes**
Group 1: Potentially hostile to the Soviet Union: (USA, Britain, France, Japan)

Group 2: Neutral or ambivalent: (Germany, some East European states)
Group 3: Friendly to the Soviet Union: (some East European states)

## Variant 3 (Unsatisfactory Status Quo)

**Characteristics:** Potentially hostile, or hostile within CFE limitations, NATO with participation by unified Germany. Soviet bilateral agreements with selected East European states. Continued US security in Asia and the Pacific shared with Japan. This continues many of the unpleasant features of Cold War relationships.

**National Attitudes**
Group 1: Hostile or potentially hostile to Soviet Union: (NATO nations, Japan, some East European states)
Group 2: Neutral or ambivalent: (some East European states)
Group 3: Friendly to Soviet Union: (some East European states)

## Variant 4 (Worst Case)

**Characteristics:** NATO dissolved and replaced by bilateral political and military agreements between US, France and Britain. Unified, militarised revisionist Germany. Competition between Soviet Union and Germany for influence in Eastern Europe. Remilitarised, expansionist Japan and diminished US influence in Asia and the Pacific. These international relationships, to some degree, resemble conditions in the 1930s.

**National Attitudes**
Group 1: Hostile to Soviet Union: (Germany, Japan, some East European states)
Group 2*: Potentially hostile to Soviet Union: (USA, Britain, France)
Group 3*: Neutral: (some East European states)
Group 4: Friendly to Soviet Union: (some East European states)

* This is a particularly volatile relationship, in that, depending on Japanese and German policies, nations in groups 2 and 3 could become friendly with the Soviet Union.

Juxtaposed with these threat variants based on international relationships and national attitudes are a series of alternatives regarding the Soviet internal situation, which could influence them. Although there are numerous possibilities, they can be lumped into three general categories, each with a specific set of probably impacts on the threat variants and *vice versa*.
**Alternative 1:** Gorbachev or a successor succeeds in reforming the

Soviet state. This would probably entail some positive economic reform and a degree of democratisation, which could involve the outright loss of the Baltic States, Moldavia, and possibly other regions, and the evolution of a federal structure which would govern the relationship between existing republics and the Soviet Union. International variants 1 and 2 would facilitate this process, variant 3 would only marginally affect it, and variant 4 could definitely inhibit the process. On the other hand, such a process within the Soviet Union would tend to foster the development of variants 1 and 2 internationally. This alternative has no precedents.[3]

**Alternative 2:** The reforms of Gorbachev or his successor fail and either democratic revolution or authoritarian reaction ensues. Although this might occur in any circumstances for internal reasons, international variants 3 or 4 could speed this outcome. A 'democratic' revolution would be likely to fragment the Soviet Union and contribute to international variants 1 or 2. Return to a more authoritarian regime (rule by party, police, union, military, or a combination of all four) would resist national fragmentation, probably by force, and promote international variants 3 and possibly 4. In addition, there is no guarantee that continued authoritarianism would stave off ultimate revolution or reform. The precedents for this alternative are, on the one hand, February 1917 and, on the other, Stalin's authoritarianism or that of his successors.

**Alternative 3:** Gorbachev or his successors muddle through with enough reform to maintain a shaky *status quo*. In this instance the Soviet government will have to contend with continuous, long-term economic, political and ethnic problems. These internal contradictions would be exacerbated by international variants 3 and 4 and would, in turn, certainly hinder achievement of variant 1, and possibly variant 2. This characterises earlier failed Soviet attempts at reform (1954, 1960, 1970s).

If one were to distil from all four threat variants all conceivable threats, they would include the following:

## All Conceivable Threats: 1995

1. Continued full NATO threat to the Soviet Union;
2. Emergence of a hostile unified Germany;
3. Strategic nuclear and peripheral threat by the USA;
4. Residual threat from a truncated NATO;
5. Foreign support of ethnic unrest in the Soviet Union;
6. Unrest in Eastern Europe with Western intervention;
7. Unrest in Eastern Europe with Soviet domestic implications;
8. Domestic ethnic unrest;

9. Nuclear and chemical weapons proliferation in hostile or potentially hostile border states;

10. Transnational threats with military implications.

In terms of likelihood and desirability, these variants break down as follows: Variants 1 and 2 least desirable; Variant 4 desirable and most likely; Variants 3, 5, 6, 9 and 10 possible; Variants 7 and 8 probable.

Since it is awkward, if not impossible, to predict one's own demise, the Soviet General Staff must plan on the basis of some sort of stability being maintained. Likewise every threat cannot be anticipated or met. In addition it is reasonable to assume that threat variant 2, or at least variant 3, will result. If so, it is also reasonable to assume that threat variants 2 or 3 are most likely and, hence, can provide a prudent basis upon which to base military policy and strategy. In fact, it is these two variants that Soviet policy-makers and strategists are today addressing. They would like to see variant 2 result, but must prudently plan for the circumstances of variant 3. The trick is to encourage the evolution of variant 2 (or even 1) by formulating a strategy (and hence a threat for the West) which does not impel Western powers to continue variant 3, but still satisfies Soviet security needs if variant 3 should persist. In this respect, and in many others, the 1920s model looks increasingly attractive.

From threat variants 2 and 3 one can distil a finite list of possible threats, which provide a reasonable and safe basis upon which to formulate a military strategy. This pared-down list might be as follows:

### Possible Threats: 1995

1. Strategic nuclear and peripheral threat by the USA;
2. Residual threat from a reduced-strength NATO;
3. Foreign support of ethnic unrest in the Soviet Union;
4. Domestic ethnic unrest;
5. Unrest in Eastern Europe with Western intervention;
6. Unrest in Eastern Europe with Soviet domestic implications;
7. Nuclear and chemical weapons proliferation in hostile or potentially hostile border states;
8. Transnational threats with military implications.

Soviet military strategy must be prepared to cope with these potential threats.

## Military Strategy

Based on existing and potential threats and their view of the nature of future war Soviet theorists must develop a military strategy which suits the political-military aims of the state. It is not unreasonable to assume that those aims, given political and economic realities, are essentially defensive. If so, that defensive posture must be adequate to meet potential threats. We earlier suggested that the threat, a combination of threat variants 2 (satisfactory) and 3 (unsatisfactory *status quo*), consisted of eight principal elements:

1. Strategic nuclear and peripheral threat by USA;
2. Residual threat from a reduced strength NATO;
3. Foreign support of ethnic unrest in the Soviet Union;
4. Domestic ethnic unrest (internal threat);
5. Unrest in Eastern Europe with Western intervention;
6. Unrest in Eastern Europe with Soviet domestic implications;
7. Nuclear and chemical weapons proliferation in hostile or potentially hostile border states;
8. Transnational threats with military implications.

Since the last five elements are essentially internal or of an indirect nature, Soviet military strategists must deal primarily with the first three elements. The nuclear threat and the conventional threat posed by a reduced-strength NATO are familiar ones whose nature is now being altered to some extent by the arms control process, which as it develops, provides a rational mechanism for measuring and, if necessary, scaling down the seriousness of the threat. The third element, foreign support for ethnic unrest, is a new dimension, which requires further clarification and definition. It also merges with the internal issue of maintaining order within the Soviet Union, which the Soviets anticipate being a matter for internal security (MVD) forces.

Given the more complex Soviet typology of war, the three most likely threats to the Soviet Union (strategic nuclear and peripheral US threat, residual threat of NATO, and foreign support of ethnic unrest in the Soviet Union) and the two likely threat variations (number 2: demilitarisation of NATO and neutrality of Germany and number 3: *status quo* with reduced NATO military threat), Soviet strategists must determine a range of war scenarios in terms of threat, form and timing. Since variant 2 is far less threatening, it is only prudent to plan on the basis of variant 3. In increasing order of seriousness, this variant could result in the following spectrum of hostile action against the Soviet Union:

*Case 1:* covert or overt support of ethnic unrest within the Soviet Union by bordering states (China, Afghanistan, Iran, Turkey, Romania, Poland, Finland);

*Case 2:* covert or overt support of ethnic unrest or indigenous generated unrest within the Soviet Union by bordering states with great power assistance (Japan, US, Britain, France, Germany);

*Case 3:* military intervention within the Soviet Union for any reason by NATO or any combination of great powers;

*Case 4:* deliberate major conventional or nuclear attack on the Soviet Union by opposing alliances or the US in concert with other powers;

*Case 5:* attack of unpredictable scope resulting from long-term crisis between major powers and the Soviet Union.

Analysis of the first four cases within the context of current and prospective arms limitations and other political and economic negotiations argues that the likelihood of their occurring is inversely proportional to their seriousness. In short:

1. Nuclear or conventional attack by NATO or the US is unlikely and will become less so as CFE negotiations progress;
2. For the above reasons, direct Western military intervention in the Soviet Union is unlikely;
3. Probable unrest in the Soviet Union is likely to afford increasing opportunity for foreign intervention in virtually all border regions, but, in particular, in Eastern Europe, and in southern and eastern Asia;
4. Planners must keep in mind the possibility of variant 5 (creeping up to war during crisis) and tailor the Soviet strategy posture accordingly.

While the first three judgements support Soviet desires to truncate their armed forces' structure and reduce its readiness posture, uncertainties associated with the fourth possibility will act as a natural brake on this process.

Based on this analysis, the geographical aspect of the threat will change considerably. During the Cold War, the principal threat to the Soviet Union emanated from the West (Europe), and only during the late 1960s did a new threat emerge in the East (China). Thus, Soviet strategists formulated a strategic posture and war plans geared to protecting those two high-priority regions.[4] Given the altered threats, these priorities will be likely to change. While CFE agreements produce (and in fact mandate) a reduction in Soviet strategic strength oriented westward, the USSR will have to continue to maintain defences in the east and, in addition, look carefully at its defensive posture in the south. These new realities argue for increased Soviet attention to building up strategic reserves in areas outside CFE guidelines regions, such as east of the Urals.[5] While satisfying CFE requirements, a build-up east of the Urals will also help the Soviet Union cope with new strategic threats to border regions in central and eastern Asia.

This geographical reapportioning of strategic resources in response to an altered threat will require the Soviets to rethink their geographical framework for planning and conducting war — specifically the current TVD concept.

The Soviet Union must also judge how future wars will begin; specifically, to what extent traditional views on that issue remain valid today and will do so in the future? As before, the central issue remains the ability to secure the strategic initiative. The traditional view, originated during the 1920s, governed Soviet strategic thought prior to the Second World War and, although somewhat modified, remained valid during the Second World War and the Cold War. The variants were:

1. Mobilisation and concentration of forces by all contending parties prior to war;
2. Partial mobilisation and concentration prior to war, but completed during war;
3. One nation attacks to achieve operational-tactical advantage, while its opponent mobilises and concentrates;
4. One nation attacks by surprise to achieve strategic advantage before its opponent can mobilise and concentrate. The most dangerous new facet of this variant is the nuclear 'first strike'.

During the 1920s the USSR planned on the basis of variants 1 and 2 above and during the 1930s on the basis of variants 2 and 3. On the eve of the Second World War variant 4 matured in the form of German *blitzkrieg*, and the Soviets were only partially prepared to deal with it. Since the end of the Second World War, and particularly since the appearance of nuclear weapons, variants 3 and 4 become the preeminent Soviet concerns in an alliance sense, for they have forced Soviet strategists to address such concepts as 'first-strikes', which vastly increase the importance of the strategic initiative.

Soviet strategy in the early 1960s focused on denying any opposing nation or alliance a first-strike capability, and in the 1970s and 1980s the Soviet concept of the theatre-strategic offensive was designed to counter variants 3 and 4 in both a nuclear and a conventional sense.

Today, as the force reduction process unfolds, Soviet military strategists must study a wider array of variations. They must remain concerned about dealing with a nuclear first-strike in the sense of variant 4, and they must also deal with the potential for full or partial mobilisation and concentration of enemy forces during periods of crisis (a modern variation of creeping up to war). In addition, they must be prepared to deal with new variations, such as ethnic unrest and foreign support of domestic unrest with no overt mobilisation or with only partial mobilisation by a foreign power (in particular, in the case of a neighbour possessing a large peacetime standing army). In essence, they face the threat of revolutionary or guerilla war on their own territory, with or without covert foreign support. This prospect blurs the traditional threat indicator of mobilisation.

Soviet study of these questions will proceed within the context of the likely threats outlined above and the national and geographical sources and focuses of those threats. The ensuing analytical process will determine Soviet judgements regarding armed forces strength, strategic posture, strategic deployment and force generation.

## Conclusion

If Soviet military strategy continues to evolve in consonance with defensive Soviet military policy and doctrine, a Soviet strategic posture will emerge which is altogether different from that of the 1970s and early 1980s. The new posture is likely to accord with models or paradigms which the Soviets have either already openly discussed or implied. Whichever model emerges, it is clear that it will be based on thorough analysis of past Soviet strategic experiences juxtaposed against changes in the contemporary and future political and military environment. Analysis of Soviet strategic defensive experiences permits further speculation regarding other prospective models. It remains for us to judge which model is most likely to emerge and then to assess its ramifications.

The original models proposed by Kokoshin, Larionov and others are a good starting point for analysis, for they offer a thorough range of options. The first model the Soviet Union suggested, that of premeditated defence at Kursk, appeared defensive only in a superficial historical light. Closer examination revealed features which contradicted its purported defensive nature. Specifically, defensive fighting took place within the framework of a Soviet strategic offensive plan, and large Soviet strategic reserves earmarked to conduct the offensive titled the correlation of forces decisively in the USSR's favour. Soviet maintenance of similar large combat-ready forces and reserves in peacetime would contradict the principal of 'defensive sufficiency' and render the strategy clearly offensive.

The Khalkin Gol and Korean model, which the USSR advanced

after the flaws of the Kursk paradigm became apparent, better matches articulated Soviet intent. It too, however, has weaknesses which cast doubt on its suitability. Soviet strategy regarding the Japanese in 1939 was only part of a larger strategy toward the more menancing foe, Germany. While overall Soviet strategy had, as yet, not become totally defensive in Europe, clearly the Russians were adopting a defensive posture in the Far East. Restraint against the Japanese at Khalkhin Gol served the larger purpose of greater readiness against the Germans. Moreover, Soviet secret reinforcement of its forces in Mongolia and its achievement of surprise make the case of Khalkhin Gol less convincing.

Subsequently, Soviet strategists have suggested a new model based on a pre-Cold War strategy. By providing details of their 1946 Group of Forces (Germany) operational plan, they have argued that their pre-Cold War strategic posture was defensive and have provided strong hints as to the nature of their desired post-Cold War strategy in a circumstance of forward defence. This defensive model provided a valid basis for discussion of the future Soviet strategic stance, but only as long as Soviet groups of forces remained in the forward area. As balanced force reductions continue and forward forces withdraw, the justification for and credibility of this strategic posture will disappear.

When Soviet forward groups of forces complete their withdrawal to the Soviet Union, entirely new models will be required to define Soviet strategic posture and its degree of 'defensiveness' in a reshaped European balance. Two such paradigms exist, one derived from the 1920s and early 1930s and one based on conditions existing from 1935 to 1941.

The paradigm warranting most attention is that of the 1920s, when the Soviet Union assessed the threat potential of Eastern European successor states, alone or in concert with Western powers. This paradigm best represents future geopolitical, strategic, economic and military relationships within a post-CFE Europe and addresses the key issue of Soviet attitudes toward Eastern European successor states and toward new European threats. As such, it offers the most valuable insights into probable Soviet military strategy of the 1990s. The 1920s paradigm suggests the Soviets will maintain lower peacetime levels of military preparedness, supplemented by a complex mobilisation system capable of rapidly tranforming the Soviet army to a wartime footing.

Another less appealing paradigm upon which future Soviet strategy may be based is that of pre-22 June 1941, when a strong and hostile Germany in the west and Japan in the east had borders contiguous to the Soviet Union. Now that the Soviet Union has admitted that their failed 1941 pre-war strategy was defensive, the Soviet strategic posture of that period can provide a basis for thoroughly analysing future strategies for defence of the Soviet Union. While this emerging model will provide an excellent basis for evaluating military 'defensive sufficiency', it will also inherently require detailed discussion of the political and military context — namely the European political and military balance as a whole.

The model of June 1941, however, poses three problems. First, Soviet theorists have recently accorded the adoption of a 1941 model a very low degree of probability because nuclear deterrents have largely neutralised all analogous threats. Second, they have only recently admitted that their military strategy on the eve of war was defensive. Third, and most important, the defensive strategy of 1941 failed. Despite these problems, the 1941 model warrants attention. Soviet implementation of a similar strategy in a post-Cold War period will have to deal more effectively with potential threats similar to that of 1941, particularly if nuclear deterrence erodes as a valid defensive concept. Adoption of a new 1941-type strategy will provide the Soviet Union with the potential collateral benefit of being able to insist on external political and military concessions to reduce the threat and, hence, validate the strategy.

Should the Soviet Union rid itself of the ghosts of 1941, this defensive strategic paradigm or that of the 1920s has the potential for offering considerable leverage in political and military negotiations with the West. If, in fact, defensiveness failed in 1941 because the USSR seemingly underestimated the external threat, then Soviet adoption of a similar strategy in the future will require the negation of any possibility of such a threat.

Two such potential threats immediately come to mind. The first, in the form of NATO, exists today in Soviet perceptions. The second, in the form of a unified and militarily powerful Germany, within or outside of NATO, looms as a potential future threat. Each threat, in its own right, must be dealt with for a Soviet 1920s- or 1941-type strategy to be viable in the future. It is indeed possible that such a Soviet strategy could become a vehicle for resolving both problems. This strategy would be viable if the USSR (and Europeans themselves) can be convinced that NATO's military power has been reduced to clearly defensive proportions, and if a weaker NATO emerged in lieu of the creation of a larger German military establishment. This would offer better changes for future political stability in Europe through continued (although reduced) US presence, thus avoiding the major problem following the First Word War, when a power vacuum existed in Europe, which was ultimately filled by warring nations.

Whatever discussions occur about which model the Soviet Union proposes and implements, another model — Manchuria — requires tangential study. The Manchurian model stands as a classic case when a defensive force structure and posture is rapidly converted into an effective offensive one through a combination of *khitrost* (strategem), *maskirovka* (deception), and a massive covert strategic and operational regrouping of forces with the use of fortified regions to cover the mobilisation. This extreme example replicates numerous, documented cases of similar transformations during operations on the Eastern Front in the Second World War. In a future context, this model embraces the circumstances of creeping up to war over an extended period. Inherent in it are issues such as transition to war and mobilisation of the front and rear. Soviet military theorists and planners continue to assess this three-*front* strategic operation in detail. Admittedly, Manchuria was an extreme case, carried out within a particular political and military context. Yet it was representative of a host of lesser examples when a defensive or less threatening posture was secretly and effectively transformed into a major offensive threat. Although many would argue that such a transformation would be unlikely to occur in contemporary or future circumstances, prudence dictates caution. In short, verification must ensure that at all times and in all circumstances, and whatever model emerges, Soviet forces should not 'be more than they seem'.

The future shape and composition of the Soviet Union will obviously also have an impact on future Soviet military strategy. The foregoing analysis applies most directly to a Soviet state which retains control over all or most of its current territory, either on a federal basis or through confederation. Independence of the Baltic Republics, Moldavia, and some Transcaucasus territory would be likely to accelerate movement toward strategic defensiveness and concern for economic restructuring in the basically Slavic core of the new Soviet Union (RSFSR, Ukraine and Belorussia). Further fragmentation, entailing the independence of the Ukraine and/or Belorussia could severely affect Soviet status as a superpower and could produce either increased defensiveness and reform or reaction and retrenchment, based on a more virulent form of Great Russian nationalism.

The 1990s promise revolutionary changes in existing political and military relationships in Europe and, in fact, throughout the world. In large part, this revolution has occurred because of important political, economic and social pressure within the Soviet Union and Eastern Europe, which are also affecting Soviet military policy, doctrine and strategy. The most discernible effects so far have been the Soviet Union's proclamation of 'defensiveness' in its military doctrine and its ensuing search for new strategic solutions. Whatever future strategic posture the Soviet Union adopts, it will be a key element in this revolution. It will dictate the nature of future political and military relationships in Europe and the world, and the degree of stability of any new political and military structures which evolve.

The future Soviet strategic posture will, in the last analysis, reveal the true nature of Soviet military doctrine and dictate the form and mission of the Soviet army. There are issues within the realm of strategy that the Soviet Union must work out anew or refine. Among these issues are the nature of the threat; concept of future war; scope of theatres of war and military operations' peacetime military strength, dispositions, and force readiness; and strategic deployment and force generation [mobilisation] schemes. All these issues must be resolved without violating Soviet security interests, and each must facilitate smooth transition from peace to war.

Resolution of these strategic issues will have major implications at lower levels of military science, for operational and tactical concepts will be constrained and governed by strategy and the realities of contemporary and future war. Hence, operational art and tactics will emphasise concepts for non-linear warfare, manoeuvre and long-range fires and indicate greater defensiveness than previously. Force structure at all levels will likewise conform to strategic, political and budgetary constraints and become smaller, leaner, more flexible, defensively oriented and, if Soviet desires are realised, of higher quality. Most important, the force structure will be more expandable to meet wartime requirements.

All these critical issues have their roots in the past. A clearer understanding of the past will better enable us to comprehend and manage the transition to the future.

## Notes

1   In the Soviet view, military strategy is the highest realm of military art (*voennoe iskusstvo*) 'encompassing the theory and practice of preparing a country and its armed forces for war and of planning for and conducting war and strategic operations'. Within the context of national and military policy, military strategy investigates the laws, mechanisms, and strategic nature of war and methods used to conduct it, and works out theoretical bases for planning, preparing for, and conducting war and strategic operations.

2   The *nomenklatura* is the finite group of party members in rank order who occupy key party, governmental, economic, and other positions within virtually all Soviet institutions. It, in essence, represents an upper class of Communist 'nobility'.

3   One could argue that the Soviet Union faced similar conditions after it signed the Treaty of Brest – Litovsk (1918). By virtue of that treaty and other post-war conditions (civil war and Allied intervention), for varying lengths of time, the Soviet Union lost possession of the Baltic states, the Ukraine, Georgia, Armenia, Azerbaijan, the Far East, and Tanu Tuva. As soon as the Soviets regained their strength, most of these regions were re-incorporated into the Soviet Union.

4   In August 1969 the Soviet Union added a 16th military district by separating the Central Asian Military District from the Turkestan Military District, ostensibly to respond to an increased threat from China.

5   In 1989 the Soviets again combined the Central Asian and Turkestan Military

Districts. The recent combination of the Ural and Volga Military Districts into a single Ural-Volga Military District reduced the overall number of military districts to 14. This marks a diminution in the perceive threat from China, and perhaps increased Soviet concern for the southern flank.

# References

Arbatov, A. G. *Oboronitel'naia dostatochnost' i bezopasnost'* (Defensive sufficiency and security). Moscow: Znanie, 1990.

Babakov, A. *Vooruzhennye Sily SSSR posle viony* [1945 – 1986] (The Armed Forces of the USSR after the war [1945 – 1986]). Moscow: Voenizdat, 1987 in Reznichenko, V. G. 'Sovetskie vooruzhennye sily v poslevoennyi period' (Soviet armed forces in the post-war period), *Kommunist vooruzhennykh sil* (Communist in the armed forces), (January 1988), 86 – 88.

Glantz, David M. *August Storm: Soviet Tactical and Operational Combat in Manchuria. 1945*, Leavenworth Papers No. 8. Ft. Leavenworth, KS: Combat Studies Institute, 1983.

Glantz, David M. *August Storm: The Soviet 1945 Strategic Offensive in Manchuria*, Leavenworth Papers No. 7. Ft. Leavenworth, KS: Combat Studies Institute, 1983.

Glantz, David M. *Soviet Military Deception in the Second World War*. London: Frank Cass and Co Ltd., 1989.

Glantz, David M. (ed). *From the Vistula to the Oder: Soviet Offensive Operations — October 1944 — March 1945, 1985 Art of War Symposium. A Transcript of Proceedings*. Carlisle, PA: Centre for Land Warfare, US Army War College, 1986.

Iazov, D. T. 'V interesakh obshchei bezopasnosti mira' [In the interest of general security and peace], *Izvestija* [News], 27 February 1989, p. 3.

Kokoshin, A. and Larionov, V. V. 'Kurskaia bitva v svete sovremennoi oboronitel'-noi doktriny' (The Kursk battle in light of contemporary defensive doctrine), *Mirovaia ekonomika i mezhdunarodnye otnosheniia* (World economics and international relations), hereafter cited as *MEMO*, (August 1987).

Kokoshin, A., and Larionov, V. V. *Predotvrashchenie voiny* (The Prevention of war). Moscow: Progress Publishers, 1990. 'Protivostoianiia sil obshchego naznacheniia v kontekste obespecheniia strategicheskio stabil 'nosti' (The counterposition of general purpose forces in the context of strategic stability), *MEMO*, (June 1988), pp 23 – 31.

Ogarkov, V. 'Strategiia voennaia' (strategy Military), *Sovetskaia voennaia entsiklopediia* (Soviet military encyclopedia), 8 vols. Moscow: Voenizdat, 1976 – 1980, 7:555 – 556, 563.

'Operativnyi plan deistvii Gruppy sovetskikh okkupatsionnykh voisk v Germanii' (Operational plan for actions of the Group of Soviet Occupation Forces in Germany), *VIZh*, No. 2 (February 1989), 26 – 31 (with map).

Sbytov, N. A. *Voennaia mysl' y iadernyi vek* (Military thought in the nuclear era). Moscow: Voenizdat, 1990.

Sokolovsky, V. D. (ed), *Voennaia strategiia* (Military strategy), Moscow: Voenizdat, 1963).

'Soviets Shifting Military Strategy', *The Kansas City Times*, 11 March 1989, p. A9, which quotes testimony of A. A. Kokoshin in March 1989. Testimony before the US Congress; House Armed Services Committee.

Turbiville, Graham, Jr. *Trip Report – Seminar on Military Doctrine*. Ft Leavenworth, KS: Soviet Army Studies Office, 9 February 1990. *The Military Balance*. London: International Institute for Strategic Studies, 1989.

Vnotchenko, L. N. *Pobeda na dal'nem vostoke* (Victory in the Far East). Moscow: Voenizdat, 1966.

Zhurkin, V. V., Karaganov, S. A. and Kortunov, A. A. 'Vyzovy bezopostnosti – starye i novye' (Challenges to security – old and new), *Kommunist*, No. 1 (January 1988), 43.

CHAPTER 9

# Soviet Sea Power for the 1990s

## JOHN MOORE

SIR ARTHUR BRYANT wrote 'Though at no time has more history been written by highly trained and conscientious academic historians, researching and clarifying, for the benefit of fellow scholars, every detail of the past, little or nothing of it has contributed to an awareness of the broad sweep.' This analysis is, unfortunately, often true of studies which appear under the title of 'Soviet Sea Power'. A vast amount of unbelievably detailed work is produced, much enhanced by the use of modern computers. However the scope of such studies is very frequently extremely limited and the results often couched in arcane and complex language. While producing much of interest to their fellow researchers, the results achieved by these academic beavers contribute little to 'the broad sweep'.

The ultimate aim of intelligence work is the production of a balanced and objective assessment of another country's capabilities. When this is married to an estimate of that state's political intentions the result is, very simply, an indication of any likely threat to one's own kingdom, republic or alliance. The intelligence assessment of maritime affairs has to examine all aspects of sea power, an extremely wide-ranging and diffuse subject. Every historian concerned has his or her own definition of 'sea power' but, for the purposes of this chapter, it is worth considering certain major aspects as they affect the Soviet Union.

Of prime importance is the country's geographical location. Covering huge distances from West to East and North to South, the USSR has unimpeded access to only the Arctic Ocean and the north-west Pacific. While this has little effect on peacetime mercantile traffic it would, in wartime, impose considerable restrictions on naval deployments.

The attitude of the people to the sea is a matter of some considerable importance but, in this case, a clear definition of 'the people' is needed. In a union in which there are over a hundred major languages and an equal number of, if not more, life styles, it is imprudent to speak of the 260 million inhabitants as 'a people'. The inhabitant of Leningrad is continually aware of the sea but, some 2,000 miles to the south-east, a Khirgiz in Alma Ata may be unaware of its existence. Yet, though the threats to present Soviet territory have normally come from the land, the old Russian navy produced many great seamen and not a few fine commanders.

Operations at sea, despite the immense array of modern devices, still depend to a very great degree on the men (and women) who provide the ships' companies. In the case of the Soviet merchant navy these are long-service volunteers who have undergone extensive technical and practical training both on land and at sea. By comparison the junior ratings and a fair proportion of the senior ratings in the navy are conscripts from all parts of the USSR, serving for three years, the first six months of which form the training period.

The result of these two methods of manning is the provision of a homogeneous, professional force for the merchant ships while the personnel in the navy consists, in the lower grades, of young men (aged 18 – 21) from diverse races and backgrounds. Many with neither knowledge of, nor particular interest in, the sea. The emphasis which is put on such things as Navy Days, the entertainment of veterans, many sporting beards and banks of medals, the great memorials, the presentation of bouquets to visiting and bashful sailors and the conscious rewriting of the history of dubious naval incidents as well as the enhancement of successful operations is clearly aimed at a consolidation of 'tradition'.

The other main foundation of sea power is a stable economy, the lack of which has been overcome in the past in the USSR by the diversion of resources to those elements considered of overwhelming importance by the Kremlin.

Thus we find that the three main bases for the sea power of a state are deficient in the Soviet Union. Geographically the country is hemmed in, the population as a whole has little concept of the sea and the economy is in a parlous state. Yet, despite these disadvantages, the USSR has a navy second only in size to that of the USA and a merchant navy tonnage 25% larger than the American. When, to these figures are added the largest fishing fleet in the world, the biggest fleet of ice-breakers and a research and survey fleet which outnumbers the total of such ships operating under Western ensigns, there is clearly some discrepancy between traditional expectations and Soviet practice. Before considering whether this extraordinary maritime expansion can be supported in the immediate future we must inspect the reasons and the methods which have impelled it over the last 45 years.

Although the total coastline of the USSR measures some 26,000 miles, only a comparatively small section of this is available for all-the-year navigation and, therefore, the ship building and berthing. By mid-1945 it was possible to count the cost of the Great Patriotic War — 24 major ports which had been in German hands were inoperative, nearly 70% of the alongside berths in the country as well as 80% of its cargo-handling equipment and warehouse space had been destroyed. Over 4,000 wrecks littered the inland waterways. There were no functioning shipyards in the area which had been occupied by the Germans and there was a serious lack of both trained personnel and technical training establishments. The navy had lost some half of its surface ships and many of its submarines; the construction programme was destroyed, apart from a small number of vessels completed at Severodvinsk, near Archangel, and the two main Pacific yards. In the 1930s the officer corps had suffered severely at the hands of Stalin's executioners while over 400,000 sailors had been transferred to fight on land during the war. The overall technical standard of the ships surviving in 1945 was abysmally low by Allied standards — the existence of sonar and radar having only recently been discovered.

Against this background the new construction programmes planned in the immediate post-war period seem wildly optimistic. There were to be a least four aircraft carriers and four battle-cruisers, 45 cruisers, 210 (or more) destroyers, and a minimum of 1,200 submarines completed by 1965. The merchant fleet, which consisted of 573 ships of some two million deadweight tons, was to be expanded by 600,000 dwt by 1950 under the fourth Five-Year Plan. With all training having been at a standstill during the war and the vast proportion of naval sailors occupied ashore, the manning of such large numbers of ships at a time of national reconstruction presented a formidable problem.

The death of Stalin in 1953 and the subsequent variations in the leadership caused what was less a change of aim than a change in direction. The urge for expansion, the necessity for defending the homeland and the requirement to support the flanks of the army remained paramount. Khrushchev appointed Admiral Sergei Gorshkov, then aged 45, as C-in-C Soviet Navy, a post which he was to hold throughout a period of unparalleled expansion and change. The Stalin programme gave way to one in which missiles and nuclear propulsion rapidly took pride of place. Innovation with an occasional glimpse of revolutionary thought became particularly clear from 1967 onwards. Up to this time development of surface-to-surface missiles had affected the design of both surface ships and submarines, though they appeared more as appendages rather than as part of an integrated weapon system. From 1967 this all changed. The new helicopter carriers and the 'Kresta II' cruisers, showed a change of emphasis from surface action to anti-submarine operations. In 1971 the first 'Krivak' class frigate appeared, continuing the trend. This was about the point when various Western intelligence analysts were busy seeking an overall pattern of Soviet development. Pre-1967 construction was of very little help; the Soviet designers of the early 1950s were feeling their way but designs had been agreed by the early 1960s and what a mass of work had gone into these decisions! Carriers, cruisers, frigates, three classes of submarines and numerous smaller ships and craft — the design potential was clearly immense. Nor was any of them, except the 'Yankee' class of ballistic missile submarines, dependent on Western counterparts. This was all native planning, much of it the result of a vast amount of research, much of it recorded in the Soviet press. But even this did not prepare Western naval intelligence for the astonishing 'Alfa' class submarine, the first of which was completed as a prototype in 1972. It was not until 1979 that the first production model was at sea, an astounding boat with a speed of 45 knots, a maximum diving depth of 3,000 ft, using a titanium hull for greater strength, a lead-bismuth reactor for a much higher power-to-weight ratio, probably a form of super-conducting electric motor and with a complement of 40 – 45 achieved by a great deal of automation. As the prototype had been laid down in the early 1960s, the main design work belonged to the 1958 – 61 period, an astonishing effort considering that the original nuclear boat of the 'November' class had only just been commissioned at that time.

Scrutiny of the Soviet scientific press dating from the mid-1960s onwards shows the immense amount of work achieved on such subjects as hull-form, boundary layer control, elastic surfaces, magnetohydro-dynamics, drag reduction by polymers and many other apparently obscure and esoteric subjects. Western scientists also produced a con-siderable body of published works on similar themes but the important point is that, in the militarily-oriented Soviet economy, money was made available to develop practical applications of theoretical dis-coveries. One has only to study the form of Soviet submarines and compare them with their Western contemporaries to see how far this development was taken.

From the early 1970s to the present day there has been a steady progression of designs of surface ships, submarines and naval aircraft. Admiral Gorshkov's aim was a 'balanced fleet'. In 1975 he wrote; 'The development and building of surface ships are in keeping with their potential in the creation of a modern, balanced nuclear missile fleet' and by the time he handed over his post to Admiral Chernavin in December 1985 the navy had made great strides to this goal. By 1990 the fruits of the 'development and building' are to be seen in the four main fleets of the Soviet navy.

The stark figures of Orders of Battle and Deletions must, however, be viewed with caution. At one time in the mid-1930s the Royal Navy had 15 capital ships listed; what the list did not show was that five were lying alongside because there were insufficient sailors to man them. The Soviet navy has no problems over numbers. The conscripts continue to roll in but the training problem still exists and the overall standard of lower deck efficiency is still in question.

This year's deletion list in *Jane's Fighting Ships* contains 45 submarines, seven cruisers, 57 destroyers and 38 frigates — an impressive total of 147 major warships in only four years. What is does not show, though the editor emphasises it in his Foreword, is that only a very few of these ships were originally completed less than 30 – 40 years ago. Such a weeding out, similar to that undertaken in the US navy nearly 20 years ago, was long overdue and has by no means yet been completed.

A more important Table in *Jane's* is that showing the current building programme. In May 1990 this included four ballistic missile submarines, four cruise missile submarines, 12 attack nuclear boats, five diesel submarines, two aircraft carriers, one battle-cruiser, one cruiser, eight destroyers, 11 frigates, four missile corvettes, four fast attack craft, five minesweepers, one LST, 16 hovercraft and several auxiliaries. This list, by itself, shows a not inconsiderable navy, and when added to a total of some 1,700 warships of all types from ballistic missile submarines to fast attack craft it is apparent that the deletions of the last three years have made little difference to what is today a very formidable fleet. Nor is there any sign of a diminution of the building programme. The US Director of Naval Intelligence, in a recent report to Congress, stated that in 1989 the tonnage of submarines commissioned was the highest since 1980 and major warship construction at a 20-year peak.

Fifteen years ago Admiral Gorshkov listed the tasks for which the Soviet navy must be prepared:

- escort of submarines.
- anti-surface ship operations.
- amphibious assault.
- mine counter-measures.
- interdiction of sea communications.
- anti-submarine operations.
- defence against aircraft/missile attacks.
- use of all forms and types of aircraft.
- employment of all forms of unconventional ships and craft.

It is worth considering how relevant these nine tasks are today, how the emphasis may have changed and how capable the Soviet navy will be to discharge them in the 1990s. The listing is interesting in that it covers all aspects of current naval warfare except one; the logistic support of squadrons on long deployments. This is a task of continual concern to planners and one which absorbs a considerable proportion of the available escorts.

What appears to be changing is the priority given to the various tasks. The all-embracing term 'escort of submarines' stemmed from several sources — a comprehensive study of the defeat of the U-boat campaign in the Second World War, the impact of nuclear attack submarines on anti-submarine operations and the necessity to ensure the survival of the SSBNs (ballistic missile submarines). In fact a somewhat better description, though more prolix, would have been 'the use of available forces to protect the passage of submarines to their patrol areas and to ensure their subsequent protection in those areas'. This was an impossible feat in the days when SSBNs carried comparatively short-range weapons but today, with ballistic missiles reaching out 4,500 miles and cruise missiles over 2,000 miles, the undertaking is certainly a great deal easier. For both SSBNs and other submarines, chances of survival have been much improved by the considerable advances in silencing which have taken place in the last 10 years or so.

This progress may have been one of the factors which lay behind the very recent support given by Admiral Chernavin, the present C-in-C Soviet Navy, to the interdiction of merchant shipping as a primary task. These operations would be much assisted by modern satellite surveillance, providing the coverage for which Admiral Dönitz continually asked the Luftwaffe in 1939 – 45.

Anti-surface ship operations remain a major priority. The somewhat lame theory that the major reasons for this task were the defence of the 'bastions' in which SSBNs operate and the defence of Soviet territory against carrier task forces is rarely heard today. As the building programme has unfolded over the last 15 years Gorshkov's intention has become clearer. The Soviet navy will, by 1992, be able to deploy two carrier battle groups, one each in the Northern and Pacific Fleet areas. The completion of the first two of the 75,000-ton 'Ulyanovsk' class carriers in the latter half of the decade will provide a major reinforcement for anti-surface ship operations.

Admiral Gorshkov, as a young Rear-Admiral, had a great deal of personal involvement in amphibious operations in the Black Sea and Sea of Azov during the Second World War. It was, therefore, no surprise that, within two years of his appointment as C-in-C, the first purpose-built, indigenous amphibious vessels were laid down and that such operations were high on his list of priorities.

During the years 1942 – 45 the Soviet navy, whose predecessors in the Imperial Fleet had shown great interest in mine-warfare, was much involved in both mine-laying and sweeping. This was also true of all countries involved in that war but the Soviet navy, unlike most Western navies, maintained a building programme into the 1980s. Mines can be laid from ships, submarines and aircraft but their clearance requires sophisticated and specialised vessels. It is the appreciation of this fact which has kept this aspect of warfare high on the Soviet priority list.

The next four of the remaining five tasks on the list are self-evidently necessary to a navy of any pretensions but the last remains of concern and importance. In 1930 Soviet interest in the use of parachute forces led to the formation of *Spetsnaz*, a unit from which small groups were detached for special and clandestine operations. Actions in the Great Patriotic War emphasised the value of such highly trained groups but, once the war was over, *Spetsnaz* was, like the Naval Infantry, disbanded. Both were reformed, the former probably in the late 1950s and the latter in the early 1960s. Today there is a brigade of *Spetsnaz* attached to each of the four fleets and their activities well merit the term 'unconventional'.

Thus we find that the tasks are similar to those of 1975 though the priorities have been slightly reshuffled. Two vital factors have, however, been greatly improved — reconnaissance and communications. Accurate positional information on hostile deployment give time to divert, regroup or close. If the information is 'real time' the advantages are even greater and this will be the function of modern satellite reconnaissance when it reaches this standard of excellence. What this facility can do now, however, is to lessen the need for cover against hostile surface forces whose position, course and speed should be known within useful limits. What it does not, and will not, do is to provide intelligence of dived submarines. For this purpose the Soviet submarines must rely on their sonar which is still, probably, several paces behind Western ability. The towed array is now a most valuable warning device but there is no firm evidence that Soviet boats are so fitted. Modern Western sonars enjoy a high standard of signal processing to eliminate extraneous contacts. There is no firm evidence that Soviet boats are so fitted. If these two assumptions are correct then the furry-hatted submariner will have an anxious passage because no number of surface ships, equally behind-the-times in their equipment, can provide the necessary warning, being able only to produce a confusing noise barrier for their underwater colleague.

The improvements in communications have been essential to the dissemination of intelligence and the redeployment of forces. The modern development of ELF (Extremely Low Frequency) transmissions, though their transmission rate is very slow, warn a submarine of the need to reach listening depth for a swifter and more comprehensive message. But not all Soviet boats are fitted for ELF reception and surface ships have no need for this facility.

Soviet satellite communications are effective and long-ranging, a valuable adjunct in the lead-in to surface-to-surface operations. As has already been mentioned the navy is well endowed with powerful surface ships and a typical task force, drawn from current deployments to the Northern Fleet, gives some idea of this capability.

2 Aircraft Carriers (*Kiev* and *Tbilisi*)
1 Battle Cruiser (*Kirov*)
1 Cruiser (*Marshal Ustinov*)
5 DDG (*Otchyanny, Otlichny, Udaloy, Kulakov, Vasilevsky*)
3 FFG (*Rezky, Rezvy, Ryanny*)

The carrier *Tbilisi* can accommodate 24 high performance fighter aircraft and up to 18 helicopters in peacetime and, it is claimed, an overall total of 60 aircraft in wartime. In addition she mounts a group of 240-mile SSMs. (surface-to-surface missiles) — with HE or nuclear warheads — and 24 vertical-launch tubes for SAMs (surface-to-air missiles). *Kiev* carries 13 VTOSL aircraft and 21 helicopters as well as eight 300-mile SSMs, an assortment of SAMs and A/S (anti-submarine) missiles. The battle cruiser *Kirov* has 20 240-mile SSMs, 16 SAM launchers, a twin A/S missile launcher plus gun armament and three helicopters. The cruiser, *Marshal Ustinov*, carries an even heavier SSM battery of 16 300-mile missiles as well as SAMs, guns and a helicopter. The first two DDGs of the 'Sovremenny' class are designed for surface action with eight 60-mile SSMs, an assortment of SAMs and guns and a helicopter while the other three, of the 'Udaloy' class, are A/S ships with eight A/S missile launchers, SAMs and guns and two helicopters. The A/S effort is continued by the three 'Krivak' class frigates with four A/S missile launchers. SAMs and guns. None of these ships is more than 10 years old, all are capable of at least 30 knots, all, except *Tbilisi*, carry torpedoes, while there is a bewildering array of radar and ECM. If the aircraft, the sensors and the armament are well-maintained and functioning and if the ships' companies are efficient then this is a formidable fighting force.

The main strength of the amphibious forces lies in three LPDs, 38 LSTs and 39 LSMs — sufficient, allowing for a 60% availability of ships, to lift the entire Naval Infantry of 12,000 men. This would be insufficient, taking into account the wide dispersion of the ships, for more than a large raid. But, also widely dispersed, are some 120 merchant ships with inbuilt facilities for carrying troops, armour and equipment, in all some 10 divisions, although this figure has been criticised as being either too low or too high. Whichever way it is, it demonstrates a considerable lift capacity for soldiers trained in amphibious work.

The 340 MCM vessels ranging down from the 100 ocean minesweepers would, in the event of an amphibious landing, have to transfer a proportion of their strength to clear the path for the assault force. This would still, using 60% availability once more, leave enough to carry out wire, magnetic and acoustic sweeping of sufficient major ports and their approaches. Such operations would also include MCM helicopters (Mi-8 and Mi-14) but there appears to be little emphasis on mine-hunting as practised in Western navies. So once again there are indications that the navy is reasonably well supplied with hardware but, unless they become involved in NATO exercises in the future, there is little chance of assessing the efficiency of the crews.

Anti-submarine operations have been touched on already but further consideration of this vital subject is necessary. Soviet ASW doctrine has been many years in development, moving forward from the days when a shore-based command received the raw data from the hunting group, analysed it and directed operations. By the early 1970s joint operations with ships, submarines and aircraft were being exercised and, by that time, ship-borne helicopters were becoming involved. It is significant that a high proportion of Soviet naval intelligence operations have been targeted on Western submarine and ASW technology. As submarines become quieter the importance of signal processing and computer analysis increases, two fields in which the Soviets have lagged behind. How far this gap has been bridged by the activities of such traitors as the Walker group in the USA it is impossible to say and how far any current fiscal restraints in the USSR will affect research and development is unknown. But it has been apparent for some time that the Soviet authorities are as aware as their Western counterparts that the progressive silencing of submarines is making advances in acoustic detection more and more difficult. For a considerable time a fair measure of their research effort has been directed towards non-acoustic detection methods. These vary from such means as internal waves caused by a dived submarine's movement and the magnetic influence of a steel body to minute thermal changes in the ocean and chemical deposits in the wake. These are probably but a few of the avenues of interest but one thing is certain — Soviet scientists are of a very high standard and have been employed in considerable numbers on such projects for a considerable time. There is no certainty that if a non-acoustic method of ASW is perfected in the next few years it will be by the Western navies.

Current political developments, both in the USSR and the other Warsaw Pact countries, have not, so far, had any noticeable impact on the Soviet navy other than the probably cessation of building programmes such as the East German 'Parchim II' class frigates and the possibly revived Polish construction of 'Ropucha' class LSTs. But, due to the long-term aspect of warship building, evidence of change may be some time in coming. The long-standing Soviet habit of maintaining a sort of 'come-in-handy' store of elderly ships and submarines (now, like the 'Buffer's store' in a British ship, being weeded out for inspection) may be transmuted into a determination to force through the completion of what is currently on the building ways. We have already seen that this is a very considerable amount in both types and numbers and therefore represents a huge financial outlay. An analysis of the major warship programmes shows one thing very clearly: any reductions in construction should become evident by 1992 at the latest. The vital date is that of launching, thus freeing the building way, dock or whatever method is used for the next keel or prefabricated sections. Even the largest SSBNs are only some two years from being laid down to launch. Thus a 'Delta IV' laid down in 1990 could be in the water by 1992. It could be argued that building time might be extended but Western experience has been that such an expedient merely adds to the overall cost.

The aircraft-carrier programme under way at Nikolayev South yard illustrates the earlier point. *Tbilisi* was launched on 5 December 1985 and her sister, *Riga*, was laid down in the same month. The latter was launched in November 1988 and the following month the larger *Ulyanovsk* was laid down in *Riga's* place. Allowing for a somewhat longer building time for the bigger ship, she should be in the water by late 1992.

Similar simple calculations hold good for the other types of ships and submarines. Early decisions are therefore needed if the various programmes are to be reorganised. It is a matter of debate whether Admiral Chernavin's support for the interdiction of merchant shipping is a pointer to the way future plans may be laid. Gorshkov so often referred to submarines and aircraft as the navy's primary strike arms that Chernavin is merely changing emphasis on past statements but we would be excused for seeking some other motivation than a theoretical tactical enquiry.

The Soviet navy is generally seen as a huge groups of ships and submarines while the less visible SNAF (Soviet Naval Air Force) receives too little attention. The 70,000 officers and men (more than in all branches of the Royal Navy) operate nearly 1,700 aircraft which can be divided into five main divisions. The first contains 350 strike bombers and 170 fighter bombers while the second, primarily concerned with reconnaissance, electronic warfare and tanker support, numbers 250 fixed wing aircraft and 30 helicopters. The anti-submarine force of 230 fixed wing machines and 320 helicopters is closely related to the 20-strong MCM helicopter detachment. Transport and training are coped with by 320 aircraft split evenly amongst the four fleets. This is a comparatively small force compared with the inventory of over

5,000 with the USN and USMC and the basic designs of many of its larger airframes date back many years. However, in the same manner as many Soviet ships and submarines have been updated over the years, the aircraft have kept pace with both sensor and weapon development. An example is the string of variants of the huge Tu95 Bear strategic bomber which first flew in 1954. Nine different forms have appeared over the years, three of which, 'D' (reconnaissance), 'F' (Tu142) (anti-submarine) and 'J' (Elint), totalling 125 aircraft, are used only by the SNAF. Even the Mach 2 Tu22M/26 'Backfire' dates back to 1969 and the only naval aircraft with a first flight date later than 1980 are the Ka27 'Helix' helicopter and the MiG29 'Fulcrum' fighter reported as part of the air-group in *Tbilisi*.

The argument over the future of the SNAF could run like this — the navy needs aircraft; those designs which it has have proved successful over many years of confrontation; therefore retain the design, reduce overall numbers by natural wastage and, should replacements be required, up-date past designs. It would be a logical curse and a great deal of Soviet naval planning has been proved to be both pragmatic and logical. What effect the CFE talks will have on land-based SNAF aircraft remains to be seen but one further logical act would be to earmark as many 'Flankers', 'Fulcrums' and 'Frogfoots' as possible as sea-borne aircraft for *Riga* and the two 'Ulyanovsk' class carriers.

Which, in a somewhat roundabout way, leads us to the confused matter of naval arms control. 'Confused' because nobody has had the time to produce suggestions for any sensible method of reaching agreement. It is far easier to delete or reduce a type of missile, whether intercontinental or battlefield, a variety of main battle tank or fighter aircraft than it is to address oneself to types of ship which should be struck from the inventory. If it were suggested that aircraft carriers should be the first casualties, Bethesda naval hospital would be crowded with senior officers of the USN suffering from apoplexy. Delete frigates? What is a frigate? The British define a 'frigate' as a ship with a primary A/S role. But the Soviet Union has cruisers and destroyers, even 17,500 ton helicopter carriers, with precisely that role. So do we delete A/S ships? 'Not on your life', half a hundred naval staffs would cry in chorus. How about banning submarines? Wouldn't that be a logical and stabilising move? 'Well, yes', could be the reply; 'but who is going to persuade the growing number of small navies to give up their newly-acquired submarine forces which, if the major powers committed underwater *felo de se*, would rule the roost?' 'Well, let's remove missile carrying ships.' What is a missile carrying ship/craft? Anything from a 100,000-ton aircraft-carrier to a 200-ton missile craft and the latter is, so far as missiles are concerned, more lethal. So that is a dead-end.

Well let us try missiles because every type of ship/craft can now carry SSMs. Once again who is going to check on the smaller navies? What response will one have from India with the most powerful navy in the Indian Ocean? Will China be prepared to surrender its long-sought capability?

Therefore, if the naval powers, major and minor, cannot reach agreement on the reduction of numerical and capability levels — and it must be remembered that it is the simplicity of oceanic deployment which makes such an accord so difficult to achieve — what then? Would some form of limitation on deployment serve a useful purpose? Singapore's six missile corvettes have no more than 20 miles to deploy to threaten the transfer of major naval forces from the Pacific to the Indian Ocean and vice versa, should their government so decree. Oman's four fast attack craft (missile) could make the passage of the Hormuz Strait most unattractive, should their government so decree. Minor naval powers could have a decisive influence on maritime affairs and, unlike the superpower dialogue on vast nuclear weapons, any discussion of deployment must take this into account.

So, if numerical cuts are too difficult and geographical limitations illogical, what is left? We already have a system of notification of exercises. Could this be extended even to the point of having observers embarked in the ships participating in a deployment or an exercise? There would, inevitably, be problems of security which could be alleviated by a sensible choice of the observers' ship or ships. The results could well be worth the effort.

The next five years will, very probably, set the pattern for the future but they will be interlaced with a series of imponderables. A few illustrations suggest that a precipitate and wholesale reduction of Western navies could well encourage unbalanced and bellicose leaders to take action at sea. General Galtieri made his cardinal mistake in the Falklands; might Qadhafi or some like-minded rough-neck see a chance to further his ambitions in the manner of Saddam Husain? Might China's old men decide on aggressive action over their claim to the Paracels and other island groups in the South China Sea? Might some outpouring of Muslim fundamentalism threaten to disrupt foreign oil supplies? Might Israel's intransigence cause yet another imbroglio which could spill over into the approaches of the Suez Canal? These are all possibilities which would affect the maritime trade of all nations and require naval support.

The Soviet merchant navy has world-wide interests, calling at the ports of 120 countries. This trade is carried out by 17 Soviet companies which, together, manage 16% of the world's merchant tonnage. These are impressive figures at first sight but more relevant are the ages of the various elements of this fleet. Some 45% of the tonnage in this total is 15 or more years old and that is the age at which many countries ban ships from their ports; and 26% is over 20 years old. This is due to a major drop in merchant ship building during the late 1960s, 1970s and early 1980s, described by the Soviet authorities as 'a chronic shortfall during the 10th, 11th and, in particular, the 12th Five-Year Plans'. Action was taken in 1986 to introduce self-financing and cost accounting for three of the 17 shipping companies, the remainder following suit on 1 January 1987. This was the first time in the history of the USSR that the companies were given any form of independence from the Ministry of Merchant Marine (*Morflot*) and the planners in Moscow. In place of the long-standing practice, all the companies, though still subject to state targets, are given a good deal of freedom in deciding how those targets should be met. This may be part of *perestroika* but the financial fact is that hard currency is desperately needed to pay for the replacement programme.

The current situation is most unhappy; one share of foreign trade cargoes is steadily diminishing and the USSR is spending 500 million rubles of freely convertible currency each year on chartering foreign vessels. Future prospects, unless firm action is taken immediately, will be even more serious. Charter costs will rise to ˌone billion rubles annually; whilst the share of foreign trade cargoes will be reduced by some 20%; and the provision of employment for many highly qualified and expensively trained seamen will be at risk. The figures involved are daunting; it is reported that shipping in the USSR requires 85% of its earnings in convertible currency to pay for the construction of ships abroad in 'capitalist countries' in addition to chartering costs, while retaining indigenous programmes. The whole matter has been referred for ministerial decision, a situation which may imply long delays.

This parlous state of affairs may come as a surprise to those who have looked on the dozen or so major shipyards with mercantile building capability in the USSR as competent to meet national needs. The yards are there but they lack the technology and facilities to build many of the types of ships required to maintain the Soviet Union as a major world competitor. The list of countries with Soviet merchant ships on their current building order books is extensive: Finland, Germany, Greece, Malta, Poland, Portugal, Turkey and Yugoslavia. Soon Japan, Korea(s) and Singapore will join the list. In several cases the orders are considerable: in August 1989 six, 2,660 – TEU container ships were ordered in West Germany, with options for a further four — far bigger ships than the USSR had possessed previously. This could well be part of an order for 40 large multi-purpose vessels, a major drain on convertible currency resources. An example of the urgent need for new construction is the state of the largest Soviet shipping company, the

Odessa-based Black Sea Shipping Company (*Blasco*) which, on 1 January 1989, was running a fleet of 259 ships of 500dwt or above. Most of these were dry cargo vessels with an average age of 15.5 years. *Blasco* officials reckon that they will need at least 100 new ships in 1991 – 94.

It is replacement requirements such as these that has forced the adoption of increased financial flexibility. A dearth of foreign currency having coincided with a desperate need for new ships, several steps have been taken to ease the situation. In 1988 *Sovcomflot*, an organisation with access to foreign banks and charged with handling all purchases of shipping in countries other than Eastern Europe, Finland and Yugoslavia, was established. A second new organisation, *Morbank*, has the 17 shipping companies as shareholders and is designed to provide more flexible banking and more favourable rates than the state banks offered. The third step is the granting of permission to the shipping companies to set up joint ventures with foreign firms. These can cover a wide range of activities from the cleaning and painting of ships to the pooling of shipping resources, and have been welcomed by many foreign firms as well as their Soviet counterparts. The fact is that the future of Soviet merchant shipping can be secured only with external loans, foreign shipbuilding and such moves as the joint venture practices.

The last few years have seen the flagging out of Soviet ships, hitherto unprecedented. The majority of the 150, mainly smaller and less important vessels concerned are now under Cypriot registry and benefiting from the change. Large tonnage general cargo ships and roll-on/roll-off ships are usually retained under the Soviet flag.

Improvements in the modern vessels, particularly those built in foreign yards, may well cause an increasing manpower problem, not because of a lack of trained men but the very reverse. Labour-saving devices and increased automation mean smaller crews and so, in the future, we may well see not only Soviet crews in Soviet ships under foreign flags. What the reaction of foreign seamen's unions to this new slant will be is a matter for speculation — but not here.

Although the main aim of the Soviet merchant navy is commercial, with a heavy emphasis on foreign currency, the lack of land routes to the more remote coastal areas puts a premium on sea-borne support. This is particularly true of the Arctic areas and the Bering/Chukchi coasts. The 60 – 70 icebreakers play an important part in such operations which could be afforded for the major permafrost regions. A recent incident in one of the outposts may serve as a warning to those who ignore the dictates of environmental requirements in the future, as the USSR has done consistently in the past. The inhabitants of a small port on the Arctic coast refused to allow the entry of a nuclear-powered ice-breaker, one of the six for which the Ministry has laid out vast sums since the early 1970s. The argument for their construction was the need to extend the season in which the Northern Sea Route was available. There is now considerable doubt as to whether these ice-breakers are sufficiently powerful for the task and, even if they are, whether it is a necessary and viable operation.

The Soviet fishing fleet is particularly necessary for the USSR as a whole since something like a quarter of the protein intake of the population is provided from this source. The fleet consists of over 2,500 trawlers, many of the larger classes combining the duties of factory ships; there are some 120 specialised factory ships, over 600 support ships (tankers, registered cargo and passenger vessels) as well as tugs, repair ships and water carriers. This is the largest fishing operation ever known and covers every ocean and sea in the world. With the vast degree of pollution that exists in the inland seas and lakes of the USSR there can be no expectation of any easing of the wholesale plundering of the world's fish population.

In conclusion, any signs of effective reductions in the size of the Soviet navy will be slow in coming. Current deletions can be ignored as they are merely the overdue removal of elderly and out-dated ships and submarines. It will be 1992 before significant variations in the new construction programme are seen. Meanwhile the navy as a whole is well supplied with sound, seaworthy ships but the standard of those manning them remains suspect.

The Soviet merchant fleet is in urgent need of replacement building and there is no scope for expansion. Forty-five per cent of today's fleet is over 15 years old, nearly twice the world average. The provision of the necessary finance is forcing the authorities to seek foreign loans, while the inability of many Soviet yards to build to modern standards ensures that a high proportion of the required new building will be done abroad. If there are any savings made by reducing naval construction, it seems unlikely that they will affect the mercantile marine.

# CHAPTER 10

# The Influence of Technology on Soviet Doctrine

JOHN HEMSLEY

THE PREVIOUS chapters have tended to concentrate upon Soviet national concerns in the broadest sense. These have covered a range of issues regarding geopolitical futures, collective security policies, economic reforms, resource management, doctrinal development and related institutional matters, in so far as they affect the USSR. The aim of this Chapter is to investigate the degree to which future Soviet military doctrine is open to the influences of new technology. To do this it is necessary to narrow the focus to some extent and to examine how many of these technological imperatives have already become translated into practical military activity in terms of military technological development, modified force structures and likely evolving operational doctrine. All this has a direct impact upon social concepts, industrial resources and procurement, as well as military organisations.

Long before 1973, when N.A. Lomov published his textbook *Scientific-Technical Progress and the Revolution in Military Affairs*, it had been recognised by the Soviet High Command that the impact of new technology would represent a crucial element in the conduct of any military operations in the future. This factor has become increasingly critical as the sheer pace of technology has increased over the last two decades; until it is now seen in the Soviet Union as the cause of radical changes in the nature of future warfare, affecting the development of military doctrine and force structures.

The technology implications therefore need to be assessed in relation to Soviet military doctrine and, in particular, their control theory under the rubric of *upravleniya silami* (the main Soviet term for command and control, but specifically embracing the concept of integration with communication and intelligence), or perhaps more properly *upravleniya voiskami* (troop control).[1] The development of Soviet command technology can then be properly placed in the practical context of current

161

Soviet military doctrinal development. The significance of this approach will become apparent later on in this Chapter.

## Hindsight

To make a sensible evaluation, in addition to understanding the interaction between Soviet doctrine and technology with its alternating influences, we need to trace the evolution of Soviet doctrine since the end of the Second World War. What is being seen now is the practical implementation of the last of four distinctive and clearly discernible phases of military development since 1945. The first of these occurred during 1945 – 53, during which time all military operational thinking was conducted under the pervasive constraints of what was known as Stalin's five 'permanently operating factors'. These were an authoritative formulation of principles produced in 1918 and later reiterated by Stalin in 1942. The list reflects the historical experience and perceptions of the Civil War and, later, the invasion of the USSR by Nazi Germany:

- Stability of the rear
- Morale of the army
- Quantity and quality of divisions
- Arms and equipment of the army
- Organising ability of the command personnel

Weapons and equipment technology were still those of the 1944 – 45 era, although nuclear weapons were being developed behind the scenes. Nevertheless doctrine inevitably remained tied to the same dimensions of technology and tactical thought which existed at the end of the war. On this basis there was neither the requirement nor incentive to upgrade command and control structures.

The period 1953 – 60 saw the establishment of strategic nuclear weapons with the accompanying philosophies of intercontinental strikes, together with the first introduction of a tactical nuclear battlefield concept which resulted in the development of combat operations designed to cope in a nuclear environment. At this point it was deduced that a robust and redundant operational command, control and communications hierarchy was required to maintain some guarantee of continuity of control on the nuclear battlefield.

Next followed the period 1960 – 70. This was a decade which saw radical changes to the basic structure of the armed forces of the Soviet Union, largely brought about as a result of the concept of an operational and tactical nuclear battlefield so far as the ground forces were concerned. The emphasis was firmly based upon widening the technological base, with the priority almost exclusively geared to armaments, and there was a large qualitative improvement in equipment generally. It was during this time that the T-62 main battle tank, the BMP-tracked armoured personnel carrier and the M-1970 main battle tank were produced, the last two being designed particularly for a nuclear campaign in Europe. Concurrently, some far-reaching steps were taken in the field of aircraft design and the development of aerospace technology; and, perhaps most significant of all, a most impressive expansion of the Soviet navy under Admiral Gorshkov. Inevitably this revolution brought accompanying changes in command and organisational structures, along with an overhaul of training methods. Not least, however, the importance of the application of science to every facet of military work and thinking was about to permeate Soviet society, and during this period a number of high technology projects were undoubtedly on the drawing-board. This was the largely unrecognised naissance of an engineering culture which was to assume such institutional importance in the USSR. It was also a time of some national satisfaction in achieving parity with the USA; even if there was a degree of foreboding for the future, especially over what was seen as a deterioration in the strategic environment.

The final and, to some extent, continuing phase started in the early 1970s. In 1973 the Soviet High Command suffered a severe shock as a result of Egyptian command and control failures in the Yom Kippur War. These were largely due to systemic rigidities throughout the whole command and control matrix which directly reflected Soviet doctrinal teaching in this area. For the rest of that decade, the main volume and weight of Soviet discussion and work was on the technicalities of command and control, which has been systematically examined and mathematically modelled.[2] The result was a complete re-think and restructuring of the military system which has been taking place since 1980.

This period has without doubt seen the most significant changes since the Second World War. It has been dominated by scientific advances and characterised by two main occurrences which have been developing in parallel. The first of these major development has been the emergence of the theatre war concept, together with a non-nuclear or conventional option as opposed to a global nuclear war strategy. Here it must be emphasised that until the mid to late 1980s, and so far as any operations against NATO in the European theatre were concerned, any conventional option would almost certainly be conducted against what might be termed a nuclear back-drop. During this period there was some associated restructuring of Soviet services, principally in the air and air defence forces, to meet the new strategic requirements resulting from the implementation of the TVD high command structure.[3]

The second important factor lies in the impact that new and developing technology, particularly in electronics, has made on the Soviet theory and practice of warfare. Nowhere has this technological revolution been more pronounced than in the field of command and control, along with its integrated communications and automated data processing (ADP); and here, in terms of fielded technology, the USSR has long maintained a lead over NATO. Indeed the first generation automated command and control systems, although perhaps crude by Western standards, were actually operating down to divisional level in the 1970s while the British, American and French were still at the design and testing stage with their last 'Wavell', 'Tos' and 'Sycamore' tactical systems respectively. During the last 20 years automation has been introduced into the Soviet military command and control network, extending into the operational and tactical headquarters in the field and at sea, as well as into a wide range of weapon systems. The ground forces have seen the introduction of sophisticated military equipment such as the SA-8 and SA-10 air defence systems and the T-72/74 and T-80 main battle tanks.

In the early 1980s the restructuring of the Soviet air organisation in support of the ground forces coincided with the introduction of modified and new aircraft types, avionics and weapons which have led to the emergence of new techniques and tactics. The result was the formation of a true army aviation consisting of a mix of troop-carrying, ground attack and other specialist helicopters, such as the Mi-28 ('Havoc'), supported by certain dedicated, purpose-built aircraft such as the MiG-23 ('Flogger'). Meanwhile the majority of fixed-wing aircraft were regrouped into air armies under centralised control at theatre level. Aircraft, such as the MiG-29 ('Fulcrum') and SU-27 ('Flanker') incorporated the latest technology of the time with 'look-down, shoot-down' capability, as well as being able to carry out multi-role missions with a greatly enhanced performance as compared with their predecessors, particularly in terms of radius of action and improved weapons fit. Significant technological advances meant that, after a long period of tactical stagnation, the Soviet air forces were able to make serious experiments and real progress in the field of air tactics, especially in the context of multi-tasking and the ability to re-role their aircraft.

It must also be admitted that the experience of the Afghanistan campaign led to an overhaul of tactical practice. Closely allied to the improvements in the operational air capability were the enhancement in Soviet theatre surface-to-surface missile systems. For many years Soviet leaders have held that the range, accuracy and speed of missile weaponry afforded the means to revolutionise warfare and have, therefore, given high priority to maximising the capabilities of all missile systems. New technologies now permitted the qualitative improvements exhibited in a whole new spectrum of missiles such as SS-21, SS-23, SS-24 and SS-25, all of which possess greatly improved accuracy and the ability to fire a selection of warheads, ranging from nuclear and bio-chemical to advanced conventional munitions. By the end of the 1980s it was significant that these missile systems provided the capability to strike in a conventional mode against opposing command and control assets, as well as other deep targets which might be particularly vulnerable to this sort of attack. In particular it was perceived that the emergence of improved conventional munitions had raised the 'revolution in military affairs' to a new level, providing the practical capability to conduct effective TVD operations.

In summary, during this period much technologically advanced equipment has come into service with all branches of the Soviet forces, along with ADP systems providing information technology to every branch and level of the military organisation. This must be matched with the extensive restructuring which has taken place within the armed forces as a whole; from the establishment of a TVD concept designed to facilitate the planning, execution and sustainability of a global war on several geographical fronts simultaneously, to the reorganisation of tactical formations aimed at increasing operational effectiveness. The entire Soviet war machine has been overlaid by a flexible, highly-automated command, control and communications matrix, into which has been tied a comprehensive ADP information/intelligence system. Command Technology (*voennaya sistemotekhnika*) had truly come of age.

## Insight

Although this last phase has represented a continuing period of doctrinal development, it might equally be described as a time of transition reaching into the mid-1990s within the overall framework of the 'Ogarkov model'. There has been much debate recently over what has been interpreted by many in the West as the emergence of a new Soviet doctrine of 'defensive defence'. It is always difficult in any analysis of sequential development to make a clear demarcation between the ending of one phase and the beginning of another, and never more so than when attempting a contemporary commentary without the benefit of hindsight. However, the pleonasm 'defensive defence', which is in fact primarily a Western invention, actually describes the logical culmination of a doctrinal revision which has been going on within the Soviet armed forces for at least one-and-a-half decades. Evolving Soviet philosophies concerning the strategic importance of space, coupled with advanced command and control systems, are inevitably linked to doctrine, and it must be stressed that the USSR regards its strategic doctrine as a prescription for national survival.

It must also be remembered that Soviet military doctrine is essentially predictive. It is concerned with the nature of future conflict, whilst military science is seen as both shaping and validating the theory of providing the means for practical achievement and future technological development. Soviet military doctrine is firstly political in essence and then 'military-technical', and defines the nature of war by establishing principles for organisation and prescribing methods for accomplishing missions once military goals have been determined. The USSR considers its military doctrine to be scientifically founded, reflecting the objective laws of armed conflict. The conclusions of military science concerning the theory and practice of war are key factors in determining its development. This is a very formal and institutional matter; therefore it must represent the *point de depart* for any investigation into Soviet perceptions and plans for future doctrinal evolution. The most useful line of examination is undoubtedly the area of Soviet control theory and its practical application, especially in view of the recognised importance accorded to this subject. Certainly Soviet control theory is thoroughly integrated into all aspects of military thought, to the extent that it serves as a catalyst between future doctrine and emerging technology, which can therefore be used to decode much of Western uncertainty surrounding future Soviet development. Also it may well be that, in this context, the USSR is somewhat better prepared than many of the countries of the NATO alliance to meet the military structural implications arising out of a major shift in the confrontational centre of gravity away from north-west Europe, with all that this implies in terms of collective security measures, restructuring forces for a rapid reaction role, and global geostrategic command and control capabilities.

When considering 'defensivism' and its implications for Soviet doctrine, it is important not to confuse this with the idea of *razumnaya dostatochnost'* (defensive sufficiency or reliable defence), which is not, and was never intended to be, a formal military doctrine, although this is certainly a key issue in determining the degree of force multiplication that should be attributed to Soviet command and control systems. In this connection, it is worth noting that, for all the ostentatious Soviet propaganda regarding troop reductions and withdrawals, the actually military capabilities will be very little reduced in quantitative terms and, in fact, will almost certainly actually be qualitatively improved through organisational restructuring and rationalisation. In any case, any numerical reductions will be offset in the short term by improved conventional and bio-chemical weaponry, with the future being taken care of by the enormous effort being put into space as the decisive 'fourth dimension'. Soviet long-term military planning is charted well up to the year 2010. The Soviet political and military hierarchy perceive that space holds the key to probable future strategic doctrine (with laser weaponry affecting the role of nuclear weapons), enabling heavily-echeloned strategic defence to operate in an additional dimension. This would allow the USSR to outflank the USA and change the balance of forces. Meanwhile, the USSR considers that the avoidance of any major military confrontation with the West over the next 15 years is critical. In addition, the inhibition or possible cancellation of the US Strategic Defence Initiative is seen in the USSR as a course to be actively encouraged.

This strategy needs to be examined in a little more detail. First, what is the essence of the debate on the 'offence/defence' relationship? This is by no means new and goes back to the late 1960s when, despite impressive force modernisation, the Soviet military was increasingly subjected to budgetary constraints, civilian theoretical restructuring of defence policy and, in the view of the Soviet General Staff, other intrusive political interference by the Party. Therefore there is a critical disparity between Gorbachev's public announcements during the latter part of the 1980s on 'defensive restructuring', and the true military objective which entails the total integration of technology into a comprehensive strategic military framework with a global dimension. This fully-integrated model specifically includes a space component and will provide the basic element for both defence and offence, all operating within the 'high-tech' environment which has for so long characterised Soviet military thinking.

In many ways this substantiates the thesis regarding the consistency and continuity of Soviet strategic thinking. Current political imperatives apart, what we are seeing today in the Soviet Union in military terms is the logical continuation of a process of equipment rationalisation and organisational restructuring to meet a long-term strategic requirement — the emphasis being on conventional warfare fully integrated within the TVD, with space as the key to the future. This doctrine had its theoretical genesis in mid- to late-1970s when it was formulated and argued. Its practical implementation started in the early 1980s and is still going on, subject to necessary fine tuning. Many Western observers of the Soviet scene fail to appreciate the continuity displayed by the evolutionary nature of Soviet doctrine, along with the degree of debate and trial that accompanies its practical implementation. Consequently there has been a tendency to leap in with instant interpretations of 'new doctrine' when this is not necessarily the case. Technological developments are reflected in doctrinal experimentation, the one validating the other. (A classic recent example of misinterpretation is afforded by the case of Soviet trials in the mid-1980s involving resurrecting the concept of the operational manoeuvre group, which many Western analysts immediately hailed as the basis of a new Soviet operational doctrine).

Military restructuring started from the top down at the strategic and operational levels at the end of the 1970s; by the end of the 1980s the ground was being prepared to improve the tactical level by looking bottom up, in order to infuse flexibility and adaptability at the lower levels. Throughout the structure, command and control underpins the whole system. It is highly time-sensitive, and here it must never be forgotten that the Soviet High Command sees the time element as the principal measure of effectiveness.

## Foresight

Are we now, however, beginning to detect a mood of uncertainty and even scepticism regarding the predictability of future Soviet doctrine? The current explosion of technology has cast a shadow of uncertainty over the future. The sheer pace of technological advance has already begun to create some major reservations for Soviet strategic thinkers as well as Western military analysts of the Soviet military scene. The problem is the extent to which future Soviet doctrine will be able to be usefully predictive over the long term, using the hitherto established stereotypes and norms. This is an important question which both Soviet strategic thinkers and Western military analysts urgently need to fathom. To answer this, it seems that we need to find some kind of litmus test that will help to decode some kind of future pattern for long-term doctrinal prediction.

The central element in Soviet strategic and operational thinking is the concept of performance or *effektivnost'* (effectiveness). This element represents the sum of a number of different but interrelated factors which will vary in type and weighting depending upon whether they are applied at the macro-politico-strategic level or the micro-military-operational level.[4] We know that concern over the effects of time constraints on operations is a major Soviet preoccupation. Consequently much of Soviet military technological application has been directed at improving command and control techniques to enhance performance by reducing the effects of the time factor. Since command and control systems represent a key component which can be quantified in this Soviet prerequisite for *effektivnost'*, it could well represent a reliable and useful gauge by which to measure performance. For instance, Soviet military modelling would relate the relationship of effectiveness with time in the form of a syllogistic equation, such as: time = $C^3I$ = EFFECTIVENESS = efficiency = defensive sufficiency.

The link here is the component of 'command, control, communications and intelligence generation'. The relevance of this approach lies in its affinity with established Soviet strategic aspirations; therefore it could be said to establish a rationale, as well as a degree of provenance, for

Soviet military command and control praxis. For the past 30 years there has been a continuing recognition of the urgent need to improve decision-making techniques, particularly in the military sphere, both at the higher echelons and the lower executive levels. To take one example, the adoption of automation at all levels throughout the command hierarchy and management process has facilitated scientific forecasting, thus leading to the application of operational research as the main means of balancing the requirements for military growth against expenditure. In other words, this has played an important part in facilitating the predictive nature of doctrine.

In order to consider the implications in terms of operational control, one only has to follow the Soviet approach to the IADA (information/analysis/decision/action) cycle, which will be familiar to most Western readers in the form shown at Figure 10.1. Computers now play a vital role in all four major functions of this cycle. Initially they manage the automated reception, filtering and correlation of a mass of information, which is then fed into a fusion centre. Here all source information is subject to a continuous cycle where it is automatically cross-referenced, supplemented, revised and matched against existing data banks and the current situation to produce a coherent intelligence evaluation for the commander. These fusion centres necessitate high rates of parallel processing, using arrays and simultaneous processing techniques, larger memory capacities, faster access and better data retention. The commander's analysis is fed into a computer where decisions are tested

FIG 10.1
Information/Analysis/Decision/Action Cycle

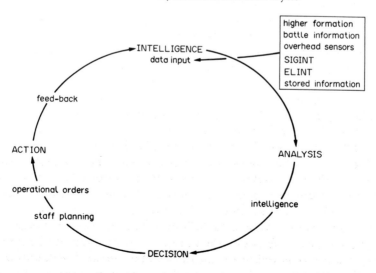

against algorithms for combat models and effectiveness criteria. The staff produce and promulgate the detailed operational plan. This work may be carried out in a number of networked 'battle planning centres' involving regrouping (*peregruppirovka*) (implying both cross-posting and re-subordination), weaponeering, integrated artillery fire planning and air support tasking, the co-ordination of the reconnaissance-strike complex, logistic planning, movement, rear area real estate management and damage control. All these staff planning functions readily lend themselves to automation in order to enhance command and control in terms of increased firepower and mobility, facilitating the breakthrough and encirclement operations which, in turn, are fundamental to the effective employment of follow-up or deep penetration forces. All this accords with Soviet doctrine, while at the same time placing very high demands upon command and control systems, particularly in a rugged and demanding military environment, which makes the whole subject of the application of computers and information technology to military tasks somewhat esoteric.

The aim of this Chapter is to present Soviet technological achievements within the context and demands of Soviet control theory as a possible indicator of the direction in which doctrine may develop. Mention was made earlier of the tendency for Soviet planners to opt for fielded technology, which frequently represents a lower technological state-of-the-art than that reached by Western research and development, to meet the same specification; for instance, the Moscow anti-ballistic missile defence was operational long before the American SDI concept was even formulated. Similarly, the USSR has a reputable signal-processing capability with a mix of optical and electrical, and we in the West tend to forget that the Russians will design and install equipment to meet their particular purposes. Therefore it by no means follows that Soviet perceptions and requirements will necessarily match the Western approach towards a similar problem. There is a very well-established relationship between engineering design and practical application; we should consider carefully whether this should not be the bench-mark against which we need to evaluate and judge command and control architectures.

For example, the technical application of Soviet information systems can be clearly illustrated by the underground strategic electro-optical communications links which have been in operation for several years between Moscow, the military districts and groups of forces stationed outside metropolitan USSR. These fibre-optic links are capable of accepting large data packages with a very high degree of security. Due to the fact that there is less attentuation on fibre-optic cable than metal, fewer repeater stations are required, perhaps one for every 100km for low capacity channels. Research into automatic amplification triggering and the use of heavy metal fluorides in the manufacture of fibre-optic cables promises even greater reliability in the future at less cost with unrepeated links. Similarly the data flow can be increased by using a multilight laser (*ie*, by transmitting red, green and blue light). Some Western analysts have speculated whether the move towards fibre-optics and ceramics has been caused by a shortage of copper in the USSR. This, however, is most unlikely: the functions of optical systems do offer a number of advantages. They offer a high rate of processing and are therefore most suitable for arrays and also for carrying sensor information for guidance control in weapons systems and avionics. Optical engineering is analogous to radio optical engineering and image-processing. Compared to digital systems, it has better memory capacity, gives faster access and better data retention. Optical systems are also better at filtering when faced with a mass of information, and are suited to 'queuing' problems. Although analogue systems give a less than 100% accuracy, they are good for 'fuzzy logic'. Fibre-optic cable also offer a great number of advantages: it is light-weight and cheap, besides being immune to the effects of electromagnetic pulse and interference, and also difficult to intercept through tapping into without detection.

It is interesting that Soviet communications technology has been criticised in the West for its reliance on analogue systems which, until recently, have been considered inferior and less accurate when compared to digital processing. For instance, back in the 1970s, Soviet airborne synthetic aperture radar was translating radar pictures to film which was then scanned optically. In fact, for the remainder of this decade, and throughout the 1980s, the USSR continued using dumped film as an interim measure while they waited for laser and more suitable high capacity, real-time downlinks to become available. Although analogue systems may be less flexible, they have a high rate of processing and the capability for holographic reconstruction gives them a degree of jam resistance. Before the end of the 1980s the Soviet *Salyut* satellite was transmitting holograms from orbit to ground. Indeed the enormous investment that has been made in Soviet research and development for a wide range of military and civil space projects is a measure of the importance attached to this area of technology.

In addition, we should perhaps remember that, despite their supposed technological inferiority, Soviet research and development (and in some cases application) is appreciably advanced on such projects as artificial intelligence and expert systems; the application of strategic reflexive control theory; advanced robotics and machine intelligence; computer simulation modelling; laser communications and electro-optics; advanced sensors, particularly AD radar sensors; laser radars and netting of radar systems (again especially for air defence); genetic engineering; hypersonics; aerodynamics and advanced materials; kinetic energy weapons, aimed at disabling space-based systems as well as destroying ballistic and cruise missiles in flight; and signature reduction (*ie* 'Stealth'), along with appropriate countermeasures.[5] Certainly Soviet investigations into directed energy covers a wide range of research, including particle beam, very low frequency acoustics and electrical discharge, gas-dynamic, chemical-pulsed lasers. In the field of tactical weaponry, the 1980s saw the introduction of a range of submunitions for many of the larger calibre, long-range delivery systems and, in particular, some significant advances in the development of air-blast technology.[6] Using new reactive materials such as boron hydride ($B^{10}H^{14}$), Soviet scientists are claiming single-shot kill probabilities of between 0.9 and 1.0 for these improved conventional weapons.

However, apart from the effort being put into the Soviet space programme, perhaps the greatest concern for the West lies in much of the advanced work being carried out in the field of genetic engineering, especially in its application to battlefield bio-chemical weapons. This covers the whole spectrum from highly toxic pathogens to sophisticated bio-regulators and non-lethal psychosomatic incapacitants. In addition, the Soviet chemical industry is researching deeply into penetrants and discipline breakers, based on organofluorine compounds involving substances such as freons and genetrons, which are aimed at defeating current standard chemical defensive equipment. During the 1990s the perfection of a wide range of bio-technically derived novel agents, many with tailored characteristics of persistency and toxicity for use in specific situations and suitable for delivery by existing weapons systems, is forecast by Soviet military planners as representing a quantum leap in military potential. There is plenty of evidence that bio-chemical warfare forms an integral part of Soviet operational doctrine, being viewed as a cheap and effective option which can be optimised to meet many of the threats posed by Western high technology projects. All this accords with an evolving Soviet policy of assymetric response. The selectivity and precision of persistency offered by the latest 'novel' agents has allowed the USSR to re-rank bio-chemical weapons into their conventional inventory. This, along with the awesome effects of air-blast technology, has resulted in the Soviet High Command placing a decreasing dependence on battlefield nuclear weapons, which they consider will become largely redundant in the early 1990s. By this time they will possess the ability to conduct military operations with a TVD on almost any scale under purely conventional conditions, without resorting to tactical nuclear weapons.

In short, we are witnessing in the USSR the development of a large 'engineering culture' which points to any future doctrine being based firmly upon technology. Nevertheless, deficiencies in command and control at the tactical level of the ground forces is a major concern facing the Soviet High Command. It is both an educational and an organisational problem. Many middle-ranking and senior officers in command and staff appointments lack the technical background to cope with the complexities presented by new technology. There are also associated difficulties presented by the span of command, reflecting the overload on the staff at regimental level and a lack of well-trained officers and senior NCOs at battalion level. New organisational structures at the tactical level will provide a better base for an integrated combined arms formation, with the ability for the rapid concentration of mass at the higher level as a result of improved command and control responsiveness.

Notwithstanding all this, as the Soviet ground forces discovered in the 1970s, at the level of battlefield management both cybernetic and ergonomic problems impose a practical limit on the proliferation of very sophisticated control systems. It requires little imagination to appreciate that the difficulties inherent in macro-systems, such as strategic missile forces and major air defence systems, are immeasurably more tractable than those relating to tactical handling. In terms of battlefield information technology, the USSR sees its greatest area of difficulty lying first and foremost in the reporting system, with anomalies between generation and automated evaluation. In addition, there are some clearly recognised vulnerabilities in a number of other areas regarding the maintenance of high technology equipment, professional and technical training, headquarters' structures (referring particularly to the size and quality of signals support units, in addition to those employed in HQ staff functions), handling procedures coupled with the volume of data input/output for processing, as well as the effects of electronic warfare and electronic counter-measures.

Up to the end of the 1980s, although equipment may not always have represented the latest state in research and development, there has been a deliberate policy of maintaining a steady output of deployed military technology, which has at least given both staffs and workers the opportunity to gain hands-on experience in operating equipments. It has also provided an important user feed-back to the design and development centres. Such a policy requires a considerable and visible front and expenditure; consequently likely cut-backs in Soviet defence spending will almost certainly be reflected by a decline in sequential production. This could lead in the future to a series of technology leaps in deployed systems, which would be more difficult to detect during the research and design stage without the benefit of watching a continuity of development through fielded experience. On the other hand, it will prove expensive in terms of redesign costs and quality control as has been proved in the United States.

To summarise, it is clear that command technology (*voennaya sistemotekhnika*) is totally integrated into Soviet doctrine, and has therefore become a major dimension in the Soviet perception of their system's effectiveness. They see the measure of the control cycle as a yardstick of efficiency. Operational research is now an eclectic mix of ergonomics, military engineering psychology and cybernetics. Overall, Soviet integrated command and control structures display some undoubted strengths as well as weaknesses; however, their effectiveness can only truly be assessed by evaluating the whole, rather than by comparing specific technology levels with those of the West on the basis of comparing like systems. In general terms, Soviet command and control architecture at the strategic and higher operational levels has a high degree of flexibility, redundancy, security, interoperability and survivability. However at the lower military tactical levels, while weapons control systems are generally successful, there are still many problems to be overcome. The Soviet military system assumes a high degree of professional and technical competence throughout the structure. For a variety of reasons, it is unlikely that the present system will be able to translate effectively the direction from a flexible highly-automated, higher command, attempting to conduct a fast moving battle, to form tactical coherence out of a confused, real-time battlefield. Soviet operational and doctrinal concepts are essentially dynamic; the question is whether inherent systemic deficiencies will allow these to achieve the desired performance or effectiveness. The key is the measure of the gap between technological achievement and operator capability. Nevertheless, in many areas, the Soviet ground force staffs have at least had more 'hands-on' experience at this tactical level than the NATO equivalent. Vulnerabilities cannot be identified with individual equipments; the crux is whether the 'system' will work on the day. Here, of course, the only real test can be comparing the result of military operations against an enemy also employing a comparable sophisticated technology.

There is obviously a close interaction between doctrine and technology; indeed the application of new technologies to military systems in general seems increasingly likely to blur the distinctions between offence and defence. However, apart from a burgeoning technology, there are many other factors which will determine the development, substance and style of Soviet military doctrine for the first part of the 21st century. These will involve global political strategies, threat perceptions, internal security and force structures affected by tight economic constraints, international arms control agreements and the changing nature of warfare. Nevertheless, as we enter the 1990s, it would appear now that technological considerations are dominating the development of doctrine to the extent of sweeping away many of the old perceptions and norms. If this means that they may no longer apply in the predictive sense, new methods of analysis and assessment will be required. Because it bridges the gap between doctrine and technology, a study of the practical applications of Soviet control theory could permit some form of quantitative assessment. This might provide one useful key by which the future may be unlocked, but it will demand a rigorous understanding of the nature of Soviet control theory, together with a clear appreciation of both its successes and failure in application.

## Notes

[1] In the West, the terms $C^2$, $C^3$, and $C^3I$ are used to denote command and control; command, control & communications; and command, control, communications and intelligence respectively. The ultimate in redundant semantics is the acronym $C^4I$ standing for command, control, communications, computers and intelligence. Since computers are only a tool in the same sense as a pencil or map, moreover command and control systems infer a communication means together with an integrated intelligence cycle on which to base the decision-making process, I have used the term command and control throughout, except where it is necessary to be particularly specific. In the USSR, the term *kommandovanie* is not used, but distinction is made between *automatizirovannaya sistema upravlenie oruzhiyem (ASUO)* (automated control of weapons systems) and *automatizirovannaya sistema upravlenie voiskami (ASUV)* (automation of command and control systems).

[2] Although MSU Sakarov started systems analysis and ADP technology in 1967, the real groundwork was laid in 1973 by Kulikov who came close to understanding the full scope of the problem.

[3] *Teatr voyennykh deistvii* (TVD), trans. Theatre of Strategic Military Action.

[4] Some of the relevant factors which might be considered when constructing a military 'performance' influence model are: attainment of goal; command & control; doctrine; effectiveness; enemy loss coefficient; historical experience; initiative; leadership; manpower & reinforcements; morale; own losses; political direction; stocks & 'armament norms'; tactics; technology; temp; training; weapons & equipment. (These have not been listed in order of importance, as their 'weighting' value in relation to one another will not necessarily become evident until after the model has been constructed.)

[5] The USSR is applying long-wave radar and infra-red detection measures to counter 'Stealth' technology. In addition, the Soviet navy use of 'Stealth' is well advanced.

[6] Classed as 'improved (or advanced) conventional weapons', fuel-air and air-blast munitions obtain the effects of blast over a local area equal to a small battlefield nuclear weapon, but without causing any radiation hazard. Fuel-air munitions react to use up the available oxygen; reactive surround warheads use a material such as aluminium (used in early research) to tamp the explosive to increase its intensity. The significance of such weapons is that they are classified as conventional munitions, while producing the area effects of a nuclear explosion without leaving any residual radiation.

## References

Akhromeyev, S.F., (ed.), *Voennyi entsiklopedicheski slovar'*, Moscow, Voenizdat, 1986.

**176**     The Lost Empire

Alekseyev, V., 'Characteristic Features of Contemporary Naval Battles', *Morskov sbornik*, No. 10, October 1986.

Altukhov, P.K., et al. *Osnovi Teorii Upravleniya Voiskami*, Moscow Voenizdat, 1984.

Bogart, P., 'Soviet Military Space Programmes', *International Defence Review*, Vol. 23, No. 1, 1990.

Derevyanko, P.M. (ed.), *Problemy revolyutsii v voennom dele*, Moscow, Voenizdat, 1965.

Erickson, J., 'Some Speculations on Soviet Military Restructuring', Unpublished Paper, Edinburgh University, February 1989.

Erickson, J., 'Victory Cannot be Computed', *Journal of the Royal Signals Institution*, Vol. XIX, No. 4, Summer 1990.

Fritz, F., 'Soviet C² Information Systems: Theories, Concepts, Evaluations', originally printed in *Oesterreichse Militärische itschrift* and reprinted in *Signal Journal* (AFCEA), December 1988.

Gorbachev, M.S., *Perestroika*, William Collins Sons & Co., London, 1987.

Grinkevitch, D., 'The Times Factor in Battle', *Voyennii vestnik*, No. 11, November 1986.

Kass, I. and Boli, F.C., 'Dangerous Terrain: Gorbachev's New Thinking', *Signal Journal*, (AFCEA), December 1988.

Kipp, J.W., 'From Foresight to Forecasting: the Russian and Soviet Military Experience', *Stratech Study SS88 – 1*, Centre for Strategic Technology, Texas A&M University, 1988.

Krasnov, A., 'The Cost of Lost Minutes', *Aviatsiia i kosmonavtika*, No. 10, October 1986.

Lomov, N.A., (ed.), *Scientific-Technical Progress and the Revolution in Military Affairs*, Moscow, Voenizdat, 1973, (USAF trans.).

Maltsev, Ye., (ed.), 'The Communist Party of the Soviet Union — the Organiser of the Defence of the Socialist Fatherland', trans. in *Strategic Digest*, Spring 1976.

Morozov, I., et al., 'Opportunities and Problems in Mastering Computer Technology', *Kommunist vooruzhennykh sil*, April 1987.

Ogarkov, N.V., *Vsegda v gotovnosti k zashchite otechestva*, Moscow, Voenizdat, 1982.

Ogarkov, N.V., 'The Defence of Socialism: the Experience of History and the Present Day, *Krasnaya zvezda*, 9 May, 1984.

Ogarkov, N.V., *Istoria uchit bditelnosti*, Moscow, Voenizdat, 1985.

Pollock, M.A., Stubbs, K.D., Thomas, R.E., and Waddell, S.R., *Soviet Optical Data Processing and its Suitability for Troop Control*. Study published by the Centre for Strategic Technology, Texas Engineering Experiment Station of the Texas A&M University System, College Station, January 1990.

Reznichenko, V.G., et al., *Taktika*, (2nd Edition), Moscow, Voenizdat, 1987.

Reznichenko, V.G., 'The Soviet Armed Forces in the Post-War Period', *Kommunist vooruzhennykh sil*, No. 1, 1988.

Stöhr, R., et al., *Chemische Kampstoffe und Schutz vor Chemische Kempstoffen*, Militärverlag der Deutschen Demokratischen Republik, 1985.

Westwood, J.T., 'Evolution and Change in C³ Requirements and Criteria: Soviet Perestroika, US Responsiveness', Lecture to US Naval Academy, June 1990.

# PART III

CHAPTER 11

# Man, the Economy and the Environment

ZE'EV WOLFSON and HENRY SPETTER

IT IS not accidental that from the outset the epoch of *glasnost'* evoked growing opposition to the Communist regimes in the Soviet Union and some East European countries from environmentally-oriented groups and citizens. Under the prevailing political conditions in those countries, where outright political protests would be considered as anti-Communist propaganda the slogans of protection of the habitat, man and nation were acceptable. But they mainly reflected the deep concern of ordinary citizens to preserve their health and welfare. The public concern about the dangerous level of pollution and degradation of nature triggered the development of nationalist and anti-government protests on a wide scale, particularly in the Baltic republics, Armenia and the Ukraine. Subsequently such politically backward regions as Central Asia and Siberia also placed the environmental issue at the top of their political agenda.

The new Supreme Soviet of the USSR can be taken as an indicator of the widespread concern with the environmental problems. During the elections in the first sessions of the Congress of People's Deputies in June 1989 nearly 90% of all speakers stressed the importance of radical measures for combating pollution and, in particular, saving the Aral Sea, the Baikal lake, the Volga and many other areas facing ecological disaster. In 1988 – 89 several government decrees were adopted; budget allocations for environmental protection were increased in 1988 by 11.3%.[1]

It should be pointed out that most of these programmes were well conceived and much more practical in their approach than in the pre-Gorbachev era. An All-Union Committee on Environmental Protection (*Goskompriroda*) was set up, whose chairman, Professor Nikolai Vorontsov, is not a Party member. The appointment of the head of this committee is the prerogative of the Supreme Soviet as is the

179

appointment of the Prosecutor-General. The Supreme Soviet created an Environmental Board on which the most active and most radical reformers were represented. This Board enjoys the wide support in Soviet ecological circles.

However, despite these measures, the degradation of the environment continues, even according to official reports. Air, water and soil pollution increased against the background of the stagnation of industrial production, especially in the chemical, oil and the fertiliser industries, and ferrous and non-ferrous metallurgy and automobile production.[2]

In spite of growing public concern and alarm, the amount of polluted waste water dumped in the Volga river in recent years has increased fourfold, in the Azov Sea, threefold, and even more than doubled in Lake Baikal. The Deputy Prosecutor-General, V. Andreev, who publicised these data, blamed the deterioration of the ecological situation on the increasing irresponsibility and carelessness of the medium level economic managers. Andreev stressed also the moral aspects of the problem, qualifying the managers' attitude towards the existing laws as 'distorted morality'. It turns out that the ordinary citizen expends more effort on circumventing the regulations than abiding by them.

Similar trends were discernible in Poland in the early 1980s when industrial output decreased sharply and pollution and waste increased in spite of the efforts of the authorities and higher budget allocations for environmental protection. It is not the purpose of this Chapter to go into details of the economic factors which prevent the improvement of the environmental situation, but it is a fact that Soviet ecological experts have little hope of a significant improvement of the ecological situation. The Congress of People's Deputies reflected this pessimistic mood; at its second session in December 1989 the majority of speakers did not mention the ecological issue at all and at the third session in February 1990 only 5% of them referred to environmental issues.

It is obvious that significant progress in the ecological field can be expected only after fundamental changes in the economic systems as well in the political institutions; for example, if power is conferred on the local Soviets to deal with the problems on the local level. Meanwhile, until the political and economic reforms are implemented and yield the results, the ecological situation in the field seems likely to get worse. Here one should mention some differences in the understanding of environmental problems between the East and the West. In the West environment means environment — landscape, water systems, flora and fauna — and only afterwards public health. In the Soviet reality the basic meaning of environmental problems is public health. Let us examine the environmental problems in the Soviet Union from this viewpoint.

## Public Health Hazards

Undoubtedly, the consequences of the Chernobyl nuclear explosion occupy a foremost place. It is clear that previous estimates of Soviet officials, which were accepted by many international experts, on the limited effect of radiation on the population were basically incorrect or manipulated. According to new official data provided by the Ukrainian Ministry of Public Health, about one and a half million people are affected by radiation on a potentially dangerous scale. An additional 600,000 people were irradiated during the constant efforts to clean up the settlements affected by radiation in the Ukraine, Belorussia, the Briansk and Kaluga regions of Russia. The reported cases of leukaemia are very limited. However, an increasing number of blood diseases, heart attacks, liver diseases can be attributed to the radiation effect.[3] Changes of the immunological system of millions of people may facilitate the rapid development of more common diseases among the population in Ukraine, Belorussia and other affected areas. In the opinion of Zhores Medvedev, the population in numerous regions subsequently evacuated had already received high doses of radiation.[4] The problem of Chernobyl is complicated by the fact that it is not possible to stop the spread of radioactivity by dust, flying winds, water streams and contaminated agricultural products. As a result, more and more territories and inhabitants are affected by a low-dose of radiation (mainly by long-lived particles of strontium and caesium).

The Chernobyl disaster was a turning point in the Soviet public's awareness of the real scale of the environmental damage. In the West realisation of the dangers of pollution was developed over a relatively long period. Gradually institutes were created for reducing the effect of pollution on the health of population. In the Soviet Union they quickly came to appreciate the seriousness of the situation in the two years after Chernobyl. The ecological crisis was no longer on the threshold but had already entered the living-rooms of most Soviet people. It is a commonly held belief that every case of cancer, the increase in infant mortality and other diseases are a direct or indirect consequence of the increased radiation from Chernobyl or other nuclear plants and military facilities. However, this is an exaggerated perception. So far only preliminary research on this topic has been carried out in the USSR. According to some estimates of Soviet experts, 80% of all diseases of the population of the Soviet Union relate directly or indirectly to various environmental factors. These figures appeared for the first time in the report of the current state of the Soviet environment prepared by the Environmental Board of the Supreme Soviet of the USSR, which released a long list of shocking facts and figures of public health, summarised in the following paragraphs.[5]

The Ministry of Public Health of the USSR analysed data for 184
Soviet cities with a high level of industrial pollution. The results
showed that excessive concentration of at least one pollutant has
led to a 70% increase in sickness rate (while for some age groups
the figure is as high as 300%). The character of disease is uniquely
determined by the industry predominating in each given city. In
the area with the heaviest pesticide load the average sickness rate
among children under six is five times as high as in ecologically
pure areas. A direct link has been established between pesticide
concentrations and tuberculosis, infant mortality, and death due
to cirrhosis of the liver and chronic hepatitis. Especially alarming
are the public health figures on environmental disaster areas —
the Aral Sea basin, the industrial regions of the Urals, southern
Siberia, and parts of the Ukraine. The overall water pollution in
the Aral basin has caused an almost 100% rate of hepatitis, and
a mortality rate double the average level for the USSR.

According to World Health Organisation reports, in the world
at large an average person loses two teeth by age 40; the average
Moscow resident loses six.

In Aktiubinsk (southern Kazakhstan), a site of intensive chemical
production, various forms of cancer occur six times as often as in
the outlying rural areas. The link between the sickness rate and
environmental pollution becomes especially notable when comparing various areas within large urban centres. Thus, residents
of Alma-Ata (the capital of Kazakhstan) suffer from 2.4 times as
many respiratory diseases, and 4.5 times as many nervous and
sensory disorders, as those living in the relatively pollution-free
suburbs. Children living along the Sadovoe Kol'tso — Moscow's
most polluted freeway — have six times the sickness rate of those
residing in ecologically safer areas of the city.

Besides the general increase in sickness rate, environmental
pollution gives rise to unusual, previously unknown diseases. In
1987, in the Ukrainian city of Chernovtsy, 200 children of various
ages began to lose all or most of their hair. Intensive medical tests
have so far failed to discover what had caused this epidemic. In
1988 – 89 similar cases of balding among children were registered
in north-eastern Estonia, Zaporozh'e (the Ukraine), Zlatoust
(the Urals), Moscow, and Biisk (Siberia). Another example is
given from the Bashkirian city of Salavat (one of the largest centres
of the oil and chemical industry) where in 1985 increasing
numbers of children were suffering from uncontrollable nervous
twitching. The specific cause of this malady remained undiscovered.
These tics usually disappeared after the child had spent some time
away from the city. The city is so polluted that vegetables grown

seven kilometres into the countryside still contain large amounts of benzol, styrol, and xylene. One in every three children living near Salavat's refinery is undersized, and monthly increases of infant mortality are directly proportionate to high levels of air-pollution.

A protein and vitamin concentrate called BVK which Soviet industry has been manufacturing for the past 20 years also relates to a grave health problem. This is a protein paste produced by breeding micro-organisms on oil paraffins. It is used as a food supplement in pig and poultry farming. In 1989 eight factories produced about one million tons of BVK. It was found that in every city where BVK was produced children developed a unique form of allergy nicknamed *bykovka* after Bykov, the Minister of Macrobiological Industry and an active supporter of BVK production.

The authors of this report conclude that, by increasing the health budget, and the number of hospitals and doctors, the Soviet Union is fighting the symptoms and not the disease. The fight will only become effective when it addresses the real cause of the high sickness rate by striving to improve the environment.

## Ecological Impact on Social Development

The deterioration of public health on such a wide scale cannot be limited to physiological parameters alone. It has also great psychological and social implications. Besides the increasing rate of psychiatric illnesses due to heavy contamination by pesticides and nitrates of foodstuffs and water, there are also clear indications of psychological depression in the ecological disaster areas. In the summer of 1989 a number of physicians from Moscow, Kiev and other regions were sent to Karakalpakia and Turkmenistan to assist in the birth clinics. This medical assistance had a positive effect on the infant mortality rate in these places for a certain period, but the doctors stressed the apathetic mood of the mothers and their lack of concern for their own health and that of their babies. Of course, this apathy can be explained by their poor physical conditions.[6]

In the centre of the copper industry in South Ural-Karabash cancer diseases reached 338 per 100,000 inhabitants against an average rate for the USSR of 129; even in the area of the nuclear tests site in Semipalatinsk this rate is about 186. The correspondent of *Moscow News* reported that in Karabash the number of healthy children is negligible. Half of the young draftees are considered unfit for military service, and half of the remainder are hardly suitable for service in auxiliary units. The parents of these youths have no illusions about their tragic future. However, they lack motivation to move away from the region, or to protest and request immediate measures for improvement of the situation.[7]

In the Altai region the number of deformed and stillborn infants drastically increased in the 1989 – 90 winter and experts subsequently attributed this to the enormous concentration of heavy metals in the soil and water. In the town of Barnaul particles of mercury were evident in drinking water, and only since then have the authorities tried to improve the water pipe system.[8]

The chief paediatrician in the Soviet Ministry of Public Health considers this neglect and indifference to toxic pollution as a suicidal tendency in social behaviour. The high concentration of DDT and other toxical chemicals in many regions of Central Asia have become routine and the responsible authorities try to solve the problem only in emergency cases, such as the reported 2,000-fold concentration in the soil in the Fergana area.[9]

Although the recent decrees of the Soviet government on environmental management have met with approval throughout the country, so far evidence of pollution problems being solved is rare. True, ecological groups and movements at grass roots level have been formed in many parts of the Soviet Union, but again they can boast success only in very limited cases, like the Baltic republics. In many regions people do not believe that real progress is possible in the near future. Of course this pessimistic mood of people is based on environmental factors but also has repercussions on the economic and social situation, particularly in the low level of productivity due to the weariness of unhealthy workers. The same is true for many high school and university students.

Within the framework of this analysis particular attention needs to be paid to the environmental impact on the Soviet army. As has been shown, the number of physically and mentally healthy conscripts decreases every year not only in Central Asia but also in the Ural, Volga river and Siberian regions which have been considered as the mainstay of Soviet military power and have now become areas of severe ecological crisis. Of course the Chernobyl nuclear explosion and its long-term residual effects had a serious impact on the psychological state of the Soviet army, particularly on those units concerned with nuclear weapons. This includes a long list of units and divisions — rocket troops, long-range strategic forces, nuclear submarines and units involved in guarding nuclear facilities at all stages of nuclear production — from the extraction of uranium to dumping of nuclear waste. The army personnel entrusted with chemical warfare, as well as with large phased-array radars, is also concerned about the possible health damage from contact with these materials and facilities. It is obvious from the scrutiny of publications that the decontamination units (so-called chemical defence units of the Soviet army) have demonstrated their lack of discipline, co-ordination and professional incompetence.[10] The measuring devices in many cases are incapable of providing early warning on dangerous radiation and pollution levels because of poor design and maintenance. The officers and their families are increasingly worried and are becoming reluctant to serve in areas with any kind of nuclear facilities. Requests for transfer to other areas less threatened by pollution are becoming ever more common. The military command set out commissions of investigation into the major cases of pollution, but people do not trust their findings and recommendations. The military authorities permitted the publication of reports on problems of radioactivity in uranium mines and other nuclear facilities, including those in the 'top secret' town of Zero, near Chelyabinsk. But public concern is still growing and faith in the authorities' capacity to solve the long-standing ecological problems is constantly diminishing.[11] In some naval bases in the Far East, such as Sovietskaya Gavan', the protest of local residents and families of military people obstruct the normal operation and repair work of nuclear submarines.[12]

Therefore, it should come as no surprise if a serious 'brain drain' takes place from the ecologically unsafe units and bases. Even the recruitment of new soldiers to these units is likely to become a major problem.

## Ecological Impact on Economy

There is consensus among most Soviet ecologists and Western experts that the ecological degradation has grave consequences for the state of public health and the social climate. Recently there are ever more references to the degradation of the entire nation (Russia, Belorussia, Armenia, Uzbekistan, etc.) as a result of severe contamination of the water, food, soil and air.[13]

Health deterioration in turn impairs industrial production, agricultural production and the entire economic performance. But other aspects which have a direct impact on industrial and agricultural production should also be noted.

In the region of the Kursk magnetic conglomerate, for example, quarries cover tens of thousands of hectares of valuable black earth. Tens of thousands more hectares of the most fertile land have disappeared for ever as a consequence of the destruction of the ground water system, soil salination and erosion. The situation is similar in south-west Belorussia where potassium extraction has destroyed fertile soil and led to the destruction of forests, orchards and gardens.[14] To date, the whole subject of environmental degradation as an economic factor has not been adequately analysed in the Soviet Union, although there are three main areas in which the degradation of nature has inflicted direct losses to the economy — first, resistance to the siting and construction of nuclear power plants and hydro-power stations; second, losses in the chemical, pharmaceutical and paper industries as a result of the shut-down of the most polluting plants; third, technological problems in the industrial development of the more heavily polluted areas.

For a long time, the Soviet authorities put the main emphasis on the setting up of nuclear power plants, with a view to increasing the energy output. Starting from 1987, the protest movement against nuclear power spread in many regions. The authorities wanted to calm the public by asserting that they had taken measures for increasing the safety of nuclear energy production. Some operational instructions were altered in order to tighten up discipline and bring down the number of accidents to a minimum. However, Soviet experts and public figures kept on emphasising that the crucial issue was the irresponsible behaviour of the personnel and inefficient management, not the lack of high technology.[15] The writer Valentin Rasputin disclosed that in some areas of the Kalinin nuclear plant alcohol is strictly forbidden, and asked whether that meant that the use of limited quantities of vodka is acceptable in other areas of the plant? What kind of trust can be expected under such circumstances?[16]

As a result of strong protests, the Armenian nuclear power plant near Erevan was shut down and the construction of the Crimean nuclear power plant was halted, despite the hundreds of millions of rubles already invested in this project. Several other projects involving nuclear power stations were stopped at the first stage of construction or design (Krasnodar, Kazan, Yaroslavl, Baku). The Supreme Soviet of the Ukraine recently decided gradually to close down the nuclear reactors in Chernobyl and other nuclear power plants.

The Soviet government will now have to look for other sources of energy to cover the deficiency in industry, transport, urban consumption, etc. However, the disastrous consequences following the construction of numerous hydropower stations and water reservoirs on the Volga in the past years have left a bad taste, and now plans to set up big new hydropower stations on the Amur, Enissei and other rivers have encountered unprecedented opposition from the public and the local authorities.

Losses in the chemical and pharmaceutical industries as a result of the shut-down of plants have been widely discussed in the Soviet media. The situation is dramatic indeed. Even though the Soviet pharmaceuticals ministry (*Minmedprom*) only meets 40% of the nation's needs as it is, environmental protests have forced many plants to close because they are unable to meet the most elementary environmental standards. *Meditsinskaya gazeta*, the USSR's main medical newspaper, commented: in the public view, *Minmedprom* is like a leper. The cutbacks have worsened shortages of antibiotics, cardiovascular preparations, and painkillers. Some drugs have simply disappeared from the market. Moreover, it was reported that opposition had thwarted the construction and renovation of 23 pharmaceutical plants in 1989. Soviet citizens fear *Minmedprom* so much that it is having trouble boosting the production of disposable syringes, desperately needed to stem the spread of AIDS in Soviet hospitals. While accusing the opposition of 'green extremism', the head of *Minmedprom* conceded to the Soviet parliament in December that, until his ministry cleans up its reputation 'they won't give us a breather'.[18]

According to some reports, in recent months up to 1,000 enterprises have been shut down in all sectors of the economy — from paper and pencils to metallurgy and chemicals — causing a loss in production to the tune of 10 billion rubles. But no accurate estimate of the real economic damage can be made due to the lack of precise data. Obviously, Soviet government officials and managers of enterprises are apt to attribute their own weaknesses and failures to 'green extremists'. In some cases the losses in paper output were compensated by increasing the output of other paper plants. At the same time it is evident that nearly every product is in short supply and even a slight decrease in production has far-reaching repercussions on the economic and social situation. The endless disputes and long queues at pharmacies which lack even such elementary medicines as aspirin, and the closure of *Novy Mir* the literary journal, due to lack of paper, are striking examples of our assertion.

Technological problems related to environmental protection are an important adverse factor in almost every sector of industrial and agricultural production, from pharmaceuticals to pesticides. But one should emphasise those aspects of the economy which have a direct impact on the major strategic sectors. Energy output is a case in point. The electricity output from nuclear and hydropower plants has already been discussed, but what of the gas and fuel output. One of the richest gas deposits in the world is the Yamal peninsula in the far north of Western Siberia. Efforts are being made to substitute gas for coal and heavy oil, in order to decrease the air pollution level in many Soviet cities. Even lorry engines are being converted to gas fuel (though with modest success). With the growing importance of gas, the primary importance of the Yamal gas deposits is being highlighted. At the same time the geological and environmental conditions make it an extremely complicated task to develop these gas deposits. Briefly, the Yamal peninsula is a huge ice block covered by a thin layer of soil. When gas tries to break through the deep layers of ice, the latter melts and the soil sinks, consequently fires are a common phenomenon in the gas drilling areas. Accidents have been reported where 50-metre high drilling installations sank in the newly-created swamps after such fires. Scientists and ecologists warned several years ago about the improper exploitation of the Yamal gas deposits. Soviet experts advised that neglect of the specific ecological norms might lead to the total collapse of the Yamal peninsula.[19] They have good reason for such a warning because in West Siberia the exploitation of some oil and gas deposits is exceedingly expensive and almost impossible due to the encroachment of the swamps on the tundra districts. It appears that the climatic conditions are becoming harsher in these areas — winters get longer and summers shorter, thereby increasing the economic and social costs of this project.[20] Consequently, in 1989 the Soviet government decreed a halt to all preparations for large-scale gas extraction until better technologies are developed and applied in Yamal. In this decree the Soviet government again emphasised the need for using proper vehicles that would prevent the destruction of the tundra. Soviet ecologists report that millions of square kilometres of tundra have been destroyed, mainly due to the improper use of cross-country vehicles, and transformed into swamps and lifeless tracts of land.

The disastrous predicament facing minorities in the north as a result of drastic changes in their habitat are being discussed at endless conferences and meetings. The respect for the right of these minorities to determine the industrial development of their area, including Yamal, was fully recognised by the Soviet authorities. Nevertheless, after the publication of the decree on halting the preparations for exploitation of the Yamal gas deposits, work was renewed. Experts estimate that several years are needed for the invention and implementation of new 'environmentally friendly' technologies in Yamal. Here the contradiction between the policy of *glasnost'* and the practice of *perestroika* is blatant. All structures dealing with energy and raw material extraction are poorly adapted to implement the required changes. The new sophisticated technologies are not utilised in the environmental protection sphere for many reasons, but most especially because higher environmental performance is still not economically rewarded; the training of specialists is also inadequate.[21]

Similar factors can be observed in the project of development of the oil fields in the Tengiz region of the north-east Caspian coast. The geological conditions in these oil fields are very unfavourable — oil is under pressure up to 900 atmospheres. It consists of up to 25% hydrosulphur. The oil deposits in Tengiz were discovered in the early 1980s and in 1986, in one drilling test, a stream of oil gushed forth — the biggest in the history of oil extraction. Simultaneously a big fire occurred which was put down only 14 months later with the assistance of American experts. The landscape in the Tengiz area is semi-desert and highly vulnerable to cross-country vehicles and other kinds of industrial impact, on nearly the same scale as the tundra. The waters of the Caspian Sea provide additional complications as well as seismic instability. Full development of this project, with an output of 12 million tonnes of oil annually, will increase the risk of earthquakes.[22] According to the estimates of Soviet ecologists, an earthquake would cause an enormous quantity of hydrosulphur to be emitted, thus endangering the population over an area of thousands of square kilometres. They forecast a catastrophe of Chernobyl dimensions.

In early 1990 the Committee for Environmental Protection suc-ceeded in cancelling the budget allocations for all development projects in the Tengiz area until a full ecological survey is carried out and guarantees are provided for the full implementation of all recom-mendations.[23] However, the fate of the Tengiz project is similar to that of Yamal. During Gorbachev's visit to the United States an agree-ment was signed on the Tengiz project between the Soviet Union and a group of American companies, with a total value of 10 billion dollars. In addition to oil extraction, petrochemical and polymer production facilities will be built (the biggest in the Eastern hemisphere) near the Caspian Sea. Soviet officials stated that Chevron oil company has the proper technology for oil extraction suitable to the conditions in Tengiz. It is true that Chevron operated in San-Ramon, South California with such facilities without accidents, thus preventing serious environmental damage. In this case, unlike Yamal, the Soviet Union will receive the sophisticated technology for such an operation, along with water and oil protection facilities.

However, the problem of the proper maintenance of sophisticated technology is no less critical than inventions of 'environmentally friendly' technologies. Soviet oil, gas and chemical industries have a long record of failures in the effective operation of Western technology, especially in such an unproductive area as that of environmental protection. Only a few hundred kilometres west of Tengiz, the huge Astrakhan gas and condensation plant was commissioned. A French system for output control was purchased for this plant, but now the Soviet press reports that in many of the facilities there is a shortage of thermometers and other simple measuring devices at the various stages of the production cycle. In this way the highly-sophisticated computerised control systems are ineffective and incapable of preventing the emis-sion of polluted gases in the atmosphere. The concentration of these gases in the nearby settlements is so high that some inhabitants have constantly worn gas masks.[24] The output of gas throughout the world is now becoming more expensive due to the increased cost of environmental protection. The Soviet Union is no exception to this trend, as Soviet authorities are compelled to allocate ever greater funds to this purpose. However, although the costs are increasing, the population still suffers the effects of heavy pollution. At the first stage of development of the Tengiz project there are already numerous reports of diseases caused by polluted drinking water, air pollution and the reluctance of workers to stay in the nearby settlements.[25]

The poor operation and training of specialists becomes an even more complicated problem against the background of rising ethnic tensions. The Tengiz area belongs to Kazakhstan, and Kazakh authorities are interested in joint venture with a US company on condition that local Kazakh manpower gradually replaces the American personnel in a few years. This is natural, taking into account the big unemployment in Kazakhstan and other Central Asian republics. Besides, the Russian qualified workers and technicians are now intent on leaving the Muslim areas, and the problem of training and transfer of technical know-how of the local generation of worker will become ever more acute.

The impact of national tensions on the ecological situation in the Soviet Union touches upon a very complicated issue, not only because of the irrationality of national conflicts but also owing to the effect of these tensions in all spheres of Soviet economic and social life. Since the national conflicts aggravate the anarchy and disintegration of the Soviet economy, they handicap the functioning of the environmental protection structures. Numerous illustrations can be provided of this, including the ending of agreements on water management between the neighbouring republics and the liquidation of natural protection reserves 'created by Moscow'. The most conspicuous example is the case of the conflict between Azerbaijan and Armenia. Because of the Azerbaijan blockade, Armenia did not receive any kind of fuel in 1990; consequently the inhabitants started to fell the forests in the natural preserves (in Armenia the forest area was only 4% of the territory).

## Conclusions

The fact is that pollution and destruction of the environment has become one the most powerful constraints hampering the utilisation of natural resources and energy in the USSR. In effect, it has become a serious obstacle to Soviet recovery from the present economic crisis. Ecological problems played a significant role in the development of *glasnost'* and the growing political activities of Soviet citizens. From an historical viewpoint, this role may be regarded positively; but pragmatically, in the everyday life of the ordinary Soviet citizen, the ecological factor considerably aggravates his social and economic problems.

Most of this analysis has been devoted to the impact of pollution on public health. It can be summed up as follows;

- air, water and soil pollution has become a serious factor in the physical degradation of the population, perhaps more serious than the shortage of foodstuffs;
- ecological pollution both directly (through psychotropic kinds of pollution) and indirectly (through causing widespread diseases) fosters social demoralisation and apathy;
- physical and psychological degradation can be observed among all social strata, including the armed forces;
- ecological pollution is a perennial factor which will affect the health of the population for generations to come (even after an improvement in the present ecological situation).

The Chernobyl disaster is just the greatest of many other minor nuclear accidents for which society will have to pay in the shape of numerous tragic cases of defective and sick children, and the high costs of their maintenance and treatment. Meanwhile, Soviet society is unwilling to sacrifice anything for such social needs, because it believes that there is no room for any more sacrifice. In one of the sociological polls recently conducted in the USSR, four out of five citizens (mainly women) demanded the destruction of defective children and urged that no further money should be wasted on their maintenance.[26]

Six decades ago the Soviet empire was established over a huge territory, larger than any other empire in history. The Soviet Union possessed the richest natural resources in the world — fertile land, forests, fresh water, oil, metal and gold deposits. The idea of boundless space and inexhaustible resources was one of the main theses of Soviet propaganda which created the illusion of the unlimited opportunities, the superiority of Communism and, ultimately, of its triumph over all other social systems. The availability of huge natural wealth buttressed the false belief in inevitable success held by generations of Soviet people.

On the other hand, the vast Russian areas, where all pollution seemingly vanished, were actually concealing the ecological crisis in the USSR in the last decades. By the early 1980s this ideology was completely discredited and the accumulative capacity of space had been almost completely exhausted. Today it is almost impossible to find clean landscapes, rivers and lakes in the vicinity of Moscow, Leningrad and the Ukraine which are safe for fishing or bathing. In this era of *glasnost'* the mass media not only supply the average Soviet citizen with a flow of information on the disastrous aftermath of Chernobyl; on the babies with rotten black teeth[27]; on the reduction of longevity; the toxic vegetables and fruit. They also show convincingly that it is not possible to expect a serious improvement in the state of the environment in the USSR over the next 10 years.

Stalin can be accused of genocide and ecocide; one can go further back to Lenin and Marx; but it is irrefutable that the vastest and richest part of the globe has been destroyed; it is covered with wounds which are probably incurable. Today Soviet ecologists are eager to study the experience of the capitalist countries in environmental management. Soviet politicians and public figures turn to the West for help with a view to setting up hard currency funds for the rescue of the Volga, Baikal, Aral, the Black Sea, the Azov and Caspian Sea, and many other areas.

The degradation of the environment in the USSR not only leads to the fundamental degradation of part of its very society, which represent its human resources; but it also has a negative effect on all other spheres of activity — from national self-consciousness to the economy. Therefore, it can be safely maintained that ecological issues have become a major obstacle to the transformation of the Soviet Union into a modern productive society reflecting the Western economic pattern. Sadly, it is probably safe to predict that this problem will last for a long time, possibly well into the twenty-first century.

## Notes

[1]  11.11 billion rubles against 9.93 billion in 1987. (*Okhrana okruzhayuschei sredy i ratzionalnoe ispolzovaniye prirodnyh resursov v SSSR. Statisticheskiy Sbornik. M.* 1989, p.9).

[2]  According to data as mentioned above the period 1986 – 88 the effluent of untreated waste-water increased nearly twice — from 15.1% to 28.6% of all waste-water subject to purification. The volume of waste, particularly municipal waste and waste of the mining industries has also increased considerably. *Statisticheskiy Sbornik*, p. 63, 143. On the other hand according to the latest data, there is a critical downward trend in the supply of energy and other raw materials in the USSR. Economic Newsletter, Russian Research Center, Harvard University, Vol. XIV, No. 12. 15 August 1990, p. 1 – 2.

[3]  See *Pravda Ukrainy*, 22 February 1990, p. 2. Also: *Krasnaya Zvezda* 26 April 1990, p. 2. *Pravda*, 1 March 1990, p. 4

[4]  Report by Z. Medvedev on the IV World Congress for Soviet and E. European Studies, Harrogate, England, 22 July 1990.

[5]  A. Yablokov. 'The Current State of the Soviet Environment'. *Environmental Policy Review*, Vol. 4, No. 1,1990, pp. 8 – 10. See also: 'Bolez n' Bykova', 'Pod Ygrozoy Deti', *Literaturnaya Gazeta*, 23 August 1989.

[6]  'Desant', *Sem'ia*, No. 40, 1989, p. 8. Also: 'K sluzbe ne prigoden', *Trud*, 20 April 1990, p. 4.

[7]  Yu. Tepliakov. *Escho dyshish, Ural . . .*, *Moscow News*, (in Russian) 24 March, 1990, p. 8 – 9.

[8]  *Trud*, 20 April 1990, p. 4.

[9]  *Pravda Vostoka*, 4 March 1989, p. 2. It is worth noting that such a case is not an exception. In the Aniva Gulf on Sakhalin island, the registered concentration of cadmium compounds amounts to 1,980 times the tolerable level. (V. Rasputin. Sumerki Cheloveka) *Literaturnuy Irkutsk* No. 12, 1989 p. 34).

[10]  E. Zhuravlev and E. Klepikov, '*Problemy voennoi ekologii*', *Krasnaya zvezda*, 8 August 1989, p. 2. Also 'The Chernobyl Accident from the Viewpoint of a Soviet Army Radiologist'. *Environmental Policy Review*, Vol. 3, No. 1. 1989. pp. 2 – 4.

[11]  *Krasnaya Zvezda*, 17 July 1990, p. 4. *Pravda*, 3 March 1990, p. 4. *Krasnaya Zvezda*, 6 March 1990, p. 4. *Trud*, 20 July 1990, p. 2

[12]  '*Gde horonit' atomohody.*' *Krasnaya Zvezda*, 28 June 1990, p. 2. '*Ostorozhno — reaktor*'. *Izvestiya*, 16 July 1990, p. 6.

[13]  M. Lemeshev, 'Ecologo-ekonomicheskaia otsenka nauchnotekhnicheskogo progressa', *Voprosy Ekonomiki*, No. 3, 1987, pp. 31 – 39.

[14]  *Literaturnaya Gazeta*, 2 March 1988, p. II.

[15]  *Literaturnaya Gazeta*, 25 January 1989, p. 8 *Sovietskaia Rossiya*, 21 May 1989, p. 3. *Pravda*, 20 July 1990, p. 3

[16]  V. Rasputin. Sumerki Cheloveka. *Literaturnyi Irkutsk*, No. 12, 1989, p. 30.

[17]  *Pravda*, 20 July 1990, p. 3

[18]  D. J. Peterson. 'A Wave of Environmentalism Shakes the Soviet Union', *Report on the USSR*, Vol. 2, No. 25, 22 June 1990, p. 8.

[19]  Yu. Golubchikov, *Ustoychivost' severnyh ekosistem*, (reprint) Moscow State University, 1989.

[20]  Z. Wolfson. 'The environmental risk of the developing oil and gas industry in Western Siberia;. *Sibérie I*, Questions Sibériennes Paris, 1985. pp. 194 – 195.

[21]  V. Larin. 'Aral. . . Baikal. . . Yamal?' *Strana i mir*, München, No. 2. 1990, p. 79 – 81.

[22]  F. Novikov. '*Diktat tsentra i bezvlastie Soveta*'. *Pravda*, 13 March 1989, p. 3. *Prikaspiyskaia komyna* (Gur'ev) 21 June 1989.

[23]  *Kazakhstanskaia Pravda*, 2 February 1998, p. 2.

[24]  *Sovietskaia Rossiya*, 12 March 1990, p. 4.

[25]  *Druzhba*, (Tengiz regional newspaper), 23 June 1989, p. 1 – 3.

[26]  *Sem'ia*, No. 2. 1990, p. 25.

[27]  A. Cherkasova, '*Karta trevogi nashey*', *Znanie — sila*, No. 1, 1990, p. 27.

CHAPTER 12

# Defence Economic Planning

JAMES T. WESTWOOD

FOR ALL except specialists the subject of economics, in this instance defence economics, is arcane. Yet, the relevance of economics to a nation's past, present and future military ability and potential is at once essential and primary. Economic resources, their management and the outcomes of economic processes determine all military quantities and qualities. The distribution and allocation of economic resources, representing whimsy, deliberate decision-making and forecasting or both, shape and define a nation's military force structure, modernisation, readiness and scientific and technological (S&T) prowess.

The fact of a large armed force possessed of potentially superior firepower does not, in itself, necessarily indicate a nation with concomitantly large and effectively-managed economic resources and responses nor a nation necessarily bent on aggression. Indeed, it may indicate a nation, such as the USSR, possessed of a large geographic area to defend, together with actual economic resources smaller and less differentiated than its adversaries, which commits to its defence an inordinately large share of its national economic resources. For such a nation defence economic efficiency — and effectiveness — may be secondary to defence economic size and survivability. The Soviet Union has never claimed that its defence economy is either efficient or effective: in fact, it has claimed the contrary, and not only since the advent of *perestroika*. For nearly three centuries, Russia and subsequently the Soviet Union have maintained exceptionally large and costly armed forces, never in an economically efficient manner. By the late 1980s the USSR maintained an armed forces nearly 60% larger in manpower than that of the USA on an income base of between 28% – 51% of the USA.[1]

Many wonder how the economy of the USSR, seemingly so suddenly, began in 1989 to fracture and collapse, increasingly unable to support its defence establishment. In fact, this collapse was not sudden; it has been a long time coming and has a long time yet to run. The present attempt to restructure the economic underpinnings of the Soviet armed forces was both predictable and prognosticated. It is remarkable (if not also embarrassing) that the West so feared and so long and expensively prepared itself to withstand Soviet armed forces resting on so weak and contrived an economic base. US Senator Daniel Moynihan is reported to have said on 16 July 1990 that if more precise estimates of Soviet economic weakness had been available. 'I think we would have behaved differently'.[2]

Although the economy of the USSR is peculiar, little understood and today in disarray, it is the premise of this Chapter that the USSR's economic resources and management mechanisms are the first cause and the final result of Soviet security policy shifts in the 1990s. Because Soviet defence economic planning is obtuse but essential, I shall first address that subject, before discussing the military decade ahead as seen from the defence economic perspective.

## Mechanisms of USSR Defence Economic Planning

The first step in predicting future USSR security policy as it affects the defence establishment is to understand that the entire Soviet economy is divided into two primary groups: production resources (called Group A) and consumption resources (called Group B), the former comprising about 70% of all national resources and the latter about 30%. As in the economy at large, so in the defence establishment, hardware (machines, machine building, equipment of all kinds) and research and development (R&D) resources belong to Group A. Military operations (and rudimentary equipment upkeep), with its consumption of fuel, lubricants, food, administrative supplies, and notably, troop labour, belong to Group B.[3]

Transfers of resources (material or monetary) between the two groups do not occur; for example, savings in one group are not transferable to the other group, but Group B consumption cutbacks in the armed forces, such as those taken during the *perestroika* period, may be taken up in other parts (*ie*, civil) of Group B. Again, for example, fuel not used by the armed forces in training may be made available for transporting agricultural products from fields to consumers. Thus, the unusual cutting back during 1986 – 90 of all Soviet armed forces training and exercising operations, rather than being a response to Western strategy initiatives, has, instead a planned economic component and rationale affected by shortages in consumable supplies, such as fuel, *vis-à-vis* the press of general requirements.[4]

Secondly, until 1963 all Soviet machinery and equipment (including tanks, ships, aircraft, weapons, etc.) were treated financially and economically as gross durable goods, *ie*, as one-time, long-term, undepreciated assets. From 1963, all equipment was treated as depreciated net capital goods with a prescribed, cost-discountable lifetime. For military equipment this lifetime was a minimum of 30 years service, after which it became conserved storage in reserve. By 1970 – 71, it began to be painfully obvious to the Soviet Defence Ministry that maintenance and storage costs of this long-term, depreciated and growingly massive assortment of largely unused military 'insurance' machinery (eg, thousands of tanks of vintage design) was taking up about 5% of the annual defence budgets.[5]

In 1984 – 85 it was decided that, *all* old machinery would be retired at accelerated rates concomitant with acquisitions of smaller numbers of modern 'high-technology' machinery, whether, for example, military or civil trucks, locomotives or computers. This nationwide programme was expertly discussed, is a centre-piece of *perestroika*, and impacted all old military machinery. Thus, from sources such as Faltsman (1985), one could foresee three years in advance Gorbachev's making a virtue of necessity by his otherwise startling announcement of 7 December 1988 of Soviet unilateral arms reductions.[6] By knowing the USSR national planning scheme and organisation, the method of accounting and by examining evidence such as Faltsman and Makarevskiy (1987), it was possible to forecast the numbers, types and ages of military weapons which Gorbachev offered to eliminate over the remaining period of the then current Five-Year Plan (1986 – 90).[7]

The USSR's national planning process provides for all structure, modernisation, R&D and operations of the Soviet armed forces. (See *Table 12.1*). In the periodicity shown here, each quinquennial is divided into five calendar budgeting years and each budget year is divided into four goal-tracking quarters. These lesser increments are used to schedule economic activity, collect performance data (much of which is incomplete or corrupted) and to measure results en route to the quinquennial targets.

A 15-year forecast, which accompanies each Five-Year-Plan and is slid forward by five years at the beginning of each numbered quinquennial, is taken with extreme seriousness in the Soviet defence establishment and throughout the national economy into which defence resourcing is highly integrated and poorly differentiated. Draft planning for the subsequent Plan and forecast is carried out during the fourth and fifth years of a current plan period, eg, in 1989 – 90 for the 1991 – 95 Five-Year-Plan.

In close co-operation with the Military-Industrial Commission, military force structure, modernisation, R&D and readiness planning begins in the General Staff of the Armed Forces with the analysis and generation of requirements, a long-standing practice now being formalised. This results in a defence budget estimate called the *smeta* and these requirements drive the funding of the defence budget. The accompanying

TABLE 12.1 *USSR National Planning & Forecasting Periodicity*

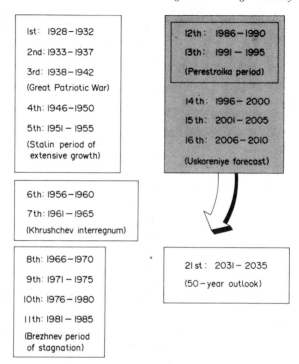

15-year armed forces forecast is based on official General Staff estimates and net assessments of which there are interesting available examples.[8] During plan drafting, the five individual services submit training, exercise and logistical plans for the upcoming five-year period according to General Staff guidance which prescribes a single, unified, all-service readiness and modernisation theme for the next quinquennial. (For 1986 – 90, for the first time, there was no war preparation training theme as such, in part owing to the trimming of military Group B resources applicable to the 12th Five-Year-Plan.) The military service headquarters schedule all military operations by quarters and years within the quinquennial according to dictates of climate, the semi-annual conscription and troop rotations, service-prescribed proficiencies, and the military training theme. All draft planning feeds together by regulation of the General Staff. The General Staff and the Military-Industrial Commission plan all hardware procurement and military R&D in the 15-year forecast; for instance during 1984 – 85 for the period through to the year 2000. (In 1987, for the first time, additional forecasting was introduced to 25-year and 50-year future marks.)[9]

During plan drafting periods Soviet military literature widely discusses the issues, themes, programmes, procurements, standards, expected values and preparations under consideration for the next plan and forecast periods. Senior Commanders and R&D researchers, analysts and planners from the military academies and institutes widely participate in this scheduled debate.

Hitherto, this process worked the same way in the armed forces of the non-Soviet Warsaw Pact nations whose national plans were interlocked with those of the Soviet Union. Among all the Warsaw Pact nations, the plans/forecasts are approved finally by the quinquennial Communist Party congresses occurring ordinarily during the first quarter of each new Five-Year plan period. Because of long lead times, military hardware acquisition and R&D programmes are approved out to 10 or 15 horizons.

During subsequent acquisition periods, major programme changes coming to light as unanticipated in previous planning by the armed forces have to be appealed on an exceptional basis to the Central Committee (some also to its Politburo) of the Communist Party. Understandably because of penalties, such changes are rare and of exceptional importance to foreign analysts and policy staffs. The Soviet system has a low tolerance of excessive deviation which explains not only its excessive commitments to state security but also its excessive and perennial commitment to planning and forecasting.

All recent evidence shows that this planning structure and process will continue to be used by Soviet planners and forecasters into the 21st century. There is an intent to make 'the Plan' more of a guidance and less of a prescriptive instrument; to suppress annual fluctuations of targets in favour of greater attention to five-year targets; and to extend forecasting horizons to 20, 25, and 50-year marks. The latest Soviet *perestroika* textbooks for educating managers reveal the unbroken pattern of planning and anticipate a measure of distributed planning and production responsibility as among central and regional ('territorial') authorities.[10]

Unlike money in the West, rubles in the USSR measure *only* cost; they do not measure value. In a Marxist-Leninist economy, only labour, materials and products measure value, and production of the means of production is considered the most valuable economic process. To a large extent, the ruble account of the Soviet defence budget (and of the whole national income) are artifacts of convenience, giving authorities a running view of financially-represented resource allocations, especially of expenditures.

Because they track relatively disfavoured consumption in a production-dominated economy, ruble-denominated accounts are most accurate and detailed for the costs and expenditures of Group B resources and are least accurate and most generalised for Group A resources, in particular for R&D resources, which are unrecognisably assimilated within Group A. According to USSR Prime Minister Nikolai Ryzhkov in 1989, 75% of all Soviet R&D budget allocation is for defence R&D.[11]

## The USSR's Defence Budget

The defence budget is the single bridge spanning what the Soviet Union says about warfare (in this case the military doctrine), what they build in the way of armed forces (force structure and modernisation) and what they do with what they build against what they say (readiness training and operations). Over time, the defence budget is the single link connecting the Soviet armed forces of the past to those of the future through those of the present.

This defence budget, for some years the subject of intensive study and controversy in the West (and in Japan and China), more recently became a subject of analysis and debate in the Soviet Union itself.

Because the defence budget is completely integrated, or absorbed, into the USSR's national economic planning and forecasting process, it is a highly valuable and eminently useful predictive instrument for assessing the future of the Soviet defence establishment according to the indigenous projection horizons of the USSR's national planning cycle.

It has been difficult for Western political and economic minds to regard seriously this Soviet predilection for mid- to long-range planning, but the purposefulness with which the Soviet Union and its Communist Party undertake this prognostication is supported by the size and complexity of the national planning and forecasting apparatus. Even though the effectiveness of this single, centralised planning process is rightly questioned by many foreign and Soviet authorities and critics, it persists largely unaltered under *perestroika* and amid the extensive political and social upheavals of the last two years.

The Soviet defence budget is highly integrated and undifferentiated within the USSR's national Five-Year Plan, that Plan's accompanying 15-year forecast and in the State budget, which together affect and, indeed, effect the whole of what may be called 'the Soviet System'. Arguably, the Plan may be said to *be* the system, a system which can be modelled according to relationships existing among politico-economic control, comparison, regulation, processing and monitoring elements tied together by feedback and control mechanisms.[12]

Apart from how well or how poorly this system functions, it is remarkable that the Soviet national planning process and its defence budget component have gone largely unused as an analytical tool and an instrument of prediction by Western defence analysts, policy support staffs and, thus, by decision-makers, during this generation.

The USSR's defence budget is one of few measurement devices

against which an otherwise self-fulfilling Soviet military doctrine may be checked and calibrated. If Soviet military doctrine is about the future of defence and warfare, the defence budget should be the means by which foreign observers can gauge that future.

To use such tools, provided by the Soviets according to their own values and methods, is to achieve a major breakthrough in Soviet studies by bringing to an almost entirely interpretative science, additional properties and revelations of prediction. Because Soviet planners point to something does not mean that they necessarily have it in hand, or will in the future act as planned; it does mean they are following a precise, structured method for acquiring or improving a capability. In itself, Soviet defence planning does not denote unequivocally an intention to employ a capability, but it does denote and describe a plan, and therein lies its virtue for Western and other foreign prediction and interpretation.

Intuitive assessing of the future has always been useful, but, at its heart, it is an act of guessing; method, in particular the native method of Soviet defence planners, will focus and arbitrate intuition to improve accuracy and precision, provided that the analysis is informed by differences among procedures, prospects and actual results.[13]

It has been widely believed that, in contrast to Western practices, the Soviet defence budget is a 'state secret', purposefully hidden from foreign observers and from most of the USSR's population — at least until 1987 – 90 when the Soviet government began openly to discuss its entire defence budget for the years 1988 – 91. Prior to that time, the USSR's published defence budget was a small ruble sum, representing only the known annual allocations and accounting for military operations and not the much higher and unknown amounts for force structure, modernisation and R&D.[14]

That Soviet officials purposefully and directly concealed and misrepresented the defence budget over many years was only partially and indirectly the case. Even though General-Major Sergei S. Filimonov, head of the USSR Main Military Censorship Office, recently stated that Soviet economic, scientific and technical, commercial and military secrets have legal protection, a law was introduced in the Supreme Soviet and passed on 1 August 1990 to loosen constraints on that legal protection. (Such state secrets are listed on a serially-numbered, annual 'List of Materials and Information Forbidden for Open Publication'. In the mid-1970s this list forbade publication of such 'military secrets' as the ruble figure for investment in the Baikur-Amur Magistral railroad and the numerical output of any tractor factory, which also produces tanks.[15])

The reason Soviet officials are now discussing in their national legislature, media and at conferences what purports to be the entire defence budget has far more to do with *perestroika* planning than with *glasnost'*. Before 1988, Soviet officials had no real quantitative measure of the financially-representable portion of the national budget expended on defence and could not have provided direct evidence of what they themselves did not account. To attempt to define accurately the share of the USSR's net material product (NMP) supporting defence was an unrewarding task because the Soviets themselves did not have such information.[16]

What they did know by accounting were large — but not all — expenditures as measured in materials and labour terms (such as tons, hours, etc.), the preferred basis of accounting in a Marxist-Leninist non-market economy; however even in those terms, the Soviet accounting system was not able to identify accurate or inclusively-comprehensive allocations and expenditures for defence procurements and, especially, not for military R&D which is particularly undifferentiated in Group A of the USSR national economic resources.

Why should there be such lack of precision? Apart from the fact that Soviet officials generally have had no responsibilities for public scrutiny of accounts and no body of independent auditing, this lack of definition derives almost entirely from the highly integrated, undifferentiated and simplified planning, production and consumption processes and mechanisms of the Soviet economy introduced over 50 years ago by Stalin's third chief planner, N. A. Voznesensky; a process of inexactitude subsequently institutionalised and closely followed with no significant deviations for over half a century. Harrison's 1985 landmark study, *Soviet Planning in Peace and War, 1938 – 45*, is necessary reading for a more consummate understanding of the defence economics of the USSR which *perestroika* now seeks to change than it is feasible to present here. The system which Harrison describes began in 1938 and has not yet greatly changed.[17]

The USSR's defence budget is kneaded into the larger dough of the national budget in a manner so enfolded that, beyond an early planning point, defence items are not separately recognisable. Supporting not only the Soviet armed forces but also foreign clients and allies, the defence budget was never intended to be precise and differentiated. In 1990, it still was not.

The methods and principles which Voznesensky established in the late 1930s and carried through the Second World War were subsequently codified over 40 years of the Cold War, with no requirement to keep accounts except in gross terms. Capitalist planners and financial authorities would not tolerate such accounting, but Soviet authorities have tolerated them well. Now, however, the *perestroika* leadership pays an onerous price for such lack of accurate and detailed information as it tries to introduce detail, frankness and candour (*glasnost'*) into the economy and its accounting processes.

It is that massive non-market economic process to which Westerners actually allude when describing the contemporary Soviet economy as being run on a wartime basis during peacetime. What actually is implied is that hitherto there have been no alternatives. This single, enfolded, massive, centrally-planned and administered economic system, in which defence efforts have been principal but unpartitioned, perennially works to distribute extensive material and labour shortages under conditions of maximal infra-structural tautness while producing hundreds to thousands of copies of rigorously standardised, single-purpose, military equipments, most of which are obsolescent when they are produced.[18]

## Science and Technology in the Soviet Armed Forces

Probably by 1980, certainly by 1985, the Soviet system had deprived the Soviet armed forces, as well as the nation as a whole, of any indigenous, high-technology future as that term is generally understood. This happened because Soviet basic (fundamental) science was deprived of all but some 10% of the country's total science and engineering resources over a period of at least the last 20 years, and actually much longer. About 90% of the USSR's total national science and technology (S&T) resources were, in practice, allocated to producing engineering and technological capabilities.[19] Soviet basic science was denied resources which otherwise would have continued to support a robust, competitive, continually-growing technological future.

The Chairman of the Soviet Academy of Sciences and his colleagues have tried to correct this incredible imbalance but, through the draft planning of 1989 – 90 for the period 1991 – 5, were able to garner from the current Chief Planner, Yuri Maslyukov (a career official in Soviet defence production and policies and a former Chairman of the Military-Industrial Commission), less than a 5% increase in the S&T resources to be allotted to basic science during 1991 – 5. A distribution of those Soviet state resources for science and engineering which averaged 1:9 respectively over at least the period 1971 – 85 will stand at about 1:12 for the coming plan period, a ratio insufficient to correct, much less redress the problem of a negative technological future.[20] Even to the extent that Soviet leaders and planners recognise the disaster implicit in this ratio, they seem unable — perhaps also unwilling — to act decisively and expertly to correct the problem. In part, this reluctance may stem from the ultimate rationale of *perestroika*, which is not reform or transformation for its own sake but rather to the end of *uskoreniye*, in other words technological (*vice* scientific) acceleration. Though producing great scientists of international acclaim, the Soviet Union cannot manage science in effective ways that have future technological pay-offs. Instead they continue to forge ahead seeking the holy grail of technological prowess while forsaking the science which yields it. Odom (1985) wrote that it was not clear whether or not high-technology would take hold in the Soviet armed forces but in all probability it could not do so 'without extensive access to Western economies and R&D communities'.[21]

## *Perestroika* and the Armed Forces

As the US Central Intelligence Agency and the Defence Intelligence Agency predicted in March 1986 at the outset of *perestroika*, the Soviet military leadership initially favoured Gorbachev's reforms because of the end-goal of a technological acceleration which presumably would invigorate and re-vitalise Soviet military equipment and weapons systems. '. . . the real test of Gorbachev's support will come in two or three years when renewed demands for expanding and renovating defence industries begin. . .'[22]

Originally, elements of the USSR's military leadership may not only have anticipated reforms but also encouraged Gorbachev and his political coterie in the quest for, and the vision of, national economic restructuring according to the '*Perestroika* Plan', envisaging the period 1986 – 95 during which large amounts of obsolescent and obsolete military equipment would be traded off for new and more modern equipment of the future. The essence of that military economic strategy was to apply savings realised from discarding large stocks of old equipment to sharply increased military R&D without decreasing the overall defence budget. Essentially, they would have traded the old of the past for the new of the future based on force structure procurement savings redirected to R&D.

Given the methods of Soviet planning and economic organisation, this was an eminently rational idea. During 1986 – 88, it appeared that the strategy was sound and would work, but, by early 1989, the politically centrist Soviet leadership had lost not only the support of the military leadership but also control over the armed forces as the country passed into a period of dissolution, disorder, chaos, civil war and a sometimes vocal if not also violent revolution; indeed a general breakdown of social, political and economical order reminiscent of Russian history in 1904 – 24.[23]

References to Figures 12.1 and 12.2 and Table 12.2 data (on which the Figures' curves are based) show the policy and planning fluctuations of the Soviet defence budget over the last three Five-Year Plan periods, projected through the next two Plans according to the statistical mean across the 1976 – 90 period.[24] The 15-year forecast through 1990 would have been prognosticated during the national

TABLE 12.2 USSR DEFENCE BUDGET FINANCIAL DATA: 10th, 11th & 12th Five-Year Plans (in billions of rubles with percentage of the total budget per year included). These data key figures 1 and 2.

| | 1976 | 1977 | 1978 | 1979 | 1980 | 1981 | 1982 | 1983 | 1984 | 1985 | 1986 | 1987 | 1988 | 1989 | 1990 | Average |
|---|---|---|---|---|---|---|---|---|---|---|---|---|---|---|---|---|
| **Force structure (procurement & modernisation) ie, Group A for armaments, equipment and military construction or 'accumulation'** | | | | | | | | | | | | | | | | |
| | 36.7 | 38.6 | 39.8 | 40.5 | 37.3 | 43.6 | 42.5 | 45.8 | 48.2 | — | — | — | — | 37.2 | 34.8 | 40.4 |
| % | 68.5 | 67.5 | 66.3 | 65.4 | 64.1 | 66.4 | 65.7 | 66.1 | 59.7 | — | — | 42.0 | — | 45.1 | 48.9 | 60.5 |
| **Military RDT&E including design, ie, Group A for all R&D plus T&E plus other, miscellaneous non-material 'accumulation'** | | | | | | | | | | | | | | | | |
| | 6.0 | 6.2 | 6.5 | 6.8 | 7.6 | 7.7 | 7.8 | 8.2 | 9.3 | — | — | — | — | 22.8 | 14.5 | 9.4 |
| % | 11.2 | 10.8 | 10.8 | 11.0 | 13.1 | 11.7 | 12.1 | 11.9 | 11.5 | — | — | 20.0 | — | 27.6 | 20.4 | 14.3 |
| **Readiness Operations ie, Group B for all armed forces labour consumables, limited upkeep of equipment and pensions or 'consumption'** | | | | | | | | | | | | | | | | |
| | 10.9 | 12.4 | 13.7 | 14.6 | 13.3 | 14.4 | 14.4 | 15.3 | 23.2 | 21.5 | 22.2 | 22.5 | 22.5 | 22.5 | 21.8 | 17.7 |
| % | 20.3 | 21.7 | 22.8 | 23.6 | 22.9 | 21.9 | 22.3 | 22.1 | 28.7 | 21.5 | — | 38.0 | — | 27.3 | 30.7 | 24.9 |
| **TOTAL DEFENCE BUDGET** | | | | | | | | | | | | | | | | |
| | 53.6 | 57.2 | 60.0 | 61.9 | 58.2 | 65.7 | 64.7 | 69.3 | 80.7 | — | — | — | — | 8.25 | 71.1 | 65.9 |

*Notes* (1) In May, 1989, Gorbachev gave the projected total defence budget for 1991 as R72.5b.
(2) All 1989 and 1990 data in this table are taken directly from Soviet sources as stated under *glasnost*. Data of 1976 through 1984 are analytically derived and inferred from USSR national income accounts by K. Mochizuki (Japan, 1987) and collated and condensed by Westwood (USA, 1990). These 1976–84 data therefore are estimative and not contained in Soviet accounts. The 1985–88 data for readiness were published in and are taken from Soviet account.

FIGURE 12.1 Soviet Defence Budget as a Measure of Military Doctrine; total budget with force structure, military R&D and readiness operations components shown separately.

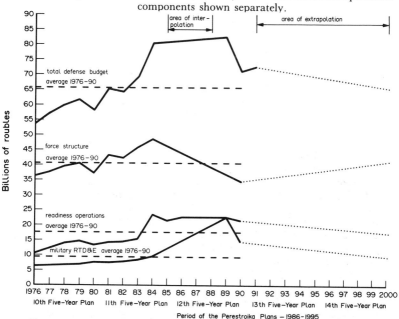

FIGURE 12.2 Soviet Defence Budget Trend; Percentage of Total Budget by Components to illustrate trade-off decisions as an empirical measure of Soviet military doctrine

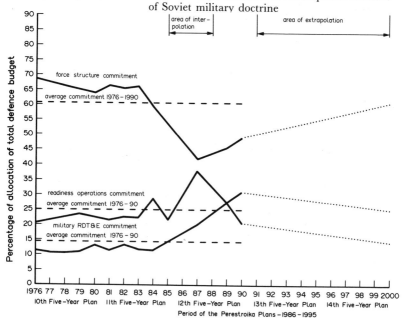

planning activity of 1974 – 75, *before* the decade of flattening of Soviet military hardware procurement pointed to in the CIA/DIA reports of 1986. Indeed, as Prime Minister Ryzhkov stated in 1989, the Soviet defence budget had been planned to grow at a rate faster than the growth of national income during 1986 – 90.[25]

Figures 12.1 and 12.2 are exercises in the use of Soviet quantitative decision-making data to test qualitative Soviet defence doctrine. In particular, Figure 12.2 reveals the trade-offs between force structure and R&D in Group A and the military demands on excessive shortages of labour and consumable supplies in national Group B resources over the long term, as discussed above. Many interesting insights can be gleaned from studying these curves within the context of the Soviet defence planning system. For example, not only may the Group A trade-off between procurement and R&D from 1983 through 1988 be seen but also how the sharp increase in R&D from 1984 anticipates the upturn in procurement three years later. It will be observed how the curves are at their respective mean values almost entirely and only during the 11th Five-Year Plan (1981 – 85), the halcyon years of the Soviet armed forces' push for force modernisation. It also may be seen that, whereas the overall defence budget (in ruble terms) declines from 1989 through 1995, more importantly, the percentage to R&D declines as the percentage to force structure inclines. Over the same period, Soviet-announced target goals for overall defence budget shrinkage during 1989 – 95 do not change those trends and relationships.

In essence, what one observes in these Figures is a national defence planning process which reverts, historically and in spite of *perestroika*, to resource force structure at the expense of sustained force modernisation — modernisation which otherwise can be guaranteed only by sustaining R&D over a leading period of at least 10 to 15 years. What is seen is what is expected: a nation whose economy is so production-dominated that it cannot effectively resource and manage science; a nation where military consumption for readiness is seen to exceed its mean throughout the original *perestroika* plan period (1986 – 95) at the expense of extremely hard-pressing civil requirements.

Over the last three years, the published Soviet defence budget data are not so approximate that they disguise the very recent disaffection of the Soviet armed forces with the original *perestroika* plan — a plan on which the armed forces hung their own strategy of *uskoreniye*. Defence budget data indicates that, since mid-1989, the USSR's armed forces leadership has forsaken its earlier commitment to trading off past force structure for future force modernisation, lately forecasting a defence budget which returns them to the procurement-dominated programmes of the pre-*perestroika* past. One may conjecture that the defence establishment's leadership is all too painfully aware that the continuous denuding of basic sciences resources in the USSR since the 1930s presumes no rectification in the 1990s and that the armed forces, ridding themselves of costly, outmoded equipment in large numbers, is better off in relative terms if it continues to pursue a large force structure of single-purpose systems according to traditional methods and means. The defence budget data and other recent evidence of the discontent of the Soviet armed forces' leadership show a destiny of largely unmitigated entropy as the empire becomes ever more lost. The armed forces were not for long serious about *perestroika*, and, even when they were (1981 – 88), sought to co-opt it to their own peculiar ends.

Gorbachev's statement in May 1989 that the defence budget was 'frozen' in 1987 – 88 is not supported by the Soviet data itself, unless he was speaking only of its Group B portion. Is Gorbachev dissembling or is his information inaccurate and incomplete? In 1989 Gorbachev intimated that the 1991 defence budget could be 72.5bn. rubles, a figure higher than the 1990 defence budget of 71.1bn.[26]

## Defence Industry Conversion

Yet, what of 'conversion', the Soviet restructuring which converts certain defence production capacities to civil products, converting old tanks into snow ploughs and fire-fighting vehicles, missile platforms into construction cranes (military construction?) and missile exhaust nozzles into flower pots?

First, one should not confuse Soviet civil products with civilian consumer products. The latter are items such as hosiery, soap, matches, gasoline, birth control products, home furnishings and food. By late 1988, senior Soviet military officers were still advocating the consumption savings campaign which they began in 1985.

Second, it should be kept in mind that 'conversion' is something of a misnomer in as much as about 40% of Soviet defence capacity has been producing non-defence products for many years, turning out vacuum cleaners, refrigerators, automobiles, television sets and baby carriages in large numbers, as well as tractors, locomotives and mining equipment — none of which have corrected the ineluctable feeding, lingerie or hygiene problems of the USSR.

In December 1989, Prime Minister Ryzhkov placed the major burden of resuscitating the USSR national economy on the defence industry by means of the conversion programme, the goal being to direct 'excess' defence production capacity at the light and food industries. Forty-six per cent conversion in those areas is targeted for 1991; over 60% by end 1995 during a period (1991 – 95) when it is hoped to reduce the 1989 total defence budget by one-third to one-half.[27]

No sooner was the conversion programme for 1991 – 95 announced than the expected difficulties came under discussion. One example is illustrative: 'Radio engineering plants . . . are in no hurry to produce . . . stereo tape recorders . . . sound systems . . . colour television sets, VCRs . . . and radio-controlled toys.'[28] By the end of 1989, complaints were heard in the Second Congress of People's Deputies that 'together with mounting economic confusion . . . conversion has been an additional heavy burden on the state enterprises'.[29]

Unlike Hewett's (1988) conclusions, we infer here that the Soviet Union cannot, by traditional methods, ever enjoy both guns and butter, if by 'butter', one connotes contemporary, widely-distributed technological sufficiency.[30] Kassel (1986) estimated that even were the USSR to improve significantly its computer R&D and production, it still might not be able to close its high technology gap with the developed nations.[31] The interminable economic and S&T shortfalls of the USSR are not the fault of the present centrist, visionary leadership. The Soviet economy is undifferentiated as between defence and both civil and civilian accumulations and consumption. Accounting data often are imprecise or irremediably corrupted, providing misleading information. Historical economic processes set in motion in the 1930s run on into maximal entropy in the 1990s. That Gorbachev's second chief planner has had a career in the presumably more efficient defence industry helps little when the single, national planning methodology remains unaltered and when the design and manufacturing of military hardware overall is no more capable or scientifically endowed than is the general production of which it is a large part. What ails the Soviet economy in general ails the defence economy in particular.

Soviet economist, O. T. Bogomolov (1989), describes this overpowering problem thus:

> The results of 1989 point to an aggravation of the economic crisis. The growing difficulties in supply and the deterioration in the quality of life have caused strikes in many regions of the country. The problems of relations between different ethnic groups are becoming more acute as a result of economic difficulties. A redistribution of budget investment in favour of housing, health care and education, light industry and the food industries has not yet produced tangible results. There has been no radical improvement in agriculture. The *per capita* output of foodstuffs is not increasing and the country still depends on 40 – 50 million tonnes of grain imports annually.
>
> The reform of the Soviet economy is burdened with problems accumulated over the previous period. The most serious implications of these are associated with significant disturbances in the structure of social production; the low quality and technical level

of many products; high production costs; and the insufficient skills and inappropriate approach and discipline of the workforce. The poor performance of agriculture and in the manufacture of consumer goods, combined with a hypertrophied development of heavy industry, constitute some of the fundamental defects of our economy. However, heavy industry itself developed irrationally: machine building, advanced chemistry and electronics are still underdeveloped.

The reason is the continuing strict control on the part of ministries, the lack of a wholesale-trade market and the imperfections of the price and tax systems. Appeals for the economic independence of mines, for increases in coal prices, for the right of free sale of production output which exceeds the obligatory quantities required by the state ...

The success of *perestroika* is highly dependent on the extent to which two harmful diseases are brought under control. These are inflation and the shadow economy that nourishes corruption. The state budget has for a long time been in deficit which this year is expected to amount to 100 bn rubles or 11% of the gross domestic product (GDP). This is the consequence of a rapid growth of expenditures and a considerable reduction of budget revenues; the latter having declined principally as a result of the fall in prices of Soviet exports and cuts in the state production of alcohol. The budget deficit is compensated by the issue on money and credit not backed by goods. The state debt is growing. The public looks to spend its money on the commodities it requires, but does not find them. The commodity hunger is growing ever more acute despite an increasing output of deficit goods.[32]

## Come the Revolution

In March 1990, the Supreme Soviet passed a law revising, up-dating and clarifying the duties and responsibilities of the 'Internal-Security Troops of the Ministry of the Internal Affairs in Protecting Public Order'. As the weather warmed, the people increasingly took their disillusion and discontent into the streets. Many expected that the USSR overall would degenerate into a state of classical, thorough-going revolution not unlike the French Revolution of 1789. One eminent Sovietologist (Bialer, 1990) in a remarkable essay shows this breakdown and overthrow of order to have begun in 1989.[33] It will probably persist for a decade or more. Unofficially the Soviets themselves richly describe this tumult as consisting of chaos, civil war, and disintegration; officially they call it transformation.

The attempt of this or any subsequent government to deal with this wide-spread upheaval of the old order cannot be confined for very long to the employment of only the Troops of the Ministry of Internal Affairs. The armed forces, acting by government order, or on their own (as during 1917 – 18), surely must be employed eventually to secure facilities, restore order, suppress ethnic and nationality revolts, operate communications and transportation infrastructures and so forth. Economically, such extensive military operations even now are placing heavy demands on already scarce supplies, in particular fuel, food, electricity, exacerbating the very problems which security forces would attempt to correct. 'Public order' military operations, extenuated by operations reactive to fears, perceived or real, of foreign intervention, foreign surveillance — or even attack — during a vulnerable period, would drive military expenditures in Group B out of tolerance, requiring recourse, on an emergency basis, to more than the one-third share of 'state reserves' normally claimed by the armed forces. Moreover, manpower demands (Group B) of all security forces would be driving up by the requirements of a civil war. Under such conditions, the Soviet armed forces might not be reducing their overall manpower as they, themselves, predicted in 1988 – 90. Even though Garthoff (1990) showed that announced Soviet armed forces reductions would be, by January 1991, 'very close to the number at the time Khrushchev announced his force reduction in January 1960', current circumstances inside the USSR are dictating otherwise.[34]

## Alternative Futures

Widespread disorder, disunity, distortion and governmental instability in the USSR over years to come will have a negative impact on the national planning mechanisms and on the production facilities which support the defence establishment for systems acquisitions programmes and for military R&D. In 1989 – 90, traditional long-term, deliberate military planning in the USSR was increasingly being supplanted by short-term, *ad hoc* crisis planning even as the armed forces sought to wrest back their established role in arms control and in systematic long-range planning.[35]

Although the fat now is in the fire, it is instructive to examine the prospects and implications for equipping and training the Soviet armed forces if political and social upheaval should not further develop. Under the original plans and goals of the military-adapted *perestroika* and its once-inevitable companion, *uskoreniye*, the defence budget allocation to military readiness operations for 1986 – 95 would still have run above its 1976 – 90 average. Were there to have been no extraordinary demands on military readiness in the 1990s, the Soviet armed forces expected to adopt an exercise theme during 1991 – 95 to test and train according to the three basic models of the new defensive doctrine which were studied during the 1984 – 88 reassessment period: the celebrated Khalgin'gol (1939), Kursk (1943) and Korean War stalemate period (1951 – 52). The first two involve an inevitable counteroffensive, a fact overlooked by some foreign analysts. (Nominally, the counter-offensive begins on the 21st day after commencement of the defended attack.) The third involves preparations for nuclear warfare. Khalgin'gol is a relatively small-scale, somewhat quickly-organised, single-front or army-level defence with a counter-offensive which drives the enemy out but does not intrude into enemy territory. Kursk is much larger, a multi-front defence of a geographically large area, systematically prepared by extensive fortifications over several weeks to months (even years), followed by a massive counter-offensive into the enemy's territory, relying on extensive armour and artillery operations in both the defensive and the offensive phases.

Under 'normal circumstances', the Khalgin'gol scenario would have been (or still might be) played in exercises during the 13th Five-Year Plan and the Kursk scenario exercised during the 14th Five-Year Plan. Khalgin'gol is less threatening to foreign observers, and many have been experimentally rehearsed in exercises as early as 1988.

During the temporary period (1984 – 88) of recalculation and re-orientation of Soviet military doctrine, strategy and resourcing, two remarkable and representative works of contrasting themes appeared, each in 10,000 copies: *Fortifications, Past and Present* (1987) and *Tank Armies in the Offensive* (1988). The former is a consummate engineering study of 'the science of strengthening the terrain in the interest of winning victory over the enemy. . .' and mentions defensive operations as lasting 14 to 21 days. The second, and much longer work, mentions defensive operations not at all.[36] *Fortifications* appears to be based on the Korean War model; *Tank Armies* on the Kursk model.

In the Group A portion, where 69% of the Soviet defence budget was distributed for 1990, (against an average of 61% for 1976 – 90), insights into alternative futures come not only from logic about the changed requirements of a defensive doctrine and from the parameters of continuing force re-structuring and scaling-down, but also from General of Army, M. A. Moiseyev, Chief of the General Staff, and from General of Army V. Shabanov, since 1978 Deputy Minister of Defence for Armaments, who is the senior weapons system acquisition manager of the USSR's defence ministry.

That the long-term deprivation of resources for the perpetuation of basic science in the USSR has already resulted in a non-technological future of the armed forces is shown in an interview with Deputy Defence Minister Shabanov (1989) wherein he discusses the obsolescence of 'modern' Soviet military equipment and systems, their lack of reliability and their lag in development, specifying 'radar weapons, infra-red-imaging, night-vision instruments and communications and control equipment'. 'Reliability', he says, 'is bothering us particularly'. Kirilenko (1990) confirms the specific lags *vis-à-vis* Western developments.[37]

On matters of *uskoreniye* in the Soviet armed forces, the military leadership is perplexed and inconsistent. Yazov (1988) and Plekhanov (1989) are specific about trading old qualities for new qualities, but later Yazov (1990) said: 'you can't have quality without quantity'.[38]

Since 1989, several Soviet authorities have said that the next two to four years would be the most confused and difficult along the road to realising the reforms. In 1988, Marshal Akromeyev said it would take three years to see results of defence resource decisions. Deputy Prime Minister Abalkin has said repeatedly that real results will not be seen until the year 2000. In late 1989 and early 1990, the CIA and DIA hastened to revise downward their 1987 and 1988 estimates of Soviet defence spending.[39] A US intelligence community report to President Bush in May 1989 said that the USSR was reversing a long-term pattern of military spending growth which would continue for from five to seven years.[40] Aslund, Lee and Holzman have criticised CIA studies of Soviet defence economics.[41]

A four-volume study prepared for Gorbachev in 1984 – 85 by the Soviet Institute of World Economics and International Relations made a thorough analysis of world affairs concluding that future trends were anti-military.[42] In August 1989, Soviet economist S.Ye. Blagovolin published a lengthy analysis of the costs of Soviet military power wherein he suggested that the infamous 'defence burden' had not yet been reduced.[43] Given the previous discussion of the armed forces' revised outlook, Blagovolin's comment is not surprising.

More specifically, what did Soviet defence authorities plan and programme for the 1991 – 2005 technological enrichment of the armed forces? As predicted in 1987 by the present author, for example, the steady evolutionary pattern of Soviet armour development would be broken by 1990. This prediction was confirmed in the 1990 Net Assessment of the US Joint Chiefs of Staff which noted that the rate and types of tank production have decreased and devolved.[44] Development of combat aircraft has been affected similarly.

In a masterwork on defence economics in the USSR, Colonel S. A. Bartenev, a Doctor of Economic Science discusses (1986) the key relationship between national economy and military capability in the USSR. He writes:

> Today, it is not just individual discoveries...but primarily the common front of scientific and technological progress and its

material foundation which are having an ever-increasing effect upon the development of the armed forces. Scientific discoveries ...embrace...all type of weapons...,which links science, production and military affairs in a...chain-like manner.

Shabanov (1986) emphasises maintaining strategic nuclear parity based on the single, integrated, three-part 'strategic nuclear force' discussed by the present author (1984) and by Goure (1986), mentioning 'interaction' and 'a highly efficient control system'.[46] Shabanov separately discusses Soviet 'general purpose forces developing within the limits necessary for defence'. With the 1986 – 90 plan and the 1991 – 2000 forecast in hand, he highlights ground forces improvements in IFVs, $C^3I$, artillery and combat helicopters. He stresses the new programme in theatre-wide air defence based on 'multiple anti-aircraft missile complexes', limits naval missions to 'operational tasks' and mentions the current and initial programme of fielding an automated planning and $C^3$ system. He cites the 'many problems associated with military hardware' in the case 'of hostilities with a technically strong enemy' against which he suggests Soviet 'principles of operations' will compensate — a Stalin-like notion of military principles.[47]

Yasyukov (1986) discusses how Soviet 'military building takes place in the spirit of general Soviet state building...' To invigorate the Soviet armed forces in the future, he leans heavily on the promise of *perestroika* and *uskoreniye* in machine building, electronics, nuclear power, laser technology and information science and pays considerable attention to revising training and education.[48] Donnelly's (1988) study for the US Institute of Defence Analysis underscores the 'pressure to improve the efficiency of (the) training system', and says 'we can expect to see the fielding of smaller quantities of technically-improved weapons systems...' accompanied by 'significant reorganisation'. He finds, however, that 'the development of weapons based on new physical principles is still in the realm of military science fiction, in that it may...be decades before this comes to pass.[49]

In July 1988, Shabanov was among the first to prognosticate a reduced Soviet defence budget, starting in the current Five-Year Plan. He forecast the revisions in tank and aircraft production mentioned above and the then-imminent appearance of the improved SS – 18 (MOD 5) as merely of a replacement of old parts. He played down artillery and tactical/theatre ballistic missiles and said that enlarged resources would be applied to air defence and reconnaissance systems.[50]

Moiseyev (1989) said that the overall defence budget would shrink by 14.2% and its Group A part by 19.5% in 1989 – 90, the total number of combined-arms divisions being cut by almost half and the number of major exercises reduced during 1990. He said that tactical

nuclear missiles withdrawn from Central Europe would not be modernised and that SS – 21 (SPIDER) would not be substituted for SS –
1B/C (SCUD). He added that promising designs for new strike
weapons systems were being cancelled and suggested that production
of weapons was being traded off for improved reliability, calling attention to new high-priority R&D directions.[51] Elsewhere, Moiseyev
detailed the future of Soviet $C^3$ systems.[52]

Yazov (1989) avers that at future stages in the reduction of strategic
weapons, 'their latent potentials should be equal...' He believes that
Soviet and Western conventional forces must be rendered 'incapable
of offensive operations'. He points to 'structural transformations' already
carried out, and states: 'We have reconsidered our strategy...From
here on the Soviet armed forces will concentrate on defensive operations
to repel aggression'. He says that the operational manoeuvre groups
(OMG) on the 1980s 'are to be disbanded'. Chervov (1990) suggests
that the previous planned and exercised offensive into Scandinavia is
of greatly reduced importance in view of contemplated (by early 1991)
reductions of tanks in the Leningrad Military District (LMD) (by one-
half, already carried out) and a cut of one-third in troops, tanks and
artillery of both the LMD and the Baltic Military District (BMD).[53]

Some three weeks after Yazov's commentary, Prime Minister Ryzhkov
discussed the priority development of Soviet fundamental research and
the creation of scientific, planning and design reserves. He said that
funding of basic science in 1991 would be 1.3 times that for 1990,
though in ruble total not as a percentage of total S&T resources. He
suggested that a 19.5% decrease in Group A military production is
confined to *offensive* systems, including SSBMs.[54]

If we keep in mind that military Group A economic resources includes
military construction, we can infer that savings in offensive weapons
production may be applied to future new construction of fortifications
as described by Levykin in 1987. Indeed, it was this new construction
which fomented the violent civil unrest in Azerbaijan in late 1989 as
the USSR build new defensive barriers and structures along the border
with Iran.

During the last few years, Soviet military and political authorities
discussed shortening the average military systems acquisition time of
10 to 15 years by between a third and a half, tracing the trend of
fundamentally new types of weapons and combat technology from
1971, the original forecast of which would have extended through
1985.

Ryzhkov outlined the second and third stage of *perestroika* as consisting of a 1990 – 92 normative period followed by a 1993 – 95 performance period. Early in 1990, faced with increasing urgency and beset
by discontent, Gorbachev undertook to by-pass the normative period by

advancing, in the second half of 1990, directly to the performance period.

Should the present convolution stabilise without endangering 'the Plan', one may expect by the year 2000 to see newly-built fortified areas inside the USSR, (more in the South and in the Far East than in the West) and widespread acquisition of counter-mobility systems. The weight of air strategy and air systems will transfer from air offence to air defence, according to planning begun in 1984 – 85. Results will present target-poor as against target-rich potential battlefields.

For the current $C^2$ system development programme, begun in basic research in 1956, one may expect not new programmes but improvements to the existing one, which was once forecast to run its course through 1990. A feature of these improvements will be the addition of decision support systems as originally developed in the US in the early 1980s.

From 1984 – 85, the Soviet navy was planned to experience the development of a new programme to deliver numerous new diesel-electric-powered attack submarines, as against continuing SSN/SSGN programmes and to witness continued applied science research in a novel approach to non-acoustic detection and tracking of submarines based on interesting geophysical principles and phenomena — a research programme begun in 1986 with expected pay-off for ASW applications by 2001 – 05.

Significant new attention is being given to Soviet military history, sociology, psychology and para-psychology treated as sciences. There is an understanding of the requirements to reduce the numbers of military systems operators and maintenance personnel by increasing systems automation. There is an all-out effort underway to proliferate microcomputers in the Soviet armed forces.

From the standpoint of the Soviet defence budget, perhaps the most fruitful way of divining the future of the Soviet armed forces is by studying the trends, programmes and proportions in and of military R&D. A 1981 CIA report described this particular analysis as being difficult and uncertain, while showing Soviet military R&D to be large and growing over the period 1971 – 80.[55] In 1986, Soviet military scientists spoke of applying basic research to the invention of advanced combat equipment, paying particular attention to technological break-throughs (*skachok*) in creating new kinds of weapons.[56]

In 1989, US Secretary of Defence Richard Cheney said of Soviet military R&D:

> We haven't seen any significant drop-off there, whether we are talking about strategic systems or new aircraft, new ships, improved submarine systems and so forth. The efforts that have been under-way in the past seem to be continuing apace without any slowing at this point.[57]

## Conclusion

The Soviet Union faces two serious and endemic problems in terms of overall defence economic resourcing and technological capability: a short-term problem through 1995 of personnel reductions in force (12% in 1989 – 90), resettlements, re-assignments, retraining and future employments; and equipment disposal and re-configuration of the demands of increased military training, security and public-order operations on national readiness resources and reserves, already greatly strained. Almost certainly troop morale will have serious, near-term repercussions apart from the ethnic divisions in the armed forces. The results of the spring 1990 semi-annual call-up of conscripts in the USSR drew highly unfavourable comments from top Soviet military leaders. Conscript shortages numbering many thousands were being reported by Soviet sources in 1990.

A long-term military budget and finance problem looms large. It concerns ruble convertibility, deficit financing and price reforms in the USSR. In 1989 Defence Minister Yazov pointed out that because of a non-market state economy, Soviet weapons system cost only a quarter of comparable Western systems.[58] In 1990 Chief of Staff Moiseyev discussed the sharply rising cost of military modernisation.[59] Early in 1989, Gorbachev stated that national budgetary problems were so acute that 'we will have to look to our expenditures on defence'.[60] Aganbegyan, long a critic of Soviet defence resourcing, complained in 1989 that the Soviet military budget reflects an old pricing system which sells armaments at a loss.[61]

Shelton's (1989) surprising study of the deficit gap in the USSR's national budget, ranging from 20% in the 1970s to over 30% by the late 1980s, was confirmed in 1989 and 1990 by senior Soviet political, economic and financial authorities, who called the deficit 'state problem number one' and the 'gravest heritage' of the Brezhnev years.[62] This deficit bears as heavily on Soviet defence economics as on the general economy, where revenues fall well short of expenditures.

A 1990 radical national price reform proposal, tied to a 'marketing' of the Soviet economy, could deregulate up to 70% of all prices, while consumables prices, such as energy and transportation, would continue to be subsidised. By mid-1990 precise calculations had not been made, but estimates showed the impact would be an immediate doubling of prices.

In January 1990, Gorbachev said that 83% of the USSR's national income is expended on consumption and non-production construction[63] — in an economy which devotes only some 30% of resources and capacities to Group B. This implies that in 1990 about 50% of Soviet civil and military consumption may already be deficit-financed. By

1995 the general USSR deficit, augured by price reforms, whether incremental or compelled, could send the carefully-crafted, artfully-forecasted Soviet defence budget into a tail-spin and a subsequent crash from which it would not recover in what remains of this century. In the worst case, this would place the Soviet armed forces in the unenviable position of having virtually to pillage the USSR economy for what they can get on an *ad hoc* basis.

Western defence policies did not drive Soviet defence to its present point. The Soviet system did it to itself. Given the constraints of a non-market economy, highly-vested military claimant interests, an inadequate and perverse accounting system, an excessive budget deficit and an historic, undifferentiated command economy, the end to which the Soviet system has now come was predictable years ago.

For the 1990s, the Soviet defence establishment has no options remaining. The once-new trends and directions in military R&D of 1981 – 88 were abandoned by 1989. The general debilitation of basic science in the USSR over many years has already deprived today's Soviet armed forces of yesterday's technological future. The armed forces will try to save what it can, preserving as best it can its traditional claim on production resources while under-resourcing military R&D and drawing more heavily than it otherwise would on scarce, dwindling consumption resources as increasing internal disorder develops.

The burden of defence on the USSR's revenues has been very large — 25% of the state budget in recent years, according to Foreign Minister Edouard Shevardnadze (1990), who reckoned opportunity costs thus forgone at 240 – 250 bn. rubles for the 12th Five-Year Plan (1986 – 90) alone.[64] The USSR budget deficit for 1989 was nearly 45% of that opportunity cost, and that cost was nearly 79% of the USSR's total national debt for 1989. In the short run, price reforms and the extraordinary budget deficit can only exacerbate an otherwise overdrawn, production-dominated USSR defence budget. A nation paying for its international trade imports with its gold reserves and selling its diamonds on the world market is a nation in final desperation. Even were basic science to be funded above its historic margin, the 'brain-drain' of Soviet scientists emigrating or remaining abroad, and also migrating continuously from research institutions to industry within the USSR, will continue to deplete the armed forces of the talents most critically required to affect any meaningful *uskoreniye* in the defence establishment.

Finally, the current period of revolution, civil war, break-down or order and collapse of the Soviet system has only just begun to run its course in the USSR. The last such era in Russian/Soviet history lasted two decades (1904 – 24) during which the armed forces were vanquished and decimated in two major foreign wars, incurred the interventions of four major foreign powers' military forces (over 100,000 foreign troops) inside the USSR and experienced a devastating civil war. During the last quarter of the 19th century and the first 15 years of this century, Tzarist Russia incurred mounting indebtedness to foreign creditors and a budget deficit which it was unable to pay or to eradicate. By 1900 an economic crisis prevailed in Russia and, from 1905, measures to invigorate production were paid for at the price of depressed consumption and consumer satisfaction. This endemic problem was 'solved' by the Bolsheviks' repudiation of all the deposed Tzar's debts. McConnell (1988) notes that Gorbachev's first *perestroika* plan (1986 – 90) 'suggests that more investment in engineering is to be paid. . . by less consumption and less investment in social programmes'. In 1986, Soviet economic management authorities described the intent of the national five-year planning process to maintain labour and material, production capacity and financial and budget balances in the USSR national economy. Such 'balances' did not occur in the last Tzarist period nor do they in the late Communist period.[65]

Until the USSR has passed through the entire period of national convulsion and convolution which it has recently entered, defence economic planning will first devolve before it can revolve. Nevertheless, it is not now premature to ask what the phoenix will be like in 10 or 15 years.

## Notes

[1] Expert studies have produced varying differences of this comparison, often because GNP is used as the universal standard when, in fact, the USSR economy cannot be assessed in terms of GNP but only in its own net material product (NMP) terms. See M. Wines, 'CIA Accused of Overestimating Soviet Economy', *New York Times*, 23 July 1990, p. A6 and R. Pear, 'Soviet Experts Say Their Economy Is Worse Than US Has Estimated', *New York Times*, 24 April 1990, p. A14.

[2] W. Gertz, 'Analyst Faults CIA for Going Astray on Soviet Spending', *Washington Times*, 17 July 1990, p. A5 and M. Wines, 'CIA Accused of Overestimating Soviet Economy', *New York Times*, 23 July 1990, p. A6.

[3] It is imperative to understand this two-group split to predict Soviet economic accounting and behaviour. See A. Yeshov, *Organisation of Statistics in the USSR* (Moscow: Progress Publishers, 1965); C. Krylov, *The Soviet Economy* (Lexington: Lexington Books, 1979) and T. Ryabishkin, *Economic Statistics* (Moscow, 1966) p. 176.

[4] J. Westwood, 'USSR's 12th Five-Year Plan and Its Zero-Growth Defence Budget', in D. Jones, ed., *Soviet Armed Forces Review Annual* (Gulf Breeze: Academic International Press, 1989).

[5] Lecture of Prof. Peter Wiles, University of London, AAASS World Congress III, Washington, DC, 31 October 1985 including Wiles' paper, 'Soviet Military Finance'. See also: B. Rumer, 'A Note on Independent Investment Behaviour and the Diversion of Funds from Repairs to New Capacity', *Soviet Studies*, January 1987, pp. 116 – 121.

[6] V. Faltsman, 'The Economics of Scientific and Technical Progress: Ways of Changing Machine Building', *Economy and Organisation of Industrial Production*, No. 12, 1985, pp. 3 – 20.

[7] Gen.-Maj. V. Makarevskiy, 'On Reasonable Sufficiency, Fragile Parity and International Security', *New York Times*, 3 July 1987, pp. 18 – 19.

[8] Numerous central military staffs around the world use this same basic approach to forecasting requirements, *viz.*, the generation of estimates and net assessments. See Gen.-Col. F. Gayvoronskiy, ed., *The Evolution of Military Art: Stages, Tendencies and Principles* (Moscow: Military Publishing House, 1987) which established the Soviet armed forces' rationale for its support of *perestroika* based on the principle of trading off old force structure for increased military R&D resourcing, a position reversed two years later.

[9] A lucid, terse explanation of Soviet and Warsaw Pact deliberate planning is Gen.-Maj. J. Sejna and Dr. J. Douglass, Jr., *Decision-Making in Communist Countries: An Inside View* (Washington, DC: Pergamon-Brassey's, 1986 Ch. 5 On the long-range forecast to 25 – 50 years, see S. V. Moiseyev, *et al*, *Economics of the Instrument Building Industry* (Moscow: *Machinostroyeniye*, 1988), pp. 64 – 65.)

[10] *Fundamentals of Scientific Management of the Socialist Economy* (Moscow: Progress Publishers, 1989). See, eg, Chs 3 and 8.

[11] Interview of N. Ryzhkov, 'Difficult Transitions', *Soviet Life*, October 1989, p. 4. In 1989, USSR official data showed the military budget to be 12% of national income.

[12] This model is introduced and developed by Dr. Daniel Howland of the US Air Force's Foreign Technology Division, Wright-Patterson AFB, Ohio, and applied by the present analyst, eg, J. Westwood, 'Modeling a Changing Soviet System: Survival, Success or Failure?' 58th Military Operations Research Society Symposium, US Naval Academy, 12 – 14 June 1990.

[13] See interview of S. G. Guchmazov, head of the Department of Defence Industries of the USSR Council of Ministers in *Governmental Herald*, No. 25 (December), 1989, pp. 6 – 7.

[14] This was well understood at least a decade before the Soviets 'admitted' that the published defence budget had been only that for operations until 1988. See, eg, R. Leggett and S. Rabin, 'A Note on the Meaning of the Soviet Defence Budget', *Soviet Studies*, October 1978, pp. 557 – 66.

[15] Interview with S. Filinov, 'From Competent Sources: Military Censorship: What Is Permitted and What Is Not', *Izvestiya*, 27 November 1989, p. 2; P. Almond, 'Soviet Manual Tells What Gets in Print', *Washington Times*, 5 January 1985, p. B5; E. Pond, *From the Yaroslavsky Station: Russia Perceived* (New York: Universe Books, 1981) pp. 64 – 66.

[16] 'Carlucci-Yazov Talks Boost Soviet Image', *Jane's Defence Weekly*, 26 March 1988, p. 561: O. Bogomolov quoted in R. Pear, 'Soviet Experts Say Their Economy is Worse Than US Has Estimated', *New York Times*, 24th April 1990, p. A14; A. Beichman quoting former US Secretary of Defence F. Carlucci in 'A Hard Look at Soviet Forces', *Washington Times*, September 1988, p. F4; B. Rayzberg, 'Lecture for All: Is it Easy to Beat Swords into Plowshares?', *Nedelya*, No. 8, 1989, p. 6

[17] Mark Harrison, *Soviet Planning in Peace and War, 1938 – 1945* (Cambridge: Cambridge University Press, 1985).

[18] M. Checinski, 'The Economics of Defence in the USSR', *Survey*, Spring 1985, pp. 70 – 78.

[19] This remarkable quantification is found first in G. Marchuk (President, Soviet Academy of Sciences), 'Re-organising the Scientific Activity of Academic Institutions', *Herald of the Academy of Sciences*, No. 1, 1987

[20] This marginal change in the S&T resourcing ratio is a calculated correlation

between the 1971 – 89 average ratio and the published allocations for 1990. See V. Pavlov, 'On the State Budget for 1990', *Economic Gazette*, No. 40, 1989, pp. 9 – 13. See also 'Soviet Scientists Tell It Like It Is', *Physics Today*, September 1988, pp. 97 – 99.

21 W. Odom, 'Soviet Force Posture: Dilemmas and Directions', *Problems of Communism*, July – August, 1985, p. 11. See also 'Dilemmas and Directions in Soviet Force Development Policy', Kennan Institute for Advanced Russian Studies, Report No. 196, 30 January 1985.

22 F. Hiatt, 'Soviet Arms Outlay Steady, CIA Asserts', *Washington Post*, 31 March 1986, p. A3.

23 This fissure between the national political and military leadership is reflected *inter alia* not only in Soviet defence budget decisions but also in recent remarks by eminent personages such as Chief of the General Staff, Gen. Moiseyev, and the Director of USSR State Historical Archives, Dr. Afanasiev. See interview with Gen. M. A. Moiseyev, *Red Star*, 15 March 1990, p. 1 – 2 and remarks by Dr. Yu Afanasiev at Georgetown University, Washington DC, on 29 May 1990, in response to a question by the present writer that whereas Soviet armed forces are not monolithic, they also are no longer fully controlled by the USSR President nor by the CPSU; that no USSR official completely controls the armed forces.

24 Table 12.2 data are taken from a variety of original Soviet sources of 1988 – 90 and from analytical data in works such as C. Jacobson, ed., *The Soviet Defence Enigma* (Oxford: Oxford University Press, 1987). See especially K. Mochizuki, 'Estimating Soviet Defence Expenditures from National Accounts'.

25 N. Ryzhkov, 'On the Programme of Upcoming Work of the USSR Government', *Izvestiya*, 8 June 1989, pp. 1 – 3.

26 M. Gorbachev, speech before Congress of People's Deputies, 30 May 1989 (Moscow television).

27 N. Ryzhkov, 'Effectiveness, Consolidation and Reform: The Path to a Healthy Economy', *Economic Gazette*, No. 51, 1989, pp. 8 – 13. The 40% existing baseline has been cited by Marshal Akhromeyev (1988), Gen. Arkhipov (1989) and by V. Semenov (1984) who said the baseline was 42% in the 1970s.

28 A. Kleva, 'Tank Plant Stalls With Conversion', *Izvestiya*, 18 October 1989, p. 2. Among numerous discussions of the uncertainty of and lack of enthusiasm for conversion is V. Ulyanov, 'Aviation Industry Seeks Restitution of Losses from Conversion', *Economic Gazette*, No. 30, 1989, p. 9

29 Speech by B. V. Gidaspov, Congress of People's Deputies, 16 December 1989 (Moscow television).

30 E. Hewett, *Reforming the Soviet Economy* (Washington, DC: The Brookings Institution, 1988), Ch 8.

31 S. Kassel, 'A New Force in the Soviet Computer Industry: The Reorganisation of the USSR Academy of Sciences in the Computer Field', (Santa Monica: RAND Corporation, 1986) (N – 2486 – ARPA), p. 33.

32 O. Bogomolov, 'The Origins of Change in the Soviet Union', *The Strategic Implications of Change in the Soviet Union* (London: International Institute of Strategic Studies Adelphi Paper No. 247, Winter 1989 – 90) pp. 18 – 19.

33 S. Bialer, 'The Passing of the Soviet Order', *Survival*, March/April 1990, pp. 17 – 21.

34 R. Garthoff, 'Estimating Soviet Military Force Levels', *International Security*, Spring 1990, p. 108.

35 Among numerous items of evidence is an interview of Marshal D. Yazov, Minister of Defence, *Izvestiya*, 1 July 1990, p. 2 and reports such as M. Sieff, 'Gorbachev Orders Paramilitary Forces to Disarm', *Washington Times*, 26 July 1990, p. A7.

[36] V. Levykin, *Fortifications, Past and Present* (Moscow: Military Publishing House, 1987); I. Ananyev, *Tank Armies in the Offensive: According to the Experience of the Great Patriotic War* (Moscow: Military Publishing House, 1988).

[37] V. Shabanov, 'Directions for Improvement, Peaceful Conversion of Military Equipment', *Red Star*, 18 August 1989, pp. 1 – 2; G. Kirilenko, 'Refuting Critics of USSR's Surplus Military Power', *Red Star*, 21 March 1990, p. 2

[38] V. Plekhanov, 'On Guard for Socialism and Peace', *Under the Banner of Leninism*, January 1989, pp. 49 – 52; Yazov as quoted by M. Dobbs, 'Soviet Army's New Battlefield: The Political Front', *Washington Post*. 15 April 1990, p. A28. See also V. Karpov quoted in 'Moscow Appoints New Military Chief', *Washington Times*, 16 December 1988, p. A8.

[39] D. Oberdorfer, 'US Intelligence Report Sees Soviet Economy as "Abysmal" '. *Washington Post*, 21 April 1990, pp. A1 and A20.

[40] P. Tyer, R. Smith, 'Bush alerted in May to Soviet Military Cuts', *Washington Post*, 11 December 1989, p. A21.

[41] W. Brookes, 'Surprised Because of Bum CIA Data', *Washington Times*, February 1990, p. F1; F. Holzman, 'Politics and Guess Work', *International Security*, Fall 1989; 'How CIA Concocts Soviet Defence Numbers', *New York Times*, 25 October 1989, p. A30; 'Are We Falling Behind the Soviets', *Atlantic*, 23 July 1983; W. Gertz, 'Analyst Faults CIA for Going Astray on Soviet Spending', *Washington Times*, 17 July 1990, p. A5.

[42] Reported in D. Remnick 'Gorbachev's Policy: Turning A Weak Hand into Grand Strategy', *Washington Post*, 18 February 1990, p. A35.

[43] S. Blagovolin, 'The How and Why of Military Power', *World Economics and International Relations*, No. 8, 1989, pp. 5 – 19.

[44] J. Westwood, 'Looking Ahead to the Next Soviet MBT', *Jane's Defence Weekly*, 10 October 1987, pp. 817 – 819 and D. Rosenbaum, 'US Sees Threats to Soviet Economy', *New York Times*, 21 April 1990, p. A4.

[45] S. Bartenev, *Economic Conflict in Warfare* (Moscow: Military Publishing House, 1986), p. 6.

[46] J. Westwood, 'Integration of the Soviet Navy: The Strategic Offensive Force Case', in *Proceedings of a Conference on Soviet Military Personnel and Organisation* (College Station: Centre for Strategic Technology of Texas A&M University, 1985, pp; 73 – 100; D. Goure, $C^3$ and the New Soviet Nuclear Forces', *Signal*, December 1986, pp. 86 – 90.

[47] V. Shabanov, 'The Material Basis of Defense Might', *Red Star,* 15 August 1986, pp. 2 – 3.

[48] M. Yasyukov, 'The 27th CPSU Congress: Questions of Defence Policy', *Red Star*, 3 December 1986, pp. 2 – 3.

[49] C. Donnelly, *Future Trends in Soviet Military-Technical Policy* (RMA Sandhurst, June 1988), p. 18.

[50] Reported in R. Smith, 'Arms Budget Cut, Soviet Says', *Washington Post*, 27 July 1988, pp. A1 and A18.

[51] M. Moiseyev, 'From a Defensive Doctrine Position', *Red Star*, 10 February 1989; 'Standing Guard Over Peace and Socialism', *Red Star*, 23 February 1989; 'Military Restructuring Campaign Technology Improvement Goals', *Pravda*, 13 March 1989, p. 5. see also: 'Weapons Production Cutback', *Jane's Defence Weekly*, 8 April 1989, p. 611.

[52] M. Moiseyev, *Red Star*, 23 February 1989.

[53] D. Yazov, *Red Star*, 13 April 1989 and 9 August 1989. Interview of N. Chervov, 'Doctrine of Reasonable Defence Sufficiency', *Trud*, 28 February 1990.

[54] N. Ryzhkov, *Izvestiya*, 14 December 1989.

Defence Economic Planning

[55] 'Soviet and US Defence Activities, 1971 – 80: A Dollar Cost Comparison', Central Intelligence Agency, Director of Public Affairs, January 1987 (SR81 – 10005), p. 3.

[56] 'The 27th Party Congress on Further Strengthening the Country's Defence Capability, and Increasing the Combat Readiness of the Armed Forces', *Military History Journal* (Moscow: April 1986, pp. 6 – 7.

[57] 'Secretary of Defence on Soviet Military Power', *Colloquy* (Annapolis: Security Affairs Support Association) December 1989, p. 10

[58] 'A Chat With Moscow's Defence Minister', *US News and World Report*, 13 March 1989, p. 28; 'The Defence Minister Sounds Off', *Life*, November 1988, p. 44.

[59] Interview of Gen. M. Moiseyev, *Izvestiya*, 22 February 1990, p. 3.

[60] Quoted in 'Gorbachev: Economic Woes Sap Faith in Reform', *Washington Times*, 9 January 1989, p. A10.

[61] Quoted in M. Sieff and D. Sands, 'Soviet Economist Talks Rubles, Sense', *Washington Times*, 1989, p. A8.

[62] J. Shelton, *The Coming Soviet Crash* (Glencoe: Free Press, 1989); D. Remnick, 'Soviet Officials Detail Budget, Paint Grim Economic Picture', *Washington Post*, 28 October 1988, pp. A1 and A25; N. Ryzhkov, 'On the Program of Upcoming Work of the USSR Government', *Izvestiya*, 8 June 1989, pp. 1 – 3; 'Gorbachev: Economic Woes Sap Faith in Reform', *Washington Times*, 9 January 1989, p. A10. See also M. Dobbs, 'Soviet Admit Massive Deficit. . .', *Washington Post*, 8 June 1989, p. A25; A. Kireyev, 'Controversial Notes: What to Spend on Defence?' *Ogonek*, No. 19, 1989, pp. 6 – 8.

[63] *Pravda*, 19 January 1990, p. 1

[64] Speech of E. Shevardnadze of 3 July 1990 at 28th Congress, CPSU quoted in W. Keller, *New York Times*, 4 July 1990, p. A6.

[65] P. Gatrell, *The Tzarist Economy, 1850 – 1917*, (London: B. T. Batsford, 1986), pp. 141 – 187 and 222 – 230; J. McConnell, 'SDI, The Soviet Investment Debate and Soviet Military Policy', *Strategic Review*, Winter 1988, p. 57; A. Irkhin, V. Suvovov and V. Shchepetov, *Management of Fleets and Ports* (Moscow, 1986).

# CHAPTER 13

# Relations with Eastern Europe

IVÁN VOLGYES

FOR THE USSR the 1980s ended badly. Its economy was disintegrating, the shops were empty, its people were killing each other. Its long commitment to the ideology of Communism disappeared piecemeal, having already been stripped by no longer tenable tenets of its outmoded premises. And, on top of everything, its empire — both internal and external — was falling apart.

The purpose of this Chapter is to study one aspect of that disintegration: the end of the Soviet Empire in Eastern Europe and the emergence of new relationships in that troubled region. First, we will examine the results of Soviet developments, earmarked by Gorbachev's policies regarding Eastern Europe, and secondly, consider a specific case study: the changing relationship between the USSR and Hungary. In the third and fourth parts we will examine the impact of the dissolution of the Warsaw Pact through analysing Soviet interests in Eastern Europe and the real interests of the East European states in reformulating their relations with Russia and/or the USSR. Finally, we will try to draw a few conclusions about Soviet/Russian–East European relations in the 1990s.

## Gorbachev and the Changing Landscape in Eastern Europe

In surveying Soviet–East European relations in the closing years of the 1980s, one is tempted to attribute the tumultuous changes that occurred during these years to the personality and policies of Mikhail Sergeevich Gorbachev. It is attractive to accept such an assessment, for without Gorbachev's desire for liberalisation and his pursuit of policies that in the public mind are simply subsumed under the categories of *glasnost'*, *uskoreniye* and *perestroika*, the Soviet empire would not have fallen apart, and Communism as an ideology would not have come to a screeching halt. It may be tempting and perhaps even comforting to accept such a view of the events of the last few years, but it would wrong to do so.

The fallacy of such an assessment becomes clear when two factors are taken into consideration: that Gorbachev did not envision the collapse of either the Soviet empire or the Soviet system; and that the policies he formulated never really emerged as a coherent set of activities, aims or purposes. That Gorbachev did not envision a collapse can be seen in his policies that were aimed at strengthening the system, 'modernising' it to fit the needs of a modern age and its requirements for the performance of an efficient world power. Those policies were both causal — seeking to remedy a badly performing system — and causative — responding to the crises of the 1980s with the obsolete, instinctive reactions characterised by earlier regimes. That his policies were marked by a lack of cohesiveness — a trait quite contrary, in fact, to the views of many an ancient Kremlinologist — can be noted in their emergence as haphazard responses to an ever-growing crisis, especially to the challenges of inertia and forced situational logic. In this respect, too, they were causal: those unplanned responses resulted in highly unpredictable situations. Yet, they were also causative: their very unplanned nature generated ever greater needs for further reformulation of policy.

Gorbachev's, or perhaps more properly stated, the Soviet leadership's policies *vis-à-vis* Eastern Europe are no exception to these observations, which hold true both in the political and in the military spheres. When the Soviet leadership passed the baton to Gorbachev, it had no ready prescription for Eastern Europe except the maintenance of the *status quo*. The Soviet élite was content to keep the Warsaw Pact intact and continue the economic, political and military alliances into the foreseeable future.

Yet, the impact of the Soviet 'liberalisation' programme soon found a ready response, especially in those countries of the region where articulation among the fledgling opposition had been the greatest; the most acute being Poland and Hungary. Here, the call for 'changing the methods of rule' and the accompanying charge toward a more efficient and more modern system were quickly coupled with the desire to alter the political basis of rule; the dictatorial Polish or the paternalistic Hungarian methods of controlling a restrained polity. The restraint on activity in both cases, however, was not entirely domestically generated, such as the fear for the employment of military force in Poland or the co-optive/coercive balance in Hungary, but also externally referenced. In both cases, the local leadership implied, either threateningly or cynically, that the Soviet leadership stood in the way of further reforms. In short, in both places the local regimes used the factors of fear and the external reference of a coercive limitation as justification for the maintenance of Communist power in the hands of the local Communist élite.

The Gorbachev reforms, if indeed these sets of policies could conceivably amount to ideals of a 'reformist' course, undermined these meta-legitimating devices of the local élites. With Gorbachev engaged in reforms and talking of democratisation, there was no longer any reason for the local élites not to engage in even further reforms. In the case of Eastern Europe generally, the move for change was also influenced by a particular Soviet response to the challenge of 'democratisation'. By 1988 – 89 it became clear across the region that the stultified mummies and satraps, accustomed to the traditional methods of rule across the region — including even Kadar! — were unable to engage in real change. A Honecker, a Husak, a Ceauşescu or a Zhivkov at best could engage in some vague promise of liberalisation, but certainly neither could nor would match the pace of experimentation that the accelerated Soviet disintegration was bringing about. The élites, fully realising that their rule was based on the threat of coercive force from both domestic and outside sources, could only urge caution and simply try to limit change to symbolic measures.

Herein lay the dilemma for East European leaders. Reliant both on the power of the local coercive forces and on the Soviet blessing for their positions, they simply could not reject the call of the Soviet élite for change. Yet the wiser of them realised that, if they engaged in reform, their days — both figuratively and perhaps, literally — would be numbered. In this sense, their Catch 22 was real: to satisfy the Soviet course and keep the Soviet blessing, they had to change; but if they changed, they felt — correctly, as it turned out — that they would rapidly be ousted from power by the people.

In the end, nearly all of them, with the exception of Ceauşescu, hoped that the Soviet leadership itself would opt for stability in the region by backing with force those measures deemed necessary by the East European élites to control their recalcitrant populations. In order to justify their half-hearted responses to the Soviet call for reform, the dark spectres of 'counter-revolution' and '1956' were revived in various forms for the Soviet élites. The message was clear: the only alternative to their rule was a disintegration of the Communist system. Here, too, that analysis proved to be quite correct.

Yet, Eastern Europe was becoming of limited importance to Gorbachev and his administration as the USSR struggled to maintain a superpower status that was feared to be slipping away. The only way to keep up with a 'Star Wars-gazing' technologically advanced, modernising US was a 'new detente', a new relationship among the superpowers through which the USSR's rapidly declining superpower status could be reinvigorated. In this game, Eastern Europe no longer played the traditional central role of a sphere of occupation or influence where the presence of unquestioned Communist rule served as a guarantee of Soviet interests. Eastern Europe and its Communist rulers suddenly found themselves to be members of a supporting cast whose presence was becoming less and less important as the popularity and influence of the main character — Gorbachev — increased.

In this sense, then, Gorbachev's fixation with the centrality of a Soviet-US relationship doomed the East European élites. A military crackdown, involving bloodshed in the streets of Prague, Budapest, or Warsaw, was certain to destroy the chance for such a positive relationship with Washington, and thereby to endanger the Soviet quest for modernisation and great power status for the 21st century. The price of détente appeared to be the end of rigid Communism in the region; the liberal Gorbachev had to be willing to pay it.

The Soviet view is amply documented by a multitude of interviews with those within the various Communist parties who desired more liberal administration in the Eastern European states. It involved the abandonment of support for the 'fossils' or 'mummies' and was intended to bring to power 'reform Communists', people similar to Gorbachev in bent and ideology. A transfer of power to the reform Communists, ranging from Gysi to Nyers, Modrow and Mladenov, was a logical step for Gorbachev to contemplate in order to secure a more liberal external empire. Hence, the Soviet withdrawal of support from the recalcitrant old men of a bygone age was expected to usher in a new era of 'Communism with a human face'. That such a thing was impossible to achieve, of course, never occurred to any of those planning the transformation.

However people in Eastern Europe already understood that far better than the Communist leaders. And suddenly, they saw quite clearly that the king was naked, in that Soviet power would no longer back the recalcitrant 'old guard'. Once the people felt that Soviet troops would not be used to back the local militias' continued enforcement of the conservative élites, they sped in a headlong rush to abandon Communism altogether. Just as the Battle for Strahov Hill in 1968 signalled the end of Stalinism in Czechoslovakia, the Battle on Wenceslas Square in 1989 sounded the death-knell for the Communist system.

## The Grey Revolution:
## Hungary and the Warsaw Pact

This proposition can be illustrated by looking at the intricate collapse of the Hungarian Communist political system. While certainly not typical, Hungary's delicately crafted experiment in political transformation shows the centrality of the Soviet hesitation, uncertainty and retreat, as much as the ever-growing conviction of a thin political élite of activists that 1956 would not happen again in 1989. As such,

Hungary's example provides an illustration of divergence in threat perception and interpretation between the earlier Soviet rulers and those in power today.

In retrospect, Hungary's dismantling of Communism, in the larger perspective of region-wide development, appears to be a rather grey compromise-based, boring, and perhaps, even 'un-Hungarian' affair. Power was peacefully transferred to the reform Communists. They dismantled the Party by abandoning its commitment to democratic centralism, to a monopolistic party, to a planned economy, to a Praetorian Guard, to the *nomenklatura* — in short, to all of the trappings of power of the Communist apparat. The reform Communists shepherded a peaceful transformation, blocked the hardliners from using force, negotiated power arrangements with a splintered opposition, helped in the formation of a multi-party system, and even prepared for the first, really free elections the country had had in more than 40 years. Of course, no reform Communist leader in the region expected the tremendous popular defeat they were to be dealt by a population that simply had had enough of Communist rule. In fact, most thought that the people would be content with a truly reformist rule. The reformers failed to realise that history rarely stops on the way out to tip the doorman.

But before the final curtain, fate stepped in and handed the Hungarian reform Communists an opportunity to perform a momentous deed. Inundated by hapless fleeing East Germans, the Communist government of Miklos Nemeth, disregarding the 'solemn commitments' of the Warsaw Treaty, opened Hungary's borders with Austria. East German citizens could suddenly travel to the West without the 'proper' identification papers that had kept them as caged birds within the zoo of Communism. Citing 'humanitarian considerations' and principles 'contained in various international conventions', Foreign Minister Gyula Horn and the reform Communists, with one simple move, made the Warsaw Pact irrelevant.

It can, of course, be argued that it was not Horn and the Hungarians, but the courage of the East Germans in fleeing tyranny that was ultimately responsible for the destruction of the Warsaw Pact. But the fact is that Horn's was an act of statesmanship, defying every known principle that had hitherto guided cohesive Warsaw Pact behaviour. Whether or not he had advance clearance from Moscow is immaterial, although reliable sources state unequivocally that Horn and his government simply gauged the Soviet preoccupation with the USSR's internal and external crises correctly, and felt secure enough to take the gamble. Whatever the basis of his action, the fact remains that it was Horn's decision that relegated the Pact to the relics of the past.

With the move toward democracy in the region, the Pact was bound to die anyway; it simply outlived its usefulness in Hungary as else-where. In the first place, the perception of the threat from the West became ludicrous for nations were begging the West for ever further loans. Hence, the *raison d'être* of the WTO as a shield against 'Western imperialism' was suddenly gone. Second, the use of the Pact as an integrating mechanism for fraternal alliance activities acquired a sudden odium that became painfully and openly voiced: proletarians of Eastern Europe, forgive them for 1956 and 1968. Third, the Eastern European recognition of Soviet domestic preoccupations combined with the now freely articulated and newly rediscovered longing for real national sovereignty in Eastern Europe, rendered the backbone of the WTO, represented by the Soviet forces 'temporarily' stationed on foreign soil, anathema to the political existence of the new democratic states. Of what use would the Pact be for new Hungary, for democratic Czechoslovakia, or for a non-Communist Poland?

The temporary ready-made justification provided by the Soviet Union was to raise the bogey of a united Germany. The eventuality that German unification would occur with alarming alacrity once the Communists were out of power was not initially a consideration when the Soviet leaders failed to back Honecker. Of course, Soviet decision-makers had long hoped for a dissolution of NATO and, consequently, for German neutrality; therefore it was the promised fulfilment of these expectations that was now used as an explanation for the dis-solution of the WTO. But it was too late; nobody accepted that excuse and the Soviet Union had to begin the painful process of doing the best it could in a game in which it was holding largely unplayable cards. A fact that the East Europeans, but especially the Czechs and the Hungarians, already perceived. The leadership of both the Communist reformers and the newly-elected democratic government of Hungary alike realised that the country had little to fear from German unifi-cation as far as security was concerned, though they did have some reservations about West German help for the reconstruction of East Germany, since this was bound to take aid away from Hungary. Eventually, the Hungarians realised that a grateful German nation would not forget, at least for a while, who opened the golden doors. Hence, the spectre of German reunification was not a real threat that could drive them back into the arms of the Pact.

The question for Hungary was now simply to find the best method to extricate itself from the nefarious but all-encompassing existing arrangements. Popular sentiment to withdraw from the WTO was echoed by the powerful opposition party, the SzDSz (Alliance of Free Democrats), when it placed the issue on the agenda of the freely-elected, multi-party Parliament on the very first day of its existence. In its proposal, which was an eloquent restatement of Imre Nagy's desperate message of withdrawal from the WTO in the days of the 1956 revolution, the SzDSz did not simply declare a desire to withdraw; the declaration was a political statement, reflecting widespread sentiment.

Yet, it was also unnecessary and possibly even potentially dangerous. With Soviet troops already scheduled to leave the country in an orderly and expeditious manner by the middle of 1991, with every joint WTO body already close to total dissolution, with the integrated arms machinery in chaos, the declaration demanding immediate withdrawal threatened to raise the level of political confrontation with the USSR beyond an advisable level. The political wisdom that resulted in the eventual compromise reached by Parliament may have represented a minor defeat for the SzDSz in May 1990, but it was a victory in the longer term and assured the orderly dissolution of the Pact itself.

The case study presented on the process of changing the long-established practices and *modus operandi* of Soviet-Pact relations is illustrative, if not modal, of the rapid dissolution of the Soviet empire in Eastern Europe. Similar practices obtained in all of the Pact countries; only the extent and speed of the changes varied. The bottom-line always seems to be the same: both parties, the Soviet Union and the Pact members, appeared to be uncertain of the direction and speed of desired change, or the limits of Soviet patience. Threats and counter-threats of promised retaliation if the presumed limits of Soviet tolerance were exceeded; but in the end the reality that the Soviet forces were going home had become clear to everyone. It is this reality that will characterise Soviet relations with Eastern Europe in the 1990s, and those relations will clearly be the result of balance between Soviet interest in Eastern Europe and Eastern Europe's interest in maintaining contacts with the USSR.

## Soviet Interests in Eastern Europe in the 1990s

The difficulty in making prognostications at the present time concerning Soviet interests in Eastern Europe is that essential baseline data are missing. At the time of writing, the questions upon which these predictions were based remain unanswered:

Will a conservative leadership replace the present political élite, altering the foreign policy course the latter has chosen?

Will the Soviet leadership opt for domesticism and retreat into isolation to mend its shattered internal rule?

Will the Soviet empire fall apart into component units?

Will the Soviet leadership, provided the USSR remains as a Union, choose US, German and West European interests over its interests in Eastern Europe?

In the absence of answers to these questions, the task of prognosticating becomes seemingly impossible. Yet, there are a few signposts in the quest for answers; signposts that are the maxims of international relations theory. These are:

Nations have neither friends, nor enemies; nations have interests.

The first rule for heads of state is to ensure the survival and independence of the country over which they preside.

Politics is the art of the possible.

In the light of these considerations, the Soviet interests in Eastern Europe can, perhaps, be more clearly delineated.

Assuming that the USSR stays intact and that it is guided by rational men and women who adopt standards of behaviour on internal and external policies deemed normal by the world community, Soviet interests in the region appear to be comprehensible. They are:

1. A region split into independent states that cannot be united into a cohesive anti-Soviet or anti-Russian unit;

2. By extension, a region, whose states could not be incorporated into an anti-Soviet NATO bent on any military opposition to the existence of the USSR;

3. A region where the local military forces do not represent a threat to the USSR;

4. A region economically linked to the USSR as desired partners in the purchase of Soviet goods and providing goods at a lower cost than from other sources;

5. A region that can serve as a cultural bridge between the ubiquitous 'West' and the USSR (or Russia).

In the light of these considerations, the paranoia factor can be discarded, and the reality of Soviet threat perceptions more clearly established. For example, Stalin's conviction that only Communists loyal to him and the USSR could be relied on to serve Soviet interests, no longer represents a viable policy guideline for the USSR. With Western Europe and the USA no longer viewed as a threat to the USSR's experience, the *raison d'être* of a policy of occupying or controlling Eastern Europe has simply disappeared. Consequently, *realpolitik* rather than ideologically preconceived notions have begun to dominate Soviet policy formulations.

Thus, for the 1990s, Soviet interests will be concentrated on securing a politically weak region of independent East European states, with diverse and competitive policies, ensuring that a political alliance system similar to the Warsaw Pact, but potentially aimed against the USSR, will not come about. In search of such ends the Soviet leadership can be expected to establish a diversified set of relations with Eastern Europe's new political entities. While the final shape of these relations may not yet be apparent, it is probable that it will involve efforts towards:

- Seeking close contacts with the Polish state. Using the potential threat of emerging German-Polish conflict areas, such as, the German corridor, border areas, resettlement and so forth, the Soviet leadership would desire friendly relations with Poland more than with any other state of the region.
- Re-establishing closer contacts with Czechoslovakia. With the departure of Soviet soldiers from the Czech and Slovak territories in 1991, with historical memories placated by the Soviet leadership's assumption of responsibility for 1948 and 1968, with a relationship based on mutual interests, including the independence of the Czech and Slovak Federation *vis-à-vis* the power of the new Germany, such a policy has a reasonable chance for success.
- Formulating a neutral policy *vis-à-vis* Hungary. Realistically, Hungary has limited geopolitical importance to the USSR.
- Limiting Romanian irredentism in the case of Moldavia by providing enough recognition of its aspirations to avoid a major conflagration. Such counterbalance may include granting greater rights and benefits to Soviet Moldavia, joining in with the West in containing Romania's ambitions, and aiding the surrounding states (Hungary, Bulgaria) in limiting any Romanian ambitions for expansion.
- Maintaining good relations with a democratic, or non-Communist, Bulgaria. Once again, however, the Bulgarian issue is of limited interest to the USSR.

The desirability of attaining these policy orientations will, of course, once again be dependent upon wider Soviet interests; their relations

with the US, Germany, and the new Europe. Yet, in basic terms the
policies of any Soviet leaders would seek to minimise the political and
military importance of Eastern Europe as a region and maximise
Soviet relations with the component parts; the old maxim 'divide and
rule' still applies to Soviet policy considerations. Regardless of who
rules the Soviet state, it is who controls, and what form of governments
exist, in Eastern Europe (the old goals of security, weak states, competitive, unaligned forces) which must continue to dictate the activities
of the Soviet rulers. Because these goals reflect permanent Soviet interests, because they maximise Soviet independence while minimising
threats to the Soviet state and, because these goals are still attainable
even in the new Europe of the 1990s, they will be pursued.

## Eastern Europe Interests and the Soviet Union

It would be tempting simply to ignore the issue of East European
interests in the USSR as irrelevant; after all, the people of Eastern
Europe have for years fervently wished that the USSR would just 'go
away'. Now that this proposition is close to becoming a reality, many
people in the region are beginning to have second thoughts about the
prospect of declining USSR involvement. Left alone, Eastern Europe
may find that a world without the protection of the USSR is not an
altogether comfortable place.

There are several reasons for such fears being held by East European
leaders. Some are more difficult to understand and perhaps less obvious
to those who watched with joy and delight the Eastern European
transformation. The exhilaration felt by all those who abhor tyranny
as they witnessed the end of Communist rule and the first steps toward
democracy may perhaps cloud Western perceptions and attitudes.

Yet, for leaders of Eastern Europe the inheritance of four-and-a-half
decades of Communist rule continues to loom large. They find that
Communism left their systems bankrupt, as Western specialists had
long predicted. Thanks to Marxism and the Communist legacy, their
infra-structural backwardness is appalling, their industrial practices
astounding, their attitude toward work abominable, and their desire
for 'Big Daddy' to take care of their everyday needs overwhelming.
Starved for capital, lacking expertise, the East Europeans are looking
for ways to become 'Europeans' both quickly and painlessly, but are
finding that it is much less difficult to become non-Communist than to
become a European. The simple fact is that, despite all the enthusiasm
greeting them upon the collapse of the Soviet Empire, they are learning
that becoming a part of 'Europe' is not at all easy. For a Europe
already engrossed in the intricacies of unification in 1992, dealing
with the Western European neutrals means one thing; dealing with

a capital-starved, backward Eastern Europe is quite another.

Moreover, the shape of the emergent Europe raises some serious concerns for Eastern Europeans, since the Europe they see emerging is one that will be dominated by a unified Germany. However much they like the Mercedes-Germany image, the preponderant German power flooding into the region gives them cause to ponder. Not only the image of wartime tragedies, but also the reality of Germany buying Eastern Europe lock, stock and barrel is beginning to affect the thoughtful as they contemplate their future relations with the USSR.

Their view of the crippled Soviet superpower is coloured, of course, by the reality left behind: abandoned and destroyed military apartments in conditions that would nauseate even the most hardened of the old Mongolian hands, poisoned wells, environmental destruction of unimaginable extent. Such is the legacy of four decades of occupation. The adopted Soviet model, encompassing everything from machinery to housing, infrastructure and transportation, was already outmoded by the time it was installed. All that is left behind reinforces the Third World impression of the region. It will, indeed, be years before the blame for all the failures can be laid at the doors of culprits other than the Russians.

But deal with the Russians they will, as they must, while seeking to find a 'normal' way of maintaining relations. Although, once again, it is true that a great deal will depend on the future of internal alignments of Soviet power, each of these states has a *desiderata* and an interest in shaping the future of the USSR.

For Poland, the presence, or mere existence of the USSR is not a great blessing in itself but a relatively secure Union, as a counterbalance to the overwhelming presence of Germany, appears at this juncture highly desirable. Territorial demands by the new Germany pose greater potential long-term threats to Poland, whereas the Soviet Union is unlikely to harbour similar claims; only Poland could have claims on the Eastern borderlands. With the Warsaw Pact dissolved, with the sore historical tragedies of the past laid to rest (for instance, Katyn), Poland's natural interests must lie in maintaining businesslike relations with the USSR.

The Czech and Slovak Federation also has continuing interests in maintaining similar relations with the USSR. In the former's case, it is especially important to return to the maintenance of geopolitically sound ties. Here again, territorial demands do not mar the potentially good contacts that are in the interests of the Czechoslovak state.

Hungarian ties with the USSR are generally viewed as desirable because the USSR is a natural ally in curbing the territorial aspirations of Hungary's potentially most competitive and combative neighbour — Romania. Although the issue of an apology for the Soviet invasion of Hungary in 1956 remains a bone of contention, the geopolitical determinants — for example having Russia act as a potential counterbalance to an antagonistic Romania — are not negligible for any Hungarian leadership.

For Romania, the USSR will remain a contentious neighbour. Romania irredentist claims on Bessarabia/Moldavia, coupled with an increasingly fervent nationalistic population, deem it likely that Romania will work for the dissolution of the USSR and, as envisioned by some members of the Romanian leadership, the subsequent, ceding of Moldavia 'back' to Romania by a then weakened Ukraine. While other mainly economic issues demand that Romania maintain normal relations with the USSR, the territorial issues and the issue of the *irredenta* will cloud these contacts in the foreseeable future.

As to Bulgaria, regardless of the form of its government or the content of the political system, there are few or no obstacles to the maintenance of good relations between that country and the USSR. It remains, clearly, in the interests of Bulgaria to build on the good ties that characterised its relations with the USSR throughout much of the last century.

For the states of Eastern Europe as a whole, the dissolution of the Pact was, in reality, accomplished by the end of 1990. Without content, the Pact became an empty shell. There is near uniform agreement among most East Europeans that during its existence it served only as a device to guarantee Soviet interests; with the Soviet leadership apparently not feeling threatened by an imminent or impending NATO invasion, with the Cold War over, the WTO was no longer perceived as a vital organisation. Consequently, the USSR is beating a hasty and rather disorderly retreat, much to the joy of most East Europeans.

The question of post-Pact security arrangements, however, remains an urgent matter for all of the region. The WTO is gone, but its place can conceivably be taken only by one of three security arrangements: collective security guarantees under a regional umbrella organisation; mutual non-aggression treaties; or guaranteed neutrality of some or all of the states in the region. While they can operate side by side or independently of one another, these security arrangements, however made, must also involve the USSR or its successor states. Any such arrangements that do not include some participation or do not receive the acknowledgement of the Soviet leadership — as the history of much of the inter-war era attests — will invariably be unstable from the outset.

One final area of concern could be important for all the states of the region, namely economic relations with the USSR. Given the state of their own economies, they must concede that Russia will remain an important market and an important source of raw materials. Trade issues will dominate over political interests in the coming era, provided that adequate bases for mutually-acceptable economic contacts can be established and maintained. Replacing the current, extensive barter agreements with agreements based on market-value considerations is of primary importance, but that cannot take place until the economy of each of these states has been transformed to an open market economy. At that point, however, the economic determinants of mutuality will automatically begin to dictate a rationality in economic ties that will greatly influence the political contacts among both the East European and the Soviet élites.

## Conclusion

The transformation in Eastern Europe from Communism into generally democratic governments has been one of the most astounding events of the 20th century. That transformation essentially ended the subjugation of the region to the USSR and led to the emergence of independent states in Eastern Europe. With the enormous changes in the weakened Soviet state, with the accelerated movement toward European unification, and with the end of the Cold War between the USSR and the USA, the whole question of Soviet/East European relations has to be re-examined.

The liberation of Eastern Europe has been both the cause and the consequence of these changes. Stripped of its paranoia, the USSR has to recognise that it can maintain good relations with its neighbours, regardless of the political beliefs of their leaders or of the political content of their regimes. The future relationship between the military superpower of the region and its immediate Western neighbours, could once again be based only on mutual, business-like considerations.

This development should be warmly welcomed by both the West and the East alike. The Messianism of Communism as well as the substructure of the Communist empire has disappeared, it is to be hoped, for ever. Looking at our troubled age, we could, perhaps, justly gloat that so rarely in recent history have the 'good guys' won. Yet, our joy is tinged with sadness for the victims of Communism who cry out for us not to forget them: those in the unmarked graves of the Gulags, of Katyn, of Gdansk, those who suffered and died in Budapest, in Timisoara. Like those who perished in Auschwitz or Lidice, the victims of Communism also force us to remember the enormous price of man's inhumanity to man.

It must also be hoped that the future relationship between the USSR and the free states of Eastern Europe will be able to overcome the legacies of the failed era of Communism. Although the Soviet empire is lost, although the states of Eastern Europe have regained their independence, there are no reasons to expect that the relationship between the USSR and the East European independent entities will be characterised as being free of conflict in the 1990s. Conflict, after all, is endemic to international relations. The task of the élites of these states, therefore, will not be to seek total unanimity of views and interests with all the states of the region. Such unanimity can only be had either by *diktat* or by voluntary subservience, and neither should be characteristic of relations between free and independent partners. Rather, the task of the new leaders of the states ought to be the creation of a system of relations with the USSR and between each other that will, for a long time to come, serve the interests of each contracting party. Finding these interests, defining and delineating them, and putting them into concrete policies will be the task of the new statesmen of the region. Let us hope that they will be up to that task in the Europe of the 1990s.

CHAPTER 14

# Yugoslavia as an Evolutionary Model

CHRISTOPHER CVIIC

YUGOSLAVIA PUZZLES the world. Only just over a decade ago, at the time of President Tito's death in May 1980, it was a stable federation playing on the world stage a role quite out of proportion to its size and its military and economic power. Throughout the world, Yugoslavia had acquired the reputation of an innovative country. Its distinctive system of self-management — evolved since Yugoslavia's expulsion from the Soviet block at Stalin's behest in June 1948 — had become a source of inspiration for the seekers of the 'third way' between Soviet-type state socialism and free-market Western capitalism.

Now Yugoslavia, beset by grave economic problems, mounting social unrest and bitter strife among its disparate nations, seems to be well on the road to disintegration. The world, disillusioned with Yugoslavia, wants to know one thing only: whether its break-up, now taken for granted, will be peaceful or bloody. But unlike the other multinational federation in trouble, the Soviet Union, Yugoslavia is not a great power armed with nuclear weapons. Nor does it any longer have the strategic importance that it once had at the time of the Cold War, on the southern flank of NATO and the Warsaw Pact, controlling access to the Mediterranean. What happens in Yugoslavia in the future, therefore, is not a matter of great consequence to Western military planners. But even in its present reduced circumstances, Yugoslavia repays study because what happens there has many resemblances to the current situation in the Soviet Union. Yugoslavia's disintegration contains many clues for those trying to plan the future course of events in the Soviet Union.

As in the USSR, all aspects of life in Yugoslavia are seen through the prism of 'national' calculations. This explains why Yugoslavia, instead of concentrating on the economic reform agenda set for it by well-meaning outsiders, including the International Monetary Fund,

239

the World Bank, the European Community and the Western governments, follows its own complex political priorities, often apparently
flying in the face of economic logic. Of course, living standards, jobs,
pensions, health and education matter as much to Yugoslavia's multinational citizens as they do to nationally homogeneous Poland and
Hungary. But in Yugoslavia everybody is a member of a community
within the state — the ethnic nation in which personal identity is
anchored, and to which the first loyalty is owed.

Questions of national identity are politically hyper-sensitive, for the
process of national differentiation is still far from over. Tito's era saw
the birth of two 'new' nations. The Bosnian Muslims, descendants of
former Catholics and members of the heretical Bogomil sect, who had
embraced Islam during the period of Ottoman rule (1463 – 1878), were
recognised as a separate nation in the 1960s. And in 1967, establishment
of the Macedonian nation was completed. But there are those who
challenge the legitimacy of this process and deny the ethnic authen-
ticity of the Bosnian Muslims and the Macedonians, disparaging them
as 'manufactured nations'. The separate nationhood of the Montenegrins, formally reaffirmed by Titoist Yugoslavia, is also vigorously
contested.

This continuing and politically destabilising national volatility can
be illustrated most vividly. In the latest (1981) census, some 1.2 million
people (out of a total population of 22.4 million) 'renounced' their
ethnic grouping or nationhood, and declared themselves to 'Yugoslava'
— prompted by a variety of reasons, including intermarriage and political opportunism in strongly 'Yugoslav' institutions such as the army
and the diplomatic service. Hence passionate discussions, for example
about which language is to dominate in federal institutions.

At times of acute external danger — during the period from the
break with the Soviet Union in 1948 right up to Stalin's death in 1953,
for instance, and again when Soviet troops invaded Czechoslovakia
in 1968 — the broader Yugoslav framework loomed larger than the
narrower 'national' one. But such temporary exceptions simply confirm the rule that in Yugoslavia it is nation, rather than class or race,
that represents the most significant political division.

In contrast to the centralising royal regime that had ruled the country
from 1918 – 41, the Yugoslav Communists accepted the need for a
federation to accommodate the country's complex ethnic make-up.
The post-1945 federal system, made up of six republics (Bosnia and
Hercegovina, Croatia, Macedonia, Montenegro, Serbia, and Slovenia)
and two autonomous provinces (Kosovo and Vojvodina, which formed
part of Serbia), was matched by the formation of separate Communist
Party organisations: each of the republics and provinces had its own
Central or Provincial Committee.

Of course, under Tito, real power was wielded by the Politburo in Belgrade, but these separate Party organisations had significant political importance. Like the country's federal system, they represented an acknowledgement of the national aspirations of those peoples in Yugoslavia (notably the Croats, the Macedonians, the Bosnian Moslems and the Albanians) who had looked upon the pre-war, strongly centralist Serbian-dominated Yugoslavia as a threat to their identity and their national interests. Behind the formal structure of federalism, there lay the unspoken aim of evolving in the fullness of time, a simple Yugoslav nation — an aim similar to that of *sliyovnie* (melting together) of peoples in the Soviet Union.

As Yugoslavia began to decentralise during the 1950s, Party leaders in the republics and autonomous provinces began to find it politically advantageous to speak up for 'their' region, usually over such questions as allocation of investment capital from Belgrade's central funds. However, the Communist fiction of 'the primacy of class interest' was maintained. Those who showed 'nationalist tendencies' — that is, threatened to escape from the local Party leaders' control into the non-Communist intelligentsia — were kept under careful review. Each local leadership was expected to 'sweep its own doorstep first', so Serbs fought Serbian nationalists, Croats fought Croats, and so on. If a local leadership seemed to be falling into the trap of 'opportunism', going too far in espousing local interests in order to boost their popularity, Tito stepped in. . .

When the Yugoslav Communist Party became fully 'federalised' in the 1970s, the last decade of Tito's life, his unquestioned authority and charisma ensured a relatively smooth functioning of the system. (After all, the senior Party leaders owed their positions to him.) His death was therefore deeply unsettling for the whole hierarchy, despite the elaborate system of rules which he bequeathed to them. These included regular rotation of offices and rigorous observance of 'the nationality key', to prevent any one nation from falling under the domination of another — in effect, to forestall any return to the pre-1941 situation when the Serbs, Yugoslavia's largest nation, had exercised hegemonic power over non-Serbs. Many regional frustrations accumulated over the years, but for a long time none of Tito's successors dared (or felt strong enough) to challenge his rules, especially in respect of the inviolability of federalism.

All this changed in 1986, with the appointment of Slobodan Milosevic, a little known Party *apparatchik*, as boss of the Serbian Communist Party. Milosevic boldly swept aside Tito's rule tying each leadership to its particular territory. He began to speak for all of Yugoslavia's 8.1 million Serbs — not just for those in Serbia and its autonomous provinces of Kosovo and Vojvodina, but also in other republics. By articulating his fellow-Serbs' frustrations, Milosevic has reaped huge political advantages, though at considerable cost to the stability of the federal system and of Yugoslavia as a whole. He was, however, merely the catalyst for a change that was already getting under way, since each national group had for some time been reassessing the whole concept of Yugoslavia and its own position within the federation.

## The Serbs

The main frustration for the Serbs was Tito's federalism, especially as it developed in the latter period of his rule, reaching its final form in the 1974 Constitution. Their case was most clearly formulated in the memorandum drafted for the Serbian Academy of Sciences, which was leaked to the press in September 1986. Originally prepared as a contribution to the public debate about reform of the Yugoslav political and economic system in the post-Tito era, this remarkably outspoken document set out the Serb's main objections to today's Yugoslavia. Three complaints were emphasised:

1. The allegedly discriminatory policy towards Serbia in the economic field throughout the post-1945 period — reflecting that old anti-Serbian bias of the pre-1941 Communist Party of Yugoslavia and of the Communist International (Comintern) in Moscow.
2. The partition of Serbia, under the leadership of Tito (a Croat) and Edvard Kardelj, his second-in-command (a Slovene), into three parts: Serbia proper, and its autonomous provinces of Kosovo and Vojvodina which, bypassing Serbia, were allowed direct participation in decision-making at federal level.
3. The allegedly anti-Serbian policy pursued in Kosovo by local Albanian 'separatists' and 'irredentists', with support from other Yugoslav republics, resulting in a steady exodus of Serbs from this centre of Serbia's medieval state.

The authors of the draft memorandum called for reversal of what they described as the 'Strong Yugoslavia, Weak Serbia' policy, and in particular for abolition of the 1974 Constitution under which Kosovo and Vojvodina had been permitted to evolve into *de facto* republics. In non-Serb areas of Yugoslavia the memorandum met with hostile criticism, partly because of its *dirigiste* economic assumptions, but above all because it was seen as yet another manifestation of 'Great Serbian hegemonism'. Among the Serbs, however, there was widespread acceptance of the document's main thesis — that under the 'anti-Serb' Tito-Kardelj coalition, which had been in charge of Yugoslavia since 1945, the Serbs had had a raw deal. Rather like the Russians in the Soviet Union, the Serbs feel that far from being the oppressors and exploiters of non-Serbs, they themselves are the oppressed and the exploited ones in Yugoslavia. The memorandum articulated that feeling. There was no question of any Serbian rejection of Yugoslavia as an entity. What the memorandum condemned was a Yugoslavia which was seen as harmful to Serbian interests, denying the traditional *Staatsvolk* their predominant position.

Publication of the draft memorandum coincided with the appearance of numerous articles and books (they have since become a torrent), unfavourably contrasting Tito's Yugoslavia with the pre-1941 Royalist regime with its Serbian dynasty, its special position for the Serbian Orthodox Church, Serbian dominance in the army, the police, the gendarmerie, the senior ranks of the civil service, and diplomacy; and with Kosovo re-Serbianised by ex-soldiers and other settlers.

Not surprisingly, the Serbs have in recent years made a point of once again celebrating in a solemn fashion the anniversary of the founding of the Kingdom of Serbs, Croats and Slovenes — the first, royalist Yugoslavia. There is agitation in Serbia for the return of the monarchy in the shape of Prince Alexander, the son of Yugoslavia's last king, Peter II — *Karadyor dycvic*. The Serbian Orthodox Church is playing an important role in this. Equally predictably, Yugoslavia's non-Serbs have studiously ignored the anniversary, or have used it to emphasise that between 1918 and 1941 Yugoslavia's citizens had lived under a galling Serbian hegemony.

## The Slovenes

These calculations of national interest look very different to the Slovenes. Back in 1918, in the wake of the Habsburg Empire's break-up, they had felt threatened by pan-German and Italian imperialism. They were eager to become part of the new kingdom, which they saw as a powerful shield against the enemy to the west and the north. Later, the Second World War brought the Slovenes the prospect of annihilation: their nation was targeted by Hitler for extinction. After 1945, thereafter, rejoining Yugoslavia — albeit a Communist Yugoslavia — seemed only natural.

But after four-and-a-half decades of life in the new Yugoslavia, the Slovenes see an altered situation. The old danger of non-Slav imperialists gobbling them up has disappeared and Slovenia has excellent relations with Austria and Italy, its two peaceful and highly prosperous neighbours. Since 1978 it has been participating, together with Croatia, in the work of an informal, low-profile organisation (called *Alpen-Adria* in German, *Alpe-Jadran* in Croat and Slovene) whose purpose is co-operation in the fields of culture, energy, environment, sport, transport and so forth. There are other members as well: the two western regions of Hungary; five Austrian *Länder*; four northern regions of Italy; and, in West Germany, Bavaria. Through this interaction, and in other ways, the Slovenes have discovered how much they still have in common with these former regions of the Austro-Hungarian Empire.

By the same token, their new westward orientation emphasises the Slovenes' growing distance from Yugoslavia's eastern regions, which seem to bring only problems — trouble in Kosovo; energy policies harmful to the environment (Slovenia has Yugoslavia's only nuclear-power station, bitterly opposed by its Greens); resistance to economic reforms; and, most important, the threat of a new centralist regime that would curtail, or even end, Slovenia's present autonomy. Not surprisingly, the Slovenes are restless — rather like tenants in a large apartment-house who feel that the rent is too high and that they do not care for most of their neighbours.

They want out. In September 1989, Slovenia's Parliament in Ljubljana adopted a series of amendments to their republic's Constitution, including the right to secede from Yugoslavia. A year later, in September 1990, Slovenia took over the control of its territorial defence — in the face of the bitter opposition of the Yugoslav army.

## The Croats

The feeling that life in the apartment-house is becoming rather unpleasant is shared by the Croats, Yugoslavia's second largest nation. For them, too, Yugoslavia had represented in earlier years a shield against Italian aspirations. (The Croatian Adriatic coast was promised to Italy under the 1915 Treaty of London, as an inducement to join the First World War on the Entente side). Post-1918 Yugoslavia was a shattering disappointment, for they lost the autonomy they had enjoyed as one of the 'historic' nations of the Hapsburg Empire under the *Nagodba* (Compromise) signed with the Hungarians in 1868, a year after the *Ausgleich* between the Austrian and Hungarian halves of the monarchy.

The Slovenes were tucked away in Yugoslavia's Alpine north-west and further protected by their linguistic separateness, but the Croats felt extremely vulnerable to 'denationalisation' by the Serbs, who were closer to them both geographically and linguistically.

In August 1939 most Croats had welcomed Prince Paul's agreement to limited autonomy for Croatia. It would, they thought, be the first step towards a federal reorganisation of Yugoslavia. But federation was bitterly opposed by the Serbian political parties. So when Germany and Italy (assisted by Bulgaria and Hungary) attacked and dismembered

Yugoslavia in April 1941, most Croats (like the majority of Yugoslavia's other non-Serbs) were far from sorry to say good-bye to a state they had never felt to be their own. (The Serbs, in contrast, experienced Yugoslavia's collapse as a traumatic event, and even produced a Serbian variant of the 'stab-in-the-back' theory, blaming the 1941 military defeat not on the invaders' overwhelming strength and the poor organisation and leadership of the — largely Serb-officered — Royal Army, but on the 'treachery' of the Croats and other non-Serbs.)

Any joy the Croats may have felt at the demise of Yugoslavia was soon dispelled when Croatia, stripped of most of its Adriatic coast, was divided into two Occupation Zones (one German, one Italian) and placed under the notorious Ante Pavelic whose regime organised a systematic extermination of Croatia's Serbs, Jews, Gypsies, and any Croats who happened to disagree with him. Of the many thousands of Croatian Serbs who fled into the forest to save their lives, some joined the royalist *Cetniks*, but the bulk ended up in the ranks of Tito's partisans. That 1941 – 45 period left a bitter legacy of Serb mistrust towards the Croats. It is still alive today.

The post-1945 territorial settlement returned to Croatia the territories annexed by Mussolini in 1941, and also those (including Istria) which had been taken by Italy after 1918. But the Croats continued to feel ill at ease; they felt themselves to be 'a nation on probation'. Even the most innocuous manifestations of national feeling were branded as 'nationalist extremism' by the Communist authorities.

This was the fate that befell the 1967 'Language Declaration' signed on behalf of 19 Croatian cultural institutions by 140 prominent scholars, writers and other intellectuals. More than half of them were Communist Party members. They included Miroslav Krleza, Croatia's greatest living writer, a member of the Croatian Central Committee and a personal friend of Tito. The Declaration demanded Constitutional recognition and full equality for four languages — Croatian, Macedonian, Serbian and Slovene — in which all federal laws and other federal Acts were to be published; (there were then only three dominant languages: Macedonian, Serbo-Croat and Slovene). It called for the use of standard Croatian in the school and through the mass media of the Croatian republic, instead of Serbo-Croatian, which was rejected by many Croats as 'a political language'. The Declaration caused public uproar, and several of its signatories were expelled from the Party.

Worse was to come in 1971 – 72, with Tito's crushing of 'the Croatian Spring'. A large-scale purge, with many arrests, produced effects not unlike those in Czechoslovakia after the 1968 suppression of 'the Prague Spring'. Tito's purges of 'liberals' and 'technocrats' in Slovenia and Serbia in 1972 were less harsh than in Croatia, but all caused the loss of many able, modern-minded leaders.

Most Croats now have little time for Yugoslavia, but until relatively recently there has been little talk of secession. This at least partly reflects a realisation of the difficulties involved in any cutting of the umbilical cord. The greatest of these is the presence of Croatia's large Serbian minority (11.6% of its total population are Serbs, but they have a disproportionate representation in the Party and the police). In Slovenia, in 1987, 82% of all Communist Party members were Slovenes, 6.5% Serbs, and 5% Croats. In Croatia, however, 19.4% of all Party members were Serbs, while only 59.6% were Croats: and it must be assumed that a large proportion of the 17.9% who declared themselves to be 'Yugoslavs' were in fact Serbs. The Serbs of Croatia, who include a large number of old partisans and retired police and army officers, have on many occasions in the past demonstrated their opposition to any greater degree of independence for Croatia that would, willy-nilly, separate them from the rest of Yugoslavia's Serbs. They stepped up this opposition in the summer and autumn of 1990 after the election of a centre-right Croat government in May by organising a referendum in the predominantly Serbian districts of Croatia, by seizing weapons from police arms depots and, on proclaiming an 'autonomous region', setting up roadblocks and armed guards to prevent the Croat police from coming in and collecting the arms.

## The Bosnians

The 'national' problem, however, is no longer mainly a Croat-Serb affair. Under Tito's federal system, the country's other nations — the Muslims of Bosnia and Hercegovina, the Macedonians, and the Montenegrins, as well as the two biggest national minorities, the Albanians of Kosovo and the Hungarians of Vojvodina — have all been upgraded politically. They all matter now.

The disintegration of Yugoslavia would not please the two million or so Bosnian Muslims, for it would revive their old nightmare: the dreaded prospect of the division of their republic, which has a particularly complex national structure. According to the 1981 census, Muslims make up 39.5% of the population; the Serbs run them close with 32% and then come the Croats with 18.4%. Federation or confederation, Yugoslavia is a preferred solution for the Muslims.

But if division were to become reality, the Bosnian Muslims would probably throw their weight behind the idea of a link-up with Croatia and Slovenia. There are two main reasons for this: good memories of the period between 1878 – 1918 when Bosnia (together with Croatia and Slovenia) formed part of the Austro-Hungarian Empire; and a deep mistrust of the Serbs. The Bosnian republic has decided to become a member of the *Alper-Adria* group.

## The Macedonians

Under the Tito regime, Macedonia attained the status of a federal republic, with full support for development of its national institutions and language, and for its own autocephalous church separate from the Serbian Orthodox Church, which since then has successfully managed to block its recognition by other Orthodox Churches.

Abroad, the Yugoslav government has promoted recognition of the Macedonian nation, and has regularly engaged in disputes with Greece and Bulgaria over their refusal to extend recognition.

With the Bulgarians, this non-recognition arises from territorial grievances. Greece, on the other hand, believes that the present-day Macedonians are ethnically a totally different people from the ancient civilisation ruled by Philip of Macedon and Alexander the Great. They object to the 'highjacking' of a glorious name, and hence will not even recognise the academic qualifications of Greek students who take degrees at Macedonia's universities.

All this has been from the Macedonian point of view, a great improvement over the pre-1941 period, when Macedonia was simply a part of southern Serbia, and exposed to a policy of systematic Serbianisation. Not surprisingly, the Macedonians welcomed the break-up of royalist Yugoslavia in 1941, but the Bulgarians who then annexed their land proved a disappointment, while Tito's regime offered them full Macedonian nationhood.

But Macedonia is now in a parlous state economically, chiefly as a result of the mistaken investment policy pursued when a large injection of capital followed the 1961 Skopje earthquake. Even worse is its political predicament. Macedonia shares with Serbia a sense of danger from the Albanians, who make up well over a quarter of Macedonia's total population and, in its western part, which borders on Albania proper, are in a majority.

The possibility of an Albanian federal unit within Yugoslavia frightens the Macedonians: they suspect that it would include not only the Serbian province of Kosovo, but also Albanian-inhabited western Macedonia, right up to Skopje. They, too, are alarmed by the recent revival of Serbian nationalism that could, once again, seek to reconquer 'southern Serbia' — *ie* Macedonia. So they feel beleaguered from both sides. More recently, the anti-Serb feeling has grown and is the dominant political force in the republic.

## The Montenegrins

The setting-up of a separate federal republic of Montenegro in 1945 represented a victory for the Montenegrin *zelenasi* (the Greens), who take the view that, for all their close connections with the Serbs — they are, historically, considered to be a tribe of the Serbian nation — the Montenegrins are a totally separate people. However, union with Serbia is advocated by the *bjelasi* (the Whites), and it was they who prevailed in 1918 when, against strong opposition from their exiled King Nikola, Montenegro joined Yugoslavia. (The names derive from the coloured ballot-slips used in the referendum. A white slip indicated a vote for union with Yugoslavia, a green slip a vote for independence.)

Since a political coup in January 1989, Montenegro is once again under the *bjelasi*, with a leadership close to Slobodan Milosevic, who describes Montenegro and Serbia as 'two eyes in one head'. The *zelenasi* have fallen back to defensive positions, but have not yet been completely routed. Recently, Montenegro decided to follow Bosnia's example and join the *Alpen – Adria* group.

## The Hungarians

The bulk of Yugoslavia's Hungarians live in Serbia's autonomous province of Vojvodina, and account for 18.9% of its total population (54.4% of whom are Serbs). Under the Yugoslav federal system, they have enjoyed a wide degree of cultural autonomy, as well as representation within Vojvodina's power structure commensurate with their numbers.

In comparison with the maltreated Hungarians of Romania and Czechoslovakia, those in Yugoslavia have on the whole done well. However, the rise of Serbian nationalism since the mid-1980s disturbs the Vojvodina Hungarians, and could stimulate a desire to leave the Yugoslav federation and join neighbouring Hungary.

## The Albanians

The worst-treated national group in pre-1941 Yugoslavia was the ethnic Albanians. In the 1930s they even faced the possibility of mass expulsion to Turkey and Albania, although this danger was averted due to lack of funds with which to compensate those countries for the influx. The Albanians welcomed the defeat and collapse of royalist Yugoslavia in 1941, when the Italians — the Occupying Power in that area — incorporated the largely Albanian-inhabited Kosovo and western Macedonia into a 'Greater Albania' under their protectorate, providing food and arms as well as a measure of local autonomy.

Not surprisingly, therefore, few Albanians joined Tito's guerrilla struggle, still of less account than that of the Serbian *Cetniks* led by Colonel Mihailovic. The later stages of the War, however, raised the local level of support for Tito's partisans, with the prospect that Kosovo and other areas inhabited by Albanians might be incorporated into Albania proper, under the Yugoslav-supported Communist leadership of Enver Hoxha. When, at the end of the War, Kosovo was in fact returned to Yugoslavia, together with western Macedonia, there was a strong Albanian armed resistance, which continued for several years.

For two decades, Kosovo remained under a special police regime. But at least Tito's central government in Belgrade was sufficiently sensitive politically not to allow the return of the Serbian colonists who had settled in Kosovo in the 1920s and 1930s and had been chased away under the Italian Occupation.

As part of Yugoslavia's liberalisation after the fall in 1966 of Aleksandar Rankovic, the powerful Secret Police chief and Party cadre secretary who was himself a Serb by nationality, Kosovo received increased aid and autonomy. Eventually, under the 1974 Constitution, it was granted the status of an autonomous province with direct participation in the federal organs, including the (collective) federal presidency and the Party presidium. In the spring of 1981, however, after Tito's death, large-scale demonstrations erupted in Kosovo, demanding formal upgrading of the province to the status of a full republic within the Yugoslav federation. The demonstrations were crushed, and severe repression followed, but at least Kosovo retained its autonomy — until March 1989. It was then that, as a result of Serbia's victory in the battle over revision of the 1974 Constitution, the Serbian government regained control of Kosovo's courts, police, and territorial defence.

Under the newly-amended Constitution, adopted in March 1989, it is not necessary to consult Kosovo about further changes which affect its status. One of the new amendments states that these can be introduced only by the Serbian Assembly — in which Kosovo is represented but has no power of veto.

Kosovo's Albanians continue to resist. A general strike in the province in February 1989 was followed by a hunger strike by Albanian miners. When the Constitutional changes were actually adopted, first by a Kosovo Assembly ringed by army tanks on 23 March, and then on 28 March by Serbia's own Assembly, province-wide unrest lasted six days and resulted in 24 deaths. The wholesale repression which followed — including the arrest of the former Party leader of the province, Azem Vllasi, together with a group of prominent Albanians, and the internment without trial in Serbia proper of nearly 200 others — provoked international reaction. The European Parliament passed a resolution condemning the events, and dispatched a fact-finding mission. Critical resolutions were passed by the US Congress. But repression has continued, and so has Albanian unrest. Despite Serbia's parlous financial condition, plans to settle more than 100,000 Serbian colonists in Kosovo are said to be well advanced.

But in Serbia the robust Slobodan Milosevic's policy remains popular, for many Serbs instinctively see the Albanians as a modern version of their former Turkish oppressors. It was in Kosovo on 28 June 1389 that the Serbian Army, lead by Prince Lazar, was defeated by the Turks — a debacle that ushered in a humiliating five centuries of life under Turkish rule. Recovery of Kosovo was the constant hope and aim during those long years. By 1912, however, when Kosovo was at long last regained, the bulk of the Serbs had left, while the number of local Albanians had increased.

Principally because of the high birth rate, the Albanians now comprise about 90% of Kosovo's population, whereas the Serbs' share has dropped during the past 10 years to below 10%. Steady Serbian emigration from the province has also been a factor. The Serbs blame this on local Albanian 'terror', while the Albanians point out that they pay large sums of money (often in hard currency earned by Albanian *Gastarbeiter* in the West) for Serbian farms and houses; and that, in any case, the Serbs merely wish to build a better life for themselves. Kosovo is the poorest region of Yugoslavia.

## The Communist Party

Milosevic has used the Kosovo issue to build a new and aggressive type of populist movement. Throughout the summer of 1988 his followers staged a series of huge rallies throughout Serbia. Then, in October, they held one in Novi Sad, the capital of Vojvodina province, whose leaders had been resisting Milosevic's bid for its reabsorption into the Serbian republic. A new, pro-Milosevic leadership was installed in Vojvodina.

A similar attempt to bring a pro-Milosevic group to power in Montenegro failed, but the second attempt, in January 1989, met with success. The final Constitutional victory over Kosovo in March saw Milosevic's popularity rising to unprecedented heights among the Serbs — not simply those in Serbia proper, but throughout the entire federation. But his attempts to use the Serbs of Bosnia and Hercegovina (32% of the population) and in Croatia (11.6%) to destabilise the local Party leaders of those republics met with failure. By November, the Slovene authorities had banned the rally which his supporters wanted to hold in Ljubljana, the capital, on 1 December — anniversary of the founding of the first, royalist, Yugoslavia in 1918. Serbia retaliated by proclaiming a boycott of Slovene goods, and broke off all cultural relations with Slovenia.

By now, of course, Milosevic's bullying tactics had thoroughly frightened not only the Croatian and Slovene leaderships, but also those of Bosnia and Hercegovina, and even of Macedonia. His bid to push the Yugoslav Communist Party towards recentralisation at its Extraordinary Congress held in January 1990 was seen by many non-Serbs as part of a bid for total power throughout the whole of Yugoslavia. After acrimonious debates, the Slovene delegation walked out. Croatia, Bosnia, and Macedonia 'suspended' their participation when Milosevic insisted that nevertheless the Congress should continue its work.

This episode marked the *de facto* demise of the Yugoslav Communist Party — the force which Tito saw as the glue that would hold Yugoslavia together after his death. Attempts by the Milosevic group, eagerly supported by the large Party organisation in the army, to breathe new life into the corpse came to nothing owing to opposition in Croatia and Slovenia and to confusion and divisions in Bosnia and Macedonia. In any case, the political significance of the reformed Communists in Croatia and Slovenia was dramatically reduced by their defeat in free, multi-party elections in those two republics in April-May 1990. Following the reformed Communists' defeat in Croatia, the Party there split, with only its Serbian wing seeking affiliation to the 'new-old' Party in Belgrade. Faced with total failure of its 'unity' initiatives, not only in Croatia and Slovenia but also in Bosnia and Macedonia, the Serbian Party leaders gave up the unequal struggle and in June announced that the Serbian Communist Party would relaunch itself as the Serbian Socialist Party after a merger with the Socialist Alliance of Serbia, the Party's mass organisation, at a congress in July. That decision effectively marked the end of Slobodan Milosevic's attempt to gain power in Yugoslavia as a second Tito by capturing the control of the Yugoslav Party. Nobody can now do this, not even a successor to Milosevic, because Tito's Party is no more.

## The Army

Could the army perhaps replace the Party as the force holding Yugoslavia together? Certainly, the Yugoslav army's officer corps is 'uniterist'; it does not want the federation to disintegrate, not least because that would also mean the end of the Yugoslav army and of their own professional careers. Some 70% of officers and non-commissioned officers are Serbs, but not necessarily automatic supporters of 'Great Serbian' chauvinism. This is even more true of the army as a whole where non-Serb conscripts are a majority. Ethnic Albanians alone make up 17% of all those currently serving in the army, according to recent Yugoslav official statistics. This is well above the Albanians' 7.7% share in the total Yugoslav population. Bosnian Muslims also have a higher share of conscripts than their share of the total population.

In both cases, the reason is the high birth-rate among both groups.

It does not require much imagination to visualise the difficulties army chiefs would encounter if they tried to stage themselves — or simply assist — a coup aimed at re-establishing a centralised Yugoslavia. Would all those Albanians, Bosnian Muslims, Croats, Slovenes and others readily obey orders to shoot at their fellow-nationals? At the very least, the army leaders could not be sure, given the present policy of mixing all nationalities right down to platoon level. All this explains why the army, though loud in condemning the country's lurch into political pluralism and not above a spot of intrigue against its favourite enemies behind the scenes, has shown marked reluctance to engage itself directly in the political process. The existence of outspoken papers such as *Mladina*, a former official Slovene youth organisation organ, which have steadily over the years fought to 'de-mythologise' the armed forces, has been a significant factor. Intriguingly, in the new conditions in Croatia and Slovenia since the non-Communists' victory there, the army chiefs have refrained from open defiance and have even shown themselves ready to open talks aimed at ensuring a greater degree of autonomy in defence matters in both republics.

Though everything suggests that as a force, capable of putting the clock back, the army has missed its chance, it might yet find itself involved. A trigger for its intervention could be the flare-up of a full-scale civil war in Kosovo if the Milosevic regime tries to carry out its plan to settle there around 100,000 Serbian colonists, with the aid of large housing and other material incentives. Another trigger could be unrest in Croatia or Bosnia, prompting calls for the protection of the Serbs from the Croat or Bosnian authorities, as part of a Milosevic-orchestrated destabilisation scenario.

### *Finis* Yugoslavia?

Does it then have to be a parting of the ways for the peoples of Yugoslavia after more than seven decades of increasingly uneasy life in their common house, interrupted by four years of enemy occupation and bitter civil war? Or could Yugoslavia evolve — as the Croats and the Slovenes say they want — into a loose confederation? A *Staatenbund*, definitely not a *Bundestaat*, is what the western half of the country is talking about. Secession was very much the talk of the opposition in Slovenia and Croatia before the 1990 elections. After their respective victories, both the *Demos* Alliance in Slovenia and the Croatian Democratic Union (*Hrvatska Demokratska Zajednica*) in Croatia are instead talking of a possible deal with the rest of Yugoslavia, provided the conditions are right. Croatia's new President and leader of HDZ, Dr Franjo Tudjman, a historian and former Tito general, has said that he is ready to talk to any credible partner, even Mr Milosevic. A deal to form a confederation has always been the aim of Mr Milan Kucan, former Slovene Party leader and now its non-party President. Croatia and Slovenia jointly suggested a project for a Yugoslav confederation to the Yugoslav collective presidency in October 1990. The idea of a confederation that would save Bosnia from partition is popular with the public, not only the majority Muslims and the minority (20%) Croats but also among some of its Serbs, the second largest nationality there. Macedonia needs Yugoslavia to survive. So it is up to Serbia. It has the key to Yugoslavia's survival.

Mr Milosevic's difficulty is that he has promised a lot and delivered little. Kosovo's Albanians remain unreconciled to their forcible re-integration into Serbia. Kosovo is in a state of creeping civil insur-rections. Under pressure from world (notably American) opinion, the Serbian government in Belgrade has been obliged to release top Albanian figures from prison — not only the former Kosovo Party leader, Azem Vllasi, but also Adem Demaqi, known as Yugoslavia's Nelson Mandela on account of his 29 years in Yugoslavia's prisons for Albanian nationalism. Serbian emigration from Kosovo continues. The 'auto-nomist' forces in Vojvodina, defeated in the 1988 coup that toppled the then unpopular leadership, are regrouping, reinvigorated by the growing public discontent with the carpet-baggers from Belgrade. Attempts to destabilise both Bosnia and Croatia by stirring unrest among the Serbs in those two republics since the middle of 1989 have strengthened anti-Serb feeling there, both among the Croats and the Muslims, Milosevic's aggressive policy has also antagonised Macedonia.

Within Serbia proper, the main challenge to Milosevic comes from the ultra-nationalists like Vuk Draskovic, a Serb from Bosnia who campaigns from an openly anti-Communist platform for the rehabili-tation of General Draza Mihailovic, leader of Serbia royalist guerrillas during the Second World War who was captured and executed by the Communists in 1946. Draskovic advocates a 'Greater Serbia' that would take in not only Macedonia and Montenegro (as well as, of course, Kosovo and Vojvodina) but also Bosnia and large parts of Croatia.

Despite this, Milosevic and his Socialist (re-named Communist) party won a convincing election victory in Serbia in December 1990. The party's control of the media was a factor as was widespread ballot-rigging, but more important was the population's fear of change on which the ruling party (like earlier in the year those in Bulgaria and Romania) was able to play. Large pay increases were awarded all round on the eve of the Serbian election and continuing full employ-ment was promised. An additional factor in the Milosevic victory was the near-total boycott of the Serbian election by the Kosovo Albanians in protest against the official refusal to register 'ethnic' parties. This gave the Milosevic Socialists control of the Kosovo province seats on the basis of the Serb vote only (less than 10% of Kosovo's total population).

Ante Markovic, the popular federal prime minister, who had managed to get inflation down from an annual rate of 2,500% in December 1989 to virtually zero in May 1990 by pegging the new hard Yugoslav dinar to the D-Mark, launched in mid-1990 his own party to fight for his economic programme in the Yugoslav federal election. That was scheduled for the end of 1990 but was then quietly put off, without a new target date being fixed, amid disagreements about how such an election was to be organised and what kind of assembly would emerge from it. The Markovic party participated in the Serbian as well as Bosnian and Macedonian elections (which also took place at the end of 1990) but its showing was poor in all three.

All of Yugoslavia's six republics now have governments elected at multiparty elections and thus, in principle, with the mandate to negotiate about the country's future. But the elections have demonstrated the wide gap between Croatia and Serbia, on the one hand, which want a loose confederation and will secede if that is not available and, on the other, Serbia and Montenegro which favour a federation with a powerful centre. Bosnia and Macedonia lean towards the confederal option but are anxious for some common framework to be preserved for the whole of Yugoslavia.

The chances of a grand *Ausgleich*, not unlike that negotiated between the two halves of the Habsburg Monarchy in 1867 and followed by one between Croatia and Hungary in 1868, being achieved in the foreseeable future are not good. The main reason is the opposition to it not only by the Milosevic group but also of the leadership of the Yugoslav army. As in the Soviet Union, the army has made clear its determination to preserve both socialism and the country's unity. A group of army officers, some of them still on the active list, launched a new Communist party of Yugoslavia in November 1990 to fight for those aims. The army's crackdown in Croatia in the first half of 1991, timed to coincide with the steadily escalating Serb rebellion against the Croat authorities, threatened to plunge the whole of Yugoslavia into civil war.

Those developments contributed to the increasing marginalisation of the federal prime minister, Ante Markovic. His authority received an extra blow from the monetary coup carried out in December 1990 by the Serbian government and which enabled it to appropriate illegally half of the fresh money supply for the whole of Yugoslavia for 1991, worth about $1.4 billion.

But even if a deal of sorts emerges, enabling Yugoslavia to continue in some form, there should be no illusion that the outcome will necessarily be solid and long-lasting. Like the Soviet Union, Yugoslavia is a country built across a great divide of cultures and civilisations. The line dividing the Roman Empire into its eastern and western parts cuts right across today's Yugoslavia, running from north to south. Yugoslavia's peoples would not, given another chance, re-invent it. One day, Yugoslavia will probably dissolve its ties, as Norway and Sweden did in 1905. Meanwhile, what is wanted is not ideal solutions but damage-limitation.

In previous times, the West would have wanted to support a strong leader — any strong leader — to 'keep the country together', whether or not its inhabitants wanted to remain in each other's embrace. Now that Yugoslavia is no longer strategically so important in the East – West balance, there is more room for holding back, for keeping an open mind about what is happening there. Western policy, including that of Yugoslavia's close neighbours, Austria, Italy and Greece, can these days afford a more active attitude than they could in the competitive atmosphere of the Cold War, offering such help (including mediation) as is needed and possible, but avoiding giving the impression to the peoples of Yugoslavia that outsiders need Yugoslavia more than they do. Above all, those outsiders should refrain from indulging in nostalgia for the days when Tito ruled. It is now clear that Yugoslavia's unity under Tito was imposed from within by him and his Party and from outside by the discipline of the Cold War. It should not be the West's business to try to keep Yugoslavia — or the Soviet Union — in being.

CHAPTER 15

# Arms Control and Limitations

LYNN HANSEN

IN EUROPE and North America the apparent willingness of the Soviet Union significantly to reduce its armed forces, both unilaterally and through the medium of arms control agreements, has evoked interest, approbation, and no small amount of sheer amazement. It is not a simple task to address arms control and the Soviet military in a short chapter, nor is it clear that anyone in the West — or the East for that matter — can really understand the attitudes and motivations which drive Soviet leaders to take certain courses of action. Arms control is at once an esoteric and an abstruse subject, seldom understood, even by its practitioners in all its aspects. Clearly, the revolutionary year of 1989 must be seen in its political essence to be fully understood. But while it has been dominated by politics, the military-security repercussions deserve the most careful scrutiny.

This chapter briefly addresses the Soviet military and conventional arms control. It does not address nuclear arms control or the strategic balance. Beginning with the briefest examination of the now defunct Mutual and Balanced Force Reduction (MBFR) talks, it progresses to a consideration of Gorbachev's unilateral withdrawal project and then provides the major outlines of the negotiations on Conventional Forces in Europe (CFE). Finally, it delves gently into possible reasons for the phenomenon of Soviet willingness to accept deep cuts in conventional forces.

## MBFR Negotiations

On 31 January, 1973 the seven member states of the Warsaw Treaty Organisation and 12 members of the North Atlantic Alliance (France, Portugal, and Iceland did not attend) began preparatory talks for the Vienna negotiations on Mutual and Balanced Forces Reductions in Europe. Sixteen years and 493 plenary sessions later, on 2 February 1989, the MBFR negotiations ended without a single agreement.

The 1973 Western MBFR proposal aimed at the withdrawal from Eastern Europe of one tank army: five tank divisions, 1,700 main battle tanks, 76,000 troops and all other conventional armaments organic to the tank army. When two years of negotiations failed to produce agreement, NATO offered to sweeten the pot with a new package deal placed on the table on 16 December, 1975. This involved proposing Option III, which had already been developed in rudimentary form in 1973. In addition to the withdrawal of 29,000 American troops, this option offered the withdrawal of 1,000 nuclear warheads, together with 90 delivery systems: 54 F-4 Phantom aircraft and 35 launchers for Pershing I short-range ballistic missiles. In addition, the West offered to agree to include air force manpower in the negotiations with the provision that ground force levels would not exceed 700,000 and to set the combined ground and air force personnel levels on both sides at 900,000. Even this new approach failed to capture Soviet agreement. From that point on, various proposals and counter-proposals were offered; none was able to bring the two sides all the way to agreement.

## Gorbachev's Unilateral Withdrawals

On 7 December, 1988 — not quite two months before the demise of MBFR — President Gorbachev strode to the rostrum at the 43rd Session of the General Assembly of the United Nations and announced projected *unilateral* reductions of Soviet armed forces that exceeded by almost 20% the most ambitious NATO proposals in MBFR. Ten years earlier, in 1979, the Soviet Union had unilaterally removed a tank division and 1,000 obsolete tanks from East Germany. Part of a restructuring plan which left the Soviets with more troops and greater firepower, this unilateral withdrawal did little to convince the West that Moscow was interested in conventional arms control in Europe. It is therefore not surprising that Gorbachev's 1988 statement on unilateral reductions was greeted with scepticism because of its unprecedented scope. It projected disbandment in six tank divisions and four independent tank regiments, 10,000 tanks (including 5,300 from forward area units) and 500,000 troops (240,000 from the eastern USSR and Eastern Europe).

Totally outside any formal arms reduction agreement, these projected unilateral reductions, when completed, would be sufficient in themselves substantially to alter the military equation in Central Europe. Soviet surprise attack, the most feared as well as the most questioned scenario for the initiation of war in Europe, was all but eliminated by this intrepid move by Gorbachev.

## CFE Talks

Despite the military significance of Gorbachev's move, it did not promise to correct the existing disparity in conventional armed forces in Europe. Therefore, throughout 1988 representatives of the 23 NATO and Warsaw Pact states met in Vienna to hammer out a mandate for new negotiations on conventional armed forces in Europe (CFE). Finally, on 10 January, 1989 a mandate was agreed.

According to the mandate, the objectives of the new negotiations were: 1) to strengthen stability and security in Europe through the establishment of a stable and secure balance of conventional armed forces, to include conventional armaments and equipment, at lower levels; 2) the elimination of disparities prejudicial to stability and security; and 3) the elimination, as a matter of priority, of the capability for launching surprise attack and for initiating large-scale offensive action. Nuclear weapons were not to be a subject of the negotiations and neither naval forces nor chemical weapons would be addressed.

**Data:** The second of the three agreed objectives for CFE was to establish parity in key weapons systems. This implied a willingness to exchange and verify data on the relevant armed forces of all participating states, and was an important departure from past practice. From 1976 onward in the MBFR negotiations, the question of a data discrepancy between NATO estimates of Warsaw Pact manpower and the Pact's 'official' data had plagued the talks because Western manpower estimates for the Pact exceeded the Eastern data by approximately 200,000. However, a new era of openness may have been ushered in with the Warsaw Pact data presented on 30 January, 1989 as Table 15.1 illustrates.

TABLE 15.1 *Personnel*

|                | WTO Data | NATO Data | Difference |
| -------------- | -------- | --------- | ---------- |
| East Germany   | 154,200  | 120,000   | + 32,200   |
| Poland         | 277,000  | 230,000   | + 47,000   |
| Czechoslovakia | 173,600  | 145,000   | + 28,600   |
| TOTAL          | 604,800  | 495,000   | + 107,800  |

In 1976, Eastern representatives had insisted that the total number of Warsaw Treaty ground force personnel in the three countries listed above was 805,000. Adding approximately 476,000 Soviet stationed ground troops in the same area to the figures above would provide a total number of about 1,080,800 or about 92,800 more than NATO estimates in 1976.[1]

### Area of Application

For all practical purposes, the 1983 Concluding Document of the Madrid CSCE Follow-up Meeting established the area for future arms reductions talks in Europe. As set forth in the Madrid mandate for the Stockholm Conference, confidence-building measures would no longer be applicable only to the first 250km of Soviet territory, but would apply to the whole of Europe, from the Atlantic to the Urals. This set the precedent which was built upon in the mandate for the CFE negotiations. Thus with the ending of MBFR, arms reduction talks were no longer restricted to the Federal Republic of Germany, the Netherlands, Belgium and Luxembourg in the West and East Germany, Poland and Czechoslovakia in the East. In CFE all the European territory of members of both alliances would be included in the area of application.[2]

### Stability

The second agreed objective in the CFE mandate stressed that parity should be established in the levels of armaments and equipment most prejudicial to security and stability. For the Western participants, this meant tanks, artillery systems, and armoured combat vehicles (ACVs) — especially armoured infantry fighting vehicles (AIFVs), such as the Soviet BMP and the US M-2 Bradley. The data exchanges on these categories were as revealing as those relating to personnel. Whereas, some European politicians had criticised governments for exaggerating the size of Warsaw Pact forces, the Pact's own data showed that the West had underestimated the total numbers. Using tanks as the example (data for artillery and ACVs also exceeded Western estimates) the following Table illustrates the difference.

TABLE 15.2 *Tanks*

|  | WTO Data | NATO Data | Difference |
|---|---|---|---|
| East Germany | 3,140 | 3,000 | + 140 |
| Poland | 3,330 | 3,400 | − 70 |
| Czechoslovakia | 4,585 | 3,800 | + 785 |
| Hungary | 1,435 | 1,300 | + 135 |
| Bulgaria | 2,200 | 1,800 | + 400 |
| Romania | 3,200 | 1,200 | + 2,000 |
| USSR | 41,580 | 37,000 | + 4,580 |
| TOTAL | 59,470 | 51,500 | + 7,970 |

The NATO data do not include approximately 2,600 light tanks (such as the T-34 and PT-76) which are included in the WTO data. Factoring light tanks into the total numbers, it is still evident that NATO's estimates were approximately 5,300 tanks lower than the data provided by the WTO on 30 January, 1989.

NATO's proposal, introduced on 6 March, 1989 in the CFE negotiations, was based on the conviction that the concentration of forces in the CFE area of application was the highest ever known in peacetime and represented the greatest destructive potential ever assembled. Therefore, overall levels of forces needed to be substantially reduced, particularly those armaments most relevant to surprise attack and large-scale offensive action. For the West this meant tanks, artillery and armoured combat vehicles. Rapid mobility, high firepower and the ability to seize and hold territory inherent in those systems made them particularly threatening to stability in Europe.

To implement the reductions required to meet the mandate's agreed objectives, NATO proposed a set of rules. To a large extent, WTO states subsequently accepted these rules as a basis for the CFE negotiations; consequently, their proposed numbers are included in the following Tables.

TABLE 15.3 *NATO proposed Structure of CFE Agreement*

*Rule 1: Overall Limits* — Without respect to alliances, the overall total of weapons in each of three categories will at no time exceed:

|               | NATO   | WTO    |
|---------------|--------|--------|
| Tanks         | 40,000 | 40,000 |
| Artillery     | 33,000 | 48,000 |
| Armoured Veh. | 56,000 | 56,000 |

*Rule 2: Sufficiency* — No one country should be allowed to dominate Europe by force of arms; no single state should therefore retain more than a fixed percentage of the overall limits established in Rule 1.

|               | NATO           | WTO                              |
|---------------|----------------|----------------------------------|
| Tanks         | 12,000 (30%)   | 14,000 (35%)                     |
| Artillery     | 9,900 (30%)    | 17,000 (35.4%) — of WTO          |
| Armoured Veh. | 16,800 (30%)   | 18,000 (32.1%) proposed limits   |

*Rule 3: Stationed Forces* — Limiting the overall number and nationality of forces will not in itself affect the stationing of armaments outside national boundaries; therefore, among countries belonging to a treaty of alliance, neither side will station armaments outside national territory in active units exceeding the following levels:

|               | NATO  | WTO   |
|---------------|-------|-------|
| Tanks         | 3,200 | 4,500 |
| Artillery     | 1,700 | 4,000 |
| Armoured Veh. | 6,000 | 7,500 |

*continued*

TABLE 15.3 *continued*

*Rule 4: Regional Sub-limits* — In the areas described below, each group of states shall not exceed the following levels.

(a) Within the whole of Europe (Zone 4.1):

|  | NATO | WTO |
|---|---|---|
| Tanks | 20,000 | 20,000 |
| Artillery | 16,500 | 24,000 |
| Armoured Veh. | 28,000 | 28,000 |

(b) Within the area consisting of Belgium, Denmark, West Germany, France, Italy, Luxembourg, the Netherlands, Portugal, Spain, the United Kingdom, Czechoslovakia, East Germany, Hungary, Poland, and the territory of the USSR comprising the Baltic, Belorussian, Carpathian, Moscow, Volga, and Ural Military Districts in active units (Zone 4.2):

|  | NATO | WTO (accepted concept of zonal limits, but constructed zones differently) |
|---|---|---|
| Tanks | 11,300 | |
| Artillery | 9,000 | |
| Armoured Veh. | 20,000 | |

(c) Within the area consisting of Belgium, Denmark, West Germany, France, Italy, Luxembourg, the Netherlands, the United Kingdom, Czechoslovakia, East Germany, Hungary, Poland, and the territory of the USSR comprising the Baltic, Belorussian, and Carpathian Military Districts in active units (Zone 4.3):

|  | NATO | WTO (accepted concept of zonal limits, but constructed zones differently) |
|---|---|---|
| Tanks | 10,300 | |
| Artillery | 7,600 | |
| Armoured Veh. | 18,000 | |

(d) Within the area consisting of Belgium, West Germany, Luxembourg, the Netherlands, Czechoslovakia, East Germany, and Poland in active units (Zone 4.4):

|  | NATO | WTO |
|---|---|---|
| Tanks | 8,000 | 8,700 |
| Artillery | 4,500 | 7,600 |
| Armoured Veh. | 11,000 | 14,500 |

*Rule 5: Information Exchange* — Each year, holdings of armaments and equipment subject to treaty provisions would be notified and disaggregated down to battalion level. This measure would also apply to personnel in both combat and combat support units. Any change of notified unit structures above battalion level, or any measure resulting in an increase in personnel strength in such units, would be subject to notification.

In their proposal of 9 March 1989, WTO states suggested that asymmetries and imbalances in the number of personnel be negotiated as well as those in the main types of armaments. And to NATO's armament categories, the WTO added combat helicopters and 'tactical strike aircraft'. The scope of reductions envisioned by the Warsaw

Treaty states — to levels 10 – 15% below the lowest level possessed by either alliance — appeared to be compatible with the general outlines of the NATO proposal. In his address at the opening of the CFE negotiations in Vienna, Soviet Foreign Minister Shevardnadze signalled a willingness to accept the major premises of the Western approach. Still, he offered a more comprehensive and long-term agenda than was reflected in the Western proposal. He urged that successful negotiation of a first stage agreement be followed by a second stage in which the two sides would agree to cut armed forces by another 25% along with organic movements. This stage would be followed by a third in which the sides would agree to ceilings on all other forms of armaments and restructure their forces to give them a purely defensive character.

For its part, NATO had not included aircraft and helicopters in its initial proposal because of the difficulties involved in establishing agreed counting rules and definitions which could find universal application in a negotiation involving 23 different states. However, on the eve of the NATO 40th anniversary summit, President Bush proposed including all combat aircraft based on land and combat helicopters in the negotiations, with the proviso that parity would be reached at about 15% below NATO levels. He also proposed that the United States and the Soviet Union agree that neither country could station more than 275,000 of its ground and air force personnel outside of its national territory in the area of application. These proposals were adopted by the North Atlantic Council on 29 May, 1989 and became an official part of the Western proposal.

Under the May 1989 manpower proposal, the United States would withdraw approximately 30,000 troops or 20% of US ground and air combat manpower in Europe. The Soviet Union, on the other hand, would withdraw in excess of 300,000 troops.

After both Hungary and Czechoslovakia had reached agreement with the Soviet Union on the total withdrawal of Soviet forces from these two countries by the end of 1991, it became clear that 275,000 stationed troops was more than the situation justified. Therefore, at the Ottawa Open Skies Conference, on 12 – 14 February 1990, US Secretary of State Baker and Soviet Foreign Minister Shevardnadze agreed to lower the figure to 195,000 each for stationed US and Soviet troops in the Central Zone[3] The United States was allowed an additional 30,000 troops outside the Central Zone in Europe.

### Aircraft

The new Western proposal on aircraft proved to be more problematic for the Soviet military. As previously noted, the Soviet arms control proposal to include aircraft had been aimed at a category called 'tactical strike aircraft'. Their proposal was calculated on the basis of data which excluded all Soviet air defence aircraft, land-based naval air, trainers, and aircraft assigned to strategic air armies. Using data based on these calculations, the Soviets proposed parity in tactical strike aircraft at 4,700. Reductions required by each side based on this data approach would be as shown in Table 15.4.

TABLE 15.4 *Aircraft Reductions based on Soviet Data*[4] *and NATO Data*

|  | WTO DATA | | NATO DATA | |
|  | WTO | NATO | WTO | NATO |
| --- | --- | --- | --- | --- |
| Total Combat Aircraft | 7,876 | 7,130 | 12,280 | 5,355 |
| Excluding Air Defence | 6,047 | 7,080 | — | — |
| Excluding Air Defence and Naval | 5,355 | 5,450 | — | — |
| Proposed Ceiling | 4,700 | 4,700 | 5,200 | 5,200 |
| Required Reductions | 655 | 750 | 7,080 | 155 |

By their count, the Soviet Union had exempted from aircraft totals the 1,829 air defence aircraft which they claimed were incapable of operating against ground targets as well as 692 naval combat aircraft. Moreover, no aircraft assigned to the strategic air armies or combat-capable trainers were included in Soviet aircraft counts.[5] Also, all Soviet strategic aircraft with intercontinental missions (Tu-95 BEAR, Tu-160 BLACKJACK) were excluded from the Soviet count.

The Western definition of aircraft to be included in the negotiation covered all combat-capable aircraft based on land. This included not only those aircraft assigned to Soviet Naval Aviation, but also the aircraft belonging to the Air Armies in the area of application as well as the strategic bombers with an intercontinental mission (since they were combat-capable aircraft based on land in the area of application) as well as more than 1,500 combat-capable trainers. Adding strategic aircraft and trainers to the January 1989 figure of 7,896 for combat aircraft would bring the total to well over 12,000 aircraft. Accordingly, to reach parity at the level of about 5,200 aircraft, as called for in the Western proposal, Warsaw Treaty states would have to reduce and destroy more than half their current inventory.

The West subsequently moderated its demands by allowing an additional 500 aircraft above the ceiling for air defence aircraft and exempting primary trainers (albeit not dual-seat combat trainer aircraft). Strategic aircraft were to be treated in accordance with the provisions of the mandate, which excluded nuclear systems. The Soviet response was to triple the extra allotment for air defence aircraft, impose a 1,500 allotment above ceiling for combat-capable trainers, and insist on excluding land-based naval aircraft from the negotiations. For the

West, this meant establishing a ceiling more than 2,000 aircraft higher than the NATO inventory, theoretically providing the West an entitlement to add aircraft. This did not seem to be a prudent arms control position for Western states to adopt. In apparent recognition of the complexity of the issue, the Soviet Union later proposed that aircraft reductions in the first phase of the CFE Negotiations be limited to establishing parity in US and Soviet stationed aircraft in the area of application at 500 aircraft each. This was apparently done with the full understanding that such a proposition would have no appeal to the West. Accordingly, on 7 April 1990 Foreign Minister Shevardnadze noted at the conclusion of the ministerial meetings held in Washington that if such an approach were unacceptable, aircraft might have to be dealt with in a later phase of the negotiations.

### *Helicopters*

The variety of helicopter airframes found in Europe made this category of reductions extremely complicated. Within the various military organisations, some are used in the attack role, some in the combat support role, and some in the transport role. Adding further complications is the utilisation of the same basic airframe in a variety of civilian roles. Both East and West agreed to place a ceiling on the number of pure attack helicopters. Systems such as the Mi-8 HIP which have been modified to perform the attack role could be recategorisd by converting them to combat support helicopters. This incurred a strict data reporting and verification regime to keep track of former attack helicopters recategorised in this way. The data reporting system would also apply to those helicopters which have not functioned in the attack role, especially when variants of the same type of airframe have been equipped for attack. With these complicated provisions, all Mi-8 HIND, Mi-28 HAVOC and the HOKUM Soviet helicopters would be captured in a 1,900 ceiling, whereas all other military helicopters functioning in a combat support role would be subject to data-reporting requirements.

## Changes in Military Thinking

Why, after 16 years of unfruitful MBFR negotiations, during which the Soviet army continually modernised and enhanced its combat potential, have Soviet leaders voiced willingness to take such significant reductions? There is no definitive answer. Traditional answers to the question involved references to economic difficulties, new thinking among Soviet leaders, *perestroika* and *glasnost'*. Each of these explanations has a legitimate place in attempting to understand the phenomenon of Soviet political development as the world faces the last decade of this century.

In addition, however, there are at least three other factors which bear more directly on the General Staff's acceptance of the enormous cuts they have sanctioned in the Soviet armed forces: nuclear deterrence, a dismal performance in Afghanistan, and the nature of the future battlefield.

## Deterrence

NATO's strategy of flexible response provided for the use of nuclear weapons to repel an invasion by superior conventional forces. Built into this strategy was the concept of an escalation ladder which meant that as the situation worsened, greater use could be made of Western nuclear systems progressing from European-based weapons up to and including the intercontinental strategic systems of the United States. Although NATO had many times stated its policy that none of its weapons would ever be used except in response to aggression, Soviet analysts continued to regard the strategy of flexible response as a first-use doctrine. NATO's deployment of Pershing-II and ground-launched cruise missiles (GLCMs) in 1984 elevated the threat already inherent in Soviet understanding of NATO strategy. The old strategy of intimidation had backfired. It was time to face the reality that deterrence works.

Much of Soviet strategy for Europe had been based on the perception that the initial period of a contemporary war would be conventional. The development of principles of operational art which sought victory through quick and decisive offensive operations had placed its demands on the so-called building (*stroitel'stva*) — the organisation, structure and equipping — of the armed forces. In many respects this was a bottomless pit into which countless scarce resources were poured without the certainty of victory because nuclear weapons could negate success on the conventional battlefield.

Accepting the fact, not the philosophy, of nuclear deterrence led to a series of conclusions: 1) there can be no winners in a nuclear war; 2) war can no longer be an instrument of politics in Europe as long as nuclear weapons are present; 3) the offensive nature evident in the structure and disposition of the Soviet armed forces undercuts Moscow's political objectives for Europe and strengthens the hand of those in NATO who insist on ever stronger defences; it therefore made political sense to reduce the image of the threat; and 4) deep cuts in the Soviet military posture are required before the arms control process can lead to the desired de-nuclearisation or partial de-nuclearisation of Western Europe.

## Afghanistan

No military force is comfortable with accepting defeat. The Soviet withdrawal from Afghanistan was an admission that the Soviet armed forces could not be used as an effective instrument in pursuing political objectives. As with every military force in the world, the reasons for lack of success had to be identified. The resulting introspection disclosed a more general and widespread malaise within the Soviet military than had been understood at the top. Lack of discipline, poor military proficiency, drug abuse, low morale, and the inability to use military technology effectively were identified key deficiencies.

Exactly what steps will be taken to rectify the situation is unclear, but it is certain that the military leadership wants a more professional and efficient military. In general, this has meant an emphasis on quality rather than quantity. Older officers and those without record of effective leadership were marked for expulsion, some through retirement, others through some procedural means. Leaner and meaner is descriptive, if 'meaner' is taken to mean more efficient as well as more effective.

## The Future Battlefield

Within the Soviet military frame of reference, military doctrine deals with the past, the present and the immediate future. On the other hand, Soviet military science focuses on the more distant future and on weapons that do not, as yet, exist. Yet, there is no real dichotomy between these two disciplines; indeed one complements the other.

A recent reprinting of a 1946 speech by General Rotmistrov (in the September 1985 issue of the *Military Historical Journal*) is an example of the meshing of military doctrine and military science. It referred to an analysis of armour operations on the Belorussian Front during the Berlin operation which concluded that Soviet force structure was too tank-heavy and lacked the combined arms balance necessary to conduct successful operations in an urbanised, hilly and forested Central Europe. Indicative of the internal debates within the Soviet General Staff during the 1980s, this speech helped argue the case for the restructuring of the Soviet army which has accompanied the unilateral withdrawals announced by President Gorbachev.

After the restructuring, Soviet tank divisions will no longer consist of three tank regiments and one motorised regiment, but will comprise two tank regiments and two motorised rifle regiments. The total number of tanks in this new 'square division' will decrease about 20% from approximately 330 to 264 tanks. Engineer, artillery and air defence sub-units are to increase. An even more dramatic reduction, approximately 40% in tank numbers — from 270 to 162 is to take place within motorised rifle divisions. Previously, such a division was comprised of three motorised rifle regiments and one tank regiment. The restructured motor rifle division will lose its tank regiment altogether and its independent tank battalion will become a motorised rifle regiment. This restructuring has made large numbers of tanks redundant, particularly within motorised rifle divisions. Thus, some 3,100 of the approximately 5,300 tanks announced in the Soviet unilateral reductions were to come from the restructuring of motorised rifle units.

TABLE 15.5 *Restructuring of Soviet Divisions*

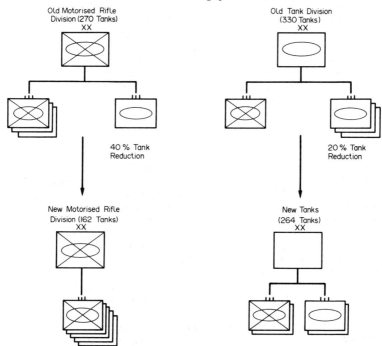

This restructuring of Soviet divisions is, of course, in response to changes in Soviet military doctrine. They reflect the military and political reappraisals of the threat, the political environment, and the character of potential future enemy. In the context of the past, the present and the immediate future, these changes signal a gradual change from an offensively-oriented force structure and deployment to a more defensively-oriented force. For example, Generals Chervov and Batenin acknowledged that five of the six divisions to be withdrawn unilaterally were operational manoeuvre group divisions, thereby contradicting an earlier statement by the former Chief of Staff of the Warsaw Pact, General Gribkov, to the effect that there were no such things as operational manoeuvre groups. Residual forces will also be smaller, of that there is no doubt. But they will be better equipped and more efficient in their overall structure and organisation. No new T-80 or T-72 tanks are scheduled for destruction and the production of new model tanks will not cease. As noted by the C-in-C of the Western Group of Forces, General Snetkov, large numbers of T-64s are to be stored beyond the Ural Mountains in the Asian areas of the USSR. But thousands of tanks that are now as much as 50 years old will be destroyed; consider that a T-34 was designed in 1934 and widely used in the final years of the Second World War and the PT-76 amphibious tank is nearly as old. T-54s, T-55, T-62s constitute the bulk of those tanks to be destroyed. These old tanks are expensive to maintain and generally ineffective on the modern battlefield.

Looking beyond the present and the immediate future, military science looks at the longer term future. It is predictive. It deals with questions of technology. In 1982 Marshal Ogarkov, then Chief of the Soviet General Staff, noted that the history of warfare and of military art attests to the fact that changes in military affairs are dictated by changes in weapons and equipment. It is advances in technology, he asserted, which forcibly and against the will of military command authorities produce revolutionary changes in the mode of waging combat. He also drew attention to the relative vulnerability of tanks on the contemporary and future battlefield in the face of emerging technologies and warned of the dangers in ignoring this trend. The bottom line is that Soviet enthusiasm for the tank-heavy battlefield of the past is waning as military science contemplates the future potential of military technology. The destruction of 30,000 – 40,000 obsolete tanks, coupled with the retention (either in storage or in operational units) of more modern T-64s, T-72s, and T-80s is a relatively small price to pay if it brings greater investment in future technology. This could be the trade-off which the Soviet General Staff has found acceptable.

## Into the 1990s

In the first half of this decade, the Soviet army will change over to its new structure, accommodating itself to a new doctrine, a revised military art, arms control, and political developments in Eastern Europe. In so doing, the system will experience significant turbulence. By mid-decade, however, things should have settled down to the point where the trend-lines will become more perceptible.

It has already become clear that the Soviet armed forces will be smaller in the 1990s than in the 1980s. The 500,000-man reduction predicted by Gorbachev could be doubled as a consequence of arms control, events in Eastern Europe, and internal adjustments designed to invigorate the economy. Standards for induction into the armed forces will be raised as the army moves cautiously from its sociological role as school of the nation towards the assumption of a more professional military character. Universal conscription will remain in theory, but it will be more selective. In addition, incentives will be found to keep larger numbers of inductees on active duty as they master the technological skills necessary to a modern army. There may be even more radical moves towards creating a professional nucleus for a smaller military force with the notion of a conscript army being eroded in the interests of retaining those who have mastered increasingly complex military technology. And more and more manoeuvre formations and units will be manned at cadre levels, thus increasing the importance of mobilisation.

Accompanying the shrinking size of the regular Soviet armed forces will be an increased emphasis on paramilitary forces. Internal security forces are apt to be equipped with increasingly capable hardware, probably falling short of taking on the trappings of a full-fledged military force, but nonetheless significantly increasing their capability to cope with internal disturbance. Their ability to perform combat against external enemies will need watching. Indeed, it is possible that the paradox will be created where there is greater separation between paramilitary and military forces to protect the former from arms control requirements while at the same time there is greater integration in strategic planning to take advantage of increased capabilities.

As has been repeatedly emphasised, the most significant trend to watch will be the acquisition and mastery of ever more sophisticated military technology. Research into space technology will intensify, reflecting a long-held Soviet view regarding the importance of space to the battlefield on the ground. Little of this is likely to be overtly visible during the first half of the decade, but bit by bit Soviet dedication to the acquisition of technological prowess is sure to become evident.

What seems important to understand is that the Soviet General Staff has engaged in arms control and the restructuring of the Soviet armed forces in accordance with the dictates and conclusions of Soviet military science. Thus for military reasons, key forward-looking elements of the Soviet military have aligned themselves with President Gorbachev to meet the exigencies of the period in which the Soviet Union finds itself. Often, it may seem to the Soviet military that Gorbachev moves with a velocity it is unaccustomed to, but in the end, Soviet military science is probably one of his staunchest allies, even within the field of arms control.

## Notes

[1] All data comparisons in this Chapter are made on the basis of US Congressional Record, S 2764, dated 16 March 1989.

2  In the case of Turkey, the area of application includes the territory of Turkey north and west of the following line: the point of intersection of the border with the 39th parallel, Muradiye, Patnos, Karayazi, Tekman, Kemaliye, Feke, Ceyhan, Dogankent, Gözne and thence to the sea.

3  West Germany, the Benelux Countries, Denmark, East Germany, Poland, Czechoslovakia and Hungary.

4  Based on Warsaw Pact Tables of the Correlation of Forces, released on 30 January 1989.

5  Four air armies are relevant here: the 4th in Vinnitsa (Ukraine), the 24th in Legnica (Poland) the 36th in Moscow, and the 46th in Smolensk. Aircraft assigned to the Air Armies include Tu-16 BADGER, Tu-22 BLINDER, Tu-22M BACKFIRE, Su-24 FENCER, and MiG-23/27 FLOGGER. Total number of aircraft is considerably in excess of 1,000.

# Conclusions

JOHN HEMSLEY

THIS COLLECTION of essays about the Soviet Union not only covers a wide syllabus, but has been contributed by a diverse group of authors from a number of countries. All authors were given a free hand over their approach to the subject. Therefore it can neither be expected, nor would it have been desirable, that they would arrive at a consensus on every topic. Nevertheless, it falls to me as Editor to attempt to draw together the salient points of these collected writings.

This task has been made easier by the fact that there is a remarkable thread of consistency running through most of what has been written. Where there is a conflict of opinion, this is a matter of interpretation. In any case, as there are usually several different ways of looking at a problem, it would clearly be an impertinence for me to make any adjudication. The reader must make his own judgement from what has been said and why it has been said, bearing in mind that it has been a bold enterprise to invite anyone to peer into the future at a time of such immense, rapid and, in many cases, unpredictable change in the Soviet Union. The restriction on the length of each contribution has provided an additional constraint upon the authors.

When considering the unfolding events in the USSR and Eastern Europe, there are clearly several questions which need to be answered. Perhaps the most critical of these is how difficult do the apparent rapid changes make it to understand what is really going on in the Soviet Union? It is important not to forget the nature of Communism and its dialectic theory before legitimately asking to what extent the system has really changed in that country. In any case what is the nature of change and how much is for internal or how much for external consumption? To what extent did Gorbachev open a Pandora's box, and did he actually envisage during 1987 – 88 just how far the effects of *glasnost'* and *perestroika* were likely to go? Is it possible for us to separate military from politico-economic *perestroika* and, in particular, are we really looking at a new and formulated military doctrine?

To answer these questions, an examination of Soviet political futures and an understanding of their political strategy is required. What do Soviet policy-makers perceive as their major concerns and priorities which might help us to investigate the dynamics governing present and future restructuring? Certainly we need to establish the determinants of Soviet military power, along with any alteration to the military balance arising out of the application of new technologies, properly to analyse whether or not the USSR really still represents any medium- or long-term threat to the West? The purpose of this book has been to address all these questions, as a result of which certain broad areas of agreement have emerged concerning the processes of present change and likely future developments in the Soviet Union of tomorrow.

The heart of the economic crisis facing the USSR clearly lies in the systemic deficiencies inherent in civilian resource management, allocation, administration and transport. This has given rise to a whole menu of inter-related problems. Resolving these issues without plunging the whole system into irretrievable chaos is the top priority for any Soviet leader. An already stagnant economy is in total recession and continues to labour under a discredited system of centralised planning. This has led to a flourishing black economy, as Soviet industry breaks down under the intolerable load of a suffocating bureaucracy, inhibited by problems of inadequate energy supplies, an inefficient distribution and transportation system with an under-developed supporting infrastructure, poor investment and the lack of an internationally-negotiable currency. The bureaucracy itself exercises an all-pervasive state monopoly over every aspect of economic planning and implementation. It is over-centralised and consists of a self-perpetuating *nomenklatura* operating a system of widely-applied and inflexible norms with an unprecedented degree of privileged self-interest.

We have probably reached no firm conclusion in this book on whether or not any of the plans for fundamental economic reform will actually work. Resource allocation, distribution and incentives all need to be radically improved to increase industrial and agricultural production output. In fact the present economic system is likely to prove unreformable, since what is needed is a completely new set of values. One of the major objectives of *perestroika* is to get Soviet society to accept this. In this context, Soviet thinking has tended to be traditional but abstract; historically, capitalism has had no place in Russian life. There is little tradition of an enterprise culture. Much of this can be attributed to the dominant role played by the Russian Orthodox church which experienced no 'reformation', even after secularisation in the 18th and 19th centuries. Ecclesiastical orthodoxy permeated most Russian philosophy and thought until the Bolshevik Revolution, effectively stifling the development of any strong mercantile caste. The proletariat dictatorship which then followed positively killed off all possibility of any economic reform along entrepreneurial lines for the next 70 years.

Closely linked with these circumstances, and indeed largely arising out of them, is the environmental degradation which has occurred throughout much of the USSR. It is no over-statement to describe this as a catastrophe of monumental long-term proportions which threatens to engulf the peoples of the Soviet Union, along with future generations, with its implications for health, agriculture, the economy, ecology, future resource prospects and political stability. The economic consequences of numerous ecological disasters, all arising from the gross mismanagement inherent in the Soviet planning and administrative system, cover almost the whole environmental spectrum. The well-documented list paints a truly horrific picture which includes the pollution of coastal waters and the Arctic ice-cap; deforestation on a massive scale, the creation of dust bowls; extensive freshwater contamination and depletion; numerous cases of major disequilibrium caused in large regions of permafrost; huge areas of erosion created through sediment yield acceleration; a wide degree of pollution and toxic hazard caused by nuclear and chemical industrial fall-out, coupled with a wholesale loss of habitat and the extinction of many species of flora and fauna. This profligate contempt for nature has all been graphically described in this volume; certainly the impact upon future Soviet economic and agrarian strategy must not be underestimated.

Indeed the perennial problems besetting Soviet agriculture have long since become accepted as an inevitability, with a succession of poor harvests being predictably blamed on the weather. And yet, prior to the First World War and the Bolshevik Revolution, the country was the largest producer of grain in the world. The lamentable inability to meet the latent agricultural potential in the USSR is a monument to the failure of the imposed Stalinist system of *kolkhozy* (collectivisation) and *sovkhozy* (state farms), together with the denial of resources which would have mechanised and modernised farming methods, in favour of the establishment of heavy industry. Thus a lack of incentives, obsolescent and badly maintained agricultural equipment (particularly, once again, transport), and labour shortages have combined to produce a chronic state of empty shelves in the cities and near famine conditions in certain areas. Many of the labour difficulties in the USSR stem from shortages in certain skills and maldistribution of manpower due mainly to demographic problems. The wide range of nationalities, with their different languages and diverse ethnic cultures, lead to difficulties for the non-Russian speaking elements, particularly in the context of technological education. Certainly this has long been recognised as a major problem in the armed forces, for instance, where, for sound policy reasons, a broad ethnic intermix is desirable.

Added to this catalogue of concerns facing the Soviet central leadership there is the long-feared spectre of social unrest brought about by mass public dissatisfaction, fuelled by the new-found freedom of expression offered by *glasnost'*. Indeed the advent of modern communications technology (radio, satellite television and so forth) meant that this was almost inevitable as the Soviet general public became increasingly aware of events and conditions outside the borders of the USSR and openly critical of deficiencies within. So far the most visible discontent has been directed at the general failure of the state to meet the rising level of public expectation for consumer goods. This disillusionment has now become a matter of public debate in metropolitan USSR, covering not only anxieties over the breakdown of the retail distribution system but also what is universally perceived as the total failure of associated management techniques. Many of these problems existed well before 1985; however, a rising disquiet now exists in the republics over the degree to which centrally-inspired projects have caused major environmental contamination, putting at risk the health and prosperity of local populations. There has been considerable vocal protest at the disregard by central government for the rights, safety and interests of regional republics. It could be said that the ecological movement grew into the first cognitive revolution; *glasnost'* providing the means of expression as a true political option when civil populations perceived that central government was uncaring over these issues.

All this has resulted in a spate of demands for greater autonomy by most of the republics, which in some cases has involved seeking a complete split with the Soviet Union. These difficulties have led to the emergence of latent nationalism within the republics of the Union, to some extent reflecting nationalistic trends in Eastern Europe — and accompanied by a corresponding resurgence in the persecution of minority groups. Events in Yugoslavia, following the death of Tito and the subsequent collapse of the Communist central government, do provide a credible model, pointing to a number of possible scenarios which could be enacted in the USSR. There are significant similarities in the emerging political structures, coupled with ethnic and religious differences, all of which tend to lead towards regionalism as opposed to centralism. Movements towards federalism or outright independence might be reinforced by the feeling that NATO no longer represents a security threat. However, the institutional strength of what might be termed metropolitan Russia should not be underestimated; even the events of 1917 and their aftermath were really in the nature of a *coup d'etat* rather than a revolution. In particular, there are strong signs of an emerging Russian national assertiveness, which can hardly be identified as an isolationist movement as the Russian Federation occupies one-seventh of the world's land mass. The Russians do, however, feel themselves to be victims of the Soviet system and will therefore vote on an anti-Soviet platform. *Glasnost'* has also led to the airing of historical ethnic grievances; consequently, while a total fragmentation of the Soviet Union is probably not imminent, it is quite possible that some of the southern republics may break away in the short term, at least on a temporary basis. Nonetheless, while ethnic and religious concerns are more easily mobilised than political abstracts, they provide no substitute for consumer difficulties. The ethnic problem is easily over-emphasised and a restoration of centralism may be the only alternative in the event of a prolonged crisis.

On the international front, the long-running ideological dissension with China, what is widely seen to have been a disastrous military campaign in Afghanistan, and failures to influence the Third World in general, have all induced disillusionment resulting in a crisis of confidence in the moral and economic superiority of Communism. It is this collapse of ideology which has led to a public questioning regarding the legitimacy of the current regime.

In short, as we move into the last decade of the 20th century, the USSR may rate as a military superpower but it certainly does not appear to command the economic or political status of one. Furthermore, the Communist system is universally reckoned as having failed to deliver its promise of Utopia. However, this is paralleled by the paradox that, after seven decades of Communist totalitarianism, there is a discernible reluctance for individuals to take on the personal responsibilities implicit in a capitalist society. It is this characteristic, bred into Russian life over six centuries of autocratic rule, which may provide the present Soviet leadership with a breathing space and possibly an element of stability. Nevertheless, a major crisis of public confidence has been created in the Soviet Union, and the Soviet leadership is having to take account of this public mood of disenchantment. As de Tocqueville pointed out, the most dangerous time for bad government is when it tries to reform itself.

So what is at stake in terms of Soviet political futures? The history of both Russia and the Soviet Union shows that national security has always been the over-riding national concern. Up to now this has been achieved through a collective security strategy of 'buffer' states. Hence the justification for the Soviet claim for the politically defensive nature of their military doctrine, which is not a new concept. Over the past decade there has been a gradual shift from an east-west axis to a north-south axis. This reflects increasing Soviet concerns over their southern borders, brought about by uncertainties and escalating tensions in the Middle East, as well as continuing long-term fears over instabilities in the People's Republic of China. With NATO and Western Europe no longer perceived as a direct military danger, the more immediate concern is the internal cohesion of the Soviet empire itself. This is the new threat to security. The enormous geographical spread of the Soviet Union gives it either peripheral or direct access to North America, the Pacific rim, Asia, the Indian sub-continent, the Middle East and Europe. This presents problems as well as opportunities for Soviet long-term strategic planning which takes into account the linking of South, South-west and South-east Asia and the Far East in order to make the United States of America less relevant in world affairs. In order to implement any new global strategy for the next century, the USSR will have to optimise its assets in terms of geopolitical advantages and natural resources through political influence; by implication this means improving its economy through world trade from an established modern industrial area.

Meanwhile there are two major and closely-related areas which need to be carefully watched. The first concerns the role the USSR wishes to play in the European market of the 21st century. Do we see the USSR, in some 15 years' time, hoping to play a major part in European commercial affairs, with the vision of a socialist Europe dominated by the USSR? If so, would it not be perhaps expedient in the short term for it to off-load the economic problems of the COMECON countries on to the West? The second point relates to Slavic perceptions of the extent to which a unified Germany is likely to affect the stability of Central and Eastern Europe in, say, 25 years' time. This is historically an area which presents an economic power vacuum. There seems little chance of Russia being able to fill it before a united and expansionist Germany starts looking eastwards, driven by the imperatives of a new economic *lebensraum*. In which case, it is likely that this might prove to be the soil in which is nurtured the seeds of another cataclysmic Russo-German conflict during the first half of the 21st century?

This brings into focus the future of force development which will be determined by Soviet long-term politico-military strategic thinking. The key determinant here will always be the perception of the threat to national security. This is closely associated with anticipated changes in the character of warfare, the nature and methods of armed conflict and, *ipso facto*, the course along which future military doctrine will need to evolve in order to support political strategy.

By the end of the 1980s it was generally recognised in the Soviet Union that the social dimension of deterrence had been left out of the political and military determination; therefore the role of the military in shaping this policy has been significantly reduced, thus effectively broadening the perspective on national security. There is a growing recognition that military conflict need not inevitably escalate into global (nuclear) war; indeed, many of the new breed of Soviet civilian 'national security advisers' no longer regard this as a viable scenario.

The accent has now turned to war prevention rather than preparation for conflict, although preservation of military parity at adequate levels is seen as an important factor in averting war. Regional security arrangements depending on conventional capability are likely to be increasingly used to deter or control conflict. This has led to the announcement of a new defensive strategy, with the stress on *razumnaya dostatochnost'* (reasonable sufficiency). So far, in practical terms this has managed to steer a careful middle course between the traditional approach to Soviet foreign policy, which depended heavily on Marxist-Leninist theory, and the new political thinking with its emphasis upon avoidance of conflict as a means of resolving international political crisis.

In line with established Soviet tradition, considerable historical research and study is being conducted into finding a suitable model on which to test new doctrinal practices. The debate between the military and civilian communities is spirited and deeply divided, although the military doctrinal defensive transition goes back to the mid-1970s. The tradition of continuity and consistency of Soviet strategic thinking has already been stressed elsewhere in this book; however it is arguable now that the speed of changing political events must inevitably have introduced some major uncertainties. In any case the integration of new technology into planning has blurred many of the distinctions between offence and defence. Although declared Soviet military doctrine may be defensive, Soviet military art is certainly still offensive in nature; this is reflected by even a cursory study of the changes and developments in the organisational structures of the Soviet armed forces. Semantics notwithstanding, evolving Soviet doctrine is searching for improvements in effectiveness through a series of continuing reforms with the emphasis on quality rather than quantity. Future force structures will therefore be smaller and lighter, with the stress being placed on proven technical sophistication as a force multiplier. In any case, since deterrence must be seen to possess viability, integrity and utility, Soviet military planners are having to look at new operational methods in order to correlate with the more comprehensive strategic concepts implicit in current new political thinking.

Chief amongst those factors influencing military doctrine is the optimisation of new applied technologies for weapon systems and command technology, as well as projects under advanced research — most particularly those relating to the use of space as a fourth dimension for military operations. While continuing for the time being to maintain an effective strategic nuclear force (which accounted for approximately one-fifth of the 1989 total defence budget), the reduced utility being accorded to nuclear weapons in the tactical and operational spheres will lead to their being replaced by an advanced space-based military support system, with both a defensive and offensive potential. This contributes a wide spread of strategic and operational capabilities, ranging from reconnaissance and strike through to command, control and communications. However, it has yet to be proved whether new Soviet force structures are capable of using and operating effectively such advanced technologies, even if an ailing Soviet economy can continue to afford them. In addition, there seems to be an increasing interest in formulating asymmetric responses to Western strategic profiles in order to make up imbalances in technological capabilities and expertise.

Doctrinal evolution is also tightly bound up with a number of developments in such fields as reflexive control, deep deception, radical force restructuring (enhanced by new technologies), improved sustainability for TVD operational force levels, and moves towards more professional, all-regular armed services. The last is likely to be accelerated as a result of the widespread draft evasion experienced at the end of 1990 and during the first part of 1991; although this social reaction against military service was probably only to be expected with the advent of *glasnost* following decades of enforced military conscription. This to some extent parallels the sort of rejection of the establishment experienced by the USA following the Vietnam War. But above all, it is the character of Soviet military thinking over the next decade which will provide the West with a useful indication of USSR's evolving view of its future strategic role.

The investment priority accorded to military defence-spending since the Second World War has placed an increasingly intolerable burden on the whole Soviet economy. The defence industry is the most technologically capable of all Soviet industries, especially in terms of quality control. The effect of this has been to unbalance completely the whole economic structure of the new country, although the defence industry has to some extent always been involved in certain civilian tasks. It has always been difficult to place an accurate figure on military expenditure; however, future defence budget allocations for production of military hardware is being drastically curtailed. Clearly the greatest single constraint upon the military over the next few years is going to be financial. Already there has begun to be a shift from the emphasis on resource allocation for military sector expenditure towards investment in civilian production. This particularly applies to the labour redeployment policy of transferring technically-trained manpower from military enterprises into the civilian market. Nevertheless, despite the fiscal cutbacks, the military research and development base remains well-founded, with the technical ability to maintain a credible force modernisation programme well into the foreseeable future. However, financial savings will probably now have to be found through increased efficiency if there is not to be substantial retrenchment in many areas of important research activity. In addition, certain military projects are increasingly being scheduled for diversion to civilian application. On the other hand, there is a degree of convergence between certain civilian and military requirements, especially in those dual-purpose industries such as 'informatics' which is seen as one of the main factors affecting economics performance. Time will tell if this planned transition between the two sectors of the economy will make a significant contribution to the consumer market, although it may well turn out to provide a degree of hidden support for military technological development.

A key issue over the next few years will be whether or not a serious institutional conflict occurs between the Soviet military and civilian sectors. There has never been, however, any tradition of direct military involvement in political control. Therefore, short of a total breakdown in law and order resulting in anarchy, there is little likelihood of a military *coup d'etat*. In the area of arms control there has already been a political policy shift towards the increasing involvement of civilians with the specific aim of diluting the power of the military. This perhaps emphasises the importance of arms control negotiations in transmitting comprehensible messages to the other side. The concept of 'defensive sufficiency' became declared Soviet military doctrine in 1987, although it is doubtful whether many understood at the time exactly what this meant. Although the concept of 'superiority' was specifically excluded, the debate included other concepts relating to minimum strategies, asymmetric reductions, parity, political meanings and the future of military reform. The development of mutual trust has always been the major stumbling block between East and West; the West now needs to understand and reciprocate the Soviet intellectual approach to new political thinking if real progress is to be made in the field of international relations.

To some extent *glasnost'* has assisted in resolving many of (but by no means all) the problems of verification. But these are times of accelerating change and the future of arms control has to be seen against this backdrop. Certainly continuing negotiations will provide a useful mechanism for the resolution of immediate concerns and problems between East and West, despite many technical problems.

In summary, one is perhaps left with an overwhelming impression of the enormous problems facing the USSR in almost every sphere, coupled with the uneven nature of their abilities and performance. The Soviet Union is undoubtedly facing a difficult time in terms of political and economic stability as it embarks on the last decade of this century. The pressures for political change throughout the Union are primarily social and economic. *Perestroika* is first and foremost a domestic issue (having been labelled 'new thinking' in the international forum) and to this extent, even after five years, the Soviet people are still working out what it means. In addition, they largely remain prisoners of their own experience and consequently their perceptions still relate to Marxist-Leninist theory. Therefore it is still necessary to look for the dialectic link between internal domestic and foreign policy of the USSR.

The most imprudent course for the West would be to underestimate the potential capability of the USSR. There is always a danger of confusing style with substance. Despite the inefficient planning and direction, and notwithstanding poor resource management, it must be remembered that one of the most remarkable aspects of the Soviet achievement over the past 60 years has been the transformation of an essentially backward agrarian economy into what is now the second largest industrial power in the world. Similarly Soviet military capability has in no way diminished; it still retains considerable potential, and is likely to do so for a long time to come. Only if socio-economic reforms really take hold are we likely to see a decline in the predominantly military culture.

The Soviet Empire may be crumbling; but it is perhaps surprising that it has survived for so long, having only been held together by a bankrupt ideology, imposed by the *nomenklatura* and Russian ethnic minorities deployed outside the Russian Federation. However, this is the second dismantling of the Russian Empire; after 1917 the Bolsheviks restored the Empire by force. As then, the perception of change is invariably greater than the change itself, therefore the relationship between political, economic, military and social perspectives needs to be very carefully examined. There is a solid institutional tradition in the USSR which, amongst other things, is concerned with formulating research and planning well forward into the next century. We do not know what is contained in hidden agendas. There may be no prospectus for global domination, but there are certainly deliberations over a policy for global access. Moreover it is this consuetudinal attitude in the northern states which in the long run is most likely to motivate the non-Muslim republics to remain in the Union. The military remains one of the few institutions which cuts across ethnic, national and cultural lines. Military restructuring is aimed at responding to the authority of new centralist doctrinal requirements through the rationalisation of resources, with an increasing emphasis on optimising potential rather than numbers. *Glasnost'* has highlighted the conflict between authoritarianism and democratisation: there has been real movement towards electoral reform, and signs of a transformation of the Soviet environmental lobby. Superimposed across all this is a lively and intellectually coherent debate on economic, cultural, technical and environmental issues facing the Union. As it enters the 21st century the

fundamental imperatives for the Soviet Union will remain its national
security, institutional integrity and the pursuit of international recognition for legitimacy.

The future prospects of the USSR would seem to be limited to
variations on one of three main possibilities. The first of these is a total
collapse of central law and order, leading to a state of anarchy throughout much of the Union. Soviet institutions are likely to be strong
enough to withstand the pressures that would cause such a catastrophe.
In any case this sort of situation would hardly be in the interests of any
of the established forces of government within the USSR, and it is
probably the only scenario in which the Soviet military and KGB
troops would actively intervene independently to prevent chaos and
preserve the national rule of law. This would inevitably imply a rapid
return to totalitarian rule of some sort. The second option is for the
USSR to continue to muddle along, basing its hopes on economic
salvation on a series of continuing reforms. This would most likely
result in a succession of short-term measures aimed at economic crisis
management and political damage limitation. Such policies would be
based on expediency, since they would inevitably be formulated as a
reaction to events rather than being designed to create any long-term
economic social and political restructuring programme. One likely
outcome of adopting such a course would be the exploitation of natural
resources in the form of selling raw materials overseas to raise hard
foreign currency, with the inevitable ecological ill effects this would
have on the local environment.

The third possibility facing the USSR is a total or partial dismantling
of the Union itself in the short- or medium-term. One plausible con-
figuration could involve a tighter, leaner 'Russia' following the secession
of the southern states of Kazakhstan, Turkmenia, Uzbekistan, Tadjik-
stan, Kirghizia and possibly Azerbaijan. Not all the Soviet states
necessarily see economic viability or a sustainable security resulting
from independence. For instance, Moldavia is more likely to opt to
remain with the Union, as absorption into Romania would currently
result in even lower living standards. So far as Armenia is concerned,
independence is clearly untenable and a transfer to Turkish sovereignty
would be seen as a case of jumping out of the frying pan into the fire.
In the longer term, the Baltic states of Estonia, Latvia and Lithuania
would almost certainly remain within some sort of looser federation
controlled from Moscow. Belorussia has a close affinity with the Slavic
aspirations of the RSFSR and would almost certainly join with it;
whilst, notwithstanding their powerful nationalist traditions, Georgia
and the Ukraine would look with justifiable concern at a Union led by
a powerful RSFSR of which they were not a part.

Whilst the Russian Federation may see a number of advantages in shedding responsibility for the troublesome and unprofitable southern states of the USSR, a total breakup of the Union will continue to be strongly resisted by the centralists in Moscow, as this could provide the catalyst for major civil unrest which could slide into civil war; thus precipitating the very situation all would wish to avoid. However a smaller confederate grouping based on a regional co-operation which excludes some or all of the southern states is certainly a possibility. This, coupled with the Russian penchant for *adaptivnost'*, makes it most probable that the country will continue to feel its way forward in a state of crisis for some time to come. If the new democratic order is to take root in the Soviet Union, then either Gorbachev or his successors will need to look urgently for some unifying factor for the Soviet people, and this will have to be found internally. Failure will lead to a straight choice between a return to more authoritarian centralist rule and the unpredictability of continuing political turmoil.

Certainly it would be the ultimate irony if, while Western Europe moves closer towards integration, the USSR and Eastern Europe slide inexorably into the melting pot of political disintegration. Nevertheless history has proved consistent in demonstrating that, in Russia, things are rarely what they seem. Whatever turn events take in that vast land, the West should not be surprised to be surprised.

# Index